Human Rights in a Changing East-West Perspective

Edited by

Allan Rosas and Jan Helgesen
with the collaboration of
Donna Gomien

Pinter Publishers
London and New York

First published in Great Britain in 1990 by
Pinter Publishers Limited
25 Floral Street, London WC2E 9DS

British Library Cataloguing in Publication Data

A CIP catalogue record for this book is available from the
British Library
ISBN 0-86187-131-6

For enquiries in North America please contact
PO Box 197, New York, NY 10533

Library of Congress Cataloging-in-Publication Data
Human rights in a changing East-West perspective/edited by
   Allan Rosas & Jan Helgesen; with the collaboration of
   Donna Gomien.
      p.   cm.
      Papers from a workshop held in Turku/Åbo, Dec. 1987 and
   organized by the Tampere Peace Research Institute.
      Includes index.
      ISBN 0-86187-131-6
      1. Human rights–Congresses.   I. Rosas, Allan.   II. Helgesen,
   Jan   E.   III. Gomien, Donna.   IV. Rauhan- ja
   Konfliktintutkimuslaitos
   (Tampere, Finland)
   K3239.6 1987d
   323–dc20   90-45077
                                                                  CIP

Typeset by Witwell Ltd, Southport
Printed and Bound in Great Britain by Biddles Ltd, Guildford and
Kings Lynn

Contents

Contributors   vii

Acknowledgements   ix

Abbreviations   x

1 Introduction
  Allan Rosas and Jan Helgesen   1

2 Human Rights in the Writings of Marx and Engels
  Jukka Paastela   6

3 Democracy and Human Rights
  Allan Rosas   17

4 Freedom of Opinion and Expression
  Vojin Dimitrijevic   58

5 Universal Legal Principles of Fair Trial in Criminal
  Proceedings
  Pieter van Dijk   89

6 The Prohibition of the Death Penalty: An Emerging
  International Norm?
  Theodore S. Orlin   136

7 The Right to Work
  Christian Tomuschat   174

8 National Minorities and International Law
  I. P. Blischenko and A. H. Abashidze   202

9 Right to Peace, Right to Development, Right to a
  Healthy Environment:
  Part of the Solution or Part of the Problem?
  Gábor Kardos   216

10 Between Helsinkis—and Beyond? Human Rights in
   the CSCE Process
   Jan Helgesen   241

11 National Implementation of Human Rights
   Roman Wieruszewski   264

12 Reporting and Complaint Systems in Universal
Human Rights Treaties
Bernhard Graefrath   290

13 CSCE State Adherence to Human Rights Conventions
Lauri Hannikainen   334

Table of Cases   367

Table of Treaties   370

Index   373

Contributors

ABASHIDZE, ASLAN H. b. 1957; Ph.D. (Patrice Lumumba University, Moscow, 1989); Assistant Professor of International Law (Patrice Lumumba University).

BLISCHENKO, IGOR P. b. 1930; Dr.iur. (Moscow Institute of International Relations Law Faculty, 1965); Professor and Head of the International Law Department (Patrice Lumumba University, Moscow); Vice-President of the Association of Soviet Lawyers.

VAN DIJK, PIETER b. 1943; Dr.iur. (University of Leiden, 1976); Professor of the Law of International Organizations (Utrecht University); Chairperson of the Netherlands Advisory Committee on Human Rights and Foreign Policy; Chairperson of the Netherlands Institute of Human Rights.

DIMITRIJEVIC, VOJIN b. 1932; Dr.iur. (University of Belgrade, 1965); Professor of International Law and International Relations (University of Belgrade); Member and Vice-Chairperson of the Human Righs Committee under the International Covenant on Civil and Political Rights; President of the Yugoslav Forum for Human Rights and Legal Security of Citizens.

GRAEFRATH, BERNHARD b. 1928; Dr.iur. (Humboldt-University, Berlin, 1951); Professor of International Law (Humboldt-University, Academy of Sciences of the German Democratic Republic); Member of the Human Rights Committee under the International Covenant on Civil and Political Rights 1977–1986; Member of the UN International Law Commission.

HANNIKAINEN, LAURI b. 1942; Dr.iur. (University of Lapland, Rovaniemi, 1989); Senior Researcher, Åbo Akademi University Institute for Human Rights; Docent of International Law (University of Helsinki).

HELGESEN, JAN b. 1947; kand.jur. (University of Oslo, 1975); Assistant Professor (University of Oslo); Member of the Norwegian Advisory Board for Human Rights.

KARDOS, GABOR b. 1956; Dr.iur. (Eötvös Loránd University, Budapest, 1980); Associate Professor of International Law (Eötvös Loránd University); Scientific Secretary of the Council on Human Rights of the Hungarian UN Association.

ORLIN, THEODORE S. b. 1946; Jur.D. (State University of New York at Buffalo, 1973); Member of the New York State Bar; Associate Professor (Utica College of Syracuse University); Fulbright Professor

1989-1990 (Åbo Akademi University, Turku/Åbo).
PAASTELA, JUKKA b. 1946; Ph.D. (University of Tampere, 1986); Docent of Political Science (University of Tampere).
ROSAS, ALLAN b. 1948; Dr.iur. (University of Turku, 1976); Armfelt Professor of State Law and International Law (Åbo Akademi University, Turku/Åbo); Director of the Åbo Akademi University Institute for Human Rights; Vice-Chairperson of the Finnish Advisory Committee for International Human Rights Affairs.
TOMUSCHAT, CHRISTIAN b. 1936; Dr.iur. (University of Heidelberg, 1964); Professor of Public Law and Director of Institute of International Law (University of Bonn); Member of the Human Rights Committee under the International Covenant on Civil and Political Rights 1977-1986; Member of the UN International Law Commission.
WIERUSZEWSKI, ROMAN b. 1947; Dr.iur. (University of Poznán, 1974); Associate Professor (Poznán Human Rights Centre, Polish Academy of Sciences).

TAPRI Studies in International Relations

This series, edited jointly by Dr Vilho Harle and Dr Jyrki Käkönen of the Tampere Peace Research Institute (TAPRI) at Tampere in Finland, is based on the work of TAPRI on peace studies. The series is launched with publications from TAPRI Workshops on European Futures: Bases & Choices. The workshops have concentrated on European issues concerning international relations, security, disarmament, human rights, technology and co-operation. .

List of publications:

Vilho Harle and Pekka Sivonen (eds), *Europe in Transition: Politics and Nuclear Security*

Vilho Harle (ed.), *European Values in International Relations*

Vilho Harle and Jyrki Iivonen (eds), *Gorbachev and Europe*

Jyrki Käkönen, Steven Miller and Lev Voronkov (eds), *Vulnerable Arctic: Need for an Alternative Orientation?*

Acknowledgments

In the Spring of 1987, the Tampere Peace Research Institute (TAPRI) took the initiative to organize a workshop on 'Human Rights in an East-West Perspective' and asked us to launch the project. The workshop was part of a series of TAPRI Workshops on 'European Futures: Bases and Choices'. We wish to thank TAPRI and especially its then Director, Dr Vilho Harle, for this initiative and the encouragement and support we have experienced throughout the process.

The participants of the workshop deserve many thanks for their contributions and enthusiasm, despite the heavy commitments many of them have in other contexts. The group met in Turku/Åbo in December 1987, in Oslo in December 1988 and again in Turku in December 1989. The atmosphere of these meetings was excellent and set an example for human rights co-operation across, by now out-dated, frontiers.

At one or two meetings, our group benefited from the presence of experts who are not contributors to the book itself. We wish to thank especially Professor Thomas Buergenthal (George Washington University), Dr Krzysztof Drzewicki (University of Gdansk and Norwegian Institute of Human Rights) and Professor Torkel Opsahl (University of Oslo and Norwegian Institute of Human Rights) for their advice and encouragement.

The workshop has been co-ordinated by us on behalf of the Norwegian Institute of Human Rights (Oslo) and the Åbo Akademi University Institute for Human Rights (Turku/Åbo). Asbjørn Eide, Director of the Norwegian Institute, has been a constant source of inspiration and support. The meetings of the group would not have been possible without the painstaking work of the personnel of both institutes, especially Catarina Krause from the Åbo Akademi Institute and Ragnhild Astrup from the Norwegian Institute.

While we attempt to take some credit for the birth of this book, Donna Gomien from the Norwegian Institute has in many respects been the 'real editor'. Both in terms of language, style and substance, her contribution has been outstanding. Many thanks are also due to Johanna Bondas from the Åbo Akademi Institute, who was instrumental in the late hectic phase of the technical editing process.

A book without a true publisher is defective. Pinter Publishers in London has been an effective remedy.

Oslo and Turku/Åbo, March 1990
Jan Helgesen
Allan Rosas

Abbreviations

The listing of an abbreviation here does not necessarily imply that it, instead of the full title, is always used in the text.

CCPR	International Covenant on Civil and Political Rights
CSCE	Conference on Security and Co-Operation in Europe
doc.	document
Publ. E.C.H.R.	Publications of the European Court of Human Rights
GAOR	(UN) General Assembly Official Records
I.C.J. Reports	International Court of Justice, Reports of Judgments, Advistory Opinions and Orders
ILC	(UN) International Law Commission
ILO	International Labour Organisation
SR	Summary Records
UN	United Nations
Unesco	United Nations Educational, Scientific and Cultural Organization
UNGA	United Nations General Assembly

1 Introduction

Allan Rosas and Jan Helgesen

The European post-war period saw important differences and tensions between the human rights conceptions and policies of the East and the West. First of all, human rights as a general notion was given priority by the West, while the East tended to stress peace and disarmament as well as the inviolability of frontiers and state sovereignty. This was a conspicuous facet of the CSCE process, with the East being primarily an advocate of the first 'basket' while the West advanced the third 'basket' (see Chapter 10).

Secondly, the Eastern European socialist states tended to see human rights as benefits secured by the state rather than as rights held by the individual against the state. The interests of the individual and those of the socialist society were presumed to be in conformity with each other (Bloed and van Hoof, 1985, p. 34f.). The socialist states also emphasized the obligations of the individual towards society. Political freedoms were 'interpreted from class positions as conditions of the consolidation of the working people and the spread of socialist ideology which rules out the "freedom" of anti-socialist propaganda, the freedom to organize counter-revolutionary forces against the fundamentals of socialism' (Kartashkin, 1982, p. 633. See also Poppe, 1989, p. 24).

In the same vein, the East often focused on economic, social and cultural rights and collective rights such as the right of peoples to self-determination (Bloed and van Hoof, 1985, pp. 37f., 41f.). Among the civil and political rights, the East emphasized the right of political participation on the basis of equality, but this was done at the expense of the individual's right to challenge the social and political system and the leadership of the ruling party (Bloed and van Hoof, 1985, p. 41). The position of the West, of course, was rather the reverse, with a focus on the civil liberties of the Western liberal heritage.

Finally, the East expressed reluctance and often outright animosity towards international monitoring and control machineries, stressing the principle of non-interference, whereas many Western states supported devices such as individual complaint systems and the creation and strengthening of international monitoring bodies.

These basic observations never provided a complete picture of the various issues involved. Just to mention a few examples: The 'Western' position on the international protection of human rights was never monolithic, as the United States in particular had (and still has) a rather 'isolationist' approach towards internationally binding instruments and international control procedures. The Eastern European states, again, have together with most Western European states adhered to the great bulk of the universal human rights conventions.

On the other hand, economic, social and cultural rights were not completely unknown even in the Western national constitutions of the first half of this century or in the New Deal policy of the Roosevelt era. Among the four 'freedoms' proclaimed by President Roosevelt was 'freedom from want', a formulation also to be found in the Atlantic Charter signed by Roosevelt and Prime Minister Churchill on 14 August 1941 (Osmanczyk, 1985, p. 57).

This heritage, also reflected in the Universal Declaration of Human Rights of 1948, has at the national level been reflected in the Western European welfare state. This, however, has occurred in the context of domestic economic and social policies rather than as part of a concerted international human rights strategy. Many Western states have certainly adhered to international instruments such as the International Covenant on Economic, Social and Cultural Rights of 1966 and the European Social Charter of 1961, but this seems to have been done on the assumption that the rights enshrined therein are not internationally protected as subjective rights in the narrow sense. Some Western European states, such as the United Kingdom under Thatcher, have opposed the international promotion of economic and social rights and, since the Reagan years, the United States regarded, and to some extent still regards, economic, social and cultural rights as 'goals' or 'aspirations' rather than rights proper (*Country Reports*, 1983, p. 1475; *ibid.*, 1987, p. 3; Kirkpatrick, 1982, p. 90; Alston and Simma, 1988, p. 614).

While the Eastern European states at the international level emphasized economic, social and cultural rights, there were serious flaws in the actual protection of these rights at the national level. Paradoxically, many economic, social and cultural rights were more effectively protected in the West. And during recent years one can see some indications of a trend in Western Europe towards the interdependence of recognized human rights and the legitimate role of economic and social rights in an integrated European human rights conception.

It may be indicative that the Declaration of Fundamental Rights and Freedoms, adopted by the European Parliament on 12 April 1989 (*Human Rights Law Journal*, vol. 10 (1989), no. 1-2, p. 341), includes both civil and political rights and economic, social and cultural rights. Some economic and social rights are further explored in the Community Charter of the Fundamental Social Rights of Workers, adopted by eleven out of twelve Heads of State and Government of the member states of the European Community during the Strasbourg Summit held on 8 and 9 December 1989.

Within the Council of Europe, the Declaration on the Future Role of the Council of Europe in European Construction, adopted and signed on 5 May 1989 by the Ministers of Foreign Affairs at a meeting of the Committee of Ministers, contains as one of the three priority lines for the Council of Europe's action, the following statement: 'safeguarding and reinforcing pluralist democracy and human rights by reference to the European Convention on Human Rights and the European Social Charter'. Thus, the Social Charter is seen as an ingredient of European pluralist democracy and human rights. But it has to be added that no concrete action has been taken with respect to developing the control system, either within the context of the Social Charter or through any extension of the European Convention on Human Rights to economic and social rights.

At the same time, civil liberties and the rule of law have begun to gain ground in the East, more or less coinciding with the coming into power of Gorbachev in spring 1985. As a first step, he asserted that there are human values common to mankind which are not directly subordinate to class interests (Gorbachev, 1988, p. 146). This initial phase can be said to have brought forward 'a comprehensive socialist concept of modern anthropocentrism' (Drzewicki and Eide, 1988, p. 4). And eventually a dramatic reform process started in the Soviet Union and some other socialist countries, implying a completely new approach to civil and political rights. The highlights have included the investiture of the rule of law, both nationally and internationally (Gorbachev, 1989), and political pluralism, including the abolishment of the constitutionally dominant position of the Communist Party.

In Hungary and Poland, some legislative and other reforms had already been initiated by the mid-1980s. For instance, a Polish Constitutional Tribunal was established in 1985 (Act of 28 April 1985) as was an Ombudsman institution in 1987 (*Annual Report of the Commissioner for Civil Rights Protection*, 1988; Reid, 1988, p. 255). To take another example: the death penalty had already been abolished in the German Democratic Republic in 1987.

Needless to say, the year 1989 saw upheavals that fundamentally changed the political map of Europe. Not only did the post-war period come to an end and the ruling parties of most of the socialist states lose their dominant position, but reforms were initiated that will change the basic elements of their political and legal systems. This may imply a real shift towards the principle of the indivisibility and interdependence of all human rights, economic, social and cultural rights as well as civil and political rights.

But one cannot exclude the possibility that some of the previously socialist states will limit their focus to civil liberties in the traditional Western sense, at the expense of economic and social rights. The present editors would deplore such a trend. We believe that there are principles and ideas of a just society inherent in both 'Eastern' and 'Western' traditions which should be preserved, despite the inability of many European states to guarantee all economic and social rights in actual practice.

As this book goes to print, it is too early to assess all the impacts of recent events. The main purpose of the book is not to provide a snapshot of the situation as it stands in spring 1990 or to lay out predictions for the future. What we try to do is to analyse, from the point of view of international human rights law, some issues which have played and probably will play an important role in the promotion and protection of human rights in Europe. Some of us also bring out perspectives and scenarios for the future. Only the future itself will tell to what extent these scenarios are relevant or not.

By 'Europe', we mean the CSCE framework, including Canada and the United States. Our starting point was the East-West perspective, which since the Second World War has offered a key explanation of European human rights developments. The words 'Eastern' and 'Western' are used to describe the realities of post-war Europe, not to reflect an ideological posture or to recognize present or future blocs.

Without trying to be exhaustive, we have included a variety of different topics. There are contributions on structural and systemic perspectives (democracy and human rights) and rights of a collective nature (peoples' rights, rights of minorities). Some substantive rights of crucial importance (freedom of expression, the right to a fair trial, the right to life, the right to work) are also analysed. And four contributions focus on mechanisms for human rights promotion and protection (the CSCE process, national implementation mechanisms, international reporting and complaint systems, adherence to human rights instruments). As Marxism and its various interpretations and applications have played such a central role in the East-West human rights debate, we have also included a chapter outlining one possible interpretation of what Marx and Engels themselves had to say on human rights.

While drafts for most of the articles have been discussed by the group of authors, it goes without saying that the individual authors are solely responsible for their respective contributions. Pluralism has been our motto, not only as a desire for European human rights developments but as an underlying principle for this book.

Bibliography

Alston, Philip and Bruno Simma, 1988. 'Second Session of the UN Committee on Economic, Social and Cultural Rights', *American Journal of International Law*, vol. 82, no. 3.

Annual Report 1988 of the Polish People's Republic Commissioner for Civil Rights Protection. Warsaw: Bureau of the Commissioner for Civil Rights Protection.

Bloed, Arie and Fried van Hoof, 1985. 'Some Aspects of the Socialist View of Human Rights', in Arie Bloed and P. van Dijk (eds), *Essays on Human Rights in the Helsinki Process*. Dordrecht: Martinus Nijhoff.

Country Reports on Human Rights Practices, 1983, 1987. Reports Submitted to the Committee on Foreign Affairs, US House of Representatives, and the Committee on Foreign Relations, US Senate, by the Department of State, 98th Congress, 2nd Session, February 1984; 100th Congress, 2nd Session, February 1987. Washington: US Government Printing Office.

Drzewicki, Krzysztof and Asbjørn Eide, 1988. 'Perestroika and Glasnost: The Changing Profile of the Soviet Union Towards International Law and Human Rights', *Mennesker og Rettigheter—Nordic Journal on Human Rights*, vol. 6, no. 4.

Gorbachev, Mikhail, 1988. *Perestroika: New Thinking for Our Country and the World*. New, updated edition to include Mikhail Gorbachev's June 1988 speech to the Party Conference. London: Fontana/Collins.

Gorbachev, Mikhail, 1989. Statement at the Parliamentary Assembly of the Council of Europe, Strasbourg, 6 July 1989. *Council of Europe, Information Department*, D (89) 35, 6.7.89.

Kartashkin, Vladimir, 1982. 'The Socialist Countries and Human Rights', in Karel Vasak and Philip Alston (eds), *The International Dimensions of Human Rights*, vol. 2. Westport/Paris: Greenwood Press/Unesco.

Kirkpatrick, Jeane J., 1982. 'Establishing a Viable Human Rights Policy', in Howard J. Wiarda (ed), *Human Rights and US Human Rights Policy: Theoretical Approaches and Some Perspectives on Latin America*. Washington: American Enterprise Institute for Public Policy Research.

Osmanczyk, Edmund Jan, 1985. *The Encyclopedia of the United Nations and International Agreements*. Philadelphia/London: Taylor and Francis.

Poppe, Eberhard, 1989. 'The Development of Socialist Human Rights: History and Prospects', *GDR Committee for Human Rights Bulletin*, vol. 15, no. 1.

Reid, Colin T., 1988. 'The Polish Ombudsman', *Review of Socialist Law*, vol. 14, no. 3.

2 Human Rights in the Writings of Marx and Engels

Jukka Paastela

1. Introduction

The classical definition of human rights comes, of course, from the French Revolution where it culminated in three words: liberté, égalité, fraternité. Marx and Engels continued this tradition of enlightenment although they were 'descendants' of Rousseau rather than Voltaire. Because Marx and Engels were so deeply tied to this tradition it is appropriate to examine what content the key words of the Declaration of the Rights of Man and of the Citizen have in their writings. There are, however, many questions which are related to these key words, for example, the questions of democracy and universal suffrage. What was the meaning of these questions to the most eminent socialist theoreticians and what was the importance they ascribed to them? The question of democracy in socialist tradition, especially, is so large that it is not possible in a short chapter to examine it exhaustively, but only to refer to it briefly in the context of the examination of the 'key words' mentioned above.

2. Equality

Marx and Engels differentiated two kinds of equality: formal, bourgeois equality as expressed for instance in the slogans of the French Revolution and 'real equality', as opposed to formal equality in the conditions of capitalism. In an early text, Engels stated that the French socialists came to the 'doctrine of Community' politically (as opposed to the English who came to it practically and Germans who came to it philosophically) and that they first sought political liberty and equality, but when they found this insufficient they added 'social liberty to their political claims' (Engels, 1843, *MECW*, vol. 3, pp. 392–3). As early as 1843, the division of equality between simple political equality and broader social equality appeared in Engels. This can be explained by the fact that Engels himself came to socialist conclusions in a much more practical way than Marx. Engels studied the concrete conditions of the English working class and was also interested in various early socialist and communist movements in France and Germany. Marx, on the other hand, became a communist on the basis of philosophical meditation as can be seen in his early concept of equality, 'association, applied to land' when the earth becomes once more a true personal property of man through free labour and thus realizes the original tendency of land division, namely, equality (Marx, 1844, *MECW*, vol. 3. p. 268).

Equality and other human rights were not for Marx and Engels based on moral principles or natural rights; they were, rather, consequences of human history. The bourgeoisie was obliged to make elective principles the basis of government. It was compelled by historical law to 'recognize equality in principle' as it was compelled to create other concepts, such as the relative liberty of the press, trial by jury and the notion of equality before law. But at the same time it conserved its privilege of money and inequality between rich and poor (Engels, 1846, *MECW*, vol. 6, p. 28). The concept of history on which this kind of formula was based, was very deterministic: the bourgeoisie had, in principle, no alternative, and the role of the proletariat was to 'help' the bourgeoisie to fulfil its historical mission. In the same deterministic way, the proletariat will, according to Marx and Engels, one day replace the bourgeoisie and establish a society based on full equality, which in the *Manifesto of the Communist Party* is famously described as 'an association in which the free development of one is the condition for the free development of all' (Marx and Engels, 1848, *MECW*, vol. 6, p. 506).

Marx dealt with the question of equality profoundly only 27 years after the writing of the *Manifesto*, in his *Critique of the Gotha Programme* where he made his well-known division between the 'first' and 'second' phase of communism. In the first phase of communism, the law of value still prevails and a worker receives from society — after necessary deductions for taxes have been made — what he has given to society by his work. He gets a certificate about his work and uses the certificate to buy the means of consumption. For Marx, this kind of equality was still a 'bourgeois right', because the right of workers is 'proportional to the labour they supply'. Because labour is unequal — people always work differently — equal rights in principle are in practice unequal. Only in the second phase of communism, when the difference between mental and physical labour has vanished, and productive forces have been increased, the law of value and with it 'bourgeois right' disappear and the principle 'from each according to his abilities, to each according to his needs', can be realized (Marx, 1875, *MECW*, vol. 24, pp. 88–97).

This kind of belief was typically utopian in at least two senses. Firstly, it did not see any limits to the enlargement of productive forces and, accordingly, production. This kind of belief in limitless economic growth and progress was typical of all socialists in the nineteenth century. Secondly, Marx's conception of communism did not see any limits of human nature. The implicit assumption was that human beings will, after they have been completely emancipated,[1] necessarily behave rationally and, for instance, will not waste the common goods.

---

[1] There is no space to deal with the complex problem of emancipation in Marx in this article. For a discussion of this subject, see Paastela (1985, pp. 27–40).

3. Liberty

Marx and Engels wrote much more about freedom(s) than about equality. This was natural because struggle about civil liberties was one of the main tasks of the young workers' movement. We can differentiate two concepts of freedom in Marx and Engels, one 'abstract' which can be realized only under communism and one 'concrete', for example, freedom of the press, freedom of association, universal suffrage, or other aspects of democracy in general.

In an early work, the *German Ideology*, Marx and Engels wrote that individuals can obtain their freedom in 'real community', 'through their association' (Marx and Engels, 1845/1846, *MECW*, vol. 5, p. 78). Does this mean that Marx's and Engels' concept of human nature was thoroughly collectivist? Our answer is negative because it is *individuals* who find their freedom through association. In *Grundrisse* Marx returns to this problem, and uses Aristotle's famous description of man as *zoon politikon* and adds that he is not merely 'a social animal' but an animal that can 'isolate itself only within society' (Marx, 1857/1858, *MECW*, vol. 28, p. 18). This notion has been called, very tellingly, 'integral individualism' (Rosanvallon, 1979, p. 193). Marx's aim was not a faceless collective but a collective where individuals could develop their talents and lead a full life.

Marx defended freedom of the press during the whole course of his life. It is obvious that freedom of the press was for him a question of principle. Marx had already begun his struggle against censorship in 1842 when he was the editor of *Rheinische Zeitung*, a liberal newspaper. He saw the essence of the free press as the 'characteristic, rational, moral essence of freedom'. Censorship, he declared in his rather abstract way,

does not abolish the struggle, it makes it one-sided, it converts an open struggle into a hidden one, it converts a struggle over principles into a struggle of principle without power against power without principle. The true censorship, based on the very essence of freedom of the press is *criticism* (Marx, 1842, *MECW*, vol. 1, pp. 158–9).

When Marx wrote these lines he was not yet a communist, he was rather a radical liberal who belonged to the philosophical school of the Young Hegelians. But his principle of the freedom of the press did not change when Marx adopted communist doctrine and when he began to develop his own theories of society. He vigorously defended freedom of the press as well as other civil freedoms, for instance in the columns of the *New York Daily Tribune*, for which he was London correspondent in the 1850s. The following quotation is very typical and illustrative of his attitude to freedoms. He wrote about Prussia:

You can neither live nor die, nor marry, nor write letters, nor think, nor print, nor take to business, nor teach, nor be taught, nor get up a meeting, nor build a manufactory, nor emigrate, nor do anything without 'obrigkeitliche Erlaubnis' — permission on the part of the authorities (Marx, 1858, *MECW*, vol. 16, pp. 76–7).

There can be no doubt that Marx's aim was nothing but the abolition of this kind of bureaucratic monster forever.[2]

Marx and Engels defended freedom of the press both in bourgeois society and within the workers' movement. Marx and Engels saw it as one of the historical tasks of the bourgeoisie to establish the free press. The workers' movement, Engels declared, cannot require that 'the bourgeoisie ceases to be bourgeoisie' but it can require that the bourgeoisie follows its own principles and follows them consistently. Through the free press, the proletariat would win tools of agitation which would be very important from the point of view of its final victory (Engels, 1865, *MECW*, vol. 20, p. 77).

As to the press of the workers' movement, Engels defended its freedom, especially after the anti-socialist law was abrogated in Germany in 1890. He was very annoyed when, during the discussion about the Erfurt programme, he tried to publish one of Marx's letters that had been written in the context of the debate about the previous Gotha programme of the German Socialist Party in the party magazine *Die Neue Zeit*, and the party leadership tried to prevent publication of the letter because they thought it was too radical. He sharply condemned what he considered as attempts to submit the *Neue Zeit* to party censorship and asked 'do you differ from Puttkamer (who as the Minister of the Interior 1881–88 suppressed social democratic organs and associations) when you introduce to your own ranks a socialist law?' Engels advised the party to be 'less Prussian': 'You — the party — *need* socialist science and it cannot live without freedom of movement'. He pointed out that a large party cannot be as 'tight' as a sect and that anti-socialist law exists no longer (Engels, 1891a, *MEW*, vol. 38, pp. 90–5; see also Engels, 1891b, *MEW*, vol. 38, p. 87).

Engels' line was very consistent in regard to intra-party democracy; he defended it on principle and not only when his own — or Marx's — affairs were in question. When he understood — although incorrectly (see Bebel, 1892, p. 620) — that the German Socialist Party would 'nationalize' the press, he protested. In the party, to be sure, there must be a press but not a press which is directly dependent on the leading committee of the party or even on the party congress. The press must be, 'within the limits of party decency', able to criticize freely the programme and tactics of the party. A formally independent party press is thus necessary (Engels, 1892, *MEW*, vol. 38, pp. 517–18).

The demand for universal male suffrage was one of the earliest

---

[2] See also Fetscher (1960) on Marx's attitude to state bureaucracy.

demands of European workers' movements. We can even say that the early workers' movement was a reaction to privileges in parliamentary life which were the heritage of feudalism. This is especially the case in the English workers' movement whose first political expression was the Chartist movement. In 1838, the famous People's Charter was accepted with enthusiasm in a workers' meeting. Its main aims were equal constituencies, universal male suffrage, no discrimination against candidates, a secret ballot and payment of a fee to members of parliament (Rosenblatt, 1967, pp. 213-33). In Brussels in 1846, when they founded their first small political organization, Communist Correspondence Committee, Marx and Engels placed much hope in the realization of the People's Charter and especially universal suffrage. They believed in nothing less than the realization of workers' power in England if there existed universal male suffrage; it was for them a sufficient condition for the victory of the proletariat in England. The parliament was to be a forum in which 'the great struggle of capital and labour, of *bourgeois* and *proletarian* must be resolved' (Marx and Engels, 1846, *MECW*, vol. 6, pp. 58-9).[3] The basis of this doctrine was the quite naive belief that in the conditions of universal suffrage all or at least the main part of the proletariat would vote for the Chartist candidates and the Chartists then would have a majority in parliament.

In Germany universal male suffrage was one of the main demands of the workers' movement. It was in the central place in Ferdinand Lassalle's *Arbeiterprogramm* (1862, p. 189) which he wrote for the first modern workers' party, the *Allgemeine Deutsche Arbeiterverein*, founded in 1863. Although Marx and Engels were very critical of Lassalle, they again placed much hope in the realization of universal male suffrage, which was in fact realized in the North German Federation in 1867 and which made it possible for the workers' organizations to send six deputies to the first parliament elected by universal male suffrage. It was also at this stage that Marx and Engels became convinced that it is the task of the proletariat in every country to form a political party 'since it must express the conditions for the emancipation of the working class' (Engels, 1871, *MECW*, vol. 22, p. 278).

It was the question about the foundation of a national workers' party in every European country which split the First International in 1872. The anarchists, led by M. Bakunin, accepted neither this principle, nor universal suffrage and the workers' entry into parliaments under conditions of capitalism. Bakunin argued in 1873 that Marx understood popular government as a government elected by universal suffrage and thus for Bakunin this meant that a small minority would in fact rule. Bakunin suggested that if all 40 million

---

[3] In 1852 Marx still held a very optimistic conception about the results which universal suffrage would have in England despite the obvious decline of chartism (Marx, 1852, *MEW*, vol. 11, pp. 335-73).

Germans could participate in the government there would be no one under another's rule (Bacounine, 1873, pp. 346–7). Marx's answer to this proposition was: 'Certainly! For the system starts with the self-government of the communities' (Marx, 1874, *MECW*, vol. 24, p. 519).

This was not a declaration made by chance. Marx and Engels greatly trusted in local self-government as a model for the administration of future society. Engels, for instance, analysed Holland as one country (with England and Switzerland) where absolute monarchy was abolished in the sixteenth to eighteenth centuries, local and provincial self-government were strong and there was no 'real bureaucracy in the French or Prussian sense'. Engels stated:

This is a great advantage for the development of the national character also for later; the working people can establish with little changes the free self-government which must be our best tool in the transformation of the mode of production (Engels, 1886, *MEW*, vol. 36, p. 434).

There can be no doubt that the vision of future society was a decentralized one, where basic administration happens in small self-governmental units.

Marx's analysis of the Paris commune also supports this conclusion. The plan in the Paris commune for the future of France was based on the idea that the commune is 'the political form of even the smallest country hamlet' and that every district administers its affairs by 'an assembly of delegates in the central town', and these district assemblies again send deputies, who should be bound to fulfil their imperative mandate, to the 'National Delegation in Paris'. Marx's conclusion was: 'Nothing could be more foreign to the spirit of the Commune than to supersede universal suffrage by hierarchic investiture' (Marx, 1871, in *MECW*, vol. 22, p. 333). This is a very important statement because it shows that Marx trusted in universal suffrage also under a working-class government.

When the workers' movement progressed, election by election, in the parliamentary elections in Germany in the 1880s and 1890s, Engels drew some conclusions about the importance of universal suffrage and a democratic republic — which, of course, did not exist in Germany but which was one of the main demands of the workers' movement — for the workers. Engels saw universal suffrage as a 'yardstick of the maturity of the working class' because the extent to which it grows mature enough to emancipate itself will, to the same extent, enable it to elect its own representatives as an independent party. And 'on the day when the thermometer of universal suffrage indicates boiling point among the workers, they will know as well as the capitalists where they are' (Engels, 1884, *MEW*, vol. 21, p. 168).

For Engels the best political system was thus a democratic republic. It was in Engels' view a bridge to the new society, that is, in a democratic republic it is easiest to transform society into a socialist one, although, to be sure, Marx and Engels never made theoretical generalizations about democracy and one can argue that in their doctrine there is no real *theory* of democracy, only remarks here and there which, however, prove, I think, that Marx and Engels belong to the great Western tradition of democratic thinkers.

4. Solidarity

Solidarity, or *fraternité*, as other slogans of the French Revolution, was much used in early socialism. Etienne Cabet, one of the famous utopian socialists, wrote in 1844 in a French newspaper, *le Populaire*: 'My principle is fraternity. My system is fraternity. My science is fraternity' (Cited in Meyer, 1896, p. 549). In the writings of Marx and Engels, this principle appears especially in their programmatic texts. Three qualifications must be made. Firstly, the word 'fraternity' is not very common in the writings of Marx and Engels; secondly, solidarity or fraternity in a capitalist society is limited to the struggle of the working class against the bourgeoisie or the remnants of feudalism and thirdly, the idea of international solidarity is also limited either to the working class or to 'democrats' in general.

In nineteenth-century socialism, international solidarity was closely connected to the question of the restoration of the Polish state. This was also true for Marx and Engels, who already in an early phase of their political career were involved in the solidarity (of course this word was not in use in the nineteenth century) movement for Poland. Both men, for instance, appeared at an international meeting held in London on 29 November 1847 to celebrate the seventeenth anniversary of the Polish uprising of 1830. In Marx's speech, the word 'brotherhood' is ascribed to the bourgeoisie, for the 'bourgeois class of one country is united by brotherly ties against the proletariat of that country' and internationally the bourgeoisie of all countries are, despite their mutual competition, 'united by brotherly ties against the proletariat of all countries'. When Marx spoke about the proletariat in this context, he no longer used the word 'brotherhood', but the idea was clear: against bourgeois brotherhood the working class must place its own brotherhood, solidarity, and the 'victory of the proletariat over the bourgeoisie is at the same time the signal of liberation for all oppressed nations' (Marx and Engels, 1847, *MECW*, vol. 6, p. 388).

Engels expressed in his speech the idea which many times appeared in Marx's and Engels' writings in the late 1840s: the liberation of Germany, that is, the creation of a democratic republic in Germany, would not be possible without the liberation of Poland. Engels formulated the principle of international solidarity in his speech also at a more general level: 'A nation cannot become free and at the same time continue to oppress other nations' (*ibid.*, p. 389).

When capitalism develops, so does the strength of the proletariat.

The idea of solidarity is expressed according to the *Communist Manifesto*, in 'combinations' which the proletariat forms against exploitation by capitalists. They form 'permanent associations' and so begins 'the organization of the proletariat into a class, and consequently into political party'. However, Marx and Engels saw this not as any straightforward development because the organization is continually being upset by the competition between the workers themselves (Marx and Engels, 1848, *MECW*, vol. 6, p. 493). But it is obvious that for Marx and Engels the competition between workers was only a temporary hindrance, they were convinced that the workers would one day unite and form a unified revolutionary class.

After the *Communist Manifesto*, the most important programmatical text Marx wrote was the *Inaugural Address* of the International Working Men's Association, i.e. the First International in autumn 1864. If we compare these two texts the difference is striking. The *Communist Manifesto* presents an interpretation of human history and ends with apocalyptic prophesies about the fate of mankind. The *Inaugural Address* does not discuss such matters, but tells us, for instance, about English tax statistics. However, Marx's basic ideas are also presented in this document, although not so straightforwardly as in the *Communist Manifesto*. This is also the case with the question of solidarity or brotherhood. We again find two concepts of solidarity: fraternity between workers and international solidarity.

The workers' movement was very weak after the revolution of 1848–49 ended in the triumph of reactionary social movements. Marx described the situation as follows:

Past experience has shown how disregard of that bond of brotherhood which ought to exist between the workmen of different countries, and incite them to stand firmly by each other in all their struggles for emancipation, will be chastised by the common discomfiture of their incoherent efforts (Marx, 1864, *MECW*, vol. 20, p. 12).

It was this defect, Marx explained, which led to the formation of the new international workers' association. Marx praised the English working class for their actions during the American civil war, showing solidarity with the Northern states and sympathy towards the emancipation of slaves, and their expressions of solidarity with Poland in its struggle against Russia, 'that barbarous power'. In a nutshell, the principle of international solidarity was expressed in the following rhetorical question:

If the emancipation of the working class requires the fraternal concurrence (the German translation, made by Marx, adds there: 'of different nations'), how are they to fulfil that great mission with a foreign policy in pursuit of criminal designs, playing upon national prejudices and squandering in piratical wars the people's blood and treasure? (*ibid.*, pp. 12–13).

5. Conclusions

Marx trusted man, his rationality and his activity — perhaps far too much: if only oppressive structures of class societies which prevent the realization of human rights were to be eliminated, men could carry out their emancipation and exclude the possibility of the formation of new repressive mechanisms. Marx believed that it was possible to eliminate natural forces which had regulated the lives of men, especially, of course, economic laws which most men had had no opportunity to influence. To Marx and Engels, this was a correct perspective on human emancipation, the realization of freedom. They were determined that these forces would necessarily be eliminated because their society was irresistibly approaching some kind of boiling point where it could not continue its existence. Marx and Engels underestimated the demonic dimension of human nature. Thirst for power and domination seems to be one of the basic features of human beings. But after saying that, it must be stressed that Marx's and Engels' concept of human nature was deeply humanist. They sincerely believed in the natural capacities of human beings, that they are able to free themselves from exploitation and oppression and to establish a society where every individual has an opportunity to develop his natural abilities. Alongside the determinist element, there was a humanist element: human beings can emancipate themselves by their own efforts.

When the teachings of Marx and Engels were adopted by the workers' movement, especially in Germany, it was this determinist side of their thought which became dominant and, as a consequence, 'Marxism' became a vulgarized doctrine of predestination. All hopes were placed on the day when a revolution suddenly would break out and socialism would be realized. At the beginning of the twentieth century, the Marxist 'family' was divided into rival schools, firstly in Germany (orthodox Marxism and revisionism) and then in Russia (bolshevism and menshevism). None of these tendencies really took into consideration the humanist side of original Marxism, and where Marxists won power they created a society which was very far from Marx's ideas. For both the Leninist variant of socialism and social democratic *l'état providence* required a strong and centralized state machine. Perhaps nowadays the time is ripe to return to Marx's original ideas of self-management, self-government and self-emancipation.

Bibliography

Collections of the writings of Marx and Engels:

Marx, Karl and Friedrich Engels. *Collected Works (MECW)*. Moscow, 1975: Progress.

Marx, Karl and Friedrich Engels. *Werke (MEW)*. Berlin (DDR), 1957–1968: Dietz Verlag.

Works cited in the text:

Bacounine, Michail, 1873. *Etatisme et anarchie*, in *Archives Bakounine*. Leiden, 1967: E.J. Brill.
Bebel, August, 1892. Letter to Engels, 22 November 1892, in August Bebel, *Briefwechsel mit Friedrich Engels*. The Hague, 1965: Mouton & Co.
Engels, Friedrich, 1843. 'Progress of Social Reform on the Continent', *New Moral World*, November 1843, Collected Works, vol. 3.
—, 1846, 'The State of Germany', *The Northern Star*, 4 April 1846, Collected Works, vol. 6.
—, 1865. *Prussian Military Question and the German Workers' Party*, Collected Works, vol. 20.
—, 1871. Letter to the Spanish Federal Council of the International Working Men's Association, 13 February 1871, Collected Works, vol. 22.
—, 1884. *Der Ursprung der Familie, des Privateigentums und des Staats*, Werke, vol. 21.
—, 1886. Letter to Ferdinand Domela Nieuwenhuis, 4 February 1886, Werke vol. 36.
—, 1891a. Letter to August Bebel, 1–2 May 1891, Werke, vol. 38.
—, 1891b. Letter to Karl Kautsky, 30 April 1891, Werke, vol. 38.
—, 1982. Letter to August Bebel, 19 November 1892, Werke, vol. 38.
Fetscher, Iring, 1960. 'Marxismus und Bürokratie', *International Review of Social History*, vol. 5.
Lassalle, Ferdinand, 1862. *Arbeiterprogramm*, in Ferdinand Lassalle, *Gesamtwerke*, vol. 1. Leipzig, n.d.: Karl Fr. Dfau.
Marx, Karl, 1842. 'Proceedings of the sixth Rhine Province Assembly', *Rheinische Zeitung*, 12 May 1842, Collected Works, vol. 1.
—, 1844. *Economic and Philosophical Manuscripts of 1844*, Collected Works, vol. 3.
—, 1852. 'The Chartists', *New York Daily Tribune*, 2 August 1852, Collected Works, vol. 11.
—, 1857/1858. *Economic Manuscripts of 1857–58*, Collected Works, vol. 28.
—, 1858. 'Affairs in Prussia', *New York Daily Tribune*, 3 November 1858, Collected Works, vol. 16.
—, 1864. *Inaugural Address of the Working Men's International Association*, Collected Works, vol. 20.
—, 1874. *Notes on Bakunin's Statehood and Anarchy*, Collected Works, vol. 24.
—, 1875. *Critique of the Gotha Programme*, Collected Works, vol. 24.
Marx, Karl and Friedrich Engels, 1845/1846. *The German Ideology*, Collected Works, vol. 5.
—, 1846. 'Address of the German Democratic Communists to Mr. Feargus O'Connor, *The Northern Star*, 25 July 1846, Collected Works, vol. 6.
—, 1847. *On Poland*, Collected Works, vol. 6.
—, 1848. *Manifesto to the Communist Party*, Collected Works, vol. 6.
Meyer, Thomas, *et al.*, 1986. *Lexikon des Sozialismus*. Köln: Bund Verlag.
Paastela, Jukka, 1985. *Marx's and Engels' Concepts of the Parties and Political Organizations of the Working Class*. Acta Universitas Tamperensis, ser. A, vol. 199. Tampere: University of Tampere.

Rosanvallon, Pierre, 1979. *Le Capitalism Utopique*. Paris: Edítíons du Sevíl.
Rosenblatt, Frank F., 1967. *The Chartist Movement. In its Social and Economic Aspects*. Harlem: Frank Cass.

3 Democracy and Human Rights

Allan Rosas

1. Introductory outline

In today's human rights discourse, democracy and human rights appear as Siamese twins: they seem not only to presuppose each other but also to be genuinely intertwined. The interrelationship is already apparent in the fact that what can loosely be termed a 'right to democracy' *is* at the same time an internationally recognized human right: modern human rights instruments recognize the right to vote and other political rights and, at least indirectly, the principle of popular sovereignty. At the same time, these instruments recognize a number of 'freedoms' generally considered to be indispensable for the exercise of political rights in the narrow sense: freedom of speech, freedom of assembly and association, and so forth. This is not to say that democracy and human rights are synonymous concepts; there may certainly be tensions between majority decision-making and certain specific human rights.

The concept of democracy is no doubt problematic. It does not have a generally established meaning, in either a historical or a contemporary comparative perspective. Notions such as 'classical democracy', 'parliamentary democracy' and 'people's democracy' attest to the broad spectrum of conceptual uses. Contemporary human rights and constitutional rights literature tend to favour concepts such as 'political rights' (Nowak, 1988) or 'the right to political participation' (Steiner, 1988). And the expression 'in a democratic society', which appears in some international human rights instruments, does not lay down a specific substantive right, but relates to those instruments' limitation clauses, which modify the states' parties' competence to limit the scope of a substantive right (Vegleris, 1968; Garibaldi, 1984).

The concept of democracy has, after some hesitation, been chosen for the title of this chapter because one of our aims is to focus on *systemic* perspectives rather than a legal-dogmatic analysis of specific political rights of individuals. On the other hand, there will be a certain bias in favour of *political rights in the narrow sense*, at the expense of civil and political freedoms such as freedom of expression and the rule of law. This also implies that the chapter will not provide a full discussion on the phrase 'in a democratic society', which as was noted above appears primarily within the context of human rights limitations clauses. Moreover, our frame of reference is human rights *law*, flavoured with elements of an 'allgemeine Staatslehre' (general theory of state and law). There will thus be no attempt at a veritable sociological study of the interdependence of democracy and human rights.

Without entering into a survey of the different concepts of democracy which are to be found in the social science literature (see, for example, Anckar and Berndtson, 1984), some basic assumptions should be spelled out. A system of governance can, according to our vocabulary, be termed *democratic* only if it is based on the principle of popular sovereignty[1] and respect for the will of the people. The will of the people, again, must be allowed to express itself at regular intervals and in free and fair procedures. A necessary prerequisite is thus adherence to the government 'by' the people tradition (as distinct from government 'for' the people[2]), implying minimum requirements on decision-making *processes*, in regard both to elections and votes (political rights in the narrow sense) and to guarantees of rational and free discussion and decision-making (civil and political freedoms). Unless otherwise stated, we assume that the 'people' comprises the adult members of a given political community, in accordance with the principle of (political) equality.

In addition to the form of decision-making, a human rights-related conception of democracy seems to contain some substantive requirements for the *contents* of decisions, as, for instance, respect for minority rights. Some requirements, such as those related to the concept of the rule of law, seem to be important both as guarantees of due democratic process and as substantive requirements in and of themselves. Some of the dimensions of the concept of democracy will be considered further below, in relation to the preparatory work and application of relevant international human rights norms.

2. Historical background

While ideas of democracy and popular sovereignty are of ancient origin, a modern notion of popular sovereignty can be traced back to

---

[1] By 'popular sovereignty' we mean not only the ultimate right of the people to constitute its own political system (constitutive powers — *pouvoir constituant*, Loewenstein, 1922, p. 12) but also a right for the people to determine continuously its agreement with the system of governance and to shape, at least through representatives, the general lines of policy. This conception of popular sovereignty may thus go further than some of the classical writings on the subject (see below, at notes 2–7).

[2] Government 'for' the people, without being accompanied by government 'by' the people, may, of course, lead to dictatorial minority rule allegedly based on 'the public good', 'objective interests', etc. It will be noted that one can detect elements of the government 'for' the people tradition not only in Marxist-Leninist thought but also in the classical writings often regarded as the ideological basis of Western democracy: for example, Locke, 1690, e.g. §§ 135, 158; Rousseau, 1762, livre II. The idea of popular sovereignty, which certainly was not absent from the classical writings (at least as some form of 'ultimate' sovereignty of the people) could suggest further requirements of popular consent, however.

seventeenth- and eighteenth-century developments and the writings of such political philosophers as John Locke and Jean-Jacques Rousseau.[3] The theoretical construction was that of the popular contract, whereby the individuals gave up some of their powers to public government, but were on the other hand secured a sphere of personal freedom and 'the preservation of their property' (Locke, 1690, II §§ 124, 138) as well as a right to take part in the formation of that government.[4]

The idea of popular sovereignty is reflected in the famous documents emanating from the American and French revolutions (Hartung, 1964, pp. 36, 42, 50). There were also references, especially in the French documents, to the right to resist oppression, to the law being an expression of the general will, to the equal access of citizens to public service and to the general principle of equality. It is often held that the foundations of the various American bills of rights were primarily influenced by Locke's writings, whereas the French declarations bear more the mark of Rousseau (Nowak, 1988, p. 32).

With respect to the formulation of the principle of popular sovereignty, there are some interesting differences among the various documents. The French formulations seem particularly instructive, as they reflect the political shifts and turbulences that took place during the revolutionary years (see also Nowak, 1988, p. 33ff.). Article 3 of the Declaration on the Rights of Man and of the Citizen of 26 August 1789 states that 'the principle of sovereignty resides essentially in the nation'.[5] Article 25 of the more radical (Jacobin) Declaration of 24 June 1793 states in more unequivocal terms that 'sovereignty resides in the people'.[6] The restorative Declaration of 22 August 1795 implied a step backwards in stating that 'sovereignty resides essentially in the totality of citizens' (Article 17).[7] We can note in the last-mentioned formulation a return to the 1789 qualification 'essentially' and the deletion of the 1793 term 'people'. Compared with the 1789 Declaration, the 1795 document seems to have implied a certain atomization of the collective concept of nation (1789) to the sum total of individual citizens (1795).

Especially with the 1795 formulation, the concept of citizen

---

[3] We are well aware that there are important differences between, for example, Locke and Rousseau, see e.g. Suksi, 1988, and below, at notes 4–6.
[4] The American Declaration of Independence of 1776 proclaims 'that, to secure these rights, governments are instituted among men deriving their just powers from the consent of the governed'.
[5] Author's translation. Déclaration des Droits de l'Homme et du Citoyen du 26 août 1789, Duverger, 1964, p. 3. Art. 3: 'Le principe de toute souveraineté réside essentiellement dans la Nation. Nul corps, nul individu ne peut exercer d'autorité qui n'en émane expressément.'
[6] Duverger, 1964, p. 29. Art. 25: 'La souveraineté réside dans le peuple; elle est une et indivisible, imprescriptible et inaliénable.'
[7] Déclaration des Droits et des Devoirs de l'Homme et du Citoyen, Duverger, 1964, p. 39. Art. 17: 'La souveraineté réside essentiellement dans l'universalité des citoyens.'

becomes crucial. Whereas the 1793 Constitution constituted an unprecedented move towards the equal citizenship of all male
inhabitants, the 1791 and 1795 Constitutions restricted the concept of
citizen to a small minority of the adult population, the 'active'
citizens consisting primarily of male property-owners, and excluding
not only women but also workers, servants and other dependent
people (J. Tolonen, 1986, p. 68; Nowak, 1988, p. 38). The more
conservative outcome was closer to Locke's model, whereas it can be
argued that the abortive egalitarian proclamations of 1793
(advocated by Robespierre among others) were more in line with
Rousseau's writings (J. Tolonen, 1986, p. 65ff.).

It was only gradually, and with various steps back and forth, that
the idea of universal suffrage, and equal political rights, gained
ground. With some minor exceptions, full equality with respect to the
right to vote and to be elected was not introduced until the beginning
of the present century.[8]

The principle of equality proclaimed by the French Revolution thus
did not fully extend to political rights for a long time. In line with the
conservative restorations that took place during the nineteenth
century, there was also a tendency in many countries to deny the
status of political rights *qua* fundamental (constitutional) rights
(Nowak, 1988, p. 39ff.). And the political freedoms (political rights in
the broad sense) vital for democratic participation such as freedom of
speech, assembly and association were still often curtailed during
this period.

Not only was the category of holders of political rights restricted to
a minority of the population, and the possibility even of this
privileged group to participate freely in a democratic process limited,
but there were also attempts to circumscribe the scope and effects of
democratic decision-making.

First of all, the right to vote did, of course, apply only to the election
of 'political' bodies such as parliaments, and, with the local government reforms of the nineteenth century, local assemblies. Secondly,
various devices were constructed in most countries to hinder or
impair efforts at extending egalitarianism to property and other
economic rights. For instance, the American politician and
statesman James Madison argued for representative democracy (as
opposed to 'pure democracy') and a federal union of American states
(as opposed to smaller individual states) as a means of curbing 'a
rage for paper money, for an abolition of debts, for an equal division

---

[8]   Rokkan, 1970, p. 151ff. In Europe, Finland in 1906 became the first country to introduce
universal and equal suffrage and eligibility for men and women alike in national parliamentary
elections. The reform was all the more radical as the previous Estates were replaced by a
unicameral parliament. In the other Nordic countries, universal franchise at national level was
introduced during the period 1913–1921 and at the local level a few years earlier, as from 1908
(Denmark), *Unfinished Democracy*, 1985, p. 38.

of property, or for any other improper or wicked project' (*The Federalist Papers*, 1788, p. 77ff.). In some countries, the constitutional protection of private property implied a need for qualified majorities for legislation abolishing or restricting private ownership, with Finland still today offering an extreme example.[9]

With the rise, first of political liberalism, and later the working-class movement, many of these curtailments began to waver, especially as far as the subject population of democracy and its political and civil freedoms were concerned. In some Western states, however, one could, even after the Second World War, notice a hesitancy to recognize political rights as fundamental human rights proper. With respect to the United Kingdom, in particular, one reason for this hesitancy seems to have been an unwillingness to extend full political rights to the populations of colonies.

Some Western countries have demonstrated a reluctance to include the right to vote in their constitutional bills of rights (Nowak, 1988, p. 118ff.) and to accept the inclusion of an express right to political participation in the relevant international human rights instruments, such as the Universal Declaration of Human Rights of 1948, the European Convention on Human Rights of 1950 and the International Covenant on Civil and Political Rights of 1966 (see Section 3).

The fact that Switzerland recognized universal suffrage only in the early 1970s, and then in national elections only, and Liechtenstein in 1985, and the continuation until today of the South African *apartheid* system, are extreme examples of a certain tergiversation in Western political thought with respect to equal suffrage *and* the equating of holders of political rights with the entire adult population.

The Eastern European socialist states and socialist doctrine have been more prone at the ideological level to argue for universal norms extending the principle of equality to political rights as well. There have also been tendencies in this tradition to extend the concept of democracy beyond the public (political) sphere as this concept is delineated in Western liberal thought.

It goes without saying, however, that the Eastern European states have not until recently accepted the devices for political competition and choice (for instance, freedom of party formation) that have become part and parcel of the Western political systems during this century, and that they have stressed the individual's duties towards society and the state more forcefully than has been the case in the West. Especially after the Second World War, the terms 'democracy' have in socialist doctrine often referred to anti-Fascist political

---

[9] The right to property recognized in Article 6 of the Constitution Act of 1919 has been interpreted to offer protection also against various regulatory measures (export and import controls, price controls, etc.). Such measures *can* indeed be taken, but this, then, requires the same qualified majorities in the Parliament as are needed for constitutional amendments (if the matter cannot await the next parliamentary elections, a 5/6 majority is required), Hidén and Saraviita, 1989, p. 259.

regimes, with a stress on the obligations of these regimes to *prohibit* undesirable behaviour such as fascist propaganda and war propaganda (see Section 3 below).

While the above discussion has been primarily related to individual (political) rights, one can also note a certain tendency in the *interstate* system of the present century to assert minimum requirements for what could be termed the democratic legitimacy of *governments*. There has, for instance, at times been a trend in the foreign policy of the United States and the Central American republics to withhold recognition of a new government deemed not to have obtained sufficient popular consent (sometimes referred to as the Tobár doctrine). There has, on the other hand, also been an almost opposite tendency to accept and establish relations with whatever regime is in power (the so-called Estrada doctrine), and it can safely be concluded that, at least before the United Nations system, general international law did not provide for a legal duty of non-recognition with respect to governments which did not obtain popular consent.[10]

Democracy and the right of peoples to self-determination became key words during and after the Second World War. The Atlantic Charter, signed by United States and British leaders in 1941, referred, *inter alia*, to the 'right of all peoples to choose the form of government under which they live' (Osmanczyk, 1985, p. 56).

The UN Charter itself does not highlight the requirement of popular sovereignty and democratic processes. Although there were some discussions at the 1945 San Francisco Conference as to whether the conditions for membership should include references to the form of government of new members, Article 4 on membership refers to 'peaceloving' states only (Kelsen, 1951, p. 76). But there are, of course, some general references in the Charter to human rights and fundamental freedoms, and to the principle of self-determination. And the provisions on non-self-governing territories (Article 73 (b)) and the international trusteeship system (Article 76 (b)) contain references to the need to take into account the wishes and aspirations of the peoples concerned.

It was left to the regional organizations to spell out some requirement of 'democracy'. The Charter of the Organization of American States of 1948 declares that the solidarity and the high aims it seeks 'require the political organization of those States on the basis of the effective exercise of representative democracy' (Article 3 (d)). The Statute of the Council of Europe of 1949 requires that every member 'must accept the principles of the rule of law and of the enjoyment by

---

[10]   See, for example, O'Connell, vol. I, 1970, p. 135ff.. These issues were present in the famous *Tinoco* arbitration (Aguilar-Amory and Royal Bank of Canada Claims, Great Britain v. Costa Rica 1923), where the arbiter did look into the question as to whether the Tinoco government of Costa Rica had obtained some popular acquiescence, but where he on the other hand clearly asserted that there was no legal duty of non-recognition (*Reports of International Arbitral Awards*, 1948, vol. I, p. 369).

all persons within its jurisdiction of human rights and fundamental freedoms . . .' (Article 3). Although this provision does not mention the concept of democracy, it is stated in the Preamble that individual freedom, political liberty and the rule of law are 'principles which form the basis of all genuine democracy'. And the Preamble of the European Convention for the Protection of Human Rights and Fundamental Freedoms of 1950 states that these fundamental freedoms 'are best maintained on the one hand by an effective political democracy' and on the other hand by a common understanding and observance of the human rights upon which the fundamental freedoms depend.

3. Survey of international instruments

The first international human rights instrument to deal explicitly with what we would call the centre of the human rights aspect of democracy — the right of political participation — was the American Declaration of the Rights and Duties of Man, adopted by the Ninth International Conference of American States in 1948. Article 20 of the Declaration provides for the right of all persons having legal capacity to participate in the government of their country and to take part in popular elections. It also makes reference to the political duties of citizens.

This instrument was adopted in the spring of 1948, that is, before the Universal Declaration of Human Rights. There was a certain interaction in the preparation of the two instruments, as drafts and proposals concerning one instrument were available to the drafters of the other (Verdoodt, 1964, p. 198; Buergenthal and Norris, 1982, booklet no. 5, p. 15).

The relevant provision of the Universal Declaration, Article 21, deserves to be quoted *in extenso*:

1. Everyone has the right to take part in the government of his country, directly or through freely chosen representatives.
2. Everyone has the right to equal access to public service in his country.
3. The will of the people shall be the basis of the authority of government; this will shall be expressed in periodic and genuine elections which shall be by universal suffrage and shall be held by secret vote or by equivalent free voting procedures.

This provision is thus divided into a general participation clause ('to take part'), an equal access clause and an elections clause, the third clause being one specific realization of the first more general principle (Steiner, 1988, p. 87).

The first draft outline of the Universal Declaration considered in 1947 also contained an express provision on the right to resist oppression and tyranny (UN doc. E/CN.4/21, Annex A). This provision was finally watered down to an indirect reference in the Preamble and was then formulated not as an express right but as a statement on the importance of sustaining a regime of law so as to avoid the need for rebellion against tyranny and oppression. The efforts of some Latin American and Socialist countries to reintroduce the idea of a separate article on the right to resist tyranny and oppression did not carry the day in the Third Committee of the General Assembly (3 UN GAOR I, 3rd Committee, SR.164-165; Verdoodt, 1964, p. 311ff.).

Otherwise the original draft of 1947 did fairly well in the flux of proposals, votes and revisions which were introduced in the Commission on Human Rights and the Third Committee of the General Assembly (Verdoodt, 1964, p. 198ff.; Humphrey, 1984, p. 192). There was an unsuccessful attempt by the United Kingdom, later supported also by the United States, to have a much shorter version of Article 21, not containing any references to elections, to the will of the people as the basis of the authority of government, or to equal access to public service (UN doc. E/CN.4/99). The longer version was maintained mainly at the insistence of France, the Soviet Union and some other countries. The final version of paragraph 3, containing references both to the will of the people and to periodic and genuine elections, was adopted in the Third Committee by a large majority. The negative and abstaining votes were cast by a few Western and Latin American countries.[11]

While the United States originally had itself proposed a reference to the will of the people, phrased as an individual right (UN doc. E/CN.4/95, p. 9), in its explanation of its negative vote it stated that the formulation in the final version 'proclaimed a political principle rather than a human right'. The final text reflected a French proposal, which was based on the consideration that for minds trained in the tradition of Roman law it was illogical to state the principle as an individual right: the requirement that the authority of government be based on the will of the people was 'a collective right on the part of the people as a whole' (3 UN GAOR I, 3rd Committee, SR.131, p. 450).

Although the Soviet Union and other Eastern European countries advocated references to the will of the people, the right to resist oppression and periodic elections, they did not support efforts to introduce an express element of competitiveness and pluralism. The United States had originally proposed a formulation providing for 'a government which conforms to the will of the people, with full freedom for minority opinion to persist and, if such is the people's

---

[11] Paragraph 3 was adopted by 39 votes against 3, with 3 abstentions. Guatemala, Uruguay and probably Haiti voted against, while the United States, Ecuador and probably the United Kingdom abstained (3 UN GAOR I, 3rd Committee, SR 132-134, explanations of vote p. 472).

will, to become the effective majority' (UN doc. E/CN.4/95, p. 9), and Belgium later proposed an addition, according to which elections should be held 'with several lists' of candidates. The latter proposal drew firm opposition from the representative of the Soviet Union, who in line with the then prevalent principles of Marxist-Leninist thought stated that the Belgian amendment 'was absolutely irreconcilable with the social structure of certain Member States' and Belgium immediately withdrew its amendment.[12]

The Eastern European states (together with France and some other Western and Latin American countries) thus advocated a kind of collective right of peoples to democracy, and also what Robert Dahl in another context has called a broad *inclusiveness* of a political regime (i.e. broad popular participation and political equality, Dahl, 1971, p. 7). The Eastern European states, on the other hand, opposed express provisions on the *competitive* nature of a regime, that is, the actual existence of choices (Dahl: 'public contestation'). The position of some Western and Latin American countries was rather the opposite, in line with the traditions of Western political liberalism.

It should also be noted in this connection that Article 29, paragraph 2, of the Universal Declaration, which provides for a general limitations clause, contains a reference to 'a democratic society'. This provision does not by itself require that societies be 'democratic'. What is required is that possible *limitations* of the rights guaranteed under the Declaration meet the 'requirements of morality, public order and the general welfare in a democratic society' (Garibaldi, 1984).

In the drafting process of the Universal Declaration, the Soviet Union insisted on a wider use of the concept of democracy and, in this context, a reference to the struggle against fascism and nazism (see, for example, the Appendix to UN doc. E/800, p. 29). These efforts were not successful, and the original reference to a democratic *state* in Article 29 was replaced by the expression 'democratic society'. This was a compromise between the Soviet (and partly French) preference for using the term 'democratic State', and the preference of many Western countries to avoid the term 'democratic' altogether (for a discussion on the distinction between these two expressions see, for instance, Jacot-Guillarmod, 1987, p. 7ff.). Undoubtedly the Soviet Union sought to bring in the idea of the subordination of certain individual rights (such as freedom of speech) to the requirements of the (democratic) state and its ruling class.[13]

The hesitancy of many Western states to accept political rights fully as fundamental human rights, and to endorse the principle of

---

[12] 3 UN GAOR I, 3rd Committee, SR.132, p. 453; SR.133, p. 464; SR.134, pp. 469, 471. See also Steiner, 1988, p. 91.

[13] To quote a Soviet statement of 1948 in the Commission on Human Rights, 'it was the laws of States that fixed the limits for the exercise of human rights and freedoms', UN doc. E/CN.4/SR. 74, p. 14. See also Garibaldi, 1984, p. 57.

political equality in international instruments, was further reflected in the preparation of the *European Convention for the Protection of Human Rights and Fundamental Freedoms* (European Convention on Human Rights) of 1950. It was not possible in 1949–50 to agree on a provision on political rights in the Convention itself, with countries such as Belgium and the United Kingdom belonging to the opposition (Steiner, 1988, p. 94; Nowak, 1988, p. 142ff.). On the other hand, the European Convention, of course, recognizes a number of civil and political freedoms indispensable for the enjoyment of political rights and also contains references to a 'democratic society'. The latter reference appears within the framework of limitation clauses, in line with the solution adopted in the Universal Declaration (Vegleris, 1968, pp. 229–30).

Protocol No. 1 to the European Convention was adopted in 1952. Article 3 of this Protocol attempts to fill in the gap of the European Convention with respect to political rights. But this provision simply sets forth the requirement of 'free elections at reasonable intervals by secret ballot, under conditions which will ensure the free expression of the opinion of the people in the choice of the legislature' and does not provide for a general participation clause or any equal access clause. The emphasis is thus on representative democracy at the national level rather than on a general right of political participation.

Moreover, the elections clause is formulated as an obligation of the States Parties and not as an individual subjective right. However, the European Commission of Human Rights, and nowadays also the Court, has, through a dynamic interpretation, equated the provision with the other provisions of the European system, thus granting the individual a right of complaint. On the other hand, no violation of the elections clause has been established so far.[14]

It should be reiterated in this connection that the Statute of the Council of Europe contains references to 'genuine democracy', to the 'rule of law' and to human rights and fundamental freedoms. Democracy, as understood in the Council of Europe, 'means a pluralistic parliamentary democracy which, moreover, is characterised by respect for human rights and fundamental freedoms' (Klebes, 1988, p. 308. See also Jacot-Guillarmod, 1987; Tenekides, 1987). Political rights based on the principle of equality have gradually become generally recognized as a fundamental ingredient of this political and social regime.

Inspired by the American Convention on the Granting of Political

---

[14] The first express revision of the previous interpretation was in *W, X, Y, Z v. Belgium*, Applications no. 6745 and 6746/74 (European Commission of Human Rights). The European Court has accepted the new interpretation in the case of *Mathieu-Mohin and Clerfayt v. Belgium*, Judgment of March 2, 1987, Publ. E.C.H.R., Series A, vol. 113 (1987). See further *Digest of Strasbourg Case-Law*, vol. V, p. 829ff.; van Dijk and van Hoof, 1984, p. 355ff.; Tenekides, 1987, pp. 17–18; Nowak, 1988, pp. 148–9.

Rights to Women, adopted already in 1948, as well as by Article 21 of the Universal Declaration, the UN General Assembly in 1952 adopted a *Convention on the Political Rights of Women*, providing for the right of women to vote in all elections on equal terms with men, without any discrimination (Article 1). Here again some Western states adopted a negative or reserved position on the need for a special convention, stating that the underlying aims could be better achieved through education and information activities (but it has to be added that some socialist states, too, expressed hesitancy: Nowak, 1988, p. 130).

A more or less direct follow-up to Article 21 of the Universal Declaration is Article 25 of the *International Covenant on Civil and Political Rights*. This provision, too, contains a general participation clause, an elections clause and an equal access clause, the elections clause appearing as sub-paragraph (b) before the equal access clause (c).

Despite Article 21 of the Universal Declaration, it was not self-evident that the 1966 Covenant should include a separate article on political rights (Nowak, 1989, p. 468). Such a provision was advanced, in particular, by the Soviet Union and its allies, some Third World countries and some Western countries such as France. The original proposals were put forward by the Soviet Union (UN doc. E/CN.4/218), and a compromise text which formed the basis of what ultimately became Article 25 was, after it had been decided to draw up two separate Covenants, presented in 1953 by France and Yugoslavia.[15] Western countries such as the United Kingdom, Netherlands and Belgium at first expressed opposition or hesitancy, as they tended to view political rights more as principles than as subjective rights.

Even after it became clear in the Commission on Human Rights that the Covenant would include a provision on political rights, there was disagreement as to whether it should provide expressly for the principle of universal and equal suffrage. Many Western countries (e.g. Australia, Belgium, France, United Kingdom) again took a reserved position, but the principle was adopted in the Commission on Human Rights by 10 votes to 5, with 2 abstentions (Nowak, 1988, p. 139; Nowak, 1989, p. 470).

The whole article was adopted in the Commission by 12 votes to 1, with 4 abstentions,[16] and many years later (1961) in the Third Committee of the General Assembly by 74 votes to none, with 4

---

[15] UN doc. E/CN.4/L.224 and Bossuyt, 1987, p. 469, for further documentary references. See also Partsch, 1981, p. 238; Nowak, 1988, p. 134; Nowak, 1989, p. 470.

[16] The recorded vote was 9 votes for, 1 vote against (Belgium) and 7 abstentions. Poland, the Soviet Union and Ukraine later announced that their votes should be regarded as positive votes. The remaining states that had abstained were Australia, France, the United Kingdom and Uruguay, E/CN.4/SR.367, p. 13, SR.393, p. 10; Nowak, 1988, p. 139.

abstentions. The final near-consensus on Article 25 is underlined by the fact that only a few and fairly marginal reservations to it have been formulated by states when ratifying or acceding to the International Covenant on Civil and Political Rights (doc. CCPR/C/2/ Rev. 2, 12 May 1989; Partsch, 1981, p. 241).

There are a number of similarities between Article 21 of the Universal Declaration and Article 25 of the Covenant, but also a few interesting differences. According to the opening lines of Article 25, the rights established by the Article shall be enjoyed 'without any of the distinctions mentioned in article 2' (i.e. the non-discrimination clause of Article 2, paragraph 1) and, furthermore, 'without unreasonable restrictions'. The latter qualification is explained by the fact that the Covenant does not contain a general limitation clause like the one appearing in Article 29, paragraph 2, of the Universal Declaration.

Thus, the Covenant does not, in relation to the political rights recognized in Article 25, link the limitations clause to the expression 'in a democratic society', which in the same instrument appears in Articles 14 (legal procedures), 21 (freedom of assembly) and 22 (freedom of association). In line with her efforts in connection with the drafting of the Universal Declaration (see *supra*), it was mainly France that advocated such references.

The Soviet Union went much further in proposing to base legal procedures on 'democratic principles' and to link freedom of expression, assembly and association to the qualification that these rights be guaranteed 'in the interests of democracy' (Garibaldi, 1984, p. 59. For documentary references see Bossuyt, 1987, pp. 282, 392, 414, 424, 429). In one Soviet proposal on freedom of assembly and association, put forward already in 1949, it was even added that 'all societies, unions and other organizations of a Fascist or anti-democratic nature and their activity in whatever form shall be forbidden by law on pain of punishment' (UN doc. E/CN.4/222).

The pattern familiar from the drafting of the Universal Declaration was thus largely repeated: while the Soviet Union and other Eastern European states advocated political rights in the narrow sense and in this context the principle of political equality (or to quote Robert Dahl's expression, a large 'inclusiveness' of a political system, see *supra*), they tried to restrict political freedoms in the broader sense and hence the competitive and pluralist features of democracy ('public contestation').

Coming back to Article 25 of the Covenant, as compared with Article 21 of the Universal Declaration, perhaps the most striking difference between the two texts is the absence in Article 25 of the bold first sentence in Article 21, paragraph 3: 'The will of the people shall be the basis of the authority of government'. Article 25, paragraph 2, of the Covenant, on the other hand, requires that elections guarantee the free expression of 'the will of the electors', which may make the difference between the two provisions seem more symbolic than real.

Moreover, the two Covenants of 1966 contain an article which is not to be found in the Universal Declaration and which might, as it were, compensate for the somewhat more bleak language of Article 25 of the Covenant on Civil and Political Rights: Common Article 1 on the *right to self-determination*. This linkage between Article 1 and Article 25, which presupposes that the right to self-determination contains not only an external but also an internal aspect, requiring some basic democratic legitimacy of a political regime, will be elaborated upon in Section 4.

The *American Convention on Human Rights* of 1969 also contains a political rights provision. The similarity between Article 23 of the American Convention and Article 25 of the International Covenant on Civil and Political Rights is striking, the latter undoubtedly having influenced the text of the former (Buergenthal and Norris, booklet no. 12, p. 124; booklet no. 13, p. 55). The three sub-paragraphs a-c of Article 25 of the Covenant are repeated in the Convention with minor drafting changes only. The most apparent difference relates to the introductory limitations clause which, in the American Convention, lists as specific grounds for regulating by law the exercise of the rights recognized in paragraph 1 some considerations which would exceed the limits allowed by the Covenant.

A third regional human rights convention dealing with political rights is the *African Charter on Human and Peoples' Rights* of 1981. Article 13 of this Convention provides for a solution almost opposite to that of Protocol No. 1 to the European Convention, as it contains general participation and equal access clauses but no express elections clause. As paragraph 1 of Article 13 more or less repeats the wording of the Universal Declaration and the 1966 Covenant, i.e. that citizens have the right to participate either 'directly or through freely chosen representatives', the issue of elections is not bypassed altogether. Paragraph 3 of Article 13 contains a novel provision stating that every individual has 'the right of access to public property and services in strict equality of all persons before the law.'

Without going into the provisions of the more specialized human rights conventions, including instruments drawn up within the framework of specialized agencies such as the International Labour Organisation, one provision of particular interest should be noted: Article 7 of the *Convention on the Elimination of All Forms of Discrimination against Women* of 1979. In developing Articles 1 to 3 of the 1953 Convention on the Political Rights of Women and Article 4 of the Declaration on the Elimination of Discrimination against Women (UNGA resolution 2263 (XXII) of 1967), Article 7 of the 1979 Women's Convention grants women the equal right to vote not only in elections but also in 'public referenda', to 'participate in the formulation of government policy and the implementation thereof' and to 'participate in non-governmental organizations and associations concerned with the public and political life of the country'. Article 8 of this Convention again refers to the 'opportunity to

represent their Governments at the international level and to participate in the work of international organizations'.

The drafting of the 1979 Convention, which, in particular, drew
upon working papers prepared by the UN Secretary-General (UN doc.
E/CN.6/573, E/CN.6/591) and drafts submitted by the Philippines
and the Soviet Union, does not seem to have involved any major
political differences with respect to Articles 7 and 8.[17] In a comment
to Article 7 (then Article 8) of a 1974 draft, the United Kingdom
expressed a preference for the text of the 1967 Declaration, which was
somewhat more restrictive than the proposed text of the draft Convention, while Finland expressed some doubts concerning the
express right to participate in non-governmental organizations and
associations, as these organizations enjoy autonomy (UN doc. E/
CN.6/591, p. 20; A/32/218, p. 11). The extension of the right to
participate to public functions at the international level, ultimately
reflected in Article 8 of the Convention, seems to have originated in
an amendment submitted by the Soviet Union to Article 7 (UN doc.
A/32/218, Annex I, p. 4). While this information does not allow for
far-reaching conclusions, one can see in the drafting history of
Articles 7 and 8 some traces of the political pattern which played a
certain role in the adoption of the general political rights provisions
outlined above.

4. Self-determination, democracy and political rights

The above section on 'historical background' indicated, if not highlighted, a distinction between political rights held by individuals on
the one hand and requirements of democracy in an inter-state setting
on the other. This distinction relates to another distinction: that
between *individual* rights and *collective* rights.

It will be recalled that the reference in Article 21, paragraph 3, of
the Universal Declaration to the will of the people as the basis of the
authority of government was rephrased from an individual right to
what the author of the amendment (Professor Cassin of France)
thought should be formulated as a collective right. We also indicated
earlier that the absence of any reference to the will of the people in
Article 25 of the 1966 International Covenant on Civil and Political
Rights may be partly explained by the fact that the 1966 Covenants
instead contain common Article 1 on the right of peoples to self-
determination. The latter right (or principle) is often regarded as a
relatively clear case of a true collective right.

In this context, we understand collective rights in the narrow sense
to be rights which *cannot* be asserted by an individual acting on his

---

[17]   See, for example, UN docs. E/CN.6/589, p. 36; E/CN.6/591, p. 20; E/CN.6/608, p. 35; A/32/
218, p. 11; A/34/830.

own behalf in a legal or quasi-legal procedure. It is notable that the Human Rights Committee has not examined the merits of individual communications under the Optional Protocol to the International Covenant on Civil and Political Rights claiming violations of common Article 1.[18] On the other hand, communications invoking Article 27 of the same Covenant and relating to the protection of minorities have been declared admissible, an approach enhanced by the formulation of this Article ('persons belonging to such minorities shall not be denied . . .').

This is not yet to say that common Article 1 of the Covenants regulates the relationships between a people and its own government. Earlier on, we indicated that this is indeed the case, that the right to self-determination contains not only an external but also an *internal* element, requiring a certain minimum standard of democratic legitimacy of a political regime.

Previously it was often assumed that the primary function of common Article 1 was its anti-colonial thrust, an approach illustrated to a certain extreme by a reservation by India, according to which the words 'the right of self-determination' appearing in Article 1 'apply only to the peoples under foreign domination and that these words do not apply to sovereign independent States or to a section of a people or nation — which is the essence of national integrity' (doc. CCPR/C/2/Rev. 2, 12 May 1989, p. 22).

This reservation drew objections from France, the Federal Republic of Germany and the Netherlands on the grounds that Article 1 applies to all peoples and not only to those under foreign domination (*ibid.*, pp. 37–8), but these objections do not yet make a clear-cut case for the internal aspect of the right of self-determination. On the other hand, a textual interpretation of the Indian reservation itself might possibly allow an interpretation according to which 'peoples under foreign domination' include peoples subjugated to a regime which has usurped power without any basis in the 'will of the people', a

---

[18] In the *Mikmaq* tribal society case against Canada (communication no. 78/1980) the Committee did not expressly answer the fundamental question as to whether individual communications could be based on Article 1, as it (partly) based its decision to declare the communication inadmissible on the fact that 'the author has not proven that he is authorized to act as a representative on behalf of the Mikmaq tribal society'. In the *Kitok* case against Sweden (no. 194/1985), the Committee observed 'that the author, as an individual, could not claim to be the victim of a violation of the right of self-determination enshrined in article 1 of the Covenant. Whereas the Optional Protocol provides a recourse procedure for individuals claiming that their rights have been violated, article 1 of the Covenant deals with rights conferred upon peoples, as such'. The latter sentence would seem to indicate that the Committee would not examine under the Optional Protocol any complaints submitted by individuals on behalf of 'peoples' protected by Article 1. See also the recent *Lubicon Lake Band* Case (communication no. 167/1984), decided by the Human Rights Committee on 26 March 1990. Cf. Nowak, 1989, pp. 19–20 (with references), who mainly on the basis of the Mikmaq case holds that individuals could submit communications on behalf of peoples protected by Article 1.

regime which in so doing becomes a group of common criminals. The thrust of the reservation, then, would be an attempt to rule out an outright right of secession for a 'section' of the people, rather than the right of the people to have a government conforming to its (majority) will.

Be that as it may, the actual wording of Article 1, paragraph 1, seems to support our thesis, as it reads: 'All peoples have the right of self-determination. By virtue of that right they freely determine their political status and freely pursue their economic, social and cultural development'. The Covenants are, after all, human rights instruments, and it would be odd if they equated the identity of a 'people' with that of the government or regime claiming to represent the people, irrespective of the legitimacy of that regime. In the legal literature, there seems to be a growing case for a true human rights dimension of Article 1.[19] And the general comments on Article 1 adopted by the Human Rights Committee in 1984 seem to presuppose internal self-determination as well (doc. CCPR/C/21/Add. 3, p. 2).

Moreover, the discussions in the Third Committee of the UN General Assembly during recent years seem to have focused more and more on the internal aspect of self-determination. This is especially true of the interventions made by the members of the European Community and by the United States. In 1987, the United States even introduced a draft resolution on periodic and general elections under the agenda item dealing with self-determination (UN doc. A/C.3/42/L.15 and Rev. 1-3). As this approach met with objections from some African countries in particular, the same topic was in 1988 and 1989 presented under other agenda items and resolutions on the question of periodic elections (UNGA resolutions 43/157; 44/146) were adopted by consensus.

The case indicates that at the global level there are still political problems involved in pursuing the internal aspect of self-determination, but at the same time that there is at least a move in this direction. Some passages from an intervention of the Federal Republic of Germany in 1988 (UN GAOR, A/C.3/43/SR 7, p. 16) deserves to be quoted here:

The right of self-determination had far broader connotations than simply freedom from colonial rule and foreign domination. Article 1 . . . defined the right to self-determination as the right of all peoples freely to determine their

---

[19]   Cassese, 1979; Kiss, 1986, p. 171; Marie, 1986, p. 203; Ramcharan, 1987, p. 12; van Boven, 1987, pp. 5–6; Nowak, 1989, p. 24. In the *Western Sahara* case the International Court of Justice referred to the realization of the principle of self-determination 'through the free and genuine expression of the will of the peoples of the Territory', I.C.J. Reports, 1971, p. 60. While this advisory opinion as well as the UN General Assembly resolutions cited in it relate to a territory acceding to independence, they provide some support for the thesis that respect for the will of the people is a crucial element in the implementation of the right of self-determination in general.

political status and freely to pursue their economic, social and cultural development. The question as to how peoples could freely determine their status was answered in article 25 of the International Covenant on Civil and Political Rights. The right to self-determination was indivisible from the right of the individual to take part in the conduct of public affairs, as was very clearly stated in article 21 of the Universal Declaration of Human Rights. The exercise of the right to self-determination required the democratic process which, in turn, was inseparable from the full exercise of such human rights as the right of freedom of thought . . .

With this interpretation, which we believe is a correct reflection of the law, it is not far-fetched to assume that common Article 1 of the Covenants, together with the reference in Article 21 of the Universal Declaration to the will of the people and the indirect reference in the Preamble of the Declaration to the right to resist oppression and tyranny, set minimum standards for the democratic legitimacy of political regimes.

As to the legal relevance of this conclusion, and the relationship between Article 1 and Article 25 of the International Covenant on Civil and Political Rights, it will be noted that the right of self-determination is not expressly mentioned as a non-derogable right in Article 4 of the International Covenant on Civil and Political Rights dealing with possible derogations in times of *public emergencies threatening the life of the nation.* It is none the less difficult to perceive a public emergency which would enable a State Party to derogate from Article 1, given the general restraints on derogations contained in Article 4 (Rosas and Stenbäck, 1987, p. 225) and the fact that Article 1, in so far as it covers 'internal' self-determination, supposedly provides only for a minimum requirement of popular consent, short of the specific requirements of Article 25.[20] It is interesting to note that the American Convention on Human Rights of 1969 lists even Article 23 on the right to participate in governments as a non-derogable right.

Apart from the possibility open in some instances to individuals to assert their political rights under Article 25 of the International Covenant on Civil and Political Rights (assuming that the state in question adheres to the Optional Protocol) or Article 3 of Protocol No. 1 to the European Convention, it appears to be a matter primarily for the international system, including intergovernmental organizations, to watch over developments. As was noted above, there have

---

[20] In a communication originally made in 1982 through the UN Secretary-General to the other States Parties under Article 4, paragraph 3, Nicaragua listed also Articles 1 to 5 as provisions from which it had derogated. The legality of this sweeping suspension is already doubtful because it includes Article 4 itself (Nowak, 1989, p. 90, note 61). In later communications as from the mid-1980s, Article 1 does not appear any longer. No other state appears to have listed Article 1 as a provision derogated from International Covenant on Civil and Political Rights, doc. CCPR/C/2/Rev. 2 (12 May 1989).

from time to time been trends in the recognition policies of some governments to deny recognition to regimes deemed not to have obtained popular consent.

It is, then, probably not a violation of the UN Charter that the South African *apartheid* regime has been denied the right to represent South Africa in the UN General Assembly.[21] Nor would it necessarily have been out of order to deny, at least for an interim period, the credentials of *both* the so-called Pol Pot regime *and* the Vietnam-backed regime, which since 1979 both asserted that they were the lawful government of Kampuchea–Cambodia (Rosas *et al.*, 1984, p. 117).

The problem of Cambodia also brings up the question of the lawfulness of *armed interventions* to overthrow despotic regimes. For obvious reasons, we cannot address here the whole range of problems that the concept of intervention raises. Let us simply note first of all that there has been a tendency in recent state practice to justify the use of force against impenitent regimes by reference to the doctrine of humanitarian intervention or the principle of self-defence, in situations where there has been no imminent and formidable threat to the nationals or territory of the intervening state (*Right v. Might*, 1989). As cases like Kampuchea, Afghanistan and Grenada teach us, such interventions are bound to raise a number of political and legal objections, especially if their real objective is perceived to be the overthrow of a foreign regime merely for ideological or political reasons (for instance as an application of the by now obsolete 'Brezhnev Doctrine').[22]

There seems to have been a growing tendency to justify interventions on the ground of promoting *democracy* (Henkin, 1989, p. 44). As demonstrated by the United States intervention in Panama in December 1989, there is, on the other hand, a certain hesitancy on the part of intervening states to rely primarily and openly on this

---

[21] Tomuschat, 1984, p. 32, seems to be of the same opinion. Cf. the opinion expressed by the United States in the UN General Assembly in 1974: 'We cannot share the view that the South African delegation's credentials, having been issued by a Government elected by a minority of the inhabitants of South Africa, are invalid. There are a number of governments around the world whose representatives cannot fairly be said to represent the majority of the peoples living in their national territories, yet no one seriously suggests that their credentials should likewise be rejected. Doing so in the case of South Africa is a dangerous precedent which tomorrow could be turned against not a few in this Assembly', quoted from American Journal of International Law, vol. 68 (1974), no. 4, pp. 720–1. Compare, on the other hand, this statement with the United States justification of its intervention in Panama in December 1989, at note 23 below.

[22] The leading case in international judicature is, of course, the Case concerning *Military and Paramilitary Activities in and against Nicaragua (Nicaragua v. United States of America)*, Merits, I.C.J. Reports, 1986, p. 14. The International Court of Justice could not 'contemplate the creation of a new rule opening up a right of intervention by one State against another on the ground that the latter has opted for some particular ideology or political system'.

argument. In the UN Security Council debates on the situation in Panama, the United States justified its action as an act of self-defence under Article 51 of the UN Charter, referring also to the need to protect American lives and to defend the integrity of the Panama Canal Treaties. But in this context references were also made to the fact that the Noriega regime 'stole' the general election of May 1989 and 'repeatedly obstructed the will of the Panamanian people' and that the intervention had been approved by the 'democratically elected leadership' of the country.[23]

'Intervention for democracy' or, for that matter, intervention to prevent genocide, may have a stronger legal basis than some other forms of intervention, in that blatant disregard for the right of a people to (internal) self-determination or gross violations of fundamental human rights probably constitute serious violations of international law, and may even run counter to peremptory norms of international law (*jus cogens*).[24] On the other hand, the prohibition on the use of aggressive armed force also appears to be a peremptory norm, and in any case unilateral action to promote such a fluid concept as democracy easily opens up the way for abuses.

While 'intervention for democracy' apparently is not a legitimate form of armed action (Schachter, 1984; Henkin, 1989, p. 44. Cf. Reisman, 1984), the above developments seem to back our thesis of an emerging principle of the democratic legitimacy of governments. This principle, for instance, would allow intergovernmental organizations and their member states to deny a clearly illegitimate regime the right of representation in that organization. Within the framework of the International Covenants of 1966, the institution of inter-state complaints (which admittedly has lacked practical significance so far) covers obligations under Article 1 as well (Nowak, 1989,

---

[23] Intervention by Ambassador Pickering, UN doc. S/PV.2899. The United States representative also noted the following: 'The question before us has never been our commitment to *Panamanian* sovereignty, nor is it today, for the sovereign will of the *Panamanian* people is what we are here defending'. In another statement (S/PV.2902), he noted on the other hand that 'I am not here today to claim a right on behalf of the United States to enforce the will of history by intervening in favour of democracy where we are not welcomed. We are supporters of democracy, but not the *gendarme* of democracy, not in this hemisphere *nor* anywhere else' (note the qualification of the first sentence: 'where we are not welcomed'). A draft resolution criticizing the intervention obtained 10 votes in favour, 4 votes against and 1 abstention and thus was not adopted, as among the four negative votes were three permanent members of the Council (France, United Kingdom and United States), S/PV.2902. Nor did the United States invoke the restoration of democracy as the main legal basis for its intervention in Grenada, Schachter, 1984, p. 648.

[24] Hannikainen, 1988, pp. 717-18, argues that genocide and mass extermination, arbitrary killings and summary executions are prohibited under *jus cogens*. As to the right of self-determination, he cites 'the obligation of States to refrain from obstructing the right of dependent peoples to self-determination', apparently holding that the right of a people to 'internal' self-determination has not achieved the status of a *jus cogens* norm (see also *ibid.*, pp. 357-8).

p. 18). So does the obligation of all States Parties to submit periodic reports to the Human Rights Committee.

To infer from the above an outright legal obligation of inter-governmental organizations to deny representation, or a duty on the part of states to insist on non-recognition, is not yet easy, in view of the practice of states and inter-governmental organizations. It will be recalled, for instance, that within the framework of the Conference on Security and Co-operation in Europe there has apparently been no serious discussion on denying some particular European government the right of participation, despite the fact that the issue of minimum popular consent could certainly have been raised (for instance, with respect to Romania before the events of December 1989).

Assuming that the right of self-determination does contain an internal element, the question still remains as to the precise subject population of that right. As a collective right, it appears to relate above all to *majority* rule. This simply implies that the basic require-ment of minimum popular consent at a given time will normally be satisfied if the majority has given its consent to a particular govern-ment, and that the minority has normally not a right of resistance (at least not armed resistance, Eide, 1984) against a government which conforms to the majority will of the people.

The starting point for determining the population which (usually by a majority vote) should decide is, of course, offered by the *nation state*. This more or less self-evident assumption is reflected in the formulation of Article 21 of the Universal Declaration of Human Rights: 'Everyone has the right to take part in the government of his country . . .' Even if the seeming erosion of the European nation state (Rosas, 1989) calls for care in equating the 'people' with the citizens of a given state, the linkage between internal sovereignty and state territory will, at least for the foreseeable future, stay with us, barring, to put it in extreme terms, a loose group of people scattered around Europe from asserting the status of a subject of the right of self-determination.

This is not to say, of course, that there cannot be distinct popula-tions within an established state which may assert a right of secession or a right to autonomy, nor that minority rights have no relevance in this context. Moreover, the individual political rights such as the right to vote and to be elected, and the civil and political freedoms such as freedom of expression and of assembly, grant each individual a right to challenge the majority opinion and to endeavour, through lawful means, to have it reversed.

In addition to such safeguards relating to pluralism and the rule of law, effective democracy seems to presuppose a certain social and cultural level on the part of the whole population (basic physical and social security, literacy, etc.), although it may be difficult to establish precise and definitive legal requirements in this regard (and econ-omic and social development is, of course, not a legal precondition for political and civil rights). Taking also the social and cultural

Table 3.1. A human rights framework for democracy and political rights.

I	II	III
right of popular participation	right to take part in the conduct of public affairs,	freedom of association, freedom of assembly, freedom of expression,
right to education	right to be elected and to have access to	freedom of movement, rule of law,
right to basic security	public office, right to vote	limitations 'in a democratic society'
minority rights	minority rights	minority rights
right to development	right to self-determination	

dimension into account, a human rights framework for democracy and political rights could, for instance, be structured as shown in Table 3.1.

It will be noted that the right-hand column (III) covers primarily traditional civil rights and liberties ('first generation' of human rights) while the rights listed to the left (I) can be seen as part of the category of economic, social and cultural rights ('second generation'). This distinction is, of course, reflected in some basic human rights conventions and has played a significant role in the political human rights debate between the East and the West. It should be added, however, that the so-called integrated approach, stressing the interrelation between the two categories, is gaining ground and that the question of direct applicability and justiciability does not necessarily follow the distinction (Karapuu and Rosas, 1988, p. 36).

The middle column (II) lists political rights in the narrow sense and indicates the linkage between the right to self-determination and individual political rights. It will be recalled that historically and politically, too, these rights occupy an intermediate position. Socialist doctrine has advocated political equality and a comprehensive concept of democracy, and, of course, economic, social and cultural rights (linkage between columns I and II), but has, on the other hand, curtailed choice and public contestation. Western liberalism has been hesitant to accept political rights as fundamental rights and to endorse political equality but has, especially during the present century, advocated pluralism and individual liberties (linkage between columns II and III).

In the following sections, an attempt will be made to study in somewhat greater detail four dimensions of democracy and political rights; first of all under one heading: (1) the subject population of democracy, in other words the attainment of political equality and (2) the concept of pluralist democracy and the acceptance of choices and

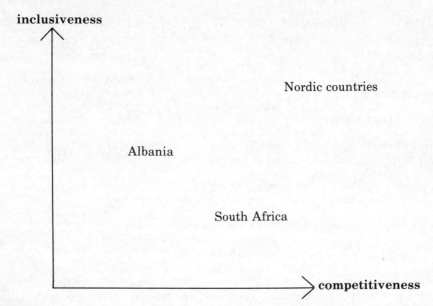

Figure 3.1.   The differences between various political systems

contestation; then under another heading: (3) the comprehensiveness (range) of democracy, in other words the question of what categories of decision-making are encompassed by the democratic process and (4) the question of 'active', as opposed to 'passive' democracy.

5. Towards inclusive and competitive democracy

We already referred above to Robert Dahl's notions of the inclusiveness and competitiveness of political regimes, the former notion relating to the extent of the subject population of democracy and the principle of equality, the latter to the degree of choices and 'public contestation' or, if you like, to pluralism. One can construct the simple scheme shown in Figure 3.1 to pinpoint the differences between various political systems.

It should be emphasized that there is an interrelation between inclusiveness and equality on the one hand, and competitiveness and pluralism on the other: if, for instance in a political system recognizing and even stressing in official doctrine the principle of political equality and the right of the entire population to take part in public life, the strategies and outcomes of public policy are determined by a small elite, with no possibilities for other parts of the population to contest those policies, it is, in fact, the principle of equality that is violated. In a European setting, Albania and, at least until December 1989, Romania, have offered extreme examples of this phenomenon.[25]

One of the great achievements of the present century has been the progress made with respect of the two dimensions of inclusiveness and competitiveness. The principle of the political equality of all adult citizens has become more or less established in Europe (see Section 2 above). With the political reforms that have recently taken place in Eastern Europe, pluralism, too, is making rapid progress. There are still a number of questions, however, which invite further study and discussion.

With respect first of all to the inclusiveness of the political system, one question relates to the age-limit of 'active citizens'. The age-limit concerning the right to vote and to stand for elections has been gradually lowered and is now 18 in many countries. Should this development be continued? Should *young people* and even *children* be granted certain political rights? The new Convention on the Rights of the Child (1989), which applies to persons below the age of 18 years, does not recognize political rights in the narrow sense but contains some provisions on freedom of thought, expression, association and assembly. While this Convention is an indication of the increasing awareness of the identity of the child as an independent human being, it is not likely that the age-limit of 18 years applying to the right to vote will be generally lowered within the near future. In Finland, there has recently been some discussion as to whether families with children should be given additional votes in general elections in order to encourage families to breed more children. There is probably no future for such ideas, however, as they would run counter to the basic notion of the independent personality of all human beings.[26]

Another question relating to the subject population of democracy concerns the status of foreign residents. No international human rights instrument appears to oblige States Parties to grant the right to vote to non-citizens. In Europe, the United Kingdom and Ireland grant non-citizen residents the right to vote even in national elections, and at the local level this idea has been followed in many other countries (e.g. the Nordic countries and some Central European countries) (Rosas, 1984, p. 233ff.). In the Council of Europe, a Draft Convention on the Participation of Foreigners in Public Life at Local

---

[25] Article 26 of the Romanian Constitution provided ample illustration: 'The most advanced and conscious citizens from among the workers, peasants, intellectuals and other categories of working people unite in the RCP, the highest form of the organization of the working class, its vanguard detachment' (Blaustein and Flanz).

[26] Such systems have existed in the past, however, and in the light of the preparatory work of the International Covenant on Civil and Political Rights they would not necessarily constitute a violation of Article 25, Nowak 1989, p. 480, note 54.

Level is currently under discussion.[27] With the refugee and immigration movements in Europe, these developments should be encouraged, certainly also in an all-European framework. Residence rather than formal citizenship may in the future be the determining factor for political affiliation with a given community, be it the European Community, a state or a regional or local government.

Let us now address the question of the prevention of (political) *discrimination* and the protection of minorities (including 'political' minorities), which also brings us closer to the notions of competitiveness and pluralism. In 1961, Hernan Santa Cruz presented his 'Study of Discrimination in the Matter of Political Rights' to the UN Sub-Commission on Prevention of Discrimination and Protection of Minorities (Santa Cruz, 1962, UN doc. CN.4/Sub.2/213/Rev.1). In 1962, the Sub-Commission adopted a set of fifteen 'General Principles on Freedom and Non-Discrimination in the Matter of Political Rights'. This fairly extensive document never led to the adoption of any normative instrument or even to any substantive follow-up, which illustrates the political sensitivity involved.[28]

That some progress has later on been achieved in a European setting is illustrated by the fact that although the Helsinki Final Act of 1975 does not list political opinion as a forbidden ground of discrimination (Principle VII), the Vienna Concluding Document of 19 January 1989 mentions as one ground of prohibited discrimination 'political or other opinion' (Questions Relating to Security in Europe, Principle 13.7).

Not all restrictions on the right of political participation are necessarily forbidden discrimination. Article 25 of the International Covenant on Civil and Political Rights recognizes the possibility of restrictions which are not 'unreasonable'. In the Universal Declaration, the possibility of restrictions is recognized in the general limitations clause of Article 29, paragraph 2.

Specific restrictions on the right to vote and to stand for election,

---

[27] Council of Europe, Steering Committee for Human Rights, doc. CDDH (89) 29, 19 July 1989. On 11 October 1989 the German Constitutional Court (Bundesverfassungsgericht) decided to postpone local elections in the state of Schleswig-Holstein scheduled for March 1990, as the constitutionality of an Act of 21 February 1989 granting the right to vote to nationals from six European states which extended the same right to German citizens had been challenged, *Neue Juristische Wochenschrift* (NJW), 1989, no. 49, p. 3147. The granting of the right to vote in local elections to Nordic citizens was in Finland considered to require an amendment (23.4.1976/334) to Article 51 of the Constitution Act. According to Section 70, paragraph 3, of the Hungarian Constitution as amended in 1989, foreign citizens domiciled in Hungary shall have the right to vote in the election of local councils.

[28] The study was transmitted to the Commission on Human Rights, which was not able to consider the topic until 1973. Ultimately the study led to the adoption of Economic and Social Council resolution 1786 (LIV), which simply drew the attention of governments and other bodies to the draft general principles (*United Nations Action in the Field of Human Rights*, 1983, p. 188).

for instance the exclusion of certain professional groups[29] or the mentally ill, may thus be possible. In the European human rights system, the exclusion from the right to vote of certain special categories of persons such as non-resident citizens and so-called convicted disloyal citizens has been tolerated (*Digest of Strasbourg Case-Law*, vol. V, p. 829ff.). Sweeping exclusions, for instance of illiterates, tend to constitute violations, however (Santa Cruz, 1962, p. 10, and his Principles IV and XI, *ibid.*, p. 97; Partsch, 1981, p. 238; Nowak, 1989, pp. 478, 489). Nor is it permissible to make the right to vote dependent on property ownership or income.[30] It would seem that Article 23 of the American Convention on Human Rights of 1969 allows for more far-reaching limitations than the other instruments, as paragraph 2 of this provision lists as specific grounds for regulating by law the exercise of the rights recognized in paragraph 1 not only age, nationality, and civil and mental capacity but also 'residence, language, education' as well as 'sentencing by a competent court in criminal proceedings'.

With regard to the question of discrimination, other specific aspects of an electoral system may also come up. The elections clauses of the political rights provisions of the international instruments and their drafting history make it clear that they were intended to leave states a fairly wide margin of appreciation in devising their electoral systems. Thus, for instance, a system of majority voting in one-seat constituencies, of 'indirect' elections (meaning that the voters cast their ballots for electors, not directly for the ultimate candidates), or of special ratios for minorities or other unprivileged groups, do not, as such, run counter to the elections clauses (Santa Cruz, 1962, p. 9ff.; cf. his Principle V, p. 97; see also Partsch, 1981, p. 240; Törnudd, 1986, p. 187ff.; Steiner, 1988, p. 90). Of course, if such devices are applied to the extreme, so as in fact to substitute minority rule for majority rule, the margin of appreciation may be transgressed.

In the European human rights system, there have been several cases dealing with the specifics of electoral systems, but in no case has a violation of Article 3 of Protocol No. 1 been established (see note 14 *supra*). Thus, for instance, the simple majority system applied in the United Kingdom has been considered to be in accordance with

---

[29] But note that Mexico has deemed it necessary to formulate a reservation to Article 25, stating that its Constitution 'provides that ministers of religion shall have neither an active nor a passive vote, nor the right to form associations for political purposes', doc. CCPR&C/2/Rev. 2, 12 May 1989, p. 25.

[30] Australia originally entered a reservation to Article 25 of the International Covenant on Civil and Political Rights, accepting the principle of universal and equal suffrage only 'without prejudice to law . . . which establish franchises for municipal and other local government elections related to the sources of revenue and the functions of such government'. In 1984 this reservation was withdrawn, doc. CCPR/C/2/Rev. 2 (12 May 1989), pp. 11, 34.

Article 3. In one fairly recent case,[31] the European Court of Human Rights accepted a Belgian system under which French-speaking voters in an electoral district with a Flemish majority were, in practice, debarred from a representation of their own at the regional legislative level (the Flemish Council). The Court, as has the Commission on several occasions, spoke of 'a wide margin of appreciation' left to the Contracting States under Article 3 of Protocol No. 1. It is not to be excluded that this margin of appreciation will be narrowed down in future European case-law (Tenekides, 1987, p. 17).

The Human Rights Committee also has considered several individual communications alleging unreasonable restrictions on the exercise of the political rights recognized in Article 25 of the International Covenant on Civil and Political Rights. In most of these cases, the Committee has found a violation of this provision, as the restrictions (usually imposed against political opponents in Uruguay) have been far-reaching and coupled with restrictions on civil rights as well.[32]

Not only should individuals and minorities in opposition to the regime in power be protected against outright discrimination, but ethnic and similar minorities should also enjoy special protection, irrespective of whether they enjoy an express right of secession. Contemporary human rights law is rather weak in offering specific minority protection. There is Article 27 of the International Covenant on Civil and Political Rights, but this provision is open to different interpretations, and most other human rights instruments, including the European Convention of 1950, are almost silent on the issue.

This, of course, does not imply that one cannot extract from the totality of human rights law a certain protection of minorities. One could mention in this connection the judgment of the European Court of Human Rights in the Case of *Young, James and Webster* (Judgment of 13 August 1981, Publ. E.C.H.R., Series A, vol. 44), which, although related to the question of individual freedom v. trade union interests (the 'closed shop' system) can be given more general significance. According to the Court the expression 'in a democratic society', which as was noted above relates to the limitation clauses of the European Convention as well as some other human rights instruments, presupposes pluralism, tolerance and broad-mindedness:

Although individual interests must on occasion be subordinated to those of a group, democracy does not simply mean that the views of a majority must always prevail: a balance must be achieved which ensures the fair and proper treatment of minorities and avoids any abuse of a dominant position.

---

[31] Case of *Mathieu-Mohin and Clerfayt* (Judgment of March 2, 1987, Publ. E.C.H.R., Series A, vol. 113). The decision was taken by a vote of 13 against 5.

[32] Human Rights Committee, *Selected Decisions under the Optional Protocol*, 1985, pp. 40, 57, 61, 65, 67, 76, 88, 105. See also Nowak, 1989, pp. 474, 486ff.

In this sense, minority protection, including specific positive guarantees to ethnic, religious and other groups, can be seen as a kind of intermediate principle between the right of self-determination (which normally must be operationalized as the right of the majority to decide) and individual political and civil rights.

This also brings us to the crucial question of the elements of *pluralism* in the political system itself. In the European human rights system, it is beyond doubt that political pluralism and tolerance, respect for minority opinions and a multi-party system are today minimum requirements (Bullinger, 1985, p. 50; Jacot-Guillarmod, 1987; Klebes, 1988, p. 308). This has not always implied freedom for any political movement, as illustrated by the decision of the European Commission of Human Rights in 1957 to declare inadmissible an application by the (West) German Communist Party, which had been dissolved through a decision by the German Constitutional Court.[33]

In an all-European framework, such civil and political freedoms as freedom of speech (see Dimitrijevic's chapter in this volume) and the rule of law are today making almost dramatic progress. At the global level, freedom of expression as well as the question of periodic and genuine elections seem to be emerging subjects on the human rights agenda.[34] But does global international human rights law, for instance, require a multi-party system?

This issue, as was noted above, was briefly considered during the preparation of the Universal Declaration, with the United States and Belgium proposing express references to the need for choices. The fact that the authors, faced with opposition from the Soviet Union in particular, did not press for their proposals, and the fact that this aspect was not openly debated during the preparation of the International Covenant on Civil and Political Rights, might be taken as an indication that the global instruments do not contain an absolute prohibition of the one-party system (Nowak, 1989, pp. 475, 482).

On the other hand, Article 25 of the International Covenant on Civil and Political Rights requires that 'every citizen' shall have the

---

[33] Application 250/57 (*Kommunistische Partei Deutschland v. Federal Republic of Germany*), European Commission of Human Rights, Documents and Decisions, vol. I (1955–57), p. 222. The decision to declare the application inadmissible was based on Article 17 (although this provision does not seem to have been invoked by the Federal Republic), according to which 'nothing in this Convention may be interpreted as implying for any State, group or person any right to engage in any activity or perform any act aimed at the destruction of any of the rights and freedoms set forth herein or at their limitation to a greater extent than is provided for in the Convention'. For criticism of the decision see, for example, van Dijk and van Hoof, 1984, p. 412.

[34] See the Working Paper on 'the right to freedom of opinion and expression' prepared by Danilo Türk for the UN Sub-Commission on Prevention of Discrimination and Protection of Minorities of the Commission on Human Rights, UN doc. E/CN.4/Sub.2/1989/26 (22 June 1989) and the United States-sponsored UN General Assembly resolutions on periodic and genuine elections, below, at note 36.

right and the opportunity, 'without any of the distinctions mentioned in Article 2' (where 'political or other opinion' is mentioned as a prohibited ground of distinction), to take part in the conduct of public affairs, directly or through 'freely chosen' representatives. And elections should be 'genuine' and be held 'by secret ballot, guaranteeing the free expression of the will of the electors'. To these formulations can, of course, be added the provisions of the Covenant dealing with civil and political freedoms and the rule of law.

In considering periodic state reports, some members of the Human Rights Committee have occasionally addressed the question of competitiveness, but no definitive conclusions can be drawn from these discussions (Partsch, 1981, p. 240ff.; Steiner, 1988, pp. 91-2). The Committee has not been able to draw up so-called general comments on Article 25, which illustrates the political and legal difficulties involved.

In interpreting the Covenant on this point, one should avoid black–and–white solutions.[35] A distinction could be made, for instance, between the following alternatives:

• constitutional one-party or non-party system;
• constitutional dominant-party system;
• *de facto* one-party or dominant-party system.

It is worth noting that the one-party system is not necessarily limited to 'socialist' or 'Eastern' countries. This is even more true with respect to states that prohibit all political parties (Gastil, 1987, p. 75). A rather extreme example of an institutionalized one-party system is offered by the Constitution of Zaire (Blaustein and Flanz, 1971), which provides that the only political institution allowed is the Popular Movement of the Revolution, whose President is at the same time the President of the Republic. It is even stated that the Popular Movement 'is the Zairean Nation organized politically', and that its doctrine is 'Mobutism' (Article 33. On African one-party systems see, Eze, 1984, p. 57ff.; Babu, 1989).

Such an institutionalized one-party system is certainly difficult indeed to reconcile with the political rights recognized under Article 25, not to speak of the civil freedoms guaranteed in other parts of the Covenant (see also Principle VIII in Santa Cruz, 1962, p. 98; Partsch, 1981, p. 240; Nowak, 1989, pp. 475-6). The situation with respect to other one-party or dominant-party systems may be less clear. The 'leading role' given to one party in the constitution may imply different things in different contexts. It is interesting to note that the United States, when introducing at the 43rd session of the UN General Assembly (1988) a draft resolution on periodic and general

---

[35] There is, for instance, a continuum between 'totalitarian' and 'liberal' regimes and states can be rated along this continuum according to different criteria. See, for example, Gastil, 1987, pp. 29-35, 77.

elections, stated that the formulation 'an electoral process which accommodates distinct alternatives', while it could be interpreted in different ways, 'did not require Member States to adopt a multiparty system. In practice, it could refer to a choice among various candidates belonging to the same party' (UN GAOR A/C.3/43/SR.55, p. 16).

Since the 44th session of the UN General Assembly in 1989, the topic of 'enhancing the effectiveness of the principle of periodic and genuine elections' has been discussed under its own separate agenda item. UN General Assembly Resolution 44/146, adopted in December 1989, contains, *inter alia*, the following paragraph of some relevance for the question of competitiveness:

3. *Declares* that determining the will of the people requires an electoral process that provides an equal opportunity for all citizens to become candidates and put forward their political views, individually and in co-operation with others within constitutional and national legislation;

One cannot but note the cautious wording and the qualification at the end: 'within constitutional and national legislation'. The resolution also contains a number of other qualifications and was accompanied by resolution 44/147 initiated by Cuba, entitled 'Respect for the principles of national sovereignty and non-interference in the internal affairs of States in their electoral processes'.[36]

In so far as a one-party system could be reconciled with Article 25 and the other provisions of the Covenant, there must at least be some minimum pluralism and tolerance within the leading party as well as in the political and social system at large. In this connection, one can also note that the principle of democratic centralism, hitherto applied in states adhering to the Marxist-Leninist doctrine, has aggravated the non-pluralist nature of the one-party system, as it has impaired competitiveness within the ruling party.

With the political changes that have recently taken place in Europe, one could adumbrate an emerging 'European' human rights standard, requiring a higher degree of pluralism and competitiveness than would be the minimum requirement of the Covenant. This perspective should be further explored within the CSCE framework. At the time of writing, Albania is the only European country which clings to a formal one-party system with an express constitutional provision on the leading role of one particular party.

In this context, it should be remembered that the international human rights instruments do not require that all political activities are channelled through 'parties' in the Western European sense. The very term 'party' does not appear in these instruments. Political

---

[36] This resolution was adopted by a recorded vote of 100 to 24, with 11 abstentions, UN doc. A/44/828, 5 December 1989, p. 5.

rights may well be exercised within the framework of other associations and groupings as well.

Although constituting a rather traditional form of political democracy, general *elections* are still a crucial procedural guarantee of democracy and are also required in the International Covenant on Civil and Political Rights and Protocol No. 1 to the European Convention on Human Rights. As was noted above, the principle of periodic and genuine elections has recently been placed on the agenda of the UN General Assembly, and the topic is also under consideration in the Commission on Human Rights. In resolution 44/ 146, initiated by the United States and finally adopted by consensus, the General Assembly also:

2. *Stresses* its conviction that periodic and genuine elections are a necessary and indispensable element of sustained efforts to protect the rights and interests of the governed and that, as a matter of practical experience, the right of everyone to take part in the government of his or her country is a crucial factor in the effective enjoyment by all of a wide range of other human rights and fundamental freedoms, embracing political, economic, social and cultural rights;

There are a number of weaknesses in the resolutions on electoral processes adopted by the UN General Assembly in 1988 and 1989. It is, on the other hand, an encouraging sign that the very issue has been brought up on the global human rights agenda. It seems likely that the question will also be further explored within the European CSCE framework, given recent United States proposals on periodic elections, including a requirement that elections in the CSCE countries be open to monitoring by foreign observers.[37] During recent years, the international monitoring of elections has become fairly common at the global level as well, although it has so far been based on *ad hoc* arrangements either within the framework of the UN (Namibia 1989) or on a voluntary regional, bilateral or non-governmental basis (the Philippines, Chile, Nicaragua, the Eastern European elections of spring 1990, and so forth).

Article 25 of the Covenant also leaves room for various forms of 'direct' democracy, such as referenda and plebiscites, referring as it does in sub-paragraph (a) to the right to take part in the conduct of public affairs, 'directly or through freely chosen representatives'. Article 7 of the 1979 Convention on the Elimination of All Forms of Discrimination against Women expressly grants women the right to vote not only in elections but also in 'public referenda'. It would seem that the term 'elections' in sub-paragraph (b) should be construed broadly, which would imply that the elections requirements ('secret

---

[37] See, for example, speech by Secretary of State James A. Baker ('1990 Must Be the Year of Building Anew'), held in Prague on 7 February 1990 (Official Text, United States Information Service, Helsinki).

ballot', etc.) apply to referenda as well, at least if they are of a decisive nature (Santa Cruz, 1962, p. 9, and his Principles IV–V, p. 97). As the wording of the elections clause in Protocol No. 1 of the European Convention is more restrictive ('choice of the legislature') it is understandable that the European Commission has held that the provision was not applicable in the British consultative referendum on EEC membership (*Digest of Strasbourg Case-Law*, vol. V, p. 864, Application no. 7096/75). No human rights instrument seems to require the organizing of referenda.

6. Towards comprehensive and active democracy

Since the 1970s, there has been an increasing discussion in the West on a broader conception of political participation and democracy than mere participation in periodic elections. Concepts such as 'participatory' democracy, 'strong' democracy and decentralization and self-government have become fashionable key words (Duncan, 1983; Barber, 1984; Held and Pollitt, 1986. A survey, from a human rights practice, is offered by Steiner, 1988, p. 96ff.). This discussion seems to relate to both the scope and methods of democratic decision-making. One could speak of comprehensive democracy, meaning that democracy is extended to all forms of relevant decision-making, irrespective of whether it is regarded as law-making or not, and active democracy, meaning that the people are given a more active role than just participation in general elections at regular intervals (see Figure 3.2).

The existing human rights instruments primarily seem to address themselves to *national elections*. As was noted above, this is especially true of Protocol No. 1 to the European Convention, Article 3 of which refers to the 'choice of the legislature'. The European organs have included in the term 'legislature' regional bodies with legislative functions (Case of *Mathieu-Mohin and Clerfayt* decided in 1987 by the Court, see note 31 *supra*) but *not* regional councils without legislative powers or local government authorities competent to adopt by-laws only (*Digest of Strasbourg Case–Law*, vol. V, pp. 864–5). Article 25 of the 1966 Covenant seems broader in scope, referring as it does in sub-paragraph (a) to the right to take part 'in the conduct of public affairs' and in sub-paragraph (b) to the right to vote and to be elected 'at genuine periodic elections', without any express limitation to national elections (Partsch, 1981, p. 242ff.). It is arguable that regional and local elections, too, are covered by this formulation provided that there are local government authorities with at least quasi-legislative powers.

With respect to the European Communities, the issue of the applicability of the European elections clause to the direct elections of the European Parliament has also arisen. The Commission has not excluded the applicability of Article 3 but does not seem to have taken

comprehensive democracy

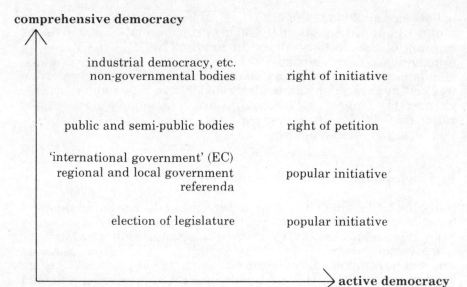

industrial democracy, etc.
non-governmental bodies   right of initiative

public and semi-public bodies   right of petition

'international government' (EC)
regional and local government   popular initiative
referenda

election of legislature   popular initiative

active democracy

Figure 3.2.   Comprehensive and active democracy.

a final stand, hinting that the outcome may depend on whether the European Parliament will be granted true legislative powers (*Digest of Strasbourg Case-Law*, vol. V, p. 865, Applications 8364/78, 8611/79, 8612/79). In this connection it should also be recalled that Article 8 of the 1979 Convention on the Elimination of All Forms of Discrimination against Women refers to the opportunity of women 'to represent their Governments at the international level and to participate in the work of international organizations'.

With respect to other types of bodies, such as public or semi-public entities (on the grey area between the public and the private sector see Modeen and Rosas, 1988; Modeen and Rosas, 1990), non-governmental organizations or commercial enterprises, there is not much to be found in existing instruments. It will be noted that in the preparation of the International Covenant on Civil and Political Rights, there was a Soviet proposal on the right of citizens to elect and be elected 'to all organs of authority'. This proposal, however, was rejected in the Commission on Human Rights, primarily out of concern about extending the elections requirement to the executive and the judiciary (Bossuyt, 1987, p. 474).

As to existing human rights norms, Article 7 of the 1979 Women's Convention seems again to provide the most interesting source material in granting women the right to 'participate in non-governmental organizations and associations concerned with the public and political life of the country'. This formulation arguably covers political parties. Especially if the political parties have a monopoly in nominating candidates to political assemblies, one could argue that the general participation clause of Article 25, together with the freedom of association clause of the International Covenant on Civil and Political Rights, require not only that there should be a right either to join existing parties or to form new ones, but also that there should be some minimum democracy *within* the parties.[38]

The 1988 Additional Protocol to the European Social Charter of 1961 contains a modest step towards *industrial democracy* by providing for the rights of workers to be informed and consulted within an undertaking concerning certain developments which could substantially affect their interests (Article 2) and to take part in the determination and improvement of the working conditions and work environment (Article 3). In addition, the Community Charter of the Fundamental Rights of Workers, adopted by eleven out of twelve Heads of State and Governments of the European Community on 9 December 1989, contains a general provision on the right of workers to 'information, consultation and participation'.

In this context, it may also be of some interest to recall Article 13 of the African Charter on Human and Peoples' Rights, which provides not only that citizens have the right to participate in the government of their country but also sets forth the right of every individual 'of access to public property and services in strict equality of all persons before the law'.

The above developments thus point to a certain broadening of the scope of the right of participation, whether this is conceived as a true political right or not. In the same vein, there is an ongoing UN study on 'popular participation', based on a study presented in 1985 by the UN Secretary-General to the Commission on Human Rights (UN doc. E/CN.4/1985/10 and Add.1-2). This study was undertaken within the broader framework of the realization of economic, social and cultural rights, but also contains a section on the right to take part in the conduct of public affairs and alludes to the broader perspectives on participation referred to above.

Moreover, the Declaration on the Right to Development, adopted by the UN General Assembly in 1986 (resolution 41/128) refers to the right of human persons 'to participate in . . . economic, social, cultural and political development' (Article 1, paragraph 1) and the duty of states to 'encourage popular participation in all spheres as an important factor in development and in the full realization of all human rights (Article 8, paragraph 2).

While the above comments have been related primarily to the scope of democracy, there seems to be even less to be said about the 'active' aspects of democracy. Of course, the general right 'to take part' in the

---

[38] Thus, the Kenyan system of nominating the candidates for parliamentary elections of the leading party, the Kenyan African National Union, through public elections (queues of voters) (*Human Rights in Developing Countries*, 1989, p. 190) is probably a violation of Article 25.

conduct of public affairs or other types of decision-making can be given a dynamic thrust, so as to point to the need not only to allow but also to encourage popular initiatives and an active involvement of various sectors of the population. This could imply both developing the institutions of popular initiative at the legislative level, including initiatives for referenda, and promoting the rights of initiative and petition at the executive level and within the semi-private and private sectors. The American Declaration of the Rights and Duties of Man of 1948 states (Article 24):

Every person has the right to submit respectful petitions to any competent authority, for reasons of either general or private interest, and the right to obtain a prompt decision thereon.

And the Declaration on the Right to Development referred to above states that the human person is the central subject of development and should be 'the active participant and beneficiary' of the right to development (Article 2). The scant references in recent instruments, both to the rights of women to participate in certain non-governmental organizations and to elements of industrial democracy, also seem to presuppose 'active' participation, and on the whole there is a close interrelation between 'comprehensive' and 'active' democracy.

While in view of the foregoing the human rights instruments in force do not yet provide for an unequivocal and general obligation to extend the scope of political rights beyond the sphere of 'public' decision-making, nor to establish legal institutions providing for outright popular initiatives, one should view the right of political participation as a 'programmatic' right, setting aspirations and new demands as societies change (Steiner, 1988, p. 129ff.). One could give the expression 'in the conduct of public affairs' appearing in Article 25 of the International Covenant on Civil and Political Rights a broad meaning, so as to include decision-making which is of a *general* interest, whether or not it forms part of 'public' affairs and the public sector in the traditional sense.

7. Summary and conclusions

The previous discussion brought out the close historical interrelationship between the development of democratic theory and corresponding legal developments. In Western liberal political thought, as well as in constitutional settings, the notion of equal political rights gained ground only slowly and has not become firmly rooted in all Western industrialized countries even today. Many of the Western states were hesitant, to say the least, to accept the inclusion of provisions on popular sovereignty, the right of peoples to self-determination and political rights in the international human rights instruments adopted since 1948. The concept of democracy has, for instance within the Council of Europe, been linked to civil and political freedoms and the rule of law, rather than to popular sovereignty and political rights in the narrow sense.

The Eastern European states adhering to Marxist conceptions advocated more strongly international human rights norms dealing with popular sovereignty, including the right of resistance, and the equal enjoyment of political rights. In regard to civil and political freedoms, however, they stressed duties rather than rights. Their conception of democracy became, also in a human rights context, linked to efforts to combat 'anti-democratic' forces, at the international level against Fascism and Neo-Fascism in particular; at the domestic level all forces deemed hostile to socialism.

Common to these two different concepts of democracy has been their emphasis on substance (the liberal state or socialism) rather than form. Democracy's *procedural* dimensions, the question of how the will of the people is to be ascertained (periodic elections, etc.), have been present but somewhat more in the background. The will of the people has, as it were, been presumed to correspond to the substantive principles of the ideal societal systems.

It has to be added, though, that democratic procedures such as general elections based on equal suffrage have entered the political life of many countries during the present century, and that these procedures have been more free and fair in the West than in other regions. The hesitancy of some Western countries to confirm these developments at the level of international human rights instruments could be explained as an ideological lag overtaken by societal events.

Moreover, the agreed texts of the political rights provisions of the universal instruments, especially Article 21 of the Universal Declaration and Article 25 of the International Covenant on Civil and Political Rights, do have a procedural rather than substantive thrust. It is understandable that indeed the procedural dimension of democracy in 1948 and 1966 offered the only possible common denominator for reaching agreement on the universal texts, with the silent understanding, on the other hand, that the requirements of competitiveness and pluralism be left somewhat fuzzy.

On balance, however, the universal norms relating to political rights were, after all, fairly radical for the times of their adoption. The normative basis for promoting democracy and political rights from a human rights perspective is in our view quite satisfactory, given also the recognition in the 1966 Covenants of the right of peoples to self-determination (which, we have concluded, contains an 'internal' aspect as well) and of civil and political freedoms and the rule of law. In the Western European human rights system, the normative basis for political rights is weaker, but this has been partly compensated for by domestic legislation and practices and the protection of civil and political freedoms by the European Convention.

At the all-European as well as at the universal level, the main problems have related to the application and implementation of political rights. The inclusiveness (principle of equality) of political systems has made headway, but their competitiveness and leeway for pluralism have in many cases not lived up to international standards. Despite the existence of the right of peoples to self-determination, even groups lacking any popular consent have been allowed to 'represent' states in international fora. From now on, the international community (rather than states acting unilaterally) should more fully recognize its responsibilities for guarding the principle of popular sovereignty.

In Europe, there has, of course, been a dramatic improvement quite recently. With one or two exceptions, there is already a consensus on a combination of inclusiveness and competitiveness which by and large meets international standards. Now the focus should be on the institutional strengthening of this consensus, as well as on the 'comprehensive' and 'active' aspects of democracy discussed in Section 6 above, and taking into account emerging normative developments such as those reflected in the 1979 Convention on the Elimination of All Forms of Discrimination against Women and the 1988 Additional Protocol to the European Social Charter.

The idea of genuine and active democratic participation, with open and informed discussion and interaction, and effective accountability, may at the present historic moment offer a common ground for democracy- and human rights–related endeavours in an all-European framework. It is important to keep up a dynamic forward-oriented process, taking into account the need to promote all aspects of relevance for democracy, such as its inclusiveness, competitiveness, comprehensiveness and 'participatoriness'. And state democracy may be gradually transformed to become 'a real "European democratic society"', not only within, but beyond a democratic State itself' (Jacot-Guillarmod, 1987, p. 30f.). Such a development may be part of a general erosion of the European nation state (Rosas, 1989). To be sure, these perspectives also bring us to the need for a broader political and societal process, where international human rights law, at best, can only provide frames of reference and stimuli.

8. Epilogue: the concept of property

The 'new forms' of democracy and political rights suggested above bring us, it would seem, to the very concept of property. It will be recalled that John Locke and others stressed the linkage between human rights and property by considering that the aim of the social contract and the task of political society was to secure the preservation of property. This linkage was made even more concrete by requiring property ownership as a precondition for the exercise of political rights.

While such limitations are unthinkable today, the linkage between democracy and property may still be with us. It should be noted, on the other hand, that for John Locke, the concept of property was given a wider meaning than is common today, encompassing not only material possessions but also life and liberty. The time may again have come for a broader conception of property, which could include some social ('new property', see Eriksson, 1989) and environmental rights.

This would imply, for instance, the extension of something akin to property rights to *res communes* (commons) such as the air and the seas, and on the other hand a relativization of ownership of possessions, especially landed property. Notions of common ownership and shared ownership, known from feudal property law (H. Tolonen, 1984, pp. 267–94), may be witnessing a certain renaissance.

Pluralist democracy, perhaps, invites visions of pluralist ownership.

Bibliography

Anckar, Dag and Erkki Berndtson (eds), 1984. *Essays on Democratic Theory.* Helsinki: The Finnish Political Science Association.

Babu, A.M., 1989. 'Human Rights and the One-Party State in Africa', *Netherlands Quarterly of Human Rights* (in continuation of the SIM Newsletter), vol. 7, no. 2.

Barber, Benjamin R., 1984. *Strong Democracy: Participatory Politics for a New Age.* Berkeley: University of California Press.

Blaustein, Albert P. and Gisbert H. Flanz, 1971. *Constitutions of the Countries of the World. A Series of Updated Texts, Constitutional Chronologies and Annotated Bibliographies.* Dobbs Ferry, NY: Oceana.

Bossuyt, Marc J., 1987. *Guide to the 'Travaux Preparatoires' of the International Covenant on Civil and Political Rights.* Dordrecht: Martinus Nijhoff.

van Boven, Theo, 1987. Report on 'Democracy, Human Rights and Solidarity', *Paper presented to the Colloquy 'Democracy and Human Rights',* Thessaloniki (Greece), 24–26 September 1987. Strasbourg: Council of Europe doc. H/Coll (87) 5.

Buergenthal, Thomas and Robert E. Norris (eds), 1982. *Human Rights — The Inter-American System.* Binders 1-3. Booklets 1-26. Dobbs Ferry, NY: Oceana.

Bullinger, M., 1985. 'Report on Freedom of Expression and Information: An Essential Element of Democracy', in *Proceedings of the Sixth International Colloquy about the European Convention on Human Rights,* organized by the Secretariat General of the Council of Europe in collaboration with the Universities of the autonomous Community of Andalusia, Seville, 13–16 November 1985. Dordrecht 1988: Martinus Nijhoff.

Cassese, Antonio, 1979. 'Political Self-Determination — Old Concepts and New Developments', in Antonio Cassese (ed), *UN Law/Fundamental Rights: Two Topics in International Law.* Alphen aan den Rijn: Sijthoff & Noordhoff.

Dahl, Robert A., 1971. *Polyarchy: Participation and Opposition.* New York: Yale University Press.

Digest of Strasbourg Case-Law relating to the European Convention on Human Rights, vols I-VI. Council of Europe. Köln 1984-1985: Carl Heymanns.

van Dijk, Pieter and G.J.H. van Hoof, 1984. *Theory and Practice of the European Convention on Human Rights.* Deventer: Kluwer.

Duncan, Graeme (ed.), 1983. *Democratic Theory and Practice.* Cambridge: Cambridge University Press.

Duverger, Maurice (ed.), 1964. *Constitutions et documents politiques.* Troisième édition. Paris: Presses Universitaires de France.

Eide, Asbjørn, in collaboration with Leif Barlaug and Chakufuwa Chihana, 1984. 'The Rights to Oppose Violations of Human Rights: Basis, Conditions and Limitations', in *Violations of Human Rights: Possible Rights of Recourse and Forms of Resistance.* Paris: Unesco.

Eriksson, Lars D., 1989. 'Sociala rättigheter som en ny form av egendom', in *Juhlakirja Jaakko Pajula. Vol. I: Ihminen ja yhteiskunta.* Helsinki: Kansaneläkelaitos (The Finnish Social Insurance Institution).

European Commission of Human Rights. *Documents and Decisions 1955-1956-1957.* Yearbook, vol. 1. The Hague 1959: Martinus Nijhoff.

Eze, Osita C., 1984. *Human Rights in Africa: Some Selected Problems.* Lagos: The Nigerian Institute of International Affairs, in co-operation with Macmillan Nigeria.

The Federalist Papers. Alexander Hamilton, James Madison, John Jay. Edited and with an Introduction by Clinton Rossiter. New York 1961: New American Library (NAL Penguin).

Garibaldi, Oscar M., 1984. 'On the Ideological Content of Human Rights Instruments: The Clause "In a Democratic Society" ', in Thomas Buergenthal (ed.), *Contemporary Issues in International Law. Essays in Honor of Louis B. Sohn.* Kehl: N.P. Engel.

Gastil, Raymond D., 1987. *Freedom in the World: Political Rights and Civil Liberties 1986-1987.* New York: Greenwood Press.

Hannikainen, Lauri, 1988. *Peremptory Norms (Jus Cogens) in International Law: Historical Development, Criteria, Present Status.* Helsinki: Finnish Lawyers' Publishing Company.

Hartung, Fritz, 1964. *Die Entwicklung der Menschen- und Bürgerrechte von 1776 bis zur Gegenwart.* 3. erweiterte Auflage. Göttingen: Musterschmidt.

Held, David and Christopher Pollitt (eds), 1986. *New Forms of Democracy.* London: Sage.

Henkin, Louis, 1989. 'The Use of Force: Law and U.S. Policy', in *Right v. Might: International Law and the Use of Force.* New York: Council of Foreign Relations.

Hidén, Mikael and Ilkka Saraviita, 1989. *Statsförfattningsrätten i huvuddrag.* Översättning av den 5. finska upplagan. Helsinki: Finnish Lawyers' Publishing Company.

Human Rights Committee, 1985. *Selected Decisions under the Optional Protocol* (second to sixteenth session). CCPR/C/OP/1. New York: United Nations.

Human Rights in Developing Countries — 1989 Yearbook. Compiled by Human Rights Institutes in Norway, Denmark, the Netherlands, Finland and Canada. Edited by Manfred Nowak and Theresa Swinehart. Kehl: N.P. Engel.

Humphrey, John P., 1984. 'Political and Related Rights', in Theodor Meron (ed.), *Human Rights in International Law: Legal and Policy Issues*, vol. I. Oxford: Clarendon Press.

Jacot-Guillarmod, O., 1987. Report on 'The Relationship between Democracy and Human Rights', *Paper presented to the Colloquy 'Democracy and Human Rights'*, Thessaloniki (Greece), 24–26 September 1987. Strasbourg: Council of Europe doc. H/Coll (87) 8.

Karapuu, Heikki and Allan Rosas, 1988. 'The Juridical Force of Economic, Social and Cultural Rights: Some Finnish Examples', *Mennesker og Rettigheter — Nordic Journal on Human Rights*, vol. 6, no. 4.

Kelsen, Hans, 1951. *The Law of the United Nations. A Critical Analysis of Its Fundamental Problems*. New York: Frederick A. Praeger.

Kiss, Alexandre, 1986. 'The Peoples' Right to Self-Determination', *Human Rights Law Journal*, vol. 7, no. 2-4.

Klebes, Heinrich, 1988. 'Human Rights and Parliamentary Democracy in the Parliamentary Assembly', in Franz Matscher and Herbert Petzold (eds), *Protecting Human Rights: The European Dimension. Studies in Honour of Gérard J. Wiarda*. Köln: Carl Heymanns.

Locke, John, 1690. *Two Treatises on Civil Government*. Preceded by Sir Robert Filmer's 'Patriarcha'. With an Introduction by Henry Morley. London 1884: George Routledge and Sons.

Loewenstein, Karl, 1922. *Volk und Parlament nach der Staatstheorie der französischen Nationalversammlung von 1789. Studien zur Dogmengeschichte der unmittelbaren Volksgesetzgebung*. Neudruck der Ausgabe München 1922. Aalen 1964: Scientia.

Marie, Jean-Bernard, 1986. 'Relations between Peoples' Rights and Human Rights: Semantic and Methodological Distinctions', *Human Rights Law Journal*, vol. 7, no. 2-4.

Modeen, Tore and Allan Rosas (eds), in co-operation with the International Institute of Administrative Sciences (Brussels), 1988. *Indirect Public Administration in Fourteen Countries — Administration publique indirecte dans quatorze pays*. Turku/Åbo: Åbo Academy Press.

Modeen, Tore and Allan Rosas (eds), in co-operation with the International Institute of Administrative Sciences (Brussels), 1990. *Indirect Public Administration in the Fields of Education and Pensions — L'administration publique indirecte. Les domaines de l'education et des pensions*. Turku/Åbo: Åbo Academy Press.

Nowak, Manfred, 1988. *Politische Grundrechte*. Forschungen aus Staat und Recht 78/79. Wien: Springer.

Nowak, Manfred, 1989. *UNO-Pakt über bürgerliche und politische Rechte und Fakultativprotokoll. CCPR-Kommentar*. Kehl: N.P. Engel.

O'Connell, D.P., 1970. *International Law*, 2nd ed. Vol. I. London: Steven & Sons.

Osmanczyk, Edmund Jan, 1985. *The Encyclopedia of the United Nations and International Agreements*. Philadelphia: Taylor and Francis.

Partsch, Karl Josef, 1981. 'Freedom of Conscience and Expression, and Political Freedoms, in Louis Henkin (ed.), *The International Bill of Rights. The Covenant on Civil and Political Rights*. New York: Columbia University Press.

Ramcharan, B.G., 1987. 'Peoples' Rights and Minorities', *Nordic Journal of International Law — Acta Scandinavica juris gentium*, vol. 56, no. 1.

Reisman, Michael W., 1984. 'Coercion and Self-Determination: Constructing

Charter Article 2(4)' (Editorial Comment), *American Journal of International Law*, vol. 78, no. 3.

Reports of International Arbitral Awards — Recueil des sentences arbitrales, vol. I. New York 1948: United Nations.

Right v. Might: International Law and the use of Force, 1989. Louis Henkin, Stanley Hofmann, Jeane J. Kirkpatrick, Allan Gerson, William D. Rogers, David J. Schefer. Foreword by John Temple Swing. New York: Council on Foreign Relations Press.

Rokkan, Stein, with Angus Campbell, Per Torsvik and Henry Valen, 1970. *Citizens, Elections, Parties: Approaches to the Comparative Study of the Processes of Development*. Oslo: Universitetsforlaget.

Rosas, Allan, 1984. 'Medborgarskap och rösträtt', in *Forhandlingene ved Det 30, nordiske juristmøtet* (Oslo, 15–17 August 1984), vol. I. Oslo: Det norske styret for Det 30. nordiske juristmøtet.

Rosas, Allan with the collaboration of a study group, 1984. 'International Law and the Kampuchea Question', in Kimmo Kiljunen (ed.), *Kampuchea: Decade of the Genocide. Report of a Finnish Inquiry Commission*. London: Zed Books.

Rosas, Allan, with the collaboration of Pär Stenbäck, 1987. 'The Frontiers of International Humanitarian Law', *Journal of Peace Research*, vol. 24, no. 3.

Rosas, Allan, 1989. 'Stat, statsmakt, statsförvaltning: Några konstitutionella iakttagelser', in *Juhlakirja Jaakko Pajula. Vol. I: Ihminen ja yhteiskunta*. Helsinki: Kansaneläkelaitos (The Finnish Social Insurance Institution).

Rousseau, Jean-Jacques, 1762. 'Du contrat social ou principes du droit politique', in *Contrat social ou principes du droit politique, précédé de Discours. Lettre à d'Alembert sur les spectacles, etc., etc*. Paris: Garnier Frères (year of publication lacking).

Santa Cruz, Hernan, 1962. *Study of Discrimination in the Matter of Political Rights* (UN doc. E/CN.4/Sub.2/213/Rev.1). New York: United Nations.

Schachter, Oscar, 1984. 'The Legality of Pro-Democratic Invasion', *American Journal of International Law*, vol. 78, no. 3.

Steiner, Henry J., 1988. 'Political Participation as a Human Right', *Harvard Human Rights Yearbook*, vol. 1.

Suksi, Markku, 1988. *Traces of Ideal Government: Exploring Legal-Philosophical Elements of Internal Sovereignty*. Turku/Åbo: Meddelanden från Ekonomisk-statsvetenskapliga fakulteten vid Åbo Akademi (A:264).

Tenekides, Georges, 1987. Report on 'The Relationship between Democracy and Human Rights'. *Paper presented to the Colloquy 'Democracy and Human Rights'*, Thessaloniki (Greece), 24–26 September 1987. Strasbourg: Council of Europe doc. H/Coll (87) 13.

Tolonen, Hannu, 1984. *Luonto ja legitimaatio. Normatiivisten asiantilojen johtaminen aristotelisen luonnosoikeustradition mukaan*. With an English Summary: 'Nature and Justification. Modes of Derivation according to the Aristotelian Tradition of Natural Law'. Helsinki: Suomalainen Lakimiesyhdistys.

Tolonen, Juha, 1986. *Stat och rätt. En studie över lagbegreppet*. Turku/Åbo: Åbo Academy Press.

Tomuschat, Christian, 1984. 'The Right of Resistance and Human Rights', in *Violations of Human Rights: Possible Rights of Recourse and Forms of Resistance*. Paris: Unesco.

Törnudd, Klaus, 1986. *Finland and the International Norms of Human Rights*. Dordrecht: Martinus Nijhoff.
Unfinished Democracy: Women in Nordic Politics, 1985. Edited by Elina Haavio-Mannila *et al.* Oxford: Pergamon Press.
United Nations Action in the Field of Human Rights, 1983 (ST/HR/2/Rev. 2). New York: United Nations.
Vegleris, Phédon Th., 1968. 'Valeur et signification de la clause "dans une société démocratique" dans la Convention européenne des Droits de l'Homme', *Revue des droits de l'homme*, vol. 1, no. 2.
Verdoodt, Albert, 1964. *Naissance et signification de la Declaration Universelle des Droits de L'homme*. Louvain: Editions Nauwelaerts.

4 Freedom of Opinion and Expression

Vojin Dimitrijevic

1. The universal standard

Freedom of opinion and expression is a cluster of rights which is not easy to define. On the one hand, it could be, at least theoretically, divided into several rights, and, on the other hand, it is related to some other rights and conditioned by them. Thus 'opinion' could be distinguished from 'expression', if we take opinion to be something existing as a thought, a mental process undetectable by others, at least until we reach the Orwellian stage of 'thought police'.

However, people have been persecuted because of their thoughts from time immemorial; the relevant state and church agencies and their environment have always been vigilant to scrutinize one's deeds as signs revealing one's thoughts, opinions, and convictions. There is no way for an ordinary human being absolutely to conceal his or her opinions, unless we have to deal with excellent practitioners of 'ketman', to use Czeslaw Milosz's famous expression (Milosz, 1953, p. 63). For example, the Inquisition tortured the victim to force him or her to confess to harbouring evil thoughts, but one normally became suspect for doing something revealing opinion, such as a person's not working on a Sabbath leading to the presumption that one secretly professed the Jewish religion (cf. Dimitrijevic, 1985, p. 48). It is practically impossible to draw a line between holding an opinion and expressing it in some way. However, as will be seen, legal instruments have pretended that it is possible to differentiate between opinion, thought and expression.

The national and international instruments concerning human rights habitually proclaim separate rights to freedom of thought, conscience and religion (see, for example, Article 18 of the International Covenant on Civil and Political Rights). Is there a difference between 'thought' and 'opinion'? Although admitting that both notions refer to internal operations of the mind, some authors believe that 'thought' may be nearer to religious and other beliefs, whereas 'opinion' is nearer to political convictions (Partsch, 1981, p. 217). This seems to be a conclusion not based on the intrinsic meaning of the words used, but on the context where they usually can be found. The conventional meaning has to be taken into account and it seems that the term 'thought' encompasses not only religious but also philosophical contents. Even if we think that opinions are predominantly political, politics and philosophy are closely related so that thoughts and opinions are not easily differentiated. Suffice it to say that a very unwelcome proof of this statement has been the consistent persecution of people who have been treated as political enemies for holding philosophical views contrary to the established philosophy which has served as the basis for the legitimacy of the government and its programmes.

Bearing all this in mind, it is advisable for the purpose of this chapter to anchor our position on a firm international standard, which is universally accepted. For a jurist at least, this is a solid starting point from which to look for an answer to the question of what is generally meant by the freedom of opinion and expression.

1.1 The Universal Declaration of Human Rights

The most widely accepted definition is certainly that contained in Article 19 of the Universal Declaration of Human Rights of 1948, most provisions of which now, after more than 40 years, represent more than just a solemn recommendation of the United Nations General Assembly. The Declaration is now generally regarded either as an authoritative interpretation of the UN Charter, or as 'general principles of law recognized by civilized nations' or as norms of customary international law (see the most recent attitudes in *Bulletin des droits de l'homme: Edition speciale*, New York: Nations Unies, 1988). Article 19 of the Declaration is affirmative and provides for four freedoms:

(a) freedom to hold opinions without interference;
(b) freedom to seek information,[1]
(c) freedom to receive information and ideas;
(d) freedom to impart information and ideas.

These freedoms are stipulated as universal, in the sense that they are not limited to the territory of the state where the human being concerned resides or exercises his or her rights. The relevance of the international flow of information remains great, but the development of electronic media makes it less and less possible to prevent that international flow. This should be borne in mind whenever one attempts to speak about divisions among groups of states (on the 'East'-'West' context, see Bloed and de Wouters d'Oplinter, 1985, p. 163).

Article 19 of the Universal Declaration contains no specific limitations to this group of freedoms, which can be explained by the desire of the drafters to have a succinct and clear statement on

---

[1] Freedom to seek information is generally understood to imply a more active attitude than the freedom to receive information and ideas. It has been exemplified in the recent developments of the right to obtain access to public files.

fundamental rights and freedoms. However, the general limitations and restrictions contained in Article 29, which were meant to balance the rights of the individual with his or her duties toward the community, apply to all rights mentioned in the Declaration. Such limitations and restrictions should conform to the following criteria:

(a) they must be determined by law;
(b) their purpose can only be the securing of due recognition and respect for the human rights and freedoms of others and the meeting of just requirements of morality, public order and the general welfare in a democratic society;
(c) no right or freedom may be exercised contrary to the purposes and principles of the United Nations.

The last restriction raises the interesting question of whether a freedom can be limited, even if there is no pre-existing law, on the basis of the UN Charter only. In any case, Article 29, paragraph 3, of the Declaration intends that the exercise of the freedom of opinion and expression must be tempered not only by duties toward the national community but also by obligations in respect of the international order.

1.2 The International Covenant on Civil and Political Rights

Universal guidance can also be sought in the International Covenant on Civil and Political Rights of 1966, which represents a part of the International Bill of Human Rights. This Covenant takes the form of an international treaty containing direct and specific obligations for participating states. However, the trouble is that so far the Covenant has not been universally accepted. Two permanent members of the UN Security Council, the United States and China, are not included among its 88 participants. This fact is important not only because of the territory and the population of these two countries, but because one of them has traditionally been labelled as belonging to the 'West' and the other to the 'East', if such designations are used predominantly ideologically, as will be done throughout this chapter (for the difficulties in using such terminology, see Dimitrijevic, 1988, p. 25). In fact, those human rights procedures in the United Nations (such as the one based on resolution 1503/XLVIII of the Economic and Social Council) which are not based on conventions still proceed on the basis of criteria contained in UN resolutions, the Universal Declaration of Human Rights holding a prominent place.[2]

The Covenant deals with freedom of opinion and expression in its

---

[2] Such is the approach of specialized non-governmental organizations. See *Information, Freedom and Censorship*, 1988.

Articles 19 and 20. The positive elements of the definition are very similar to those in the Universal Declaration. The freedoms are:

(a) to hold opinions without interference;
(b) to seek information;
(c) to receive information and ideas;
(d) to impart information and ideas;
(e) to choose the medium through which to use one's freedom— information and ideas can flow either orally, in writing or in print, in the form of art, or through any other media;
(f) there are no territorial limits to this freedom (Nowak, 1989, p. 356).

According to the Covenant, the freedom of opinion is absolute — there is no restriction on the right to hold opinions, which corresponds to the idea that thinking and holding opinions are strictly internal processes of the mind. However, the drafters of the Covenant found it necessary to indicate that the freedom of expression is a specific right, the exercise of which carries with it special duties and responsibilities. It appears to be easier to restrict this freedom than many other rights and freedoms, but only under the following conditions.

(a) that the restriction is provided by law;
(b) that the purpose of the restriction is to protect the rights and the reputation of others, the interests of the community in general, i.e. national security, public order (*ordre public*), public health and morals;
(c) that universal interests are not jeopardized by the misuse of the freedom — according to Article 20 there is a duty of all contracting states to prohibit propaganda for war and any advocacy of national, racial and religious hatred that constitutes incitement to discrimination, hostility and violence.

The following seem to be the main differences between the standards set by Article 19 in conjunction with Article 29 of the Universal Declaration and Articles 19 and 20 of the Covenant. In a positive vein, the latter unequivocally stress that the freedom of opinion is absolute and unlimited. It also evinces the richness of the freedom of expression by providing for the free choice of media, including both artistic expression and all media that may yet be invented and made available for wide use. In a more negative vein, on the other hand, permitted restrictions were made more specific and germane to the politically and morally very sensitive freedom of expression. Thus, for example, 'national security' was introduced as a possible ground for restriction, in keeping with an old tradition throughout the world.

Another, maybe ominous, addition was the French expression *ordre public*, put in brackets to explain the meaning of the English syntagm 'public order'. *Ordre public* is a rather mysterious legal term used predominantly in conflict of laws situations, where it indicates that a given rule of law, or even judicial decision, is valid and will be applied only if it conforms with the foundations and the general essence of the constitutional and legal system of the relevant state. The term has therefore frequently been translated into English as 'public policy'. Whereas 'public order' means basically absence of disorder or disturbances, *ordre public* may have political and ideological meanings, thus enabling governments to restrict the freedom of expression if it is perceived to conflict with the 'general philosophy' or socio-economic system of the state. Given the fact that many constitutions are in fact programmatic, or contain at least a statement of political and social ideals and aims, this is a real danger. The proviso of Article 29, paragraph 3, of the Universal Declaration was translated in Article 20 of the Covenant into the duty of states to legislate against propaganda for war and advocacy of national, racial and religious hatred. It should be noted that this formulation limits possible arbitrariness by ruling out restrictions through mere reference to the UN Charter and leaving it to the States Parties to pass laws prohibiting the abuse of the freedom of expression against international interests. The duty of the signatory states to prohibit such manifestations of the freedom of expression does not go so far as to ask them to make transgressions criminal offences.

It must be noted, however, that the ensemble of Articles 19 and 20 cannot serve as a safe universal standard for the contents of the freedom of expression because of the serious objections some states harbour against Article 20, and especially its paragraph 1 relating to the prohibition of propaganda for war. Many states, predominantly belonging to the 'West', have entered reservations to that Article in the belief that it unduly restricts the freedom of expression and that it is contrary to their constitutional, legal, and traditional rules guaranteeing free speech (*Human Rights. Status of International Instruments*, 1987, p. 28). In this connection, states have usually observed that the terms 'propaganda' and 'war' are not sufficiently precisely defined in order to serve as a basis for the limitation of a human right. The critics have not been persuaded by the efforts of the interpreters of the Covenant, including the Human Rights Committee, to show that 'propaganda' involves systematic efforts to promote an idea and that 'war' means only aggressive war contrary to the UN Charter (General Comment of the Human Rights Committee, A/38/40, 1983, p. 110; see Nordenstreng and Hannikainen, 1984, p. 167). Article 20, paragraph 2, of the Covenant should present fewer difficulties, since the wording of Article 4 of the International Convention on the Elimination of All Forms of Racial Discrimination of 1965 (127 participating states) is much stronger and makes any dissemination of ideas based on racial superiority and hatred punishable.

2. The 'Western' international standard

After establishing *grosso modo* the universal standards for the freedom of opinion and expression, it remains to be seen what have been the basic differences in the 'Western' and 'Eastern' approaches to the subject. As for the 'West', legal guidance is more easily sought through the study of regional treaties on human rights, which are absent in the 'East'. The Convention for the Protection of Human Rights and Fundamental Freedoms of 1950 (the European Convention on Human Rights) is particularly interesting, for it was drafted immediately after the adoption of the Universal Declaration of Human Rights and long before the work on the Covenant on Civil and Political Rights was completed (for a discussion of the relevant provisions of the European Convention see Bullinger, 1985, p. 339). In case there are any doubts about whether the European Convention epitomizes the 'Western' view of the freedoms we are studying, reference will also be made to the American Convention on Human Rights, which was signed after the Covenant, on 22 November 1969 (Buergenthal, 1984, p. 439).

2.1 The European Convention on Human Rights

Compared to the universal standard, Article 10 of the European Convention shows interesting differences (cf. Nowak, 1989, pp. 359, 363).

On the one hand, the text of the European Convention includes no express freedom to seek information, but this freedom has been interpreted into it by subsequent decisions of the competent organs. Furthermore, all media are not treated equally, and the possibility is reserved for the licensing of broadcasting, television and cinema enterprises. Although licensing does not necessarily equal restriction, this can mean, and usually has meant, state monopoly of broadcasting and television and special attention to cinematic forms of expression (including prior censorship[3]). On the other hand, the European Convention includes a different but longer list of permissible restrictions. The restrictions must be prescribed by law and are linked to the standard of 'democratic society' (on the interpretation of this term, see Bullinger, 1985, p. 342). They can be based on some grounds that are not found in the general standard: territorial integrity, preventing the disclosure of information received in confidence, and maintaining the authority and impartiality of the judiciary. 'Public order' is in the European Convention interpreted as

---

[3] In various forms and degrees prior film censorship exists in Denmark, France, Ireland, Sweden, and the United Kingdom among other Council of Europe countries. See *Information, Freedom and Censorship: The Article 19 World Report*, pp. 181, 186, 197, 225, 238.

'public safety' and 'prevention of disorder and crime', which is closer to the English term 'public order' than to the French *ordre public*. There are no provisions in the European Convention corresponding to Article 20 of the Covenant on Civil and Political Rights.

2.2 The American Convention on Human Rights

Article 13 of the American Convention is closer to the Covenant than is Article 10 of the European Convention. In the American Convention, 'opinion' is called 'thought', and is not separated from expression, even for the purposes of defining permissible limitations. The freedom to seek information is included and prior censorship is expressly forbidden except in relation to public entertainments, where it may be exercised for the sole purpose of regulating access to them for the moral protection of childhood and adolescence. Other restrictions can take place only through subsequent impositions of liability, and must be based on law in order to protect the same values as in the Covenant. The French version of *ordre public* was avoided.

It is worth noting that no American country except the United States found any offence in Article 20 of the Covenant and that Article 13 of the American Convention, obviously under the influence of the Racial Discrimination Convention, uses even stronger language, requiring that propaganda for war and advocacy of national, racial, and religious hatred be considered as offences punishable by law (paragraph 5). Of particular importance is Article 13, paragraph 3, of the American Convention, which enters the thorny field of indirect impediments to the freedom of expression. Such restrictions are prohibited by the Convention, and examples are given of the abuse of government and private controls over the supply of newsprint, radio broadcasting frequencies, or implements and equipment used in the dissemination of information.

3. The 'Eastern' constitutional standard

There are no multilateral treaties or international declarations of 'Eastern' or socialist countries regarding the freedom of opinion or expression, or regarding human rights at all. In order to match the declaratory standards of the 'West', expressed in the European and American Conventions, one has to resort to the constitutions of socialist countries and of countries closely allied to them, or claiming to 'build socialism'.

At this particular historical point, one has to approach this task with utmost care. Several reasons have to be given for the wariness to deduce from the constitutions too much, not only in terms of political reality, but also in purely legal terms. Firstly, constitutions in a number of such countries are about to be changed, and there has been a lively debate on constitutional drafts, where the chapters relating to the rights of citizens are at the centre of the concern. Secondly, changes introduced in some socialist countries appear to be contrary to the existing constitutions, which in itself makes the constitutional texts less relevant.[4] Thirdly, and this is especially the case in the Soviet Union, in addition to plans for a new constitution, the existing constitutional provisions have been reinterpreted in favour of more rights and freedoms and in the direction of a stricter construction of permissible restrictions.

Nevertheless, until the constitutions are changed (and, of course, the laws enacted under them) there is a need to get better acquainted with them, not only in order to understand the recent past in some of those countries, and the present in 'non-reformist' socialist countries, but also to meet the objections of those who tend to interpret the recent developments in some socialist countries only as political phenomena, doomed to be ephemeral unless firmly entrenched in the constitutions and relevant legislation. For the reasons quoted, instead of citing a large number of constitutional provisions, one can try to establish a number of paradigmatic features of socialist constitutions.

3.1 Socialist 'ordre public'

First and foremost, freedom of opinion and expression in the 'East' cannot be understood outside the general framework in which all rights and freedoms of citizens are located. There are general limitations that apply to all rights and freedoms, and it is characteristic that the latter are not limited by law only, but also by some kind of socialist *ordre public*, i.e. the general aim of constructing socialism. For example, according to Article 61 of the Cuban Constitution, freedoms cannot be exercised 'contrary to the decision of the Cuban people to build Socialism and Communism'. This can also be stated as a duty, as in the Mongolian Constitution: 'It is the duty of every citizen of the MRP: (a) to devote all his efforts and knowledge to the building of socialism . . .' (Article 89).

In addition to general statements, some rights are also granted conditionally, as guided rights: the legitimate purpose for their use is immediately indicated. Thus, for instance, the freedom of scientific research and the right of association are granted by Articles 45 and 51 of the Soviet Constitution 'in accordance with the aims of building communism'. This can mean two things. One of them is that the rights mentioned are needed to build communism, but given that the

---

[4]   Günter Maleuda, the Speaker of the German Democratic Republic Parliament, said that the Article of the Constitutions of his country laying down the leading role of the Socialist Unity Party 'has already been scrapped by the people'. (*The Guardian Weekly*, 2 December 1989, p. 6).

quotation comes not from the preambular part but from the operative articles of the Constitution, the more probable meaning — as confirmed by practice — is that the rights can only be exercised in conformity with this general aim. This in turn means that the citizens alone cannot determine whether or not the enjoyment of the right can take place in each specific case.

True to the collectivist concept of human rights, not only is more stress placed on collective rights (and this has also been reflected in the behaviour of diplomats from socialist countries in international fora), but the rights of the individual are explicitly submitted to the interests of the collectivity, as represented by the state: 'Enjoyment of citizens of their rights and freedoms must not be to the detriment of the interests of the society or the state . . .' (Article 39 of the Soviet Constitution). Still more explicit are the constitutions of North Korea and Albania. Article 49 of the Korean Constitution states, 'In the PDR Korea the rights and duties of citizens are based on the collectivist principle "One for all and all for one" '. And Article 68 reads 'Citizens must display a high degree of collectivist spirit'. Article 39 of the Albanian Constitution reads, '. . . The rights and duties of the citizens are established on the basis of harmonization of the interests of the individual and the socialist society, with priority given to general interests'.

There is, in the same vein, a stronger stress on duties than is contained in other constitutions. If the translations are correct, this sometimes verges on the ridiculous, as in Article 69 of the Constitution of the PDR Korea: 'It is the sacred duty and honour of citizens to work. Citizens *must voluntarily* and honestly participate in work and strictly observe labour discipline and working hours' (emphasis added). The duties in Mongolia are, among others, 'to adhere to the norms of the socialist way of life and struggle actively against all anti-social manifestations', to 'give priority to social and state interests', to 'preserve strictly state secrets and to be vigilant in respect to enemies' and 'to fulfil impeccably all . . . civic duties and to demand the same of other citizens' (Article 89). The preceding example shows that, in addition to respect for the constitution, citizens are expected to observe some other rules which do not relate only to the socialist way of life. Koreans must adhere to 'the socialist norm of life and the socialist rules of conduct' (Article 67). In the German Democratic Republic (GDR), it was 'socialist morality' (Article 19,3). In Afghanistan it is 'social behaviour and human morality' and even 'etiquette' (Article 31).

Introducing into the constitution elements that are legally hard to define underlines the political nature of the document, and at the same time gives a wide margin of appreciation to those who decide about the limits put on the enjoyment of human rights.

Constitutions of socialist states have been unabashedly partial. They were established to defend the interests of the ruling working class. It is no wonder then that discrimination is not totally prohibited. To be more precise, there are articles prohibiting discrimination against citizens, but the grounds given do not correspond to accepted international standards. Discrimination on the basis of national origin, sex and even religion is not allowed in those constitutions that have non-discrimination clauses, but prohibitions against discrimination based on political opinions are strangely absent everywhere, with the possible exception of the German Democratic Republic, where 'philosophy' figured as one of the forbidden grounds of discrimination (Article 20, paragraph 1).

Recent events and debates in socialist countries indicate that the consequences of such a deletion could be far-reaching, because the 'wrong' political opinion could result not only in limitations on political activity, but theoretically also in the withdrawal of all other rights guaranteed in the constitution, including economic and social rights. In most countries, this has fortunately not been the case, and the effect of political discrimination has been limited mostly to the so-called crime of thought, which makes it a punishable offence to express political evaluations of the situation in the country that are dissonant from the official view. In practice, such provisions of the criminal codes have not been invoked recently in some socialist countries, otherwise 'glasnost' would have been impossible (Soviet Union, Yugoslavia, Hungary, Poland), but they still remain on the books and are still vigorously invoked in some other countries (e.g. China, Romania, Cuba).

As stressed in most statements on human rights, there is theoretically no possibility of conflict between the socialist state and the individual. The state is a 'friend' of the individual, and only some bureaucrats may act otherwise. In accordance with the principle of unity of powers, the public prosecutors, or the 'Prokuratura' in most socialist countries are conceived of not only as investigating agencies that have to bring criminals before courts, but as protectors of the people. What is more important is to note that in addition to so many meta-constitutional elements in the constitution which determine the enjoyment of human rights, there has been a meta-constitutional and meta-state authority to determine what certain phrases and expressions mean. This has been the Communist Party, under its different names. The Constitution of the Soviet Union stated in its Article 6 that 'the leading and guiding force of Soviet society and the nucleus of its political system, of all state organizations and public organizations, is the Communist Party of the Soviet Union (CPSU). The CPSU exists for the people and serves the people'. In addition to a similar paragraph in its Constitution, Romania determined the composition of the elite party:

The most advanced and conscious citizens from among the workers, peasants, intellectuals and other categories of working people unite in the RCP, the highest form of the organization of the working class, its vanguard detachment (Article 26, paragraph 2).

The Mongolian constitution is somewhat more sectarian: the vanguard includes only peasants who are members of co-operatives and the 'working intelligentsia' (Article 82, paragraph 2). The distrust of the intellectuals, expressed in the term 'honest intelligentsia' has been abandoned, at least in constitutions. It is quite obvious, and this has been evident in practice, that the Communist Party, in fact its leading organs, have determined the meaning of the constitution, and consequently the limitations on the enjoyment of human rights. This explains why some changes have been possible without significant constitutional amendments. In order to understand such developments, one has had to look into party documents and decisions, but the situation is now politically different in a number of countries. However, in order to be convinced that changes are definite and durable, one must await constitutional and legal amendments. Warnings should be heeded about the possibility of a stalinist 'thermidor'.[5]

However, this is no longer the situation in some Eastern countries. In Poland, a government was installed led by a non-Communist party, in Hungary the Communist Party itself changed its name and image, and in the German Democratic Republic the elections of 18 March 1990 led to a government of the non-socialist parties. According to some authoritative sources near to the supreme leadership of the CPSU, such ideas have recently been entertained even in the Soviet Union. Thus, the chairman of the USSR Supreme Soviet Subcommittee on Constitutional Lawmaking has stated that he believed the CPSU would drop its claim to the 'leading role' in Soviet society and allow the possibility of a multi–party system's operating in the country.[6]

3.2 Restrictions on the freedom of opinion and expression

The freedom of opinion and expression has been recognized (not in its entirety, as we shall presently see) in all socialist constitutions, but not as a 'formal' and 'arbitrary' expression of individuality. More specifically, it has been subjected to another principle, which strictly speaking is not a restriction. It has been believed that the freedom of opinion and expression could serve as a useful means to promote the goals of socialism and that it should be exercised as such.

Article 50, paragraph 1, of the Soviet Constitution has been quoted above. In this Constitution, and the similar constitutions of the

---

[5]   See, for example, Stipetic, Radovan, 'Sumrak komunisticke srece' in *HSLS* (Zagreb), 23 December 1989, p. 7.

[6]   Article 19, *Commentary on Freedom of Expression and Information Issues Arising From: The Third Periodic Report of the USSR. Submitted Under Article 40 of the Covenant for Consideration by the Human Rights Committee at its October 1989 Session*, London, 1989, p. 3.

USSR's constituent republics, general interests appear to have inspired the constitution authors in granting the freedom of expression. In contrast, Article 29 of the Romanian Constitution had a negative wording: 'The freedom of speech, of the press . . . cannot be used for purposes hostile to the Socialist system and to the interests of the working people'. Although the approach is slightly different, it must be taken that socialist constitutions have generally given instructions as to the laws necessary to regulate the exercise of this freedom: the legislatures have granted wide latitude in restricting the freedom of expression when it did not coincide with the general interests, and not only when it was contrary to them. As a consequence, prior censorship was considered to be necessary and has been widely practised (Scammell, 1988, p. 8).

A further glance at this group of constitutions shows that the freedom of opinion and expression is, as a rule, defined very briefly and narrowly, usually together with the related freedom of association. Freedom of opinion and expression has thus been reduced to freedom of speech and of the press, with very few exceptions, such as the Constitution of the German Democratic Republic, which in Article 27 gave the right to every citizen 'to express his opinion freely and publicly' and guaranteed the freedom of the press, radio and television.

In none of these constitutions is there the freedom to seek and receive information and ideas, nor is there any mention of the international flow of information. As a rule, no detailed instructions exist other than the already quoted very general restrictions on these freedoms. The protection of national security, public order and morals, etc., is left to the laws, as guided by the 'general interests' expressed broadly by the constitution.

3.3 The economic aspect

An interesting feature of the constitutions of socialist states is the consideration given to the material basis for the freedom of expression in the virtual absence of privately owned media. In this respect, the Soviet Constitution has obviously served as a model: 'Exercise of these political freedoms is ensured by putting public buildings . . . at the disposal of the working people and their organizations, by broad dissemination of information, and by the opportunity to use the press, television, and radio' (Article 50, paragraph 2). Article 52 of the Cuban Constitution provides that:

The material preconditions for the exercise of this right are secured by the fact that the press, radio, television, films and other forms of mass media are state or social property and that they can never become private property. This secures their use exclusively in the service of the working people and in the interests of the society.

In this context, the Yugoslav Constitution should be mentioned, because it is based on a different concept of property than in other socialist countries. The bulk of economic enterprises in Yugoslavia are not state-owned but operate on the basis of social ownership effected through workers' self-management. The Yugoslav Constitution guarantees the freedom of thought and choice (Article 166) and freedom of the press and other media of information and public expression (Article 167). The absence of state ownership is reflected in Article 167, paragraph 3: 'Citizens, organizations, and citizens' associations may, under conditions specified by statute, publish newspapers and other publications and disseminate information through other information media.' It appears that socially owned enterprises have the exclusive right to operate other media of information and public expression than the press and the publication of books. However, in an effort to regulate the freedom to receive information, Article 168 guarantees the right to be informed and to correct published information, but it also imposes the general duty on all media 'to inform the public truthfully and objectively and to make public the opinions of and information about bodies, organizations and citizens of concern to the public'. It remains unclear who is competent to judge the truthfulness, objectivity and completeness of information and the press laws are currently under attack in Yugoslavia because they enable the courts to ban publications liable to 'misinform' citizens and 'upset the public'.

3.4 Relative unimportance of the freedom of expression and 'glasnost'

Finally, one may venture to add that the freedom of opinion and expression has been accorded rather low priority in the constitutions of socialist countries. This is an impression based on the brevity of the relevant constitutional provisions and the low place they have in chapters on the rights and duties of citizens, appearing far down the list after all economic, social, and cultural rights and many other civil and political rights. This impression can be wrong, but it has also been supported by both practice and the public pronouncements of leading figures.

Although it may be futile and possibly dangerous to theorize about hierarchies of human rights, freedom of expression is certainly very important as a means to protect other human rights and as a link between civil and political rights (Nowak, 1989, p. 356; Türk, 1989, p. 3). Restrictions on the right have been perceived as one of the causes of the difficulties of the functioning of the political and economic system in socialist countries. Very important changes in that respect are taking place just now. The whole idea of 'glasnost' is based on the need to obtain and to use more information and thus to help revive and invigorate socialism ('perestroika'), which had suffered under incompetent leadership because of the lack of democracy and had entered into economic difficulties because of the absence of motivation on the part of the populace, which is to a great extent attributable to a cavalier attitude toward the rights of the individual.

The debate on 'glasnost' has been under way in the Soviet Union for some time and it is very probably going to influence both the authorities and public opinion in other socialist countries. What should be stressed here is that the idea of 'glasnost' will certainly be reflected in the constitutions of 'East' European socialist countries. In the relevant resolution of the 19th All-Union Conference of the Soviet Communist Party, held in 1988, this intention was unequivocally expressed:

The Conference holds that glasnost has wholly justified itself, and that it should be promoted in every way in future. For that, it should be considered essential to create legal guarantees of glasnost. The right of citizens of the USSR to information should be enshrined in the constitution.

In the further text of the resolution, a rather clear blueprint for the provisions on freedom of information in the future Soviet constitution is discernible. It will be a combination of the rights of citizens, mass media, work collectives and public organizations to receive information and of the duties of the state and office holders to provide it. There is an intention to limit the powers of authorities to declare information and data official secrets. Everyone obstructing citizens in the exercise of their right to information will be made responsible. There is also a serious intention to make the list of permissible restrictions of the freedom of expression more specific, and thus to replace the very general limitations which have been abused to prevent and hamper 'glasnost'. From the text of the resolution, it can be gathered that this freedom will be restricted if it concerns state or military secrets (national security), impinges upon the legitimate rights of citizens, disrupts public order, or threatens security ('safety' is probably the better translation) public health, or morals. It will not be permissible to abuse the freedom of information to 'preach war and violence, racism, and national and religious intolerance, to propagate cruelty or to disseminate pornography' (*19th All-Union Conference*, 1988, p. 156).

The constitutional sketch given in the resolution on 'glasnost' is very close to the universal standard and it remains to be seen how it will be implemented in the constitutional changes and whether other socialist states will follow the Soviet example, as they did, with some exceptions, in the late 1970s. Hungary has already made the first resolute step in that direction in 1989, with a complete and detailed set of constitutional amendments, which amount to a *de facto* new constitution.

3.5 Direct application of international commitments

It will also be important to observe to what extent socialist countries will change their attitudes towards international human rights treaties. In that respect it will be very interesting to see whether they will emulate Hungary and ratify the Optional Protocol to the International Covenant on Civil and Political Rights and what will be the experience of Hungary if any communication from that country reaches the Human Rights Committee. The Soviet Union has already, through its Foreign Minister, announced its intention to ratify the Protocol (Amnesty International EUR 466/22/89 of October 1989, p. 6). Intimations of this kind have also been made public at least in Yugoslavia, Poland and Bulgaria.

Another development, which we are not fully able to follow here, relates to the process initiated by the Conference on Security and Co-Operation in Europe (CSCE). The results of this process, including the 1975 Final Act, have not been international treaties entailing legal obligations for the signatory states, but it is undeniable that the parts of relevant CSCE documents relating to human rights have gained tremendous importance and popularity in Eastern Europe, where the word 'Helsinki' has become synonymous with the promotion of human rights.

Chapter VII of the Helsinki Final Act has evolved since 1975 and its culmination was the Concluding Document of the Vienna Meeting, which was adopted early in 1989. While repeating the language of the Helsinki Final Act, the Vienna Document broadens the scope of the rights the signatories pledge to secure. For example, principle 11 of the Document contains a still narrower list of grounds for forbidden discrimination, while principle 13.7 has a much wider list, similar to that in the International Covenant on Civil and Political Rights. Under the separate heading, 'Human Dimension of the CSCE', the Vienna Document also introduced a new machinery to enable CSCE states to monitor respect for human rights. The first Meeting of the Conference on the Human Dimension, held in Paris from 30 May to 23 June 1989, showed that all Eastern European states except Romania were fully prepared to use the new machinery and to account publicly for the human rights situation in their countries (Dimitrijevic, 1989, pp. 205, 234; Staack, 1989, p. 533).

Finally, the changing attitudes in some socialist countries to international law in general, and to international legal provisions concerning human rights in particular, raises the question of the possible direct application of universal and European human rights standards by courts and other institutions in socialist countries, which have so far stuck to a particular 'socialist' dualist concept of international law (Graefrath, 1985, p. 1; 1988, p. 52; Kartashkin, 1982, p. 631).[7] 'New thinking' in this respect has been voiced not only by political figures (Shevardnadze, 1989, p. 2), but also in learned journals (see, for example, Tuzmukhamedov, 1988, p. 116; Vereshchetin and Miullerson, 1988, 1989), thus rendering the classical 'socialist' theory of international human rights obsolete (Drzewicki and Eide, 1988, p. 3), at least for the Soviet Union and some other countries. Although in some other socialist countries, the leaders and the theoreticians still persist in 'old thinking', we do not find it necessary to dwell any further here on the traditional 'socialist' concept of international human rights and human rights in general (one of the best exposés can be found in Bloed and van Hoof, 1985, p. 29).[8]

4. Balancing elements: law and practice

The above comparison of the 'Western' and 'Eastern' models of the freedom of opinion and expression was unfair because the former was established on the basis of regional multilateral treaties and the latter deduced from similar and typical constitutional provisions. A comparison between 'Eastern' and 'Western' constitutions will probably result in different conclusions, but a summary of the latter is much more difficult to produce and would be unmanageable within the scope of this chapter. The problem of what is the 'West' will inevitably reoccur and is harder to solve, even operationally, than the question of what is the 'East'. Are, for example, the constitutions of Chile and South Africa to be taken into account, or should it simply be said that they represent a deviation from the 'Western' model? Is it then justifiable to attribute the features of the constitutions of, say, North Korea or Romania to all socialist countries?

4.1 The 'West'

Apart from being a less compact and ideologically homogeneous group (which is now more and more questionable even for the 'East'), the countries of the West have constitutions adopted at quite different periods, ranging from the eighteenth to the twentieth centuries. If one will take examples from some older constitutions, such as the existence of state religion in Norway or the ban on political

---

[7] Kartashkin has apparently changed his mind, at least in respect of the freedom of movement: '. . . the right to leave a country is a natural right every human being has from birth . . .' (Kartashkin, 1989).

[8] Serious and impartial works on Marx's own and Marxist concepts of human rights, as they differ from the practice in the countries of 'real socialism' are few. Among them one should note Atienza, 1982, and Markovic, 1986.

pronouncements by the clergy in Mexico, or, for that matter, the absence of any entrenched charter of human rights in the unwritten constitution of the United Kingdom, one could be criticized for promoting some vestiges of history into current problems, while being lenient to the 'East' regarding human rights violations in the more recent past. However, in order partly to correct the imbalance, some problems common to many 'Western' countries in the realization of the freedom of expression have to be singled out. They mostly relate to the interpretation in law and in jurisprudence of some internationally recognized bases for restriction.

4.1.1 Defence of the order and ideology

One of the internationally recognized bases for restricting the exercise of freedom of expression is *ordre public*, which here is taken to mean the whole constitutional, political and social set-up of a given country. Limitations on the freedom of expression under this rubric take two basic forms, depending on the country in question. In common law systems, the relevant offence is sedition. According to English law 'a seditious intention means an intention to bring into contempt or excite disaffection against the government and to promote feelings of ill will between the classes' (Gifis, 1984, under 'Seditious Libel').

In countries or territories where sedition has been made a statutory offence, it is still clearer that the consequences for freedom of expression can be serious, because of the very general terms utilized. Thus, in Section 93 of the Criminal Code of the UK Dependency of Bermuda,

Sedition is defined as the importing (no intention necessary) into territorial waters any publication or representation bearing a seditious meaning, i.e. to incite disaffection, etc. for Her Majesty the Queen, or the Administration of justice, or to procure changes in the law illegally, or to arouse hostility among classes, etc. (doc. CCPR/C/32/Add. 14, paragraph 34).

In Hong Kong

Sedition is a statutory offence under the Crimes Ordinance which is committed when any person (a) does or attempts to do, or makes any preparation to do, or conspires with any person to do any act with seditious intention, or (b) utters any seditious words, or (c) prints, publishes, sells, offers for sale, distributes, displays or reproduces any seditious publication . . . (d) possesses without lawful excuse any seditious publication.

Seditious intention is an intention

(a) to bring into hatred and contempt or to incite disaffection against the person of Her Majesty or Her Heirs or Successors, or against the

Government of Hong Kong or of any other part of Her Majesty's dominions or of any territory under Her Majesty's protection . . .
(b) to incite Her Majesty's subjects or inhabitants of Hong Kong to procure the alteration, otherwise than by lawful means, of any other matter in Hong Kong as by law established or
(c) to bring into hatred or contempt or to excite disaffection against the administration of justice in Hong Kong, or . . .
(d) to promote feelings of ill-will or enmity between different classes of inhabitants of Hong Kong (CCPR/C/32/Add. 14, p. 97). (Other restrictions in the United Kingdom are reported in Eide and Skogly, 1988, p. 49)

Some governments claim that the offence of sedition can be used to respond to the exigencies of prevention of national and religious hatred, as it was done by the Government of New Zealand in its report to the Human Rights Committee (CCPR/C/10/Add. 6, paragraph 260). However, it can easily be imagined that any Marxist publication could be labelled as seditious, even if it refers to class struggle in very general and abstract terms. No reports of recent cases of this nature in democratic countries have been available but such practices from the past could be revived. Combating 'Communism' has been the common task of military dictatorships in Latin America, resulting in incarceration, torture and death of alleged Communists and leftists only on the base of their utterances and writings. The alleged Communist threat has also been the rationale for censorship in many Asian countries (Scammell, 1988, p. 9).

The United States of America, which is not bound by the International Covenant on Civil and Political Rights and for which the Conference on Security and Co-operation in Europe documents might play a bigger role than even for 'Eastern' countries, still has on the books the notorious Smith and McCarran Acts of 1940 and 1950, respectively (18 USC Section. 783, 50 USC Section 783), as well as the Communist Control Act of 1954 (50 USC, Section 841). Recently these acts have seldom been invoked, but one should remember that in the 1950s they were interpreted in a manner that threatened not only freedom of expression, but also freedom of opinion, for it was enough to 'believe' in Communism to be criminally liable (Rohrer, 1979, p. 13).

The extremes in the 'West' of Europe can be found in the still valid Criminal Code of Turkey, which was promulgated in 1938, and is believed to be a faithful copy of the fascist Criminal Code of Italy. Among others, it contains the following provisions:

Whoever makes propaganda with the purpose of establishing the domination of one social class over others, exterminating any of the social classes, overthrowing any of the established basic economic or social orders of the country, or totally exterminating the political or legal orders of the State, shall be punished by heavy imprisonment for five to ten years (Article 142.1).
If the acts in the foregoing paragraphs are committed by means of

publication, the punishment imposed shall be increased by one-half (Article 142.6).

As a result of these and similar provisions, a staggering number of journalists were tried and sentenced in Turkey.

In the five years since the end of the military rule in 1983, 2,127 journalists have been tried in 1,426 cases. At least 41 journalists are now in prison for what they have written (*Paying the Price*, 1989, p. 22).

Sentences have amounted to several hundred years in prison, and in one case the defendant was sentenced to 1,086 years, which was on appeal reduced by 300 years!

4.1.2 Defamation of the state

In most countries with a civil law tradition, the traditional offence of *lèse-majesté* has been retained, often replacing the monarch with the government. The most recent example is Article 90 (a) of the Criminal Code of the Federal Republic of Germany ('Defamation of the State and Its Symbols'), which proscribes insulting or maliciously bringing into contempt the Federal Republic of Germany and its federated states. Cases have been reported of persons being prosecuted for utterances of such a nature, without their being allowed to attempt to show that their allegations were true. For example, an author who had claimed that the police were the servants of the ruling class, which for a Marxist is a fairly common statement, was convicted. His defence was rejected, the court's holding that according to the Basic Law (Constitution) there was no ruling class in the Federal Republic and that the police were subject only to competent authorities (Amnesty International, EUR/22/02/85).

Let us again quote rough examples from the Turkish Penal Code:

Whoever uses aggressive language against the President of Turkey in his absence, shall be imprisoned for one to three years. If the aggression is done by allusion or hint . . . but if there is presumptive evidence beyond reasonable doubt that the aggression was directed toward the person of the President . . ., the aggressions shall be considered as expressly made against the President.

If this offense is committed by any means of publication, the punishment shall be increased by one-third to one-half (Article 158).

Whoever overtly insults or vilifies the Turkish nation, the Republic, the Grand National Assembly, or the moral personality of the Government or the military or security forces of the State or the moral personality of the judicial authorities, shall be punished by heavy imprisonment for one to six years (Article 159 — this offense can also be committed by hint).

This brings us to the protection of power holders, politicians and influential personalities via their protection as private individuals, in the sense believed to be basically allowed by the principle of the protection of the rights and reputations of others. It has been noted that public officials have had the sensitivity and means to prosecute with more vigour any critics of their behaviour, and especially journalists. In Norway, for instance, the provisions of Articles 247–250 of the Criminal Code ('Defamation of Character') have been used for this purpose. Traditionally, the higher up one was in the social and political hierarchy, the better one was protected. There is a new trend now, best exemplified in a number of national court rulings[9] and in the famous judgment of the European Court of Human Rights in the *Lingens* Case[10] that public personalities have to put up with harsher criticism and scrutiny than simple private individuals, because the control of their comportment is in the interest of the society and its right to receive information.

Common law countries (but not only they) face problems with blasphemy:

A common law misdemeanour to publish blasphemous matter orally or in writing. Matter is blasphemous if it denies the truth of the Christian religion or the bible or the Book of Common Prayer or the existence of God (CCPR/C/32 Add. 14, p. 97).

Similar statutory provisions persist in a number of other countries (for some examples in Finland see Suksi, 1990). Even when the authorities do not act, influential bodies, such as state education boards and school boards in the United States, act against 'blasphemous' teachings and eliminate 'blasphemous' books from public libraries. In a recent example, the California Board of Education deleted from its textbook guidelines the following sentences, as a concession to 'creationists':

There is no scientific dispute that evolution has occurred and continues to occur; this is why evolution is regarded as a scientific fact.

These sequences show that life has continually diversified through time, as older species have been replaced by newer ones (*International Herald Tribune*, 11-12 November 1989, p. 2).

---

[9] In Denmark, the process started already in the 1930s, when a court found that statements about politicians should be more liberally judged. *Information, Freedom and Censorship*, 1988, p. 178.

[10] Judgment of 8 July 1986, Publ. E.C.H.R., Series A, no. 103, p. 11. Mr Lingens, an Austrian journalist, had been sentenced on the basis of Article 111.2 of the Austrian Criminal Code (üble Nachrede) for criticizing the personality of the then Prime Minister because of his political dealings and utterances. The Court found that Austria had violated Article 10 of the European Convention on Human Rights, because the freedom of the press allowed for wider acceptable criticism as regards a politician than as regards a private individual.

This can be regarded as the 'Western' pendant to the limitations on the freedom of expression in the 'East' based on official ideology and compulsory teaching of 'Marxism' (for other examples of religious censorship see *Information, Freedom and Censorship*, 1988, p. 299).

Whereas the 'Eastern' model of the freedom we are dealing with does not encompass the freedom to seek information (which also does not appear in the European Convention), this right and the whole complex of freedom of expression seems to be seriously affected in some countries of the 'West' by the broad interpretation of the terms 'official secret' and 'national security'. Journalists have been penalized for divulging unconstitutional and immoral intentions of government officials and agencies. Thus, even after the amendments of the 1911 Official Secrets Act in the United Kingdom, unauthorized disclosure of information by an intelligence agent was made a punishable offence, with all legal defences, including the desire to blow the whistle on official wrongdoing, eliminated (*The Guardian Weekly*, 25 December 1988, p. 5), while 'government secrecy is not a given, an absolute, but a battleground', where the administrative machine 'responds to shocks, crises, diktats and dissatisfaction (Downing, 1986, p. 154).

The right of the citizen to obtain information and data from official sources and files has recently been secured in some states (with impressive results in the United States, Sweden and Finland), but it is still in its infancy in others (Kirtley, 1989, p. 65).

4.2 The 'East'

As already observed, the common feature of the constitutions of socialist countries is the subordination of all human rights to the local *ordre public*, coupled with wide powers given to the legislature and to non-state actors to interpret and limit the rights promulgated in the constitution.

4.2.1 'Hostile propaganda'

Legal restrictions have been most frequently contained in criminal codes, especially in their articles on 'enemy propaganda and agitation'. Paradigmatic in that respect are Articles 70 and 190-1 of the Criminal Code of the Russian Soviet Federal Socialist Republic (RSFSR), and the corresponding articles in the codes of all constituent Soviet republics.

Article 70 prohibited:

Agitation or propaganda carried out with the aim of undermining or weakening Soviet power or of committing particularly dangerous crimes against the State, disseminating for the said purpose slanderous fabrications which defame the Soviet State and social system, as well as circulating, preparing or harbouring, for the said purposes, literature of similar content.

And Article 190-1 made punishable the 'systematic dissemination of fabrications known to be false, discrediting the Soviet State and social system'.

We do not intend to bore the reader with documenting again the uses and abuses of these and similar provisions, not only in the Soviet Union but also in other socialist states. Publications that have been considered dangerous included seemingly innocuous works of art and documents on human rights (including international treaties ratified by the prosecuting government). The concept of 'notoriously false' statements has prevented defendants from attempting to prove that their utterances or writings were true and made in good faith. It has been unclear which objects were intended to be protected by such penal laws, and they have been interpreted in an ideological and arbitrary way. As a result, many people have been punished with stiff sentences in the Soviet Union and elsewhere. This was admitted by the governments themselves (see, for example, the Third Periodic Report of the Soviet Union to the Human Rights Committee, CCPR/C/52/Add. 6 of 2 October 1989, p. 8).

4.2.2 Preventive measures: media and secrecy

The battle against the socialist version of sedition and blasphemy has been accompanied by auxiliary provisions that deal with the position of the media and the protection of state secrets. Thus, according to the 1978 version of the 1974 Law on Press Activity of Romania, the inspiration of that act is

the sociopolitical mission of the press in implementing the general policy of the Romanian Communist Party, on building the comprehensively developed socialist society and building communism in the Socialist Republic of Romania . . . (Preamble)

Whereas a journalist could only be a person

Who militates for the application in practice of the Romanian Communist Party's policy . . ., behaves in his activity and private life in keeping with the socialist norms of ethics and equity . . . (Article 39).[11]

---

[11] In some other countries instructions of this kind have been a part of the professional code. They have been contained since 1960 in the *Handbook on Journalism* in the German Democratic Republic:

> Die Journalisten in der DDR sind frei von finanziellen Sorgen. Sie betrachten ihren Beruf als kämpferische Berufung durch das Volk und für das Volk. Sie haben mit ihrem Beruf auch ihre Gesinnung gewählt . . . Parteilichkeit für die Sache des Sozialismus, für die Sache der DDR, ist selbstverständliche Verpflichtung (*Berliner Morgenpost*, 29 October 1989, p. 65).

The Law prohibits the publication of 'materials' which

contain attacks against the socialist system, the principles of the domestic and foreign policy of the Romanian Communist Party and of the Socialist Republic of Romania, calumniate the party-state leadership, . . . include false or alarmist information and commentaries which threaten or disturb public order or are dangerous to state security (Article 69).

The widest interpretation of the idea of passing harmful information, or an extremely unspecified and exaggerated zeal for protecting state secrets could be found in Article 99 of the Penal Code of the German Democratic Republic:

Whoever, to the disadvantage of the interests of the GDR collects or makes available information *not classified as secret* to the bodies of the people named in Article 97 (a foreign power, its institutions or representatives, or a secret service or foreign organization as well as their helpers) shall be punished by two to twelve years of imprisonment (emphasis added).

In the official commentary to the Code, prepared by the GDR Ministry of Justice, it was added:

Information (is) of a general kind. The information may be true, distorted or untrue . . . whether the information is stored in notes, in the mind or in some other way is not of importance in deciding whether a crime has been committed (Article 19, German Democratic Republic, London, 1989).

This limitation relates also to the dangers which restrictions on the freedom of expression pose for scientific research and the necessary international co-operation of scientists, not only in fields that are obviously related to politics (see Ziman *et al.*, 1986).

In some countries preventive action went so far as to control firmly all possible means of disseminating information, even to a narrow audience. Instead of referring to sources that could be dismissed as unfriendly, it suffices to quote from the Romanian Decree of 1983 regulating the possession and use of typewriters and copying machines (*Bulletinul official* 21/1983 of 30 March 1983). According to the Decree, the Ministry of the Interior kept records of persons possessing and using duplicating machines and typewriters (Article 2, paragraph 1). Private persons had to have licences for the possession of typewriters and to produce them upon request of the militia, who would check how they were used and stored (Article 3, paragraphs 1 and 2). In order to own a typewriter, a private person had to get an official authorization, which would not be issued to 'persons who have a police record or those whose behaviour poses a threat to public order or state security' (Article 15, paragraph 2). Typewriters could only be repaired in workshops authorized for that purpose by the police (Article 19). They could not be rented or lent (Article 26).

4.2.3 Recent improvements

At the present time, it is more interesting to concentrate on the efforts in those societies in Eastern countries where there have been signs of serious intentions to change radically and dramatically the whole concept of human rights and, in particular and in accordance with the principle of 'glasnost', the scope of the freedom of opinion and expression. This freedom has *de facto* been widened by political decisions, under popular pressure and because of economic difficulties, but it remains to be seen how this will be reflected in constitutions and laws. We have already dealt with the blueprints for the new Soviet constitution; nevertheless, legislative efforts in the USSR deserve to be mentioned because they are illustrative both of the good intentions of the serious opposition to liberalization.

In April 1989 the Presidium of the Supreme Soviet abolished the above-cited Articles of the Penal Code of the RSFSR, but replaced them with the Decree on Criminal Responsibility for Crimes against the State, which again incriminated 'public calls for the overthrow or change' of the system or calls for the 'hindrance of the execution of Soviet laws with the aim of undermining the political and economic system of the USSR'. Another punishable offence was to 'insult or discredit state organs or public organizations' (CCPR/C/52/Add.6, p. 7). However, the Congress of People's Deputies repealed the relevant articles of the Decree and opted for incrimination only of calls for the violent overthrow of the state or the system, and also introducing milder sentences (31 July 1989):

Public calls for the violent overthrow or change of the Soviet state and social system, which is consolidated in the USSR Constitution, and also the spreading of material of such a content with this aim are punishable by deprivation of liberty for a period of up to three years or by a fine of up to 2,000 rubles (Article 19, USSR, 1989, p. 6).

At the time of writing, reports abound about the intended changes in some of the press laws.[12] They are followed by statements of the journalists and their associations (see, for example, 'Journalistic Fantasies. What Should a Draft Law on the Press Be Like', *Moscow News*, 40, 1989). In contrast to the above-cited principles of the journalist profession in the German Democratic Republic,[13] it is instructive to read the statement of the Section of the former ruling party (SED) on GDR television, broadcast on 5 November 1989, where the leaders of the Section declared:

---

[12] Not yet adopted in the Soviet Union.
[13] See note 11.

We state with profound consternation that we are co-responsible for the situation of the current crisis in the GDR. We have allowed our medium to be perverted by dirigist interventions. We have thus betrayed the confidence of many viewers and numerous collaborators. We present our excuses to the citizens of the GDR. We are determined to regain the confidence of the public, which compels us to a reexamination without self-satisfaction of our work and its results . . . (*Journal de Geneve*, 6 November 1989, p. 3).

It is not at all certain whether this trend will be followed in all socialist countries, but one does not venture to name those where the system is not likely to adopt a broader view of the freedom of opinion and expression, because changes can be abrupt and make such predictions ridiculous even before they are published. One can certainly expect that in this regard there will be two groups of socialist states, and that the hitherto unheard of practice of banning publications from other socialist countries, which started with the Soviet 'Sputnik' and 'Moscow News' in the German Democratic Republic and Cuba, will be continued (*The Guardian Weekly*, 13 August 1989, p. 7).

5. Common problems: concentration of ownership and control

In the modern world, the freedom of expression depends heavily on its economic basis. To be effective and to serve its social purpose, among which the monitoring and the protection of human rights and the promotion of democratic government play a prominent place, this freedom cannot be limited to the freedom of speech and the freedom to publish information and ideas in forms that reach very small numbers of people. Modern mass media require financial backing and sophisticated organization. In this respect, the danger of the concentration of ownership and control of the media is faced by both the 'East' and the 'West', each in its own way. In the words of the Human Rights Committee, in its General Comment 10 (19), little attention has so far been given to the fact that, because of the development of modern mass media, effective measures are necessary to prevent such control of the media as would interfere with the right of everyone to freedom of expression . . . (doc. CCPR/C/21, Add.2).[14]

It should be stressed with great intensity that the most numerous and possibly most dangerous threats to the freedom of expression do not emanate from fear of being criminally prosecuted by the state

---

[14] The drafters of the Covenant in the Third Commission of the United Nations General Assembly were fully aware of the danger of concentration of media ownership and refused suggestions that the freedom of expression be protected only against governmental interference. On the contrary, they wanted governments to undertake measures against concentration (Nowak, 1989, p. 365).

(which is of course the most visible and most easily documented fact), but from fear of losing employment and the source of income through dismissal, 'blacklisting', boycott, etc. Such measures are very pernicious because there is no open trial, there is no possibility for defence or appeal, and protests have been usually dismissed as false or fabricated. The writer and the journalist very often face powerful social, economic, and political forces that prefer to act through intimidation, which results in the worst and the least detectable kind of censorship, self-censorship (Scammell, 1988, p. 17).[15]

5.1 The 'East': state and party

In the 'East', ownership and control of the media have been generally exercised by the state and the ruling party. This statement needs some elaboration.

In a number of socialist countries, the churches have been the only non-state entities allowed to publish their own papers, periodicals and books, within the limits of the role assigned to them by the law and the government. Paradoxically, the only unorthodox opinion in many Marxist societies that has been tolerated was theism, whereas holders of atheist socialist, but non-Communist beliefs have been persecuted.

As to ownership, or, to put it more precisely, management based on ownership, economic systems in the 'East' differ. In Yugoslavia, which admittedly has been atypical, there is no state ownership and the media are self-managing enterprises where the employees decide on personnel, management and investment policies. However, information activity has been treated even in that country as an activity of special social concern, so that the media have been limited by laws on information, which impose on each newspaper, television or radio station, or publishing house a publishing council, which is only partly composed of employees and editors; the remaining members represent the 'society' and limit the scope of self-management. So far, the majority of the members of councils have been members of the League of Communists, which means that they have been in some instances under an obligation to obey superior party orders in the name of 'democratic centralism'. This is why the whole system of information in Yugoslavia, regulated by a number of federal and state laws, has been unfavourably viewed by public opinion.

In other socialist countries, there are varying degrees of self-management elements in all enterprises, including those engaged in the dissemination of information and ideas. This trend has become

---

[15] In the time of McCarthyism, only one American review stood openly against the powerful senator and his machinery. This was *The National Guardian*, an editor of which was subsequently expelled, as a foreign national, although he had not been convicted of any offence. See Downing, 1986, p. 163.

stronger. In still other countries, the most notable examples being Poland and Hungary, papers and books have been published by wholly independent parties and associations; the latter country has even allowed foreigners to buy interests in dailies with wide circulation. Such practices have come to be tolerated in Yugoslavia too, with the gradual reinterpretation of the Socialist Alliance as a true national front, not simply an adjunct of the League of Communists.

As has already been noted in the case of Yugoslavia, in all socialist countries such enterprises have been considered to be of such great public importance that their activity has not been controlled on an economic basis alone, especially where the media are not self-supporting. Ideological control has usually been shared by state and Communist Party organs. The Party may act indirectly if the medium is not its own organ, but is in the hands of national fronts, trade unions and similar organizations. However, as witnessed by the Romanian law quoted above and by Soviet institutions of prior censorship or control (such as 'Glavlit'), state and party control have very often merged and it has been, and in many cases it will be, the duty of the editors and collaborators of the media to observe the Party line or otherwise to risk demotion or the loss of employment (Scammell, 1988, p. 8).

In most socialist countries, the vast majority of editors (and certainly those who control the 'mainstream' press and the electronic media) have needed to be approved by the relevant party and national front bodies, thus giving these entities the opportunity to influence editorial policy. The media have thus been under double pressure: the state has been in the position to withdraw the funds for newsprint or frequencies if it has acted not only as a controlling mechanism but also as the owner, and the party and related organs have influenced the content of the published material through their control of personnel and through party discipline. The consequences of disobeying guidelines have been far-reaching, even disastrous.

5.2 The 'West': state and private monopolies

In the 'West' there is a basic difference between Western Europe and the countries which have tended to follow the example of the United States. In the former, electronic media started as a rule as state monopolies or at least were under state licensing powers, with all the ensuing effects, including sometimes the change of the leading personalities following a change of government. In some countries, state control has been tempered by the creation of independent supervisory bodies, where reliance has been put on the personal integrity of their members; however, these members have often been recruited from the higher echelons of the establishment and have only sporadically represented minorities, especially ideological ones. Under the impact of new technological developments, allowing for international programmes and a multitude of new stations, state monopoly appears to be more and more difficult to maintain (Bullinger, 1985, p. 342).

The written press has had more leeway, but it has been endangered by the concentration of private ownership and dependence on revenue from advertising, which is the case with privately owned electronic media outside Western Europe, and especially in the United States. Owners can effectively control editorial appointments and editorial policy, which is a relatively minor evil if there is a freedom of choice among newspapers. If, however, a whole set of dailies, weeklies, and monthlies belong to the same person or company, freedom of expression is at least in some respect limited or endangered (Bullinger, 1985, p. 356).[16]

The printed press can hardly survive solely on the income from the copies sold to the public, so that advertising plays an important, and in some countries, a tremendous role (in the United States the percentage of income from advertising is 100 for the electronic media and 75 for the written media (Bagdikian, 1983, p. 117)). Powerful advertisers can condition their contributions upon certain standards to be observed by the medium and those standards are known to have been both political and to have belonged to the realm of 'public morals'. Advertisers have been reported to have imposed their biases, conservative as a rule, on behalf of the public and its tastes and preferences.

Some observers go as far as to say that the result has been ideological streamlining and castration of the mainstream media:

This is not saying that all journalists and screenwriters are forced to follow ideological lines. There is considerable latitude for description of events and ideas in the news . . . But there is a limit to this latitude, established by conventional wisdom in journalism and broadcasting. The most obvious limit is criticism of the idea of free enterprise or of other basic business systems. Some reporters often criticize specific corporate acts, to the rage of corporate leaders. But the taboo against criticism of the system of contemporary enterprise is, in its unspoken way, almost as complete within mainstream journalism and broadcast programming in the United States as criticism of communism is explicitly forbidden in the Soviet Union (Bagdikian, 1983, p. 157; cf. Demac, 1988, p. 3).

As a result of these and many other factors in many 'Western' countries, the average reader, listener or viewer has been in recent times exposed to a rather uniform and more or less prejudiced diet of information and opinion (for the situation in Latin America see Somavia, 1981, p. 13). To be sure, there have been efforts to combat

---

[16] It is maintained that at the beginning of the 1980s some 50 companies controlled all the publishing and broadcasting in the United States (Bagdikian, 1983, p. 7). See also Schiller, 1989. There is also the danger of foreign financial control — see Bullinger, 1985, p. 359.

this. Some of them come from the state which, as in Norway, subsidizes small newspapers in order to preserve the variety of the written press (for the attitude of the Council of Europe and measures in other countries see Bullinger, 1985, p. 358) or has imposed media under its monopolistic control the duty to allot a given minimum time to the opinions of all political parties, at least prior to elections, or has promulgated laws and taken legal action against undue concentration of media ownership (for the example of France see *Information, Freedom and Censorship*, 1988, p. 183).

In other societies, wide circulation, established habits and traditions have so far prevented excessive concentration of media ownership or control. There have been attempts to uphold independent party organs (supported by membership fees) or to use modern, cheaper and more accessible duplication methods to publish and disseminate unconventional opinions and lesser known facts (which is, *mutatis mutandis*, the 'Western' version of 'samizdat'). It must be repeated, however, that 'alternative' and 'countercultural' information and views reach a very small sector of the public (naturally, depending on the country concerned), while the majority of the population remains under the mighty influence of the mainstream media which tend to use it as a criterion for the selection of news and opinions to be disseminated (Radojkovic, 1984, p. 94).

Bibliography

19th All-Union Conference of the CPSU: Documents and Materials, 1988. Moscow: Novosti Press Agency.

Atienza, Manuel, 1982. *Marx y los derechos humanos*. Madrid: Mezquita.

Bagdikian, Ben, 1983. *The Media Monopoly*. Boston: Beacon.

Bloed, Arie and Fried van Hoof, 1985. 'Some Aspects of the Socialist View of Human Rights', in Arie Bloed and Pieter van Dijk (eds), *Essays on Human Rights in the Helsinki Process*. The Hague: Martinus Nijhoff.

Bloed, Arie and Pascale C.A.E. de Wouters d'Oplinter, 1985. 'Jamming of Foreign Radio Broadcasts', in Arie Bloed and Pieter van Dijk, *Essays on Human Rights in the Helsinki Process*. The Hague: Martinus Nijhoff.

Buergenthal, Thomas, 1984. 'The Inter-American System for the Protection of Human Rights', in Theodor Meron (ed.), *Human Rights of International Law: Legal and Policy Issues*, vol. 2. Oxford: Clarendon Press.

Bullinger, Martin, 1985. 'Freedom of Expression and Information: an Essential Element of Democracy', *Human Rights Law Journal*, vol. 6, no. 2–4.

Demac, Donna A., 1988. *Liberty Denied. The Current Rise of Censorship in America*. New York: PEN American Center.

Dimitrijevic, Vojin, 1985. *Strahovlada*. Beograd: Rad.

Dimitrijevic, Vojin, 1988. *Human Rights Today*. Beograd: Medjunarodna politika.

Dimitrijevic, Vojin, 1989. 'Konferencija o evropskoj bezbednosti i saradnji', in Dusan Mrdjenovic (ed.), *Temelji moderne demokratije*. Beograd: Nova knjiga.

Downing, John, 1986. 'Government Secrecy and the Media in the United

States and Britain' in Peter Golding, Graham Murdock and Philip Schlesinger (eds), *Communicating Politics*. Leicester: Leicester University Press.

Drzewicki, Krzysztof and Asbjørn Eide, 1988. 'Perestroika and Glasnost — The Changing Profile of the Soviet Union Towards International Law and Human Rights', *Mennesker og Rettigheter* — *Nordic Journal on Human Rights*, vol. 6, no. 4.

Eide, Asbjørn and Sigrun Skogly (eds), 1988. *Human Rights and the Media*. Oslo: Norwegian Institute of Human Rights.

Gifis, S.H., 1984. *Law Dictionary*. Woodbury, NY: Barrons.

Graefrath, Bernhard, 1985. 'The Application of International Human Rights Standards to States with Different Economic, Social and Cultural Systems', in *Bulletin of Human Rights. Special Issue.*

Graefrath, Bernhard, 1988. *Menschenrechte und internationale Kooperation*. Berlin: Akademie-Verlag.

Human Rights. Status of International Instruments, 1987. New York: United Nations.

Information, Freedom and Censorship: The "Article 19" World Report, 1988. London: Longman.

Kartashkin, Vladimir, 1982. 'The Socialist Countries and Human Rights', in Karel Vasak and Philip Alston (eds), *The International Dimensions of Human Rights*. Paris: Unesco.

Kartashkin, Vladimir, 1989. 'The Doors Open Ever so Slightly', *Moscow News*, July.

Kirtley, Jane E., 1989. 'Openness in Government and Freedom of Information', in Marcus Ruskin and Chester Hartmann (eds), *Winning America: Ideas and Leadership for the 1990's*. New York: Matthew Bender.

Markovic, Mihailo, 1986. 'Differing Conceptions of Human Rights in Europe: towards a resolution', in *Philosophical Foundations of Human Rights*. Paris: Unesco.

Milosz, Czeslaw, 1953. *Zniewolny umysl*. Paris: Instytut Literacki.

Nordenstreng, Kaarle and Lauri Hannikainen, 1984. *The Mass Media Declaration of UNESCO*. Norwood, NJ: Ablex.

Nowak, Manfred, 1989. *UNO-Pakt über bürgerliche und politische Rechte und Fakultativprotokoll*, CCPR-Kommentar. Kehl: N.P. Engel.

Partsch, Karl Josef, 1981. 'Freedom of Conscience and Expression, and Political Freedoms', in Louis Henkin (ed.), *The International Bill of Rights*. New York: Columbia University Press.

Paying the Price: Freedom of Expression in Turkey, 1989. The Helsinki Watch, International Freedom to Publish Committee of the Association of American Publishers.

Radojkovic, Miroljub, 1984. *Savremeni informaciono-komunikacioni sistemi*. Beograd: Zavod za udzbenike i nastavna sredstva.

Rohrer, Daniel M., 1979. *Freedom of Speech and Human Rights*. Doboque, Iowa: Kendall/Hunt.

Scammell, Michael, 1988. 'Censorship and Its History — A Personal View', in *Information, Freedom and Censorship: The "Article 19" World Report 1988*. London: Longman.

Schiller, Herbert I., 1989. *Culture Inc.: The Corporate Takeover of Public Expression*. Oxford: Oxford University Press.

Shevardnadze, E.A., 1989. 'Vneshnaia politika i perestroika', in *Pravda*, 24 October.

Somavia, Juan, 1981. 'The Democratization of Communications', *Development Dialogue*, no. 2.
Staack, Michael, 1989. 'Fortschritte in der Menschenrechtspolitik. Perspektiven nach der KSZE-Konferenz in Paris', *Europa-Archiv*, vol. 44, no. 17.
Suksi, Markku, 1990. Ilmaisuvapauden rajoituksista — Vertailevia huomioita Suomen ja USA:n välillä, *Lakimies 3/1990*.
Türk, Danilo, 1989. *The Right to Freedom of Opinion and Expression*. Working Paper for the Sub-Commission on Prevention of Discrimination and Protection of Minorities, UN doc. E/CN/4/Sub. 2/1989/26.
Tuzmukhamedov, R.A., 1988. 'Gumanizacija mezhdunarodnogo prava', *Sovetskoe gosudarstvo i pravo*, no. 11.
Vereshchetin, V.S. and R.A. Miullerson, 1988. 'Novoe myshlenie i mezhdunarodnoe pravo', *Sovetskoe gosudarstvo i pravo*, no. 3.
Vereshchetin, V.S. and R.A. Miullerson, 1989. 'Primat mezhdunarodnogo prava v mirovoi politike', *Sovetskoe gosudarstvo i pravo*, no. 7.
Wenger, Klaus, 1989. 'Euro-Fernsehen oder Euro-Flimmern?', *Europa-Archiv*. no. 18.
Ziman, John, Paul Sieghart and John Humphrey, 1986. *The World of Science and the Rule of Law*. Oxford: Oxford University Press.

5 Universal Legal Principles of Fair Trial in Criminal Proceedings

Pieter van Dijk[1]

1. Introduction

For the full and effective implementation of international norms concerning human rights at the national level it is important that these norms have a firm basis in domestic law as well. This holds true in particular for those national legal systems where international legal norms have no internal effect (van Dijk, 1988a, pp. 634–6). But even for legal systems where international legal norms do have internal effect, this domestic legal basis may be important, especially as far as international legal norms are concerned which are not, or, in any case, are not considered by the competent national authorities to be self-executing (van Dijk, 1988a, pp. 636–8). Moreover, even in those cases where the national courts are empowered or even obliged to apply international law and give it priority over conflicting domestic law, such a domestic legal basis offers a better guarantee that the courts will indeed give full effect to the standards laid down in these norms. In fact, national courts are more familiar with their own national legal system and will, therefore, be less inclined to evade the consequences of international legal norms if these norms are integrated into that national legal system.[2] This would seem to be even more true in the case of procedural norms, since the national courts will be accustomed to conduct proceedings on the basis of domestic procedural law as a coherent system.

Consequently, even in the case of express and clear provisions in human rights treaties that have been ratified by most states in both the East and the West, for their common interpretation and application in both regions it is important to determine if and to what extent these provisions also have a common legal basis in the respective domestic legal systems. One way to determine this common domestic basis would be to examine all legal systems concerned and identify the provisions which deal with the issues under research. A very interesting and successful effort in that

---

[1] The author gratefully acknowledges the extensive research assistance by Nicholas Franssen, LL.M.
[2] On the various devices used by Dutch courts in the past to evade the consequences of the 'monistic system' laid down in the Dutch Constitution, see van Dijk, 1988a, pp. 640–1.

direction was the study directed by Bassiouni concerning the protection of human rights in the criminal process under international instruments and national constitutions, published in 1981 (hereafter Hertzberg and Zammuto, 1981). In the following study, a different approach will be followed. On the basis of some national legal documents of great historical importance, some documents based upon comparison of national legal systems, and some international treaties and other international instruments and documents, the study will determine if and to what extent general principles of law can be defined on the issue of fair trial in criminal proceedings. The hypothesis is that, if and to the extent that the international legal norms concerned reflect general principles of law, these international norms will in all likelihood also be incorporated into the domestic legal systems in one way or another, or will at least be recognized as principles to be applied at the national level by the competent authorities. Whether that is indeed the case will be verified to the extent possible on the basis of certain existing comparative studies.

Of all international human rights norms the principles of fair trial in criminal proceedings were selected for examination under this method. This was done, first of all, because of the vital importance of these principles as minimum guarantees of effective protection of the individual against the national authorities. But, moreover, these principles present a clear example of how from one single principle — i.e. the principle of fair trial — different (sub)principles may develop, some of which have become generally recognized and others of which have not (yet). The present study will, therefore, only serve as an example, on the basis of which similar research may be carried out with respect to other international human rights norms.

It is the purpose of the present study to investigate to what extent certain principles of fair trial in criminal proceedings have found universal recognition in national legal systems and/or in international law. The present author is, of course, fully aware that universal recognition in law by no means implies universal application in practice. The scope of the present study does not, however, allow for a survey of state practice in the field of criminal proceedings. In order to get a complete picture of the recognition of the principles concerned such a survey is necessary, but this would require a team of researchers. The present author has had to restrict himself in this respect to giving a few instances of friction between principles and practice in his final observations.

2. What are legal principles?

When an international lawyer discusses the concept of legal principles, he is inclined to think first and foremost of Article 38 of the Statute of the International Court of Justice, which lists among the sources of international law to be applied by the Court when deciding disputes submitted to it, 'the general principles of law recognized bycivilized nations'. This reference does not, however, help him very much to clarify further the concept of legal principles. In fact, this source of international law, mentioned in Article 38(1)(c), is of a complex and much debated character (Bin Cheng, 1953, *passim*; Bos, 1984, pp. 259–85; van Hoof, 1983, pp. 131–67; Lammerts, 1980, pp. 53–9; Vitányi, 1982, pp. 46–116). In fact, its value as an independent source of international law has even been disputed (van Hoof, 1983, pp. 132–3 and 139–51; Parry, 1965, p. 91; Verzijl, 1968, p. 62).

If one takes Article 38(1)(c) as a point of departure, one has to recognize, at least from a historical point of view, that the inclusion of general principles among the sources of international law was intended to open the possibility of filling any gaps in international law in order to prevent a *non-liquet* on the part of the Court, without requiring the Court to create new law itself. Furthermore, the drafters of the provision, when speaking of 'general principles recognized by civilized nations', were thinking mainly, if not exclusively, of those principles which were accepted by all ('civilized') nations *in foro domestico*, and not of general principles of *international* law; after all, to the extent that the latter principles had been generally recognized, there was no question of a gap in international law.[3]

It has become recognized, however, that the concept of 'general principles of law' also includes those legal principles which are not derived from national law, but are an inherent part of international law and are generally recognized as such by the states, or which have become general principles of international law through a process of induction, by analogy, from positive rules of international law (Lammerts, 1980, pp. 57–9 and 66–9 and accompanying references). In other cases, a general principle derived from national legal systems may at the same time be an inherent principle of international law. This is the case, for example, with the principle of *pacta sunt servanda* and also with certain elements of the principle of fair trial.

The latter situation will present itself mainly, albeit not exclusively, in relation to those general principles of law which are of such a fundamental character that they either constitute a necessary part of any legal system, be it national or international, or they are even basic to the concept of law.[4] In addition, however, the general principles of law comprise principles which are of a less fundamental character, but which may also be of great importance, especially in

---

[3]   See the *Procès-Verbaux* of the Proceedings of the Advisory Committee of Jurists, appointed to prepare plans for the establishment of the Permanent Court of Justice, discussed by van Hoof, 1983, pp. 136–9. See also van Dijk, 1989, pp. 3–11.

[4]   See von der Heydte, 1933, p. 290. Bos, 1984, pp. 72–3, is of the opinion that these 'necessary' principles have to be excluded from the generally recognized principles, since there is no choice as to their recognition. He, too, however, accepts that the Court has to apply them, so the issue seems to be a rather academic one.

view of the original purpose to fill certain gaps. These general principles, too, may be of a procedural nature (e.g. the *nemo bis in idem* principle or the *audi et alteram partem* principle) or may contain substantive norms (e.g. standards for indemnification in case of tort).

Thus far, the concept of general principles of law has been discussed merely from a *procedural* point of view, i.e. in relation to the question of how principles of law are created and manifest themselves as a separate source of international law. However, in investigating the legal principles of fair trial one will encounter legal principles which are laid down in treaties and/or form part of customary international law and, consequently, are not 'general principles of law' in this *procedural* sense, but indeed are legal principles in a *substantive* sense (van Hoof, 1983, pp. 148-9).

Legal principles in a substantive sense constitute a separate category of legal norms not as to their origin, but as to their contents and effect. In these respects they are to be distinguished from other categories of legal norms, i.e. legal policies on the one hand and legal rules on the other (van Dijk, 1987, pp. 13-15). They are, in general, highly abstract norms, which, if further elaboration into legal rules is lacking, serve as guidelines for the legislature, for those who apply the law, and for legal subjects, rather than as norms from which concrete rights and obligations may be inferred. They therefore imply consequences for action without prescribing particular action. In other words, legal principles in a substantive sense are 'norms of aspiration' rather than 'norms of obligation' (Jackson, 1969, p. 761). In the absence of further norms the consequences will lie particularly in the sphere of prohibitions, while in addition legal principles in a substantive sense form a guideline for, and give rise to 'aspirations' with respect to the legislature and those who are called upon to apply the law.

Legal principles in a substantive sense generally contain standards which, in the eyes of those who have formulated the principles or have incorporated them into a treaty or other legal instrument, are of an important and in many cases even of a fundamental value. Indeed, the form of a legal principle is chosen if one wishes to set an important standard, but there is not sufficient consensus about the legal ways and means to implement this standard to give it the form of a legal rule. This explains why legal principles always contain important standards. On the other hand, the importance of the standard may very well be the reason for its general character and vague formulation which gave it the form of a legal principle.

When studying the legal principles of fair trial, it is important to keep in mind the above distinction between principles in a procedural sense and principles in a substantive sense. Indeed, from some basic rules of domestic law certain basic rules of international law concerning fair trial have emerged which form part of the general principles (in a procedural sense) of the minimum standard. At the same time, international legal principles (in a substantive sense) have been formulated, both at the governmental and at the non-governmental level, which have taken their own course of development into legal rules and have simultaneously played a guiding role *vis-à-vis* the national and international law-creating and law-applying bodies. In human rights treaties, too, with respect to fair trial one finds general principles in a procedural sense with the specificity of legal rules, alongside principles in a substantive sense. And the national and international case-law based upon these treaty provisions offers the same picture. Those principles of fair trial which have not (yet) developed into legal rules are equally worth studying, since they may be very instrumental to the development of universal legal principles.

3. National legal principles of fair trial

The development of national legal principles concerning fair trial is closely connected with the development of the Anglo-American legal concept of due process.[5] This concept also has a procedural and a substantive meaning: procedural due process implies a body of legal norms and supporting institutions which require certain procedures and respect for certain values, while substantive due process embodies the principle of equality and certain limitations on the power of the state under some superior law.[6] This study of fair trial will focus on the procedural aspects of due process, and more specifically on the procedural guarantees for a person who stands trial on a charge of having committed a crime. Although these guarantees are not restricted to the trial itself, but cast their shadows before them in those phases of the criminal investigation the conduct of which also determines the ultimate fairness of the trial,[7] this study will concentrate on the guarantees of the trial itself.

For the history of the due-process concept one should perhaps go as far back as the earliest traces of the broader concept of human rights.[8] However, the first milestone for the codification of certain guarantees for due process is generally regarded to be the Magna

---

[5] See, in general, Mott, 1926. The English and the American development and practical application of the concept are not identical: Horvath, 1955, pp. 549–59.

[6] See Noor Muhammad, 1981, p. 139. See the decision of the Supreme Court of the United States in *Duncan v. Louisiana*, 1968, 381 US 479, 85 S.Ct. 1678, 14 L.Ed.2d 510.

[7] See the admissibility decision of the European Commission of Human Rights on joint Applications 8603, 8722, 8723 and 8729/79, *Crociani et al. v. Italy*, 22 Decisions and Reports p. 216 at p. 254.

[8] For these traces, see, for example, Lauterpacht, 1950, pp. 73–93; Robertson, 1982, pp. 3–14. For a critical evaluation of the traditional views concerning this history, see Szabó, 1982, pp. 11–20, and Pagels, 1979, pp. 1–8.

Carta of 1215.[9] Chapter 29 of the 1297 version, confirmed by King Edward I in its definitive form, reads as follows (Evans and Jack, 1984, p. 54):

No free man shall be taken or imprisoned or disseised of his freeholds, liberties or free customs or outlawed or exiled or in any way ruined, nor will we go or dend against him, except by the lawful judgment of his peers or by the law of the land. To no one will we sell, to no one will we deny or delay right or justice.

One has, of course, to keep in mind the circumstances under which the Magna Carta came about, especially the conflict between the English King and the barons, which was settled by the recognition on the part of the King of the historically developed rights of the free men (*homines liberi*), among which what is now called 'due process of law'[10] also figured.[11] In fact, therefore, one of the essential elements of modern due process, i.e. equality before the law, was still lacking.

The English Bill of Rights of 1689 did not contain a provision that was comparable with the one cited above, but only one concerning trial by jury (Evans and Jack, 1984, p. 354). Two other milestones in the codification of human rights, the Bill of Rights of the State of Virginia of 1776 and the Bill of Rights annexed to the 1787 Constitution of the United States of America in 1791,[12] were far more specific in this respect. The Virginia Bill of Rights, which became a model for the Bills of Rights of other States of the Union (Mott, 1926, p. 21), provides in Article VIII as follows:

That in all capital or criminal prosecutions a man hath a presumption in his favor, and to a speedy trial by an impartial jury of twelve men of his vicinage, without whose unanimous consent he cannot be found guilty; nor can he be compelled to give evidence against himself; that no man be deprived of his liberty, except by the law of the land or the judgment of his peers.

Here the 'due process of law' clause ('the law of the land') was

---

[9] This is of course especially the view of common-law lawyers. See, for example, Robertson, 1982, p. 5 and Noor Muhammad, 1981, pp. 138–9. For a less categorical view, with reference to possible sources of inspiration for the Magna Carta in this respect, see Mott, 1926, pp. 1–2, and Lauterpacht, 1950, p. 85. On parallels between the text of the Magna Carta and that of the Bible, see Silving, 1965/1966, p. 122.

[10] The expression 'due process of law' was not contained in the original text of the Magna Carta, but was probably used for the first time in its confirmation of 1354. See Mott, 1926, p. 4, note 11.

[11] For the background of the Magna Carta, see Mott, 1926, pp. 30–6. For a very critical view, see also Wyzanski, 1979, pp. 12–13, who, with a reference to J.C. Holt, speaks of 'a baronial restriction upon the King, requiring him to adhere to ancient custom and due process as established previously'.

[12] For these and other comparable constitutional enactments, see Lauterpacht, 1950, pp. 88–9.

expressly connected with the criminal trial.[13] And the Fifth and Sixth Amendments of the Federal Constitution contain the following guarantees:

V. [No person shall be] subject for the same offence to be twice put in jeopardy of life or limb; nor shall he be compelled in any criminal case to be a witness against himself . . .

VI. In all criminal prosecutions, the accused shall enjoy the right to a speedy and public trial, by an impartial jury . . ., and to be informed of the nature and cause of the accusation; to be confronted with the witnesses against him; to have compulsory process for obtaining witnesses in his favor, and to have the assistance of counsel for his defense.

Unlike those in the Magna Carta, these guarantees were applicable to all individuals.[14]

The other milestone, the French Déclaration des Droits de l'Homme et du Citoyen, which was adopted by the Assemblée Constituante in 1789 and became the preamble of the Constitution of 1791, compared rather poorly with the US provisions. Its Article 9 reads as follows:

Tout homme étant présumé innocent jusqu'à ce qu'il ait été déclaré coupable . . .[15]

These documents have been very instrumental to the incorporation of human rights into national legal systems and to the development of general principles of national law concerning human rights issues, particularly in the field of civil and political rights, including that of fair trial. One might argue, of course, that since these documents are all of Western origin, their contribution to the development of universal principles should be assessed with a good deal of scepticism. That argument should certainly be kept in mind, and research should also extend to sources outside the Western sphere of influence (see Hersch, 1969, pp. 174–94). On the other hand, one can hardly deny that the impact which these documents have had, either directly through their adoption in the legislation of other states, or indirectly *via* international documents like the Universal Declaration of Human Rights, is not restricted to the Western legal systems. And by their redefinition and adaptation, and their national and international interpretation and application in practice, the prin-

---

[13] On the identification of the 'law of the land' concept with that of 'due process of law', see Mott, 1926, pp. 5 and 589, and Noor Muhammad, 1981, p. 139.

[14] See Article I of the Virginia Bill of Rights: 'That all men are by nature free and independent, and have certain inherent rights'. However, the extension of the equal protection clause to all federal states was introduced into the American Constitution only by the Fourteenth Amendment of 1868; A.J. Peaslee, *Constitutions of Nations*, vol. IV, Second part, The Hague 1970, pp. 1208–9.

[15] For the text, see *ibid.*, vol. II, The Hague 1956, pp. 20–1.

ciples concerned may have lost their typically Western character and become more universal.

The basis for the validity of national legal principles as general principles of law is their commonality. Bin Cheng expresses this as follows:

The recognition of these principles in the municipal law of all or nearly all States gives the necessary confirmation and evidence of the juridical character of the principle concerned (Bin Cheng, 1953, p. 25; see also Kaufman Hevener and Mosher, 1978, p. 600).

It is not possible, within the framework of this study, to examine and compare all national legal systems in order to work out general principles of national law concerning fair trial. Such a comparative enterprise would certainly be worthwhile and might be fruitful, but requires the co-operation of a large group of experts.[16] On the other hand, one has to realize that 'general' in this context does not necessarily mean 'general' in a strict sense. In fact, for a legal norm to be considered a general principal of law, it is not necessary that this norm forms part of each and every legal system and is interpreted and applied everywhere in the same way. Zweigert (1969, pp. 444–5) has made this point as follows:

Le principe général du droit ne consiste pas nécessairement dans la solution admise de manière concordante par le plus grand nombre d'ordres juridiques. Le principe général du droit, au contraire, consiste dans ce qui apparaît comme la meilleure solution d'après une étude critique des solutions du droit comparé.

In the modern doctrine of comparative law it is the qualitative rather than the quantitative aspect of the rule of law emerging from the comparison that is most important; a *kritisch-wertende Vergleichung* (Ipsen, 1972, p. 113). That does not, however, alter the fact that, precisely when one is looking for *universal* principles, it is essential that these principles are supported, or at least not rejected, by a large and representative group of legal systems.

Here no more can be done than to rely on comparative studies by others and on authoritative views about the general character of certain elements of the principle of fair trial. To the extent that these studies and views have also served as a basis for the drafting of the relevant provisions in treaties, this fact may enhance the validity of their conclusions.

An early example of such a study combined with such an authoritative view is the Statement of Essential Human Rights, adopted by the American Law Institute on 24 February 1944. Its Article 7, which is

---

[16] For some of the problems involved in such an enterprise, cf. Coutts, 1966, pp. 1–20.

said to be included in substance in the constitutions of fifty countries, reads as follows (Wright, 1945, pp. 257–8):

Everyone has the right to have his criminal and civil liabilities and his rights determined without undue delay by fair public trial by a competent tribunal before which he has had opportunity for a full hearing.

This provision was put forward by Panama during the drafting of the Universal Declaration of Human Rights (UN doc. E/HR/3, p. 6).

Another example is included in the Report of the Sixth Congress on Penal Law of the Association Internationale de Droit Pénal, held in Rome from 27 September to 30 October 1953.[17] The second issue discussed at the Congress concerned the protection of individual liberty during pre-trial investigation. The rapporteur for this issue, Chevalier Braas, dealing with what in his opinion were the core elements of the right of the accused to a fair trial, stated as follows:

L'accord existe sur les principes:
1. Nul ne peur être poursuivi que dans les cas prévus par la loi et selon les formes qu'elle prescrit;
2. Nul ne peut être jugé sans avoir été dûment cité et appelé;
3. Tant qu'un prévenu n'a pas été déclaré coupable par une décision passée en force de chose jugée, il est réputé innocent;
4. Chacun a le droit de présenter sa défense en toute liberté et de discuter tous les éléments de preuve produits contre lui;
5. La preuve incombe à la partie poursuivante. Tout est de droit étroit en matière répressive et le doute bénéficie à l'inculpé;
On ne saurait concevoir doctrine plus libérale, ni plus équitable.
Ces règles posées, le restant n'est qu'application et modalité ou mise en oeuvre. Les discussions qui se produiront au Congrès ne porteront guère que sur des aménagements.

(*Revue Internationale de Droit Pénal*, vol. 24, 1953, p. 711).

These proposed core elements were not challenged during the Congress. Indeed, as Trechsel (1978, p. 543) stated 25 years later in respect of that same text:

We are therefore faced with a situation, where the basic principles are solidly accepted. The devil, however, seems to reside in the details.

Another potential reference source for a universal recognition of certain principles consists of the various regional seminars on the protection of human rights in criminal law and criminal proceedings, organized under the auspices of the United Nations in pursuance of

---

[17] For the proceedings, see *Revue Internationale de Droit Pénal*, vol. 24, 1953, pp. 597–723, and *Revue Internationale de Droit Pénal*, vol. 25, 1954, pp. 213–36.

Resolution 926 (X) of the General Assembly of 14 December 1955.[18] The first seminar, held in Baguio City, Philippines, from 17 to 28 February 1958, brought together representatives from most Asian countries.[19] The second seminar took place in Santiago de Chile from 19 to 30 May 1958 with the participation of Latin-American lawyers.[20] European lawyers from both Western and Eastern Europe came together for the third seminar, convened in Vienna from 20 June to 4 July 1960.[21] Finally, Asian lawyers discussed the issue for a second time, together with lawyers from Australia and New Zealand, at a seminar organized in Wellington from 6 to 20 February 1961.[22] Why no such seminar was organized for African lawyers is not clear. For this study, the most important factor of these seminars, which cannot be dealt with here in any detail, is the remarkable identity of the views expressed and adopted by lawyers from different regions and legal systems on the minimum guarantees of a fair trial. This consensus provides a strong indication of the universality of these guarantees.

Two conferences of the International Commission of Jurists have also been devoted to the conditions of a fair trial. These conferences were attended by participants from all continents, though not from Eastern Europe. The first conference took place in Athens from 13 to 20 June 1955 (*ICJ Bulletin*, vol. 5, 1956, pp. 3-7); the second was convened in New Delhi from 5 to 10 January 1959 (*ICJ Review*, vol. 2, no. 1, 1959, pp. 7-55). When reading the resolutions adopted at these two conferences (International Commission of Jurists, 1966, pp. 5-7, 9-13, 23-8, 30-3, 43, 65-6), one has to keep in mind that the International Commission of Jurists is not an organization focusing on the codification of principles which have already been generally recognized, but on the interpretation and implementation of principles and rules which, in the opinion of its members, ensue from the Rule of Law and the concept of human rights. This may imply that the norms recognized and applied by the Commission are of a rather progressive character and do not necessarily reflect general recognition as existing legal principles.

In Section 7 of the present study, where an attempt will be made to define the universally recognized principles, reference will be made to the above-mentioned seminars and conferences and to the principles formulated there.

---

[18] See GAOR, 10th session, Supplements 1-4, 1955, p. 55 at (m).

[19] *Seminar on the Protection of Human Rights in Criminal Law and Procedure*, UN doc. ST/ TAA/HR/2, 1958.

[20] *Seminar on the Protection of Human Rights in Criminal Law and Procedure*, UN doc. ST/ TAA/HR/3, 1958.

[21] *Seminar on the Protection of Human Rights in Criminal Procedure*, UN doc. ST/TAO/HR/8, 1960.

[22] *Seminar on the Protection of Human Rights in the Administration of Criminal Justice*, UN doc. ST/TAO/HR/10, 1961.

4. International legal principles of fair trial

Traditionally the protection of the individual under general international law is subject to the principles and rules of diplomatic protection and the various restrictions implied therein.[23] According to these principles and rules states are entitled to a certain treatment of their nationals by other states in accordance with a 'minimum standard' as this has been developed from treaties and state practice (Borchard, 1939, pp. 51–63; Roth, 1949, pp. 81–111; Jaenicke, 1971, pp. 282–9).

In this context what interests us most is the question of whether respect for certain guarantees of fair trial in cases of criminal prosecution of aliens forms part of this minimum standard. As early as 1935 this link was clearly made in the Harvard Draft Convention on Jurisdiction with Respect to Crime, Article 12 of which contains the following passage:

In exercising jurisdiction under this Convention . . . [no State shall] prosecute an alien otherwise than by fair trial before an impartial tribunal and without unreasonable delay.[24]

If the guarantees of a fair trial form part of the minimum standard, disregard for them amounts to a denial of justice, for which the state concerned is responsible *vis-à-vis* the national state of the victim (De Visscher, 1935, pp. 238–66). As is stated in Article 9 of the 1929 Harvard Draft Convention on Responsibility of States for Damage Done in their Territory to the Person or Property of Foreigners:

A State is responsible if an injury to an alien results from a denial of justice. Denial of justice exists when there is a denial, unwarranted delay or obstruction of access to courts, gross deficiency in the administration of judicial or remedial process, failure to provide those guarantees which are generally considered indispensible to the proper administration of justice, or a manifestly unjust judgment.[25]

A further elaboration of the connection between principles of fair trial and the minimum standard is to be found in the 1961 Harvard Draft Convention on the International Responsibility of States for Injuries to Aliens, which was meant to be a codification of existing customary law on the subject.[26] Article 7 provides as follows:

The denial to an alien by a tribunal or an administrative authority of a fair

---

[23] van Dijk, 1980, pp. 399–427. See also the classical study by Borchard (1919).

[24] Text in *American Journal of International Law*, vol. 29, Supplement, Part II, 1935, pp. 435–651 at p. 596; comments at pp. 596–602.

[25] Text in: *American Journal of International Law*, vol. 23, Special Supplement, 1929, pp. 131–239 at p. 173; comments at pp. 173–87.

[26] Text in: *American Journal of International Law*, vol. 55, 1961, pp. 545–84.

hearing in a proceeding involving the determination of his civil rights or obligations or of any criminal charges against him is wrongful if a decision is rendered against him or he is accorded an inadequate recovery. In determining the fairness of any hearing, it is relevant to consider whether it was held before an independent tribunal and whether the alien was denied:

(a) specific information in advance of the hearing of any claim or charge against him;

(b) adequate time to prepare his case;

(c) full opportunity to know the substance and source of any evidence against him and to contest its validity;

(d) full opportunity to have compulsory process for obtaining witnesses and evidence;

(e) full opportunity to have legal representation of his own choice;

(f) free or assisted legal representation on the same basis as nationals of the State concerned or on the basis recognized by the principal legal systems of the world, whichever standard is higher;

(g) the services of a competent interpreter during the proceedings if he cannot fully understand or speak the language used in the tribunal;

. . .

(j) disposition of his case with reasonable dispatch at all stages of the proceedings; or

(k) any other procedural right conferred by a treaty or recognized by the principal legal systems of the world.

This text would seem to imply that in the opinion of its drafters denial of any of the procedural guarantees listed there results in the hearing being unfair.

Another draft of the same year, this time within the framework of the United Nations, took the international principles of fair trial out of the context (and controversy) of the distinction between the treatment of aliens and that of nationals into the general field of human rights. This was the 1961 Draft on International Responsibility of the State for Injuries Caused in its Territory, submitted to the International Law Commission by its rapporteur on the subject of state responsibility, Garcia Amador (ILC, *Yearbook* 1961, vol. II, pp. 46–54). In the view of the rapporteur, as laid down in the Draft, a state is obliged, both in relation to its nationals and *vis-à-vis* aliens in its territory, to respect the internationally recognized fundamental human rights. According to Article 1, paragraph 2, of the Draft these human rights include:

(d) The right to a public hearing, with proper safeguards, by the competent organs of the State, in the substantiation of any criminal charge . . .;

(e) In criminal matters, the right of the accused to be presumed innocent until proved guilty; the right to be informed of the charge against him in a language which he understands; the right to present his defence personally or to be defended by a counsel of his choice; . . .; the right to be tried without delay or to be released.

(ILC, *Yearbook*, 1961, vol. II, p. 46)

Impediment of these rights by the judiciary with respect to aliens amounts to a denial of justice in the sense of Article 3, paragraph 1, of the Draft (see *ibid.*).

The above-mentioned documents concerning international principles of fair trial will also be referred to in the concluding chapter of this study.

5. International legal principles of fair trial laid down in the Nürnberg and Tokyo Charters and in the Geneva Conventions and Additional Protocols

Although, during the Second World War, the Allied Powers were determined to prosecute and punish the war criminals,[27] they were equally determined to guarantee them a fair trial. Thus, the Charter which was added to the 1945 Agreement establishing the Nürnberg Tribunal,[28] included Article 16, which provided as follows:

In order to ensure fair trial for the Defendants, the following procedure shall be followed:
(a) The Indictment shall include full particulars specifying in detail the charges against the Defendants. A copy of the Indictment and of all the documents lodged with the Indictment, translated into a language which he understands, shall be furnished to the Defendant at a reasonable time before the Trial.
(b) During any preliminary examination or trial of a Defendant he shall have the right to give any explanation relevant to the charges made against him.
(c) A preliminary examination of a Defendant and his Trial shall be conducted in, or translated into, a language which the Defendant understands.
(d) A Defendant shall have the right to conduct his own defence before the Tribunal or to have the assistance of Counsel.
(e) A Defendant shall have the right through himself or through his Counsel to present evidence at the Tribunal in support of his defence, and to cross-examine any witness called by the Prosecution.

Article 9 of the comparable Charter of the Tokyo Tribunal has a somewhat different wording. It reads as follows (Bevans, 1970, p. 29):

Procedure for Fair Trial. In order to ensure fair trial for the accused the following procedure shall be followed:
a. *Indictment.* The indictment shall consist of a plain, concise, and

---

[27] See the Declaration on German Atrocities in Occupied Europe, signed by Stalin, Roosevelt and Churchill in Moscow on 30 October 1943. Text in: United Nations, *The Charter and Judgment of the Nürnberg Tribunal — History and Analysis* (memorandum submitted by the Secretary-General, UN doc. A/CN.4/5), New York 1949, pp. 87–8.
[28] For the text of the Agreement and Charter, see *ibid.* at pp. 89–99.

adequate statement of each offense charged. Each accused shall be furnished, in adequate time for defense, a copy of the indictment, including any amendment, and of this Charter, in a language understood by the accused.

b. *Language.* The trial and related proceedings shall be conducted in English and in the language of the accused. Translations of documents and other papers shall be provided as needed and requested.

c. *Counsel for Accused.* Each accused shall have the right to be represented by counsel of his own selection, subject to the disapproval of such counsel at any time by the Tribunal. The accused shall file with the General Secretary of the Tribunal the name of his counsel. If an accused is not represented by counsel and in open court requests the appointment of counsel, the Tribunal shall designate counsel for him. In the absence of such request the Tribunal may appoint counsel for an accused if in its judgment such appointment is necessary to provide for a fair trial.

d. *Evidence for Defense.* An accused shall have the right, through himself or through his counsel (but not through both), to conduct his defense, including the right to examine any witness, subject to such reasonable restrictions as the Tribunal may determine.

e. *Production of Evidence for the Defense.* An accused may apply in writing to the Tribunal for the production of witnesses or of documents. The application shall state where the witness or document is thought to be located. It shall also state the facts proposed to be proved by the witness or the document and the relevancy of such facts to the defense. If the Tribunal grants the application the Tribunal shall be given such aid in obtaining production of the evidence as the circumstances require.

The principles laid down in the Nürnberg Charter and applied by the Nürnberg Tribunal were given a more general scope through their adoption by the UN General Assembly in 1946 (resolution 95 (I) of 11 December 1946). A year later the General Assembly charged the International Law Commission with the codification of the principles as laid down in the Nürnberg Charter and recognized by the Nürnberg Tribunal (resolution 177 (II) of 21 November 1947).[29] On the basis of a report by its rapporteur, J. Spiropoulos, the International Law Commission adopted seven principles (ILC, *Yearbook* 1950, vol. II, pp. 374-8), the fifth of which states:

Any person charged with a crime under international law has the right to a fair trial on the facts and law.

In the explanatory report of the International Law Commission it says:

In the view of the Commission the expression 'fair trial' should be understood in the light of the provisions quoted above [*i.e.*, Article 16] of the Charter of the Nürnberg Tribunal (*ibid.*, p. 376).

---

[29] Its task also included the drafting of a Code of Offences against the Peace and Security of Mankind.

And Article 6 of the Draft Code of Offences against Peace and Security, prepared by the International Law Commission (ILC, *Yearbook* 1987, vol. II, p. 5), reads as follows:

Any person charged with an offence against the peace and security of mankind shall be entitled to the guarantees extended to all human beings with regard to the law and the facts. In particular:

1. In the determination of any charge against him, he shall be entitled to a fair and public hearing by an independent and impartial tribunal duly established by law or by treaty, in accordance with the general principles of law.
2. He shall have the right to be presumed innocent until proved guilty.
3. In addition, he shall be entitled to the following guarantees:
   (a) to be informed promptly and in detail in a language which he understands of the nature and cause of the charge against him;
   (b) to have adequate time and facilities for the preparation of his defence and to communicate with counsel of his own choosing;
   (c) to be tried without undue delay;
   (d) to be tried in his presence, and to defend himself in person or through legal assistance of his own choosing; to be informed, if he does not have legal assistance, of his right; and to have legal assistance assigned to him, in any case where the interests of justice so require, and without payment by him in any such case, if he does not have sufficient means to pay for it;
   (e) to examine, or have examined, the witnesses against him and to obtain the attendance and examination of witnesses on his behalf under the same conditions as witnesses against him;
   (f) to have the free assistance of an interpreter if he cannot understand or speak the language used in court;
   (g) not to be compelled to testify against himself or to confess guilt.

Also related to the law of war are the Geneva Conventions of 1949. Geneva Convention III, concerning the treatment of prisoners of war, was preceded by the 1929 Geneva Convention Relative to the Treatment of Prisoners of War, whose Articles 61 and 62 read as follows:

Article 61.
No prisoner of war shall be sentenced without being given the opportunity to defend himself. No prisoner shall be compelled to admit that he is guilty of the offence of which he is accused.

Article 62.
The prisoner of war shall have the right to be assisted by a qualified advocate of his own choice and, if necessary, to have recourse to the offices of a competent interpreter. He shall be informed of his right by the detaining Power in good time before the hearing.

Failing a choice on the part of the prisoner, the protecting Power may procure an advocate for him. The detaining Power shall, at the request of the protecting Power, furnish to the latter a list of persons qualified to conduct the defence.

The representatives of the protecting Power shall have the right to attend the hearing of the case.

The only exception to this rule is where the hearing has to be kept secret in the interests of the safety of the State. The detaining Power would then notify the protecting Power accordingly.

Geneva Convention III also contains provisions with respect to procedural guarantees for the trial of prisoners of war by the enemy authorities: Articles 99–108.

Article 99 contains the general principles applicable to the trial of a war prisoner for crimes committed before or during his detention. It states, for example, that the accused may not be compelled to confess guilt.

Article 105 elaborates the right of the accused to defence. It sums up the following minimum guarantees:

(a) to be informed as soon as possible and in a language which he understands of the nature and cause of the charge against him;
(b) to have adequate time and facilities for the preparation of his defence;
(c) to defend himself or have the assistance of counsel of his own choosing or, if he does not have sufficient means to pay for legal assistance, to be given it free of charge;
(d) to examine or have examined witnesses against him in his presence, and to obtain the attendance and examination of witnesses on his behalf under the same conditions as witnesses against him and under the normal rules of procedure; and
(e) to ask for the free assistance of a competent interpreter if he cannot understand or speak the language used in court.

Geneva Convention IV, concerning protection of the civilian population at time of war, contains similar provisions with respect to the trial of civilians in occupied territory by the occupying powers (Articles 71–76) and the trial of civilians who have been interned in enemy territory (Article 126).

These treaty provisions require that the domestic legislation under which the trials will take place is in conformity with the minimum standard which they contain. Consequently their effect may well go beyond the specific situations to which they apply.[30]

Article 75 of the Protocol Additional to the Geneva Conventions of 12 August 1949, and Relating to the Protection of Victims of International Armed Conflicts (Protocol I), which contains fundamental guarantees to be enjoyed by persons in the power of a party to a conflict, lists in paragraph 4 the following principles:

No sentence may be passed and no penalty may be executed on a person found guilty of a penal offence related to the armed conflict except pursuant

---

[30] See common Article 3 of all four Conventions. Cf. also the last paragraph of Article 49 of Convention I, Article 50 of Convention II, Article 129 of Convention III and Article 146 of Convention IV. See also Draper, 1958, pp. 20, 23, 68, 106 and 111.

to a conviction pronounced by an impartial and regularly constituted court respecting the generally recognized principles of regular judicial procedure, which include the following:

(a) the procedure shall provide for the accused to be informed without delay of the particulars of the offence alleged against him and shall afford the accused before and during his trial all necessary rights and means of defence;

(b) no one shall be convicted of an offence except on the basis of individual penal responsibility;

(c) no one shall be accused or convicted of a criminal offence on account of any act or omission which did not constitute a criminal offence under the national or international law to which he was subject at the time when it was committed; nor shall a heavier penalty be imposed than that which was applicable at the time when the criminal offence was committed; if, after the commission of the offence, provision is made by law for the imposition of a lighter penalty, the offender shall benefit thereby;

(d) anyone charged with an offence is presumed innocent until proved guilty according to law;

(e) anyone charged with an offence shall have the right to be tried in his presence;

(f) no one shall be compelled to testify against himself or to confess guilt;

(g) anyone charged with an offence shall have the right to examine, or have examined, the witnesses against him and to obtain the attendance and examination of witnesses on his behalf under the same conditions as witnesses against him;

(h) no one shall be prosecuted or punished by the same Party for an offence in respect of which a final judgement acquitting or convicting that person has been previously pronounced under the same law and judicial procedure;

(i) anyone prosecuted for an offence shall have the right to have the judgement pronounced publicly; and

(j) a convicted person shall be advised on conviction of his judicial and other remedies and of the time-limits within which they may be exercised.

Article 6 of the Protocol II Additional to the Geneva Conventions of 12 August 1949, and Relating to the Protection of Victims of Non-International Armed Conflicts (Protocol II), deals with penal prosecutions. The second paragraph of that provision differs at some points from Article 75, paragraph 4, of Protocol I. It reads as follows:

No sentence shall be passed and no penalty shall be executed on a person found guilty of an offence except pursuant to a conviction pronounced by a court offering the essential guarantees of independence and impartiality. In particular:

(a) the procedure shall provide for an accused to be informed without delay of the particulars of the offence alleged against him and shall afford the accused before and during his trial all necessary rights and means of defence;

(b) no one shall be convicted of an offence except on the basis of individual penal responsibility;

(c) no one shall be held guilty of any criminal offence on account of any act or omission which did not constitute a criminal offence, under the law, at the time when it was committed; nor shall a heavier penalty be imposed than that which was applicable at the time when the criminal offence was committed; if, after the commission of the offence, provision is made by law for the imposition of a lighter penalty, the offender shall benefit thereby;

(d)   anyone charged with an offence is presumed innocent until proven guilty according to law;

(e)   anyone charged with an offence shall have the right to be tried in his presence;

(f)   no one shall be compelled to testify against himself or to confess guilt.

6. International legal principles of fair trial laid down in human rights treaties

The UN Commission on Human Rights, established by the Economic and Social Council in 1946 and charged, *inter alia*, with the drafting of an International Bill of Rights, included the right to a fair trial in its discussions from the very beginning. As mentioned above, Panama submitted the Statement of Essential Human Rights prepared by the American Law Institute, Article 7 of which was devoted to the fair-hearing principle, to the Commission as a starting-point for its deliberations. The first phase of the Commission's work resulted in the adoption by the UN General Assembly of the Universal Declaration of Human Rights on 10 December 1948: the vote was 48 votes in favour, none opposed, and eight abstentions. Articles 10 and 11, paragraph 1, of the Universal Declaration read as follows:

Article 10.
Everyone is entitled in full equality to a fair and public hearing by an independent and impartial tribunal, in the determination of his rights and obligations and of any criminal charge against him.
Article 11(1).
Everyone charged with a penal offence has the right to be presumed innocent until proved guilty according to law in a public trial at which he has had all the guarantees necessary for his defence.

On the basis of the Universal Declaration, the Commission continued its work on the second phase, the drafting of a human rights treaty. This eventually resulted in the adoption of two separate treaties: the International Covenant on Civil and Political Rights and the International Covenant on Economic, Social and Cultural Rights. The principles of fair trial, as elaborated during the preparatory work of the Commission, have been laid down in the former treaty, Article 14 of which provides as follows:

1.   All persons shall be equal before the courts and tribunals. In the

determination of any criminal charge against him, or of his rights and obligations in a suit at law, everyone shall be entitled to a fair and public hearing by a competent, independent and impartial tribunal established by law. The press and the public may be excluded from all or part of a trial for reasons of morals, public order (*ordre public*) or national security in a democratic society, or when the interests of the private lives of the parties so requires, or to the extent strictly necessary in the opinion of the court in special circumstances where publicity would prejudice the interests of justice; but any judgment rendered in a criminal case or in a suit at law shall be made public except where the interest of juvenile persons otherwise requires or the proceedings concern matrimonial disputes or the guardianship of children.

2.   Everyone charged with a criminal offence shall have the right to be presumed innocent until proved guilty according to law.

3.   In the determination of any criminal charge against him, everyone shall be entitled to the following minimum guarantees, in full equality:

 (a)   To be informed promptly and in detail in a language which he understands of the nature and cause of the charge against him;

 (b)   To have adequate time and facilities for the preparation of his defence and to communicate with counsel of his own choosing;

 (c)   To be tried without undue delay;

 (d)   To be tried in his presence, and to defend himself in person or through legal assistance of his own choosing; to be informed, if he does not have legal assistance, of this right; and to have legal assistance assigned to him, in any case where the interests of justice so require, and without payment by him in any such case if he does not have sufficient means to pay for it;

 (e)   To examine, or have examined, the witnesses against him and to obtain the attendance and examination of witnesses on his behalf under the same conditions as witnesses against him;

 (f)   To have the free assistance of an interpreter if he cannot understand or speak the language used in court;

 (g)   Not to be compelled to testify against himself or to confess guilt.

4.   In the case of juvenile persons, the procedure shall be such as will take account of their age and the desirability of promoting their rehabilitation.

5.   Everyone convicted of a crime shall have the right to his conviction and sentence being reviewed by a higher tribunal according to the law.

6.   When a person has by a final conviction been convicted of a criminal offence and when subsequently his conviction has been reversed or he has been pardoned on the ground that a new or newly discovered fact shows conclusively that there has been a miscarriage of justice, the person who has suffered punishment as a result of such conviction shall be compensated according to law, unless it is proved that the non-disclosure of the unknown fact in time is wholly or partly attributable to him.

7.   No one shall be liable to be tried or punished again for an offence for which he has already been finally convicted or acquitted in accordance with the law and penal procedure of each country.

At the time of the deliberations in the Commission, human rights treaties of a comparably general character were being prepared at the regional level, viz. within the frameworks of the Council of Europe and the Organization of American States. These efforts resulted in the European Convention for the Protection of Human Rights and Fundamental Freedoms and the American Convention on Human Rights respectively. Article 6 of the European Convention reads as follows:

1. In the determination of his civil rights and obligations or of any criminal charge against him, everyone is entitled to a fair and public hearing within a reasonable time by an independent and impartial tribunal established by law. Judgment shall be pronounced publicly but the press and public may be excluded from all or part of the trial in the interest of morals, public order or national security in a democratic society, where the interests of juveniles or the protection of the private life of the parties so require, or to the extent strictly necessary in the opinion of the court in special circumstances where publicity would prejudice the interests of justice.
2. Everyone charged with a criminal offence shall be presumed innocent until proved guilty according to law.
3. Everyone charged with a criminal offence has the following minimum rights:
    (a) to be informed promptly, in a language which he understands and in detail, of the nature and cause of the accusation against him;
    (b) to have adequate time and facilities for the preparation of his defence;
    (c) to defend himself in person or through legal assistance of his own choosing or, if he has not sufficient means to pay for legal assistance, to be given it free when the interests of justice so require;
    (d) to examine or have examined witnesses against him and to obtain the attendance and examination of witnesses on his behalf under the same conditions as witnesses against him;
    (e) to have the free assistance of an interpreter if he cannot understand or speak the language used in court.

Article 8 of the American Convention contains the following provisions:

1. Every person shall have the right to a hearing with due guarantees and within a reasonable time, by a competent, independent and impartial tribunal, previously established by law, in the substantiation of any accusation of a criminal nature made against him or for the determination of his rights or obligations of a civil, labour, fiscal or any other nature.
2. Every person accused of a serious crime has the right to be presumed innocent so long as his guilt has not been proven according to law. During the proceedings, every person is entitled, with full equality, to the following minimum guarantees:
    (a) the right of the accused to be assisted without charge by a translator or interpreter, if he does not understand or does not speak the language of the tribunal or court;
    (b) prior notification in detail to the accused of the charges against him;

(c) adequate time and means for the preparation of his defence;
(d) the right of the accused to defend himself personally or to be assisted by legal counsel of his own choosing, and to communicate freely and privately with legal counsel;
(e) the inalienable right to be assisted by counsel provided by the State, paid or not as the domestic law provides, if the accused does not defend himself personally or engage his own counsel within the time period established by law;
(f) the right of the defence to examine witnesses present in the court and to obtain the appearance, as witnesses of experts or other persons who may throw light on the facts;
(g) the right not to be compelled to be a witness against himself or to plead guilty; and
(h) the right to appeal the judgment to a higher court.
3. A confession of guilt by the accused shall be valid only if it is made without coercion of any kind.
4. An accused person, acquitted by a non-appealable judgment, shall not be subjected to a new trial for the same cause.
5. Criminal procedure shall be public, except in so far as may be necessary to protect the interests of justice.

Finally, mention should be made of the African Charter on Human and Peoples' Rights, which was drafted within the framework of the Organization of African Unity. Its Article 7, paragraph 1, is formulated as follows:

Every individual shall have the right to have his cause heard. This comprises:
(a) The right to an appeal to competent national organs against acts violating his fundamental rights as recognized and guaranteed by conventions, laws, regulations and customs in force;
(b) The right to be presumed innocent until proved guilty by a competent court or tribunal;
(c) The right to defence, including the right to be defended by counsel of his choice;
(d) The right to be tried within a reasonable time by an impartial court or tribunal.

Although the latter treaties are, all three of them, regional human rights instruments and, therefore, cannot be considered as independent manifestations of universal recognition of certain principles, they may nevertheless be of great importance for the determination of the universality of principles of fair trial.

On the one hand, the fact that the drafters of these regional instruments paid close attention to the text of what eventually became Article 14 of the International Covenant on Civil and Political Rights,[31] may indicate the universal values embodied in the

---

[31] For Article 6 of the European Convention, see van Dijk, 1988b, pp. 137-8. For the American Convention, see *Inter-American Yearbook on Human Rights* 1968, Chapter III: The Draft Inter-American Convention on Protection of Human Rights, especially pp. 71-91.

latter instrument. On the other hand, to the extent that the provisions of the regional treaties are identical to, or in substance the same as, Article 14 of the Covenant, this may serve to enhance further the universal recognition of the latter provision. Also, as is the case with the Covenant, the regional treaties will further develop in practice, through their national and international interpretation and application. They do so as independent 'living instruments',[32] but at the same time in close interdependence. In fact, a national court or other authority which is called upon to apply both the global and the regional treaty, will be inclined to interpret them in a uniform way, which may result in a certain harmonization of interpretation. Equally, the international bodies which are entrusted with the supervision of the implementation of one of the treaties will be inclined to pay close attention to the interpretation which other international bodies have given to comparable provisions in other treaties. This, again, may lead to greater uniformity in practice. All of these facts together mean that the Covenant and the regional human rights treaties are involved in a process of sometimes express, but most of the time implied, interaction which may enhance the universality of the recognition of the principles involved.

Consequently, in addition to a comparative study of the national legal systems, covering both the law in the books and the law in practice, a comparative study of the pertinent provisions in human rights treaties, including their interpretation in national and international case-law, should form part of the search for universal legal principles of fair trial. Indeed, the international case-law can be very instrumental in bringing about a more uniform interpretation and application of the principles concerned by national courts and other authorities, while their taking into account the case-law of other States Parties may have the same result.[33] Analysis of the national case-law of the states which are parties to the separate treaties requires co-operation of a team of experts. For the international case-law concerning Article 14 of the International Covenant and Article 6 of the European Convention, use can be made of recent very comprehensive and detailed studies.[34] These will be relied upon to some extent for the next section. For the American Convention, the

---

[32] The character of the European Convention as a 'living instrument' has been emphasized by the European Court of Human Rights in its case-law. See, for example, its judgment of 25 April 1978 in the *Tyrer Case*, Publ. E.C.H.R., Series A, vol. 26 (1978), p. 14.

[33] On this harmonizing effect, see the judgment of the European Court of Human Rights of 26 April 1979 in the *Sunday Times* Case, Publ. E.C.H.R., Series A, vol. 30 (1979), paragraph 59.

[34] For a detailed analysis of the theory and practice of the International Covenant on Civil and Political Rights, see Nowak, 1989. An English version will be published by Engel Publisher, Kehl am Rhein, in 1990. For the European Convention use can be made of van Dijk and van Hoof, 1984, of which a second edition will be published by Kluwer Publisher, Deventer, in 1990.

international case-law is still very scarce.[35] For the African Human Rights Charter it is almost non-existent, partly in view of the fact that the supervisory procedure provided for has started to function only recently.

7. Identification of universal legal principles of fair trial

On the basis of the above-mentioned treaties, other documents and (selected) scholarly opinions, an effort will be made to identify legal principles concerning fair trial which were universally recognized at the moment of the adoption of the general and regional human rights treaties. An effort will also be made to identify any such principles whose universal recognition has been enhanced both by the adoption of these treaties and the legal practice based upon them and by the adoption of later documents, and which have found further support in the conclusions of (selected) comparative studies. The year 1950, in which the European Convention was signed and the text of Article 14 of the International Covenant on Civil and Political Rights, although not yet adopted, had obtained its final wording, is taken as a dividing line.

The sources used for the identification of the principles are referred to here in their abbreviated form, as indicated in the list of sources at the end of the chapter.

7.1 Legal principles generally recognized

A fundamental principle which is very often mentioned in close connection with one or more principles of fair trial in criminal proceedings is the principle of *nullum crimen, nulla poena*, i.e. the principle that:

(1) a criminal conviction may only be based on a legal rule which existed at the time of the incriminating act or omission (*nullum crimen sine lege*); and,

(2) on account of the infringement of that rule, no heavier penalty may be imposed than the one that was applicable at the time the offence was committed (*nulla poena sine lege*).

The universal character of the principle has found support in its inclusion in the following sources:

---

[35] See Comisión Interamericana de Derechos Humanos, 1982, pp. 313, 314, 316–17, 324, 332 and 334. See also Corte Interamericana de Derechos Humanos, Opinión Consultiva OC-9/87 del 6 de Octubre de 1987: Garant as judiciales en estados de emergencia, solicitada por el Gobierno de la República Oriental del Uruguay.

Universal Declaration, Article 11(2);
Geneva Convention III, Article 99;
Orfield, p. 44;

European Convention, Article 7;
AIDP Rome, No. 1;
ICJ Athens, Resolution I, Article 3;
ICJ New Delhi, Committee III, Article 2;
1961 ILC Draft, Article 1(2)(e);
Covenant, Article 15;
American Convention, Article 9;
Protocol I, Article 75(4)(c);
Protocol II, Article 6(2);
African Charter, Article 7(2);
Bakken, p. 416.

It is submitted, however, that this principle is a fundamental precondition for a fair trial in criminal proceedings, but should not be listed among the principles of fair trial.

On the basis of an analysis of the sources mentioned in the preceding section on identification of universal legal principles of fair trial, the following principles may be said to be generally recognized:

(1) Right to a Fair Hearing (including Equality of Arms)

The principle of the right to a fair hearing may be considered the umbrella principle by which all other principles of fair trial are covered. However, the case-law has also given an independent meaning to the principle in the sense that the proceedings as a whole must present the picture of a fair hearing, apart from the fulfilment of the guarantees listed separately.[36] In that context especially, the requirement of 'equality of arms' between on the one hand the accused and on the other hand the public prosecutor is emphasized,[37] implying in particular that no elements of the examination of the case may be settled when the party is present or represented and the other is not,[38]

---

[36] See, for example, the Report of the European Commission of 15 March 1961 in the *Nielsen* Case, *Yearbook IV* (1961), p. 494 at p. 568. For Article 14 of the Covenant, see the 1959 Report of the Third Committee to the General Assembly, UN doc. A/4299, paragraph 55.

[37] See, for example, the judgment of the European Court of 6 May 1985 in the *Bönisch* Case, Publ. E.C.H.R., Series A, vol. 92 (1985), pp. 14–16.

[38] See, for example, the judgment of the European Court of 27 June 1968 in the *Neumeister* Case, Publ. E.C.H.R., Series A, vol. 8 (1968), p. 43.

that they must have the same access to the information which plays a part in the formation of the court's opinion,[39] and that they must have equal opportunities to present evidence and to contradict the evidence produced by the other.[40]

The universal character of this principle has found support in its inclusion in the following sources:

Statement of Human Rights, Article 7 ('fair trial');
1935 Harvard Draft, Article 12 ('fair trial');
Universal Declaration, Article 10 ('fair hearing');
Geneva Convention IV, Article 71(1) ('regular trial');
Orfield, p. 42 ('fair trial');

European Convention, Article 6(1) ('fair hearing');
1961 ILC Draft, Article 1(2)(d) ('with proper safeguards');
1961 Harvard Draft, Article 7 ('fair hearing');
Covenant, Article 14(1) ('fair hearing');
Harris, pp. 376-7 ('fair trial');
American Convention, Article 8(1) ('hearing with due guarantees');
Protocol I, Article 75(4) ('regular judicial procedure');
Kaufman Hevener and Mosher, pp. 610-12 ('fair hearing');
AIDP Hamburg, Resolution No. 2 ('equality of arms');
Hertzberg and Zammuto, pp. 17-18 and 20-1 ('equality of arms');
Bakken, pp. 414-17 ('equality of the parties', 'fair trial');
Draft Code of Offences, Article 6 ('fair and public hearing').

(2) Right to a Public Hearing

The public nature of proceedings helps to ensure a fair trial by protecting the litigants against arbitrary decisions and by enabling society to control the administration of justice.[41] In addition to the interest which the parties to the dispute may have in a public hearing, it serves the public interest: verifiability of, and thus confidence in, the administration of justice ('justice must not only be done; it must also be seen to be done').

On the other hand, both the interest of (one of) the parties and the public interest may require that the proceedings not be public, e.g. the

---

[39] Admissibility Decision of the European Commission on Appl. 9433/81, *X v. the Netherlands*, Decisions and Reports 27 (1982), p. 233.

[40] Judgment of the European Court of 29 May 1986 in the *Feldbrugge* Case, Publ. E.C.H.R., Series A, vol. 99 (1986), pp. 17-18.

[41] See, for instance, the judgment of the European Court of 28 June 1984 in the *Campbell and Fell* Case, Publ. E.C.H.R., Series A, vol. 80 (1984), p. 43.

protection of privacy or the protection of public order or national security. Therefore, the guarantee of a public hearing allows for certain, exhaustively listed, exceptions.[42]

The universal character of this principle has found support in its inclusion in the following sources:

	limitations?
Statement of Human Rights, Article 7;	—
Universal Declaration, Articles 10 and 11(1);	—
Geneva Convention III, Article 105(5);	yes
Geneva Convention IV, Article 74;	yes

European Convention, Article 6(1);	yes
Covenant, Article 14(1)	yes
ICJ Athens, Principle 1;	—
UN Baguio City, pp. 18–19;	yes
UN Santiago, pp. 24–5;	yes
ICJ New Delhi, Principle 9;	yes
UN Vienna, p. 20;	—
UN Wellington, pp. 22–3;	yes
1961 ILC Draft, Article 1(2)(d).	—
Harris, pp. 357–61	yes
American Convention, Article 8(5);	yes
Protocol I, Article 75(4)(i) (only with respect to the judgment);	—
Kaufman Hevener and Mosher, pp. 610 and 612;	—
Hertzberg and Zammuto, pp. 20–1;	yes
Bakken, pp. 418–20.	—

The right to have the judgment pronounced publicly is not always expressly recognized as a separate element, but may be assumed to be recognized *a fortiori*.

(3) Right to a Hearing by an Independent and Impartial Tribunal

Independence and impartiality are two qualifications which are essential for a tribunal in order to be considered as a court. Of these, the first has an objective and the second a subjective character.

For the independence of a court it is required that it can and does base its decision on its own free opinion about facts and legal grounds, without any commitment to the parties or the public authorities. Moreover, its decision should not be subject to review by any other but an authority that is independent in the same sense.[43]

---

[42] The State has to show that one of these exceptions was applicable and justified. See, for instance, view of the Human Rights Committee with respect to military-court proceedings in Uruguay: Communications 10/1977; 28 and 32/1978; 44/1979; 70, 74 and 80/1980; 159/1983; 139/1984.

[43] See, for example, the judgment of the European Court of 23 October 1985 in the *Benthem* Case,

For the impartiality of a court it is required that the court is not in any way biased with respect to the decision to be taken, does not allow itself to be influenced by information from outside the court room, by popular feeling, or by any pressure whatever, but bases its opinion on objective arguments, put forward at the trial.[44]

Since a court is often composed of more than one judge, its impartiality, being itself an objective concept, in its turn has an objective and a subjective side. The objective side refers to the question whether the court is organized or composed in such a way as to raise doubt about its impartiality, regardless of the personal attitude of the individual judges, while the subjective side concerns that personal attitude.[45]

In several documents a third qualification of the tribunal is mentioned, viz. that it must be competent and/or established by law. This implies that the accused has the right to be tried by a court previously designated by the law to judge on the charges brought against him, and not by a court established *ad hoc.*[46]

While in civil cases the right under discussion implies, at least according to the European Court,[47] the right to a court, i.e. the right of access to a court, in criminal cases it means the right to be sentenced by no authority other than a court. It does not mean the right of a victim of a crime to have the suspect prosecuted and brought before a court or to institute criminal proceedings in addition to civil proceedings.[48]

The universal character of these principles has found support in its inclusion in the following sources:

1935 Harvard Draft, Article 12;
Statement of Human Rights, Article 7 ('competent');
Universal Declaration, Article 10;
Geneva Convention IV, Article 71(1); ('competent');
Orfield, p. 42;

Publ. E.C.H.R., Series A, vol. 97 (1986), p. 18. With respect to military tribunals, see the observations by members of the Human Rights Committee in CCPR/C/SR. 127–129, 222 and 249, and the views of the Committee on Communications 28/1978 and 46/1979.

[44] See, for example, the admissibility decision of the European Commission on Application 1727/72, *Boeckmann v. Belgium*, Yearbook VI (1963), pp. 416–20. For the Human Rights Committee, see A/C.3/SR.964, paragraph 6 and A/C.3/SR.966, paragraph 21.

[45] See, for instance, the judgment of the European Court of 1 October 1982 in the *Piersack* Case, Publ. E.C.H.R., Series A, vol. 53 (1982), pp. 14–16.

[46] See, for example, the admissibility decision of the European Commission on Applications 8603, 8722, and 8729/79, *Crociani et al. v. Italy*, Decisions & Reports 22 (1981), p. 219. For Article 14 of the Covenant, see the 1959 Report of the Third Committee to the UN 59th General Assembly, UN doc. A/4299, paragraph 77.

[47] Judgment of the European Court of 21 February 1975 in the *Golder* Case, Publ. E.C.H.R., Series A, vol. 18 (1975), pp. 16–18.

[48] Admissibility decision of the European Commission on Application 8366/78, *X v. Luxembourg*, Decisions & Reports 16 (1979), p. 198.

European Convention, Article 6(1) ('. . . established by law');
UN Santiago, pp. 9-13;
UN Wellington, pp. 7-11;
1961 ILC Draft, Article 1(2)(d) ('competent organs of the State');
1961 Harvard Draft, Article 7;
Covenant, Article 14 ('competent . . . established by law');
Harris, pp. 355-6 (". . . established by law");
American Convention, Article 8(1) ('competent . . . previously established by law');
Protocol I, Article 75(4) ('regularly constituted');
Protocol II, Article 6(2);
Kaufman Hevener and Mosher, p. 610;
Hertzberg and Zammuto, pp. 18-19 ('procedures established by law');
African Charter, Article 7(1)(b) and (d) ('competent');
1982 Draft Principles on Independence;
1983 Minimum Standards of Independence;
1983 Universal Declaration on Independence;
1985 Basic Principles on Independence;
Bakken, pp. 415-17;
1988 Draft Declaration on Independence;
Draft Code of Offences, Article 6 ('competent', 'duly established by law or by treaty');
Body of Principles, Principle 4 ('judicial or other authority').

(4) Right to be Tried Within a Reasonable Time

This principle aims at keeping the period of uncertainty about whether the accused will be found guilty and, if so, about the penalty to be imposed upon him, as short as is reasonable, given the complexity of the case and the procedural guarantees to be respected.

According to the case-law under the European Convention, the beginning of the period to be considered for the determination of reasonableness is either the moment of the formal charge or the moment at which the situation of the person concerned has been substantially affected as a result of a suspicion against him, whichever is earlier.[49] The end of the relevant period is the moment at which a decision on the charge has been taken at the highest instance or has become final through the expiration of the time-limit for appeal, or when the prosecution refrains from further action. However, the certainty must concern the opinion of the court not only on the charge, but also on the penalty (see note 49).

Important factors to be taken into account to determine the reasonableness of the length of the procedure are the complexity of the case — including the difficulty in collecting data and evidence — the way

---

[49] See, for example, the judgment of the European Court of 15 July 1982 in the *Eckle* Case, Publ. E.C.H.R., Series A, vol. 51 (1982), p. 33.

in which the prosecuting authorities and courts have conducted the procedure to avoid unnecessary delays, the measures taken by the authorities to cope with an overburdened judiciary, and any behaviour of the accused that may have contributed to the delay.[50]

The universal character of this principle has found support in its inclusion in the following sources:

1929 Harvard Draft, Article 9 ('unwarranted delay');
1935 Harvard Draft, Article 12 ('without unreasonable delay');
Statement of Human Rights, Article 7 ('without undue delay');
Orfield, p. 42 ('without undue delay');

European Convention, Article 6(1) ('within a reasonable time');
ICJ Athens, Principle 4 ('reasonable');
UN Baguio City, pp. 14–15 ('avoidance of delay');
UN Santiago, p. 21 ('speedy');
UN Vienna, p. 19 ('speedy');
UN Wellington, p. 22 ('speedy');
1961 ILC Draft, Article 1(2)(e) ('without undue delay');
1961 Harvard Draft, Afticle 7(j) ('with reasonable dispatch');
Covenant, Article 14(3)(c) ('without undue delay');
American Convention, Article 8(1) ('within a reasonable time');
AIDP Hamburg, Resolution No. 3 ('speedily');
Hertzberg and Zammuto, p. 24 ('speedy trial');
African Charter, Article 7(1)(d) ('within a reasonable time');
Bakken, pp. 413–14 ('without undue delay');
Draft Code of Offences, Article 6 ('without undue delay');
Body of Principles, Principle 38 ('within a reasonable time').

(5) Right to be Presumed Innocent

The principle of the *presumptio innocentiae* is a core element of fair trial, because its violation amounts to a denial of the other elements of a fair trial.

The principle is violated if a judicial decision or a decision by another competent authority reflects the opinion, even if only by implication, that the accused is guilty, without the latter's having been proved guilty according to law and, notably, without his having had the opportunity of exercising his right of defence.[51] The

---

[50] See, for example, the judgments of the European Court of 16 July 1971 in the *Ringeisen* Case, Publ. E.C.H.R., Series A, vol. 13 (1971), p. 45; of 28 June 1978 in the *König* Case, *ibid.*, vol. 27 (1978), pp. 34–40; and of 26 October 1984 in the *De Cubber* Case, *ibid.*, vol. 86 (1984), p. 20. For Article 14 of the International Covenant see, for instance, the Case of *Pinkney v. Canada*, Communication 27/1978, paragraphs 10 and 35.

[51] Judgment of the European Court of 25 March 1983 in the *Minelli* Case, Publ. E.C.H.R., Series A, vol. 62 (1983), p. 18.

innocence of the accused has to be assumed by the court without any prejudice and the guilt has to be proved not by the court but by the prosecutor, with full opportunity for the accused to disprove the evidence put forward.[52]

This principle has also implications for the pre-trial phase: the treatment of the accused must be based on the presumption of innocence and, therefore, must not have a punitive character, while evidence collected during the pre-trial investigations must be verified during the trial by the court, with the possibility for the accused to contradict statements by witnesses and experts, and any other evidence, including his own previous confessions.[53]

The universal character of the principle has found support in its inclusion in the following sources:

(a)   burden of proof lies with the prosecuting authority

(b)   not to be compelled to testify against oneself

(c)   not to be compelled to confess guilt

1929 Geneva Convention, Article 61;c	
Universal Declaration, Article 11(1);a	
Geneva Convention III, Article 99(2);	a,b,c
Orfield, p. 45;	a

European Convention, Article 6(2);	a
AIDP Rome, Resolution No. 3;	a
ICJ Athens, Resolution I(1) and (5);	a,b,c
UN Baguio City, p. 17;	a
UN Santiago, pp. 18–19 and 22–s3;	a,b
UN New Delhi, pp. 3 and 8;	a,b
UN Vienna, p. 20;	a,c

---

[52] Judgment of the European Court of 6 December 1988 in the Case of *Barberà, Messegué and Jabardo*, Publ. E.C.H.R., Series A, vol. 146 (1988), paragraph 77. The fact that a proposal by the Philippines to include in Article 14 the International Covenant the words 'beyond reasonable doubt' was rejected (E/CN.4/SR.156, p. 6ff.) does not mean that the court should not, in case there is any doubt on its part, decide in favour of the accused according to the general principle '*in dubio pro reo*'. See the view of the Human Rights Committee on two Communications against Uruguay: 5/1977 and 8/1977.

[53] See, for example, the judgment of the European Court of 24 November 1986 in the *Unterpertinger* Case, Publ. E.C.H.R., Series A, vol. 110 (1987), pp. 14–15, and the admissibility decision of the European Commission on Application 5076/71, *X v. United Kingdom*, Collection of Decisions 40 (1972), pp. 66–7. See also Article 1 of Recommendation R(80)1 (27 June 1980) of the Committee of Ministers of the Council of Europe, on the matter of custody on remand. And see Article 10(2)(a) of the International Covenant on Civil and Political Rights.

UN Wellington, pp. 20, 23 and 24;	a
1961 ILC Draft, Article 1(2)(e);	a
Covenant, Article 14(2) and (3)(g);	a,b,c
Harris, p. 369;	a,b,c
American Convention, Article 8(2) and (2)(g);	a,b,c
Protocol I, Article 75 (4)(d) and (f);	a,b,c
Protocol II, Article 6(2);	a,b,c
AIDP Hamburg, Resolutions 1 and 5;	a,b,c
Hertzberg and Zammuto, pp. 16-18	a,b,c
African Charter, Article 7(1)(b);	a
Bakken, pp. 420-1;	a,b,c
Draft Code of Offences, Article 6;	a,b,c
Body of Principles, Principle 36.	a

(6) Right to be Informed Promptly and in Detail in a Language Which He Understands of the Nature and Cause of the Charge

This principle is closely related to that of the right of the accused to adequate defence, since his defence can only be prepared if he knows from the very beginning the nature of the charge as well as the factual and legal grounds on which it is based.[54]

The principle implies that the prosecuting authority must make all relevant information available to the suspect as soon as a decision is taken to institute criminal proceedings and any necessary translations have been made. That information must be supplemented with other information, if new facts or legal grounds are added to the charge.

The universal character of the principle has found support in its inclusion in the following sources:

Nürnberg Charter, Article 16(a);
Tokyo Charter, Article 9(a);
Geneva Convention III, Article 105;
Geneva Convention IV, Article 71;
Orfield, p. 42;

European Convention, Article 6(3)(a);
ICJ Athens, Resolution I, Article 1(a);
ICJ New Delhi, Committee III, Articles 4(2) and 6(2);
UN Vienna, p. 13;
1961 ILC Draft, Article 1(2)(e);

---

[54] See, for example, the Report of the European Commission of 2 March 1988 in the *Brozicek* Case, paragraph 65. For Article 14 of the International Covenant on Civil and Political Rights, see General Comment 13/21 of the Human Rights Committee, paragraph 8.

1961 Harvard Draft, Article 7(a);
Covenant, Article 14(3)(a);
Harris, pp. 361-3;
American Convention, Article 8(2)(b);
Protocol I, Article 75(4)(a);
Protocol II, Article 6(2);
Hertzberg and Zammuto, p. 20;
Bakken, p. 421;
Draft Code of Offences, Article 6;
Body of Principles, Principles 10, 12 and 14.

(7) Right to Adequate Time and Facilities for Defence

This principle is closely related to the preceding one and to that concerning the right to legal assistance.

According to the case-law under the European Convention, this principle concerns not only the accused but also his counsel. Therefore, in order to assess the fairness of the trial, the position of both of them has to be taken into account.[55] Thus, if an accused has special confidence in a certain lawyer who, at that moment, is very busy or absent, or if he has to change lawyers for any legitimate reason, the prosecuting authorities and the courts have to take this into account. On the other hand, the accused cannot complain about any delay caused by such problems. If appeal is open to the accused, the time-limit must be such that there is sufficient time to decide on whether to appeal and to make adequate preparation of the appeal possible.

The right to adequate facilities includes especially access to and information about all relevant documents and information,[56] and adequate possibilities for communication between the accused and counsel, even if the former is detained.[57]

The universal character of the principle has found support in the following sources:

Tokyo Charter, Article 9(e);
Universal Declaration, Article 11(1);
Geneva Convention III, Articles 99 and 105;
Geneva Convention IV, Article 72;

European Convention, Article 6(3)(b);

---

[55] See the admissibility decision of the European Commission on Application 524/59, *Ofner v. Austria*, Yearbook III (1960), p. 352.

[56] Report of the European Commission of 15 October 1987 in the *Bricmont* Case, paragraph 158. See also the view of the Human Rights Committee on Communication 158/1983, *O.F. v. Norway*, paragraph 5.5.

[57] Judgment of the European Court of 28 June 1984 in the Case of *Campbell and Fell*, Publ. E.C.H.R., Series A, vol. 80 (1984), p. 49; View of the Human Rights Committee on Communication 115/1982, *Wight v. Madagaskar*, paragraph 17.

ICJ Athens, Resolution I, Articles 1(1) and 2;
UN Santiago, pp. 19-20;
ICJ New Delhi, Committee III, Articles 6 and 7;
UN Vienna, pp. 17, 18 and 21;
UN Wellington, pp. 20-1;
1961 ILC Draft, Article 1(2)(d);
1961 Harvard Draft, Article 7(b);
Covenant, Article 14(3)(b);
Harris, p. 367;
American Convention, Article 8(2)(c);
Protocol I, Article 75(4)(a);
Protocol II, Article 6(2);
Bakken, p. 414;
Draft Code of Offences, Article 6;
Body of Principles, Principle 18.

(8) Right to Defend Oneself or Through Legal Assistance

This principle implies that the accused who does not wish to defend himself in person or who is not allowed to do so under the applicable domestic law must be enabled to have recourse to legal assistance.[58]

In most sources it is stated that the accused must be allowed free choice of counsel under the conditions set by national law for legal assistance, and that he must be given legal aid free of charge if he cannot pay for it. However, these elements are not included in all documents, not even in the American Convention or the African Charter, and they have been subjected to restrictions and reservations in other documents. Consequently, they do not form part of the generally recognized principle. However, if a certain lawyer is forced upon the accused, e.g. a military instead of a civil lawyer, the defence cannot be expected to be adequate and consequently the fair trial requirement is violated.[59]

If the accused is not assisted by a lawyer during the pre-trial phase, the requirement of a fair trial demands that the court evaluate the collected evidence during the trial, in the presence of the accused and counsel, and give them ample opportunity to contradict it.[60]

The universal character of the principle has found support in its inclusion in the following sources:

---

[58] Judgment of the European Court of 25 April 1983 in the *Pakelli* Case, Publ. E.C.H.R., Series A, vol. 64 (1983), p. 15. Although the formulation in many documents seems to suggest that the accused has the choice either to defend himself or to opt for legal assistance, in view of the fact that in many legal systems legal representation in criminal proceedings is required, it is rather doubtful that this was the intention of the drafters.

[59] View of the Human Rights Committee on Communication 110/1981, *Viana Acosta v. Uruguay*, paragraphs 13.2 and 15.

[60] See the admissibility decision of the European Commission on Application 9370/81, *G v. United Kingdom*, Decisions and Reports 35 (1984), p. 75.

	free?
1929 Geneva Convention, Articles 61 and 62;	—
Nürnberg Charter, Article 16(d);	—
Tokyo Charter, Article 9 (c) and (d);	—
Universal Declaration, Article 11;	—
Geneva Convention III, Articles 99 and 105;	—
Geneva Convention IV, Article 72;	—
Orfield, p. 42;	—

European Convention, Article 6(3)(c);	yes
AIDP Rome, Resolution No. 4;	—
ICJ Athens, Resolution I, Article 1(c);	yes
UN Baguio City, p. 16;	yes
UN Santiago, pp. 19–21;	yes
ICJ New Delhi, Committee III, Article 6(1);	—
UN Vienna, pp. 18–20;	yes
1961 ILC Draft, Article 1(2)(e);	—
1961 Harvard Draft, Article 7(e) and (f);	yes
Covenant, Article 14(3)(d);	yes
Harris, pp. 364–7;	yes
American Convention, Article 8(2)(d) and (e);	—
Protocol I, Article 75(4)(a);	—
Protocol II, Article 6(2);	—
AIDP Hamburg, Resolution No. 6;	yes
Hertzberg and Zammuto, pp. 22–3;	yes
African Charter, Article 7(1)(c);	—
Bakken, pp. 414–15;	yes
Draft Code of Offences, Article 6;	yes
Body of Principles, Principles 11 and 17.	yes

(9) Right to Examine Witnesses Against Him and to Obtain the Attendance and Examination of Witnesses on His Behalf Under the Same Conditions

This principle is closely related to that of the 'quality of arms' as an element of a fair hearing, especially as far as its second part is concerned.

The first part relates to the right of the accused to contradict the evidence against him. For that purpose he and/or his lawyer must be given ample opportunity to examine both witnesses against him and any experts whose statements are unfavourable to him. The court should restrict these opportunities only in case of manifest abuse or improper use of the right.[61]

---

[61] The case-law concerning the European Convention seems to give broader discretion to the courts in this respect, but in our opinion this is not in conformity with the guarantee aimed at by this principle. See van Dijk and van Hoof, 1990 (2nd edition of 1984 publication), with respect to Article 6(3)(d).

The second part clearly allows for discretion on the part of the court, since it only requires that the prosecutor and the accused receive equal treatment in obtaining the attendance of witnesses.[62] However, if there is no possibility at all for the accused to have witnesses on his behalf examined, there is no fair trial.[63]

If an expert appears not to be impartial, to the disadvantage of the accused, the principle requires that the latter has the right to appoint his own expert to give testimony.[64]

The universal character of the principle has found support in its inclusion in the following sources:

Nürnberg Charter, Article 16(b) and (e);
Tokyo Charter, Article 9(d) and (e);
Geneva Convention III, Article 105;
Geneva Convention IV, Article 72;
Orfield, pp. 42-3;

European Convention, Article 6(3)(d);
AIDP Rome, Resolution No. 4;
ICJ Athens, Resolution I, Article 1(d);
UN Baguio City, p. 16;
UN Santiago, p. 20;
ICJ New Delhi, Committee III, Article 6(3), (4) and (5);
UN Vienna, p. 19;
1961 Harvard Draft, Article 7(c) and (d);
Covenant, Article 14(3)(e);
Harris, p. 367;
American Convention, Article 8(2)(f);
Protocol I, Article 75(4)(g);
AIDP Hamburg, Resolution No. 2;
Hertzberg and Zammuto, p. 21;
Bakken, pp. 421-2;
Draft Code of Offences, Article 6.

(10) Right of Assistance of an Interpreter

A fair trial implies that the accused must be able to follow what is going on during his trial. Therefore, if he is not sufficiently familiar with the language used in court, he must be entitled to the assistance of an interpreter. It is not sufficient that his counsel has command of the language, since the accused must also be able to know what

---

[62] Article 8(2)(f) of the American Convention contains a more far-reaching guarantee for the accused.
[63] View of the Human Rights Committee on Communication 63/1979, *Raúl Sendic v. Uruguay*, paragraphs 12.3, 16.2 and 20.
[64] Judgment of the European Court of 6 May 1985 in the *Bönisch* Case, Publ. E.C.H.R., Series A, vol. 92 (1985), p. 15.

defence is put forward on his behalf and to participate in the preparation of his defence.

According to the European Court of Human Rights, the right of assistance of an interpreter concerns all those documents or statements in the proceedings which it is necessary for the accused to understand in order to have the benefit of a fair trial.[65] 'Proceedings' must be understood as also covering the pre-trial proceedings, since the investigations by the police, the prosecutor and the investigating judge are also very important for the accused to understand properly.[66]

The right to have the assistance of an interpreter free of charge has been recognized in most sources, but not in all. This right establishes that interpretation costs cannot be included among any other costs to be paid at the end of the proceedings, no matter what their outcome.[67]

The universal character of this principle has found support in its inclusion in the following sources:

	free?
1929 Geneva Convention, Article 62;	—
Nürnberg Charter, Article 16(c);	—
Tokyo Charter, Article 9(b);	—
Geneva Convention III, Article 105;	yes
Geneva Convention IV, Article 72;	yes

European Convention, Article 6(3)(e);	yes
ICJ Athens, Resolution I, Article 1(e);	yes
UN Baguio City, p. 17;	—
UN Vienna, p. 19;	—
UN Wellington, p. 21;	yes
1961 Harvard Draft, Article 7(g);	—
Covenant, Article 14(3)(f);	yes
Harris, pp. 368–9;	yes
American Convention, Article 8(2)(a);	yes
Hertzberg and Zammuto, p. 23;	—
Bakken, p. 421;	yes
Draft Code of Offences, Article 6;	yes

---

[65] Judgment of the European Court of 28 November 1978 in the Case of *Luedicke, Belkacem and Koç*, Publ. E.C.H.R., Series A, vol. 29 (1978), p. 20. In drafting Article 14 of the International Covenant, extension of the right to all relevant documents was rejected: Annotations prepared by the Secretary-General, UN doc. A/2929, paragraph 87.

[66] See also the Report of the European Commission of 5 May 1988 on the *Kamasinski* Case, application 9783/82, paragraph 169. It is doubtful if this extensive interpretation is generally recognized.

[67] Judgment of the European Court of 28 November 1978 in the Case of *Luedicke, Belkacem and Koç*, Publ. E.C.H.R., Series A, vol. 29 (1979), p. 19.

Body of Principles, Principle 14.   yes

(11) Right to be Tried in One's Presence

This principle has not been included expressly in all the relevant sources, but has been recognized to be implied in either the concept of a fair trial or the right of the accused to defend himself.

Indeed, it may be important for the accused to be admitted to the court room, for instance to be able to answer certain questions himself and to contradict any evidence put forward, to know what is going on and what is said in his defence, and to participate in the preparation of his defence. If his presence may be assumed to be important for the formation of the court's opinion, denial of this right violates the principle of fair hearing, unless there are urgent reasons for this denial.[68]

In Article 14 of the International Covenant, the right of the accused to be tried in his presence has been expressly included in paragraph 3(d). Several complaints about military trials in the absence of the accused have found support in views of the Human Rights Committee.[69] If, however, the accused does not appear at his trial although he has been summoned in accordance with a prescribed procedure which provides for sufficient guarantees, a trial in his absence is not in violation of the principle.[70]

The universal character of this principle has found support in its inclusion in the following sources:

1935 Harvard Draft, Article 12;
Geneva Convention III, Article 107;

European Convention, Article 6 (according to the 'Strasbourg' case-law, depending on the circumstances this right may be implied in the right to a fair trial);
UN Baguio City, p. 19;
UN Santiago, p. 25;
Covenant, Article 14(3)(d);
Harris, pp. 370-1;
American Convention, Article 8(2)(d) (probably implied in the right of the accused to defend himself personally);
Protocol I, Article 75(4)(e);
Bakken, p. 417.

---

[68] Admissibility decision of the European Commission on Application 9818/82, *Morris v. United Kingdom*, Decisions and Reports 35 (1984), pp. 121-2.
[69] See several Communications against Uruguay, e.g. 28/1974, 32/1974 and 139/1983.
[70] Judgment of the European Court of 12 February 1985 in the *Colozza* Case, Publ. E.C.H.R., Series A, vol. 89 (1985), p. 12. View of the Human Rights Committee on Communication 16/1977, *Mbenge v. Zaire*, paragraphs 14.1 and 21.

7.2 Legal principles not yet generally recognized

A comparison of the above-mentioned sources leads to the conclusion that the following principles, although expressly or impliedly laid down in one or more of the human rights treaties, are not yet generally recognized:

(12) Right of Appeal to a Higher Tribunal

Although the right of appeal in criminal cases has often been included in the relevant sources, it has been subjected to so many restrictions and reservations that it is not included among the generally recognized principles for the purposes of this study.

This principle has been included in the following sources:

Geneva Convention III, Article 106;
Geneva Convention IV, Article 73;

European Convention, Protocol VII, Article 2;
ICJ Athens, Resolution I, Article 6;
ICJ New Delhi, Committee III, Article 11;
UN Wellington, p. 27;
Covenant, Article 14(5) ('according to law');
Harris, pp. 371–2;
American Convention, Article 8(2)(h);
Hertzberg and Zammuto, p. 24.

(13) Right to Compensation in Case of Miscarriage of Justice

For this principle the same holds true: its recognition is growing, but is still not sufficiently general to include it among the generally recognized principles of fair trial.

The principle has been included in the following sources:

European Convention, Protocol VII, Article 3;
UN Santiago, p. 15;
UN Vienna, p. 23;
UN Wellington, p.28;
Covenant, Article 14(6);
Harris, pp. 372–5;
American Convention, Article 10.

(14) Principle of Ne Bis in Idem

Again, it may be said for this principle that it is still in the process of developing into a generally recognized principle. Moreover, it should be kept in mind that in those legal systems where the principle finds recognition, this is often restricted to trial within the same legal system. Since decisions by foreign courts are often not recognized, or the prosecution policy followed and punishments imposed in foreign countries are often not considered to be sufficiently effective to prevent certain serious crimes, states are reluctant to exclude the possibility of prosecuting and trying crimes under their jurisdiction which have already been prosecuted and tried in another country. It is to be assumed, therefore, that the principle laid down in international documents is restricted to retrial within the same state.

This principle has been included in the following sources:

1935 Harvard Draft, Article 13;
Geneva Convention III, Article 8;
Geneva Convention IV, Article 117;

European Convention, Protocol VII, Article 4;
ICJ New Delhi, Committee III, Article 10;
Covenant, Article 14(7);
Harris, pp. 375–6;
American Convention, Article 8(4);
Protocol I, Article 75(4)(h) ('by the same Party');
Hertzberg and Zammuto, pp. 24–5;
Bakken, p. 412.

8. Final observations

The above survey of principles of fair trial is a very global one and is also incomplete, since each of these principles could be further specified by other principles. The survey takes as a starting point the minimum guarantees for a person charged with a criminal offence, as they have been laid down in Article 14 of the International Covenant on Civil and Political Rights. However, the concept of 'fair trial' is not exhausted with these guarantees.[71] A more detailed survey of the principles and of their further specifications requires additional research on national legislation and national and international case-law in the field of criminal procedure. It is clear, however, that the more detailed and specific the survey gets, the more difficult it will be to classify the principles found as universal principles. On the other hand, it is equally clear that here lies an important task for the international supervisory organs established by each of the human rights treaties concerned. Through the interpretations laid down in

---

[71] The European Commission made this point in connection with Article 6 of the European Convention in its report of 15 March 1961 in the *Nielsen* case, *Yearbook* 1961, p. 494 at pp. 548–50.

their decisions, views or general comments,[72] as the case may be, they can and will promote a uniform interpretation of the principles laid down in the treaty concerned, and at the same time promote a harmonization of domestic law concerning criminal procedure. This will enlarge the universal contents and scope of these principles.

However, even to the extent that certain principles have been universally recognized and laid down in treaties and domestic legislation, in equivalent or identical wording, this does not guarantee their universal application. That application lies in the hands of the domestic authorities (see the contributions by Graefrath and Wieruszewski in this volume). And indeed, to a certain extent there must be room for some variations in that application, according to the legal tradition and to the political, economic and social situation prevailing in the country concerned. However, the core of the guarantees should be implemented in a uniform way, or else the purpose of their universal definition and international legal foundation would be frustrated. Here again an important supplementary role is to be played by international implementation measures; not only by the supervisory bodies established by the human rights treaties, but also — in the case of serious and systematic violations — by the political organs of the international organizations under whose auspices these universal standards have been adopted, mainly the UN Commission on Human Rights and, at its suggestion, the Economic and Social Council and the General Assembly. On the basis of the information provided by the governments concerned, by rapporteurs, committees and working groups, by individual victims and non-governmental organizations and groups, all elements of the international supervisory mechanism should act in a way which ultimately leads to *universally guaranteed* minimum standards of fair trial, both in theory and in practice.

As has been said in the introduction, the present study deals with the legal principles concerning fair criminal proceedings rather than with the practice of these proceedings in individual states. To give a survey of the latter would require a separate study, based upon analyses by experts in the national criminal law and criminal procedure of the states concerned. However, even a cursory glance at certain international sources makes it abundantly clear that national practice is not yet in conformity with the universal legal principles in many respects.

If, for the purpose of the present book, we restrict ourselves to the

---

[72] On general comments, see Professor Graefrath's contribution to this volume. Although most supervisory bodies have no formal mandate to interpret treaty provisions, interpretation is an inherent element of the review function. The fact that, for instance in the case of the Human Rights Committee, these interpretations are based upon a consensus reached within the Committee, make them highly authoritative, though not binding. On views concerning individual complaints, see *ibid.*

situation in Eastern and Western Europe, it may even be submitted that in several Eastern European countries, systematic violation of some of the core principles of fair trial has been the rule rather than the exception, at least until recently. And especially the fact that the position of the judiciary in Eastern European states has not traditionally been a fully independent one, bound as the courts have been to take the general policy of the Communist Party into consideration when arriving at their verdicts, has negatively influenced the composition of the courts and the attitude of individual judges, and has opened broad possibilities for direct or indirect interference in the administration of justice by central and local party organs.[73] More or less the same holds true for the independence of the legal profession, in view of the fact that lawyers have often been required to belong to a party-controlled body, or that legal aid has been provided by party-controlled institutions such as, for instance, trade unions.[74] Moreover, in many cases the fairness of the administration of justice could not be controlled by the press and/or the public due to extensive restrictions on the public character of trials.[75] There have also been reports of the violation of the presumption of innocence,[76] and of not allowing defence lawyers enough time to prepare cases.[77] The fact that recently the leading role of the Communist Party has formally or in fact been abolished in several Eastern European states, while guarantees of civil and political rights have been restored or enhanced, will no doubt have a positive effect on the administration of justice in those countries.

As far as Western European countries are concerned, the Strasbourg case-law relating to Article 6 of the European Convention, as well as other international sources, clearly show that there, too, practice still is not in conformity with the minimum standards of fair trial in all respects. Thus, for instance, violations have been found of the principles of fair trial in relation to the independence of

---

[73] See, for example, Human Rights Committee, Report (A/42/40), New York 1987, p. 78 with respect to Romania. For Yugoslavia, see Amnesty International, 1988, p. 225, and Petovar, 1989, *passim*. For a discussion of the boards judging petty offences, which exist at the local administration level in Poland, see Polish Helsinki Committee, 1989, *passim*. For the Soviet Union, see the reply of the USSR delegate to a question by a member of the Human Rights Committee, CCPR/C/SR.930, paragraph 50; see also *ibid.*, paragraph 48.72.6.

[74] For the German Democratic Republic, see its report submitted to the Human Rights Committee, CCPR/C/52/Add. 1, paragraph 41. In Albania, the institution of advocacy was abolished in 1967, and lawyers lost their legal status; Amnesty International, 1989, p. 212.

[75] For the German Democratic Republic, see Amnesty International, 1987, p. 293. For Romania, see Amnesty International, 1988, p. 211. For Czechoslovakia, see Human Rights Committee, Report (A/40/41), 1986, paragraph 339. For the Soviet Union, see the question raised by a member of the Human Rights Committee, CCPR/C/SR.930, paragraph 46.

[76] See, for example, with respect to Yugoslavia: Amnesty International, 1988, p. 225.

[77] See, for instance, with respect to Poland: Amnesty International, 1989, p. 228.

the trial court,[78] the submission and evaluation of evidence,[79] trial within a reasonable time[80] and the right to choose one's own lawyer.[81]

In this context it should be recognized, especially in view of the present very weak economic situation of certain European countries — as well as that of many other countries in the world — that several of the principles concerning fair trial set a standard which can be met only if the required economic conditions and the necessary legal infra-structure are present, which for several states is not the case at the present moment and will not be the case for years to come, unless large-scale external assistance is provided to that end. Consequently, universal principles can only become universally effective if universal responsibility for their implementation is assumed, not only in the form of collective supervision, but also in the form of collective assistance (van Dijk, 1984, pp. 227-8 and 235-6).

Moreover, the guarantees aimed at by the universal principles will only be effectuated in a universal and, therefore, in a non-discrim-inatory way, if the costs for the individual concerned are set and kept at a minimum. After all, if a fair trial is only guaranteed to those who have the money to 'buy' it, there is of course no guarantee at all. That is why a more general recognition of the right to *free* legal aid and *free* interpretation services is so important; only then will the equality of arms between the prosecuting authorities and the accused, and the equality before the law of all potential suspects, come closer to reality.

List of sources

1. Article 9 of the 1929 Harvard Draft Convention on Responsibility of States for Damage Done in Their Territory to the Person or Property of Foreigners, *American Journal of International Law*, vol. 23, 1929, Special Supplement, pp. 131-239 at p. 173, referred to as: *1929 Harvard Draft*.
2. Articles 61 and 62 of the 1929 Geneva Convention Relative to the Treatment of Prisoners of War, *League of Nations Treaty Series*, vol. 118, 1931-33, No. 2732 at p. 381, referred to as: *1929 Geneva Convention*.

---

[78] For Denmark, see the judgment of the European Court of Human Rights of 24 May 1989 in the *Hauschildt* Case, paragraph 52. On the system of military tribunals in Turkey, see Amnesty International, 1989, p. 235.

[79] For an example from the Netherlands, see the judgment of the European Court of Human Rights of 20 November 1989 in the *Kostovski* Case, Publ. E.C.H.R., Series A, vol. 166 (1989), paragraph 45. On Turkey and the United Kingdom, see Amnesty International, 1988, pp. 217 and 222 respectively.

[80] For Portugal, see the judgment of the European Court of Human Rights of 25 May 1989 in the Case of *Neves e Silva*, Publ. E.C.H.R., Series A, vol. 153-A, paragraphs 45-6. For Finland, see Human Rights Committee, Report (A/41/40), 1986, p. 41. For France, Italy and Turkey, see Amnesty International, 1989, pp. 218, 225 and 235 respectively.

[81] For Spain, see Amnesty International, 1988, p. 212.

3. Article 12 of the 1935 Harvard Draft Convention on Jurisdiction with Respect to Crime, *American Journal of International Law*, vol. 29, 1935, Supplement, pp. 435-651 at pp. 596-97, referred to as: *1935 Harvard Draft*.
4. Article 7 of the 1944 Statement of Essential Human Rights, adopted by the American Law Institute, Wright, Q. 1945, 'War Criminals', *American Journal of International Law*, vol. 39, pp. 257-85 at pp. 257-8, referred to as: *Statement of Human Rights*.
5. Article 16 of the 1945 Charter of the International Military Tribunal, United Nations, *The Charter and Judgments of the Nürnberg Tribunal; History and Analysis*, UN doc. A/CN.4/5, p. 96, referred to as: *Nürnberg Charter*.
6. Article 9 of the 1946 Charter of the International Military Tribunal for the Far East, Ch.I. Bevans, *Treaties and Other International Agreements of the United States of America 1776-1949*, vol. 4, Washington, DC 1970, p. 29, referred to as: *Tokyo Charter*.
7. Articles 10 and 11 of the 1948 Universal Declaration of Human Rights, United Nations, *Human Rights: A Compilation of International Instruments*, New York 1983, p. 3, hereinafter: *Universal Declaration*.
8. Articles 99 and 105 of the 1949 Geneva Convention No. III and Articles 71-76 and 126 of the 1949 Geneva Convention No. IV, *UNTS*, vol. 75, 1950, pp. 210-14, pp. 188-94 and pp. 234-6, referred to as: *Geneva Convention III* and *Geneva Convention IV*.
9. Orfield, L.B. 1950, 'What Constitutes Fair Criminal Procedure under Municipal and International Law?', *University of Pittsburgh Law Review*, vol. 12, pp. 35-46, hereinafter: *Orfield*.
10. Article 6 of the 1950 European Convention for the Protection of Human Rights and Fundamental Freedoms. Council of Europe, *European Convention on Human Rights; Collected Texts*, Strasbourg 1987, pp. 3-62 at pp. 6-7, referred to as: *European Convention*.
11. Sixth Congress of the Association Internationale de Droit Pénal, Rome 1953; Question no. 2: la protection de la liberté individuelle pendant l'instruction judiciaire, *Revue Internationale de Droit Pénal*, vol. 24, 1953, pp. 697-725, and *Revue Internationale de Droit Pénal*, vol. 25, 1954, pp. 213-36 and 243-52, referred to as: *AIDP Rome*.
12. Congress of the International Commission of Jurists, Athens 1955; Committee on Criminal Law, Resolution I, International Commission of Jurists, *The Rule of Law and Human Rights; Principles and Definitions*, Geneva 1966, pp. 23-5, referred to as: *ICJ Athens*.
13. United Nations Seminar on the Protection of Human Rights in Criminal Law and Procedure, Baguio City 1958, *UN doc. ST/TAA/HR/2*, referred to as: *UN Baguio City*.
14. United Nations Seminar on the Protection of Human Rights in Criminal Law and Procedure, Santiago de Chile 1958, *UN doc. ST/TAA/HR/3*, referred to as: *UN Santiago*.
15. Congress of the International Commission of Jurists, New Delhi 1959; Committee III, International Commission of Jurists, *The Rule of Law and Human Rights; Principles and Definitions*, Geneva, 1966, pp. 25-8, referred to as: *ICJ New Delhi*.
16. United Nations Seminar on the Protection of Human Rights in Criminal Procedure, Vienna 1960, *UN doc. ST/TAO/HR/8*, referred to as: *UN Vienna*.

17. United Nations Seminar on the Protection of Human Rights in the Administration of Criminal Justice, Wellington 1961, *UN doc. ST/TAO/ HR/10*, referred to as: *UN Wellington*.
18. Article 1, paragraph 2, of the 1961 Draft of the International Law Commission on International Responsibility of the State for Injuries Caused in its Territory to the Person or Property of Aliens, *Yearbook of the ILC* 1961, vol. II, pp. 46–54 at p. 46, referred to as: *1961 ILC Draft*.
19. Article 7 of the 1961 Harvard Draft Convention on the International Responsibility of States for Injuries to Aliens, *American Journal of International Law*, vol. 55, 1961, pp. 545–84 at p. 550, referred to as: *1961 Harvard Draft*.
20. Article 14 of the 1966 International Covenant on Civil and Political Rights, United Nations, *Human Rights: A Compilation of International Instruments*, New York 1988, pp. 24–5, referred to as: *Covenant*.
21. Harris, D. 1967, 'The Right to a Fair Trial in Criminal Proceedings as a Human Right', *International and Comparative Law Quarterly*, vol. 16, pp. 352–78, referred to as: *Harris*.
22. Article 8 of the 1969 American Convention on Human Rights, IACHR, *Basic Documents Pertaining to Human Rights in the Inter-American System*, Washington, DC 1988, pp. 29–30, referred to as: *American Convention*.
23. Article 75(4) of the 1977 Protocol I to the Geneva Conventions, *International Legal Materials*, vol. 16, 1977, p. 1424, referred to as: *Protocol I*.
24. Article 6(2) of the 1977 Protocol II to the Geneva Conventions, *International Legal Materials*, vol. 16, 1977, pp. 1445–6, referred to as: *Protocol II*.
25. Kaufman Hevener, N. and S.A. Mosher, 1978, 'General Principles of Law and the UN Covenant on Civil and Political Rights', *International & Comparative Law Quarterly*, vol. 27, pp. 596–613, referred to as: *Kaufman Hevener and Mosher*.
26. XIIth Congress of the Association Internationale de Droit Pénal, Hamburg 1979; Resolutions of Section III: The Protection of Human Rights in Criminal Proceedings, *Actes du Congrès*, Baden-Baden 1980, pp. 559–64; *Revue Internationale de Droit Pénal*, vol. 50, 1980, pp. 238–41, referred to as: *AIDP Hamburg*.
27. Hertzberg, S. and C. Zammuto, *The Protection of Human Rights in the Criminal Process under International Instruments and National Constitutions*, Association Internationale de Droit Pénal, 1981, referred to as: *Hertzberg and Zammuto*.
28. Article 7 of the 1981 African Charter on Human Rights and Peoples' Rights, *International Legal Materials*, vol. 23, 1982, pp. 58–68, referred to as: *African Charter*.
29. Draft Principles on the Independence of the Legal Profession, adopted by a Committee of Experts organized by the International Association of Penal Law and the International Commission of Jurists, Noto, Sicily, 1982, *CIJL Bulletin*, vol. 10, October 1982, pp. 29–40, referred to as: *1982 Draft Principles on Independence*.
30. Minimum Standards of Judicial Independence, adopted by the International Bar Association, New Delhi 1982, *CIJL Bulletin*, vol. 11, April 1983, pp. 53–6, referred to as: *1983 Minimum Standards of Independence*.
31. Universal Declaration on the Independence of Justice, adopted by the World Conference on the Independence of Justice, Montréal 1983, *CIJL*

Bulletin, vol. 12, October 1983, referred to as: *1983 Universal Declaration on Independence.*
32. Basic Principles on the Independence of the Judiciary, adopted by consensus by the 7th UN Congress on the Prevention of Crime and the Treatment of Offenders, Milan 1985, *CIJL Bulletin*, vol. 16, October 1985, referred to as: *1985 Basic Principles on Independence.*
33. Bakken, T., 1985, 'International Law and Human Rights for Defendants in Criminal Trials', *Indian Journal of International Law*, vol. 25, pp. 411–23, referred to as: *Bakken.*
34. Article 6 of the 1987 Draft Code of Offences against the Peace and Security of Mankind, A/42/10, referred to as: *Draft Code of Offences.*
35. Draft Declaration on the Independence and Impartiality of the Judiciary, Jurors and Assessors and the Independence of Lawyers, adopted by the UN Sub-Commission on Prevention of Discrimination and Protection of Minorities, Geneva 1988, *E/CN.4/Sub.2/1988/20/Add.1*, referred to as: *1988 Draft Declaration on Independence.*
36. Principles 4, 10, 11, 12, 14, 17, 18, 36 and 38 of the 1988 Body of Principles for the Protection of All Persons Under Any Form of Detention or Imprisonment, GA Resolution 43/173, 9 December 1988, referred to as: *Body of Principles.*

Bibliography

Amnesty International, 1987. *Report.* London.
Amnesty International, 1988. *Report.* London.
Amnesty International, 1989. *Report.* London.
Bakken, T., 1985. 'International Law and Human Rights for Defendants in Criminal Trials', *Indian Journal of International Law*, vol. 25.
Bevans, Ch.I., 1970. *Treaties and Other International Instruments of the United States of America 1776–1949*, vol. 4. Washington, DC: Department of State.
Bin Cheng, 1953. *General Principles of Law as Applied by International Courts and Tribunals*, London: Stevens.
Borchard, E.M., 1919. *The Diplomatic Protection of Citizens Abroad or The Law of International Claims.* New York: Columbia University.
Borchard, E.M., 1939. 'The "Minimum Standard" of the Treatment of Aliens', *Proceedings of the American Society of International Law*, vol. 33.
Bos, Maarten, 1984. *A Methodology of International Law.* Amsterdam: Elsevier.
Comisión Interamericana de Derechos Humanos, 1982. *Diez Años de Actividades 1971–1981.* Washington, DC: Secretaría General de la Organización de los Estados Americanos.
Coutts, J.A. (ed.), 1966. *The Accused: A Comparative Study.* London: Stevens.
De Visscher, Ch., 1935. 'Le déni de justice en droit international', *Recueil des Cours de l'Académie de Droit International*, vol. 52-II.
Dijk, P. van, 1980. *Judicial Review of Governmental Action and the Requirement of an Interest to Sue in National and International Law.* Alphen a/d Rijn: Kluwer Group.
Dijk, P. van, 1984. 'The Right to Development and Human Rights: A Matter of Equality and Priority', *Israel Yearbook on Human Rights*, vol. 14.

Dijk, P. van, 1987. 'Normative Force and Effectiveness of International Norms', *German Yearbook of International Law*, vol. 30.

Dijk, P. van, 1988a. 'Domestic Status of Human Rights Treaties and the Attitude of the Judiciary: The Dutch Case', in Manfred Nowak *et al.* (eds), *Progress in the Spirit of Human Rights; Festschrift für Felix Ermacora*. Kehl am Rhein: Engel.

Dijk, P. van, 1988b. 'The Interpretation of "Civil Rights and Obligations" by the European Court of Human Rights — one more step to take', in F. Matscher and H. Petzold (eds), *Protecting Human Rights: The European Dimension; Studies in honour of Gérard J. Wiarda*. Köln: Heymann.

Dijk, P. van, 1989. 'Equity: A Recognized Manifestation of International Law?', in W.P. Heere (ed.), *International Law and Its Sources; Liber Amicorum Maarten Bos*. Deventer: Kluwer Law and Taxation Publishers.

Dijk, P. van and G.J.H. van Hoof, 1984. *Theory and Practice of the European Convention on Human Rights*, 2nd edition 1990. Deventer: Kluwer Law and Taxation Publishers.

Draper, G.I.A.D., 1958. *The Red Cross Conventions*. New York: Praeger.

Drzemczewski, A.Z., 1983. *European Human Rights Convention in Domestic Law: A Comparative Study*. Oxford: Clarendon Press.

Evans, M. and R.I. Jack (eds), 1984. *Sources of English Legal and Constitutional History*, Chapter Four, Magna Carta. Sydney (Newton Upper Falls, Mass): Butterworths.

Harris, D., 1967. 'The Right to a Fair Trial in Criminal Proceedings as a Human Right', *International and Comparative Law Quarterly*, vol. 16.

Hersch, J. (ed.), 1969. *Birthright of Man*. Paris: Unesco.

Hertzberg, S. and C. Zammuto, 1981. *The Protection of Human Rights in the Criminal Process under International Instruments and National Constitutions*, published by the Association Internationale de Droit Pénal.

Heydte, F. von der, 1933. 'Glossen zu einer Theorie der allgemeinen Rechtsgrundsätze', *Friedenswarte*, vol. 33.

Hoof, G.J.H. van, 1983. *Rethinking the Sources of International Law*. Deventer: Kluwer Law and Taxation Publishers.

Horvath, B., 1955. 'Rights of Man: Due Process of Law and Excès de Pouvoir', *American Journal of Comparative Law*, vol. 4.

International Commission of Jurists, 1966. *The Rule of Law and Human Rights: Principles and Definitions*. Geneva: International Commission of Jurists.

Ipsen, H.P., 1972. *Europäisches Gemeinschaftsrecht*. Tübingen: Mohr.

Jackson, John H., 1969. *World Trade and the Law of GATT*. Indianapolis: Bobbs Merrill Co.

Jaenicke, G., 1971. 'Judicial Protection of the Individual within the System of International Law', in H. Mosler (ed.), *Judicial Protection against the Executive*, vol. III. Köln: Heymann.

Kaufman Hevener, N. and S.A. Mosher, 1978. 'General Principles of Law and the UN Covenant on Civil and Political Rights', *International and Comparative Law Quarterly*, vol. 27.

Lammerts, J., 1980. 'General Principles of Law Recognized by Civilized Nations', in F. Kalshoven *et al.* (eds), Essays on the Development of the International Legal Order, *Netherlands Yearbook of International Law*, vol. 11.

Lauterpacht, H., 1950. *International Law and Human Rights*. New York: Praeger.

Mott, R.L. 1926. *Due Process of Law — A Historical and Analytical Treatise of the Principles and Methods Followed by Courts in the Application of the Concept of the 'Law of the Land'.* Indianapolis: Bobbs Merrill Co.

Noor Muhammad, H.N.A., 1981. 'Due Process of Law for Persons Accused of Crime' in L. Henkin (ed.), *The International Bill of Rights: the Covenant on Civil and Political Rights.* New York: Columbia U.P.

Nowak, M., 1989. *UNO-Pakt über bürgerliche und politische Rechte und Fakultativprotokoll; CCPR-Kommentar.* Kehl am Rhein: Engel.

Orfield, L.B., 1950. 'What Constitutes Fair Criminal Procedure under Municipal and International Law?', *University of Pittsburg Law Review,* vol. 12.

Pagels, E., 1979. 'The Roots and Origins of Human Rights', in A.H. Henkin (ed.), *Human Dignity; The Internationalization of Human Rights.* New York: Dobbs Ferry.

Parry, Clive, 1965. *The Sources and Evidences of International Law.* Manchester: Manchester U.P.

Petovar, T., 1989. *Remarks on the Independence of the Judiciary in Yugoslavia,* Report presented at a seminar of the International Helsinki Federation, Warsaw, not published.

Polish Helsinki Committee, 1989. *Human and Citizen's Rights in the Polish People's Republic.* Vienna: International Helsinki Federation.

Robertson, A.H., 1982. *Human Rights in the World,* 2nd edition. Manchester: Manchester U.P.

Roth, A.H., 1949. *The Minimum Standard of International Law applied to Aliens.* Leyden: A.W. Sijthoff.

Seminar on the Protection of Human Rights in Criminal Law and Procedure, 1958. UN doc. ST/TAA/HR/2, New York.

Seminar on the Protection of Human Rights in Criminal Law and Procedure, 1958. UN doc. ST/TAA/HR/3, New York.

Seminar on the Protection of Human Rights in Criminal Procedure, 1960. UN doc. ST/TAO/HR/8, New York.

Silving, H., 1965/1966. 'The Origins of the Magna Carta', *Harvard Journal on Legislation,* vol. 3.

Szabó, I., 1982. 'Historical Foundations of Human Rights and Subsequent Developments', in K. Vasak (ed.), *The International Dimensions of Human Rights,* vol. I. Westport, Conn.: Greenwood Press.

Trechsel, S., 1978. 'Rapport Général', *Review Internationale de Droit Pénal,* vol. 49.

Verzijl, J.H.W., 1968. *International Law in Historical Perspective,* vol. I: General Subjects. Leyden: A.W. Sijthoff.

Vitányi, B., 1982. 'Les Positions Doctrinales concernant le Sens de la Notion de "Principes Généraux de Droit Reconnues par les Nations Civilisées" ', *Revue Générale de Droit International Public,* vol. 86.

Wright, Q., 1945. 'War Criminals', *American Journal of International Law,* vol. 39.

Wyzanski Jr., Ch.E., 1979. 'The Philosophical Background of the Doctrines of Human Rights', in A.H. Henkin (ed.), *Human Dignity; The Internationalization of Human Rights.* New York: Dobbs Ferry.

Zweigert, K., 1969. 'Les Principes Généraux du Droit des Etats Membres', in W.J. Ganshof van der Meersch (ed.), *Droit des communautés européennes.* Bruxelles: F. Larcier.

6 The Prohibition of the Death Penalty: An Emerging International Norm?

Theodore S. Orlin

1. Introduction

This chapter discusses whether there is 'an emerging' international norm prohibiting states from the use of the death penalty. This question stems from an earlier work presented before a Finnish-Polish Human Rights Seminar conducted in September 1989, at the Institute for Human Rights, Turku/Åbo, Finland. That paper examined the use of capital punishment in the United States, its constitutionality, and its legality within an international framework. In exploring these questions it became apparent that although the death penalty is constitutional under US law, *Gregg v. Georgia* 448 US 153, 96 S.Ct. 2909 (1976), and although the execution of the mentally retarded, *Penry v. Lynaugh*, — US —, 109 S.Ct. 2934, 106 L. Ed. 2d 256 (1989), and of sixteen year olds, *Stanford v. Kentucky*, — US —, 109 S.Ct. 2969 (1989), have been upheld by the US Supreme Court, there is some international jurisprudence that is contrary to the United States position. In the Inter-American Commission on Human Rights' (Inter-American Commission) decisions of *Roach and Pinkerton* the execution of those who had committed offences when below the age of 18 was clearly condemned, albeit indirectly:

The failure of the federal government to preempt the states as regards legislative arbitrariness throughout the United States which results in the arbitrary deprivation of life and inequality before law, is contrary to Articles I and II of the American Declaration of the Rights and Duties of Man.[1]

None the less the Inter-American Commission, in *obiter dicta*, used some interesting language and logic to suggest that perhaps the

---

[1] Resolution No. 3/87 Case 9647 United States, *Annual Report of the Inter-American Commission on Human Rights* 1986–1987, p. 147, quotation pp. 172–3. Article 1 of the American Declaration reads: 'Every human being has the right to life, liberty and the security of his person.' According to Article 2, 'all persons are equal before the law and have the rights and duties established in this Declaration, without distinction as to race, sex, language, creed or any other factor.' It should be noted that in *The Report of the Secretary-General to the Committee on Crime Prevention and Control: Implementation of the United Nations Safeguards Guaranteeing Protection of the Rights of Those Facing the Death Penalty* (E/AC.57/1988/9) (3 June 1988) the question of the executions of 18 year olds was discussed in light of the adoption of the UN safeguards which prohibit the execution of those under the age of 18 (pp. 6–7).

international legal landscape is now in flux. For example, the Commission noted:

The rule prohibiting the execution of juvenile offenders has acquired the authority of *jus cogens*, a peremptory norm of international law from which no derogation is permitted (*Annual Report*, 1986–87, p. 168).

In a discussion of *jus cogens*, the Commission reviewed Article 53 of the *Vienna Convention on the Law of Treaties* of 1969, the International Court of Justice advisory opinion on the *Reservations to the Genocide Convention, The Barcelona Traction* Case, and others, concluding that '. . . in the member States of the OAS there is recognized a norm of *jus cogens* which prohibits the State execution of children. This norm is accepted by all the States of the inter-American system, including the United States.' (*Annual Report*, 1986–87, p. 170).

The Commission, while recognizing this general prohibition of juvenile executions as *jus cogens*, limited its opinion by accepting the US argument that it may be 'emerging' but there 'does not now exist a norm of customary international law establishing 18 to be the minimum age for the imposition of the death penalty'.

The *Roach and Pinkerton* decision was not the only international legal review of the US death penalty. The European Court of Human Rights had the opportunity to review the American use of capital punishment in the *Soering* Case (1/1989/161/217); a decision that barred the extradition of a Federal German Republic national from the United Kingdom to the Commonwealth of Virginia on the grounds that the 'death row syndrome' would subject *Soering* to a violation of Article 3 of the European Convention on Human Rights. In this opinion, the European Court of Human Rights refused to accept the position of Amnesty International that the death penalty is a *per se* violation of the European Convention of Human Rights, given the existence of Article 2, paragraph 1, of the Convention which permits the death penalty, and the separate drafting of Protocol No. 6, banning the imposition of the death penalty by its signatories.[2] This was interpreted by the Court to mean that it was inappropriate to establish judicially a death penalty prohibition. None the less, the Court did not feel obliged to reject the petitioner's claim, arguing that it was quite legitimate to review capital punishment issues such as, 'disproportionality', 'conditions of detainment' and 'manner of imposition' for their conformity with the Convention.

---

[2] Amnesty's logic will be discussed later in this chapter as will Protocol No. 6. Article 3 of the European Convention reads: 'No one shall be subjected to torture or to inhuman or degrading treatment or punishment.' According to Article 2, paragraph 1, '(1) Everyone's right to life shall be protected by law. No one shall be deprived of his life intentionally save in the execution of a sentence of a court following his conviction of a crime for which this penalty is provided by law.'

Given these opinions, which limit but clearly permit the use of the death penalty by states, there are several questions that remain. For example; is there now evolving a trend that will permit future jurists to conclude that capital punishment is contrary to customary international law? If such a trend does exist, will it take on the character of being *jus cogens*, i.e. a peremptory norm of international law from which no derogation is permitted? If a trend does not exist on a universal international plane, is it possible to conclude that a regional legal norm is emerging? Further, for those arguing against the use of the death penalty, what steps would be useful to bring about such a conclusion? And finally, if an outright prohibition of capital punishment is not developing, is there some indication that some manifestations of the death penalty, for instance, age, mental status, death-row syndrome, is becoming prohibitive, thus curtailing the use of capital punishment?

It is by no means feasible in this effort to draw concrete conclusions as to these questions. This chapter will simply review from an East-West perspective the trend and status of capital punishment in human rights law, with the hope that some light may be shed on the future of the death penalty in international law.

2. The requirements of norms to become customary international law and/or *jus cogens*

When considering the status of the death penalty in international law, it is essential that the criteria for norms to become customary international law and/or *jus cogens* be understood.[3] Unfortunately, as is made clear by Lauri Hannikainen's study (1988), such precision at this point is impossible.[4] However, a review of the accepted legal theory as well as an analysis of some norms that have taken on the

---

[3] The author is aware of the difficulties and dangers of the *jus cogens* doctrine. Attempts to determine a hierarchy of international law is fraught with problems and arguably could destroy the foundations of the international legal system, e.g. sovereign equality. As Prosper Weil (1983, p. 423) argues, 'the international normative system has traditionally been characterized by its unity: whatever their object or importance, all norms are placed on the same plane, their interrelations ungoverned by any hierarchy, their breach giving rise to an international responsibility subject to one uniform regime. This unity of the normative regime is shattered by the *jus cogens* theory and the distinction between international crimes and international delicts, which introduce what Roberto Ago, as rapporteur of the International Law Commission, called 'a "normative differentiation" between two kinds of rules, and hence, of legal obligations.' None the less, given the acceptance of the *jus cogens* doctrine by international adjudicatory bodies, an understanding of *jus cogens* is critical in a discussion on international law's impact on capital punishment.

[4] See also Brownlie, 1979, pp. 514-15: 'Many problems remain: more authority exists for the category of *jus cogens* than exists for its particular content, and rules do not develop in customary law which readily correspond to the new categories.'

characteristics of customary law or *jus cogens* may be useful in assessing the present status of the death penalty. Of course the root of the legal question is the extent of the state's right to govern its jurisdiction as it sees fit and when sovereign power may be condemned, curtailed or limited by international law. Or, to use the terminology of the UN Charter (Article 2), at what point are state responses to criminal behaviour no longer 'essentially within their domestic jurisdiction', and thus outside their 'political independence' and in contravention of international law, therefore allowing legitimate international objections to the use of capital punishment?

At this point in the development of international law, examples to contrast the death penalty to other norms held to be contrary to international law are rare. This is understandable given the lack of accepted priorities in international law. As Theodor Meron points out, 'the lack of generally agreed standards makes it extremely difficult to select (such) fundamental (human) rights.' If no standard now exists to determine what are 'fundamental rights', it is clearly more difficult to determine which of those rights have attained the status of *jus cogens*. Without standards, it is impossible to categorize any internal action of a state, including its choice of punishment for criminal acts, as being contrary to international law. None the less, there are authoritative statements that some state action can be condemned as contrary to international law, for instance, slavery, apartheid, torture.[5] The right to life may also be included in this category with some qualifications still undetermined in international jurisprudence. Whether the prohibition of the death penalty ought eventually to be included on the basis of this right is the question of this chapter.

---

[5] Meron, 1986, p. 11, also states: 'Most observers would probably agree that protection of the right to life from arbitrary taking and protection of the human person from torture or egregious racial discrimination are fundamental rights. Perhaps they would also agree that the small number (irreducible core) of the rights that are deemed non-derogable under both the Political Covenant and the European and American Conventions constitute fundamental, and perhaps even peremptory norms. But that irreducible core comprises four rights only: *the right to life and the prohibitions of slavery, torture and retroactive penal measures* (emphasis added). The prospects for a consensus reaching beyond these few rights are not immediate. For instance, while for some observers, including this writer, due process rights are fundamental and indispensable for ensuring any other right, for others the rights to food and other basic needs take precedence. Superficially seductive formulae such as the notion of rights protecting the physical and mental well-being of the human person are not helpful either, because they involve clusters of rights whose components require scrutiny. Would the prohibition of indefinite preventive detention, for example, be considered fundamental?'
See also *Filartiga v. Pena-Irala* 630 F.2d 876 (1980), where the US Court of Appeals, Second Circuit, in applying the Alien Tort Statute, held: 'official torture is now prohibited by the law of nations', further holding that 'among the rights universally proclaimed by all nations, . . . is the right to be free of physical torture. Indeed, for purposes of civil liability, the torturer has become — like the pirate and slave trader before him — *hostis humani generis*, an enemy of all mankind.'

Nor should it be assumed that human rights that are now considered *jus cogens* are members of a closed group. The number of rights assuming *jus cogens* status ought not to be locked in time. Again, Meron (1987, p. 350) states:

It may also represent a step in the process that begins with the crystallization of a mere contractual norm into a principle of customary law and culminates in its elevation to *jus cogens* status (a norm of *jus cogens* can mature also through other processes). The development of the hierarchical concept of *jus cogens* reflects the quest of the international community for a normative order in which higher rights are invoked as a particularly compelling moral and legal barrier to derogations from and violations of human rights. To be sure, the Geneva Conventions already contain some norms that can be regarded as *jus cogens*.

Yet how is it possible to determine which rights are now in the process of assuming *jus cogens* status? Once again, Meron (1987, p. 363) suggests a possible methodology:

As far as lawmaking is concerned, the starting point is, of course, the practice of states. Yet in concluding noncodifying multilateral treaties even outside the humanitarian law field, norms and values are commonly asserted that differ from the actual practice of states. When it comes to human rights or humanitarian conventions — i.e., conventions whose object is to humanize the behaviour of states, groups and persons — the gap between the norms stated and actual practice tends to be especially wide.

The lawmaking process does not merely 'photograph' or declare the current state of international practice. Far from it. Rather, the lawmaking process attempts to articulate and emphasize norms and values that, in the judgment of some states, deserve promotion and acceptance by all states, so as to establish a code for the better conduct of nations.

Hence, it would appear appropriate in assessing the present status of capital punishment in international law not only to review present state practice, but to inquire if there now is, via existing or prospective multilateral agreements, a trend that would portend either the eventual end or the limitation of the death penalty.

And yet to be certain not to go too far astray, it is essential that the clearest statement of *jus cogens* be addressed in discussing the death penalty; Article 53 of the *Vienna Convention on the Law of Treaties* and its four criteria (for a discussion of these criteria, see Hannikainen, 1988, p. 3ff.):

1. They are norms of general international law.
2. They have to be accepted by the international community of states as a whole.
3. They permit no derogation.
4. They can be modified only by new peremptory norms.

It is quite obvious, given these criteria, that the use of the death penalty is *not* now prohibited by peremptory international law. Yet it may be possible to conclude that the stage is now set for an eventual conclusion that the prohibition of the death penalty will become *jus cogens*.

An obstacle in drawing any conclusion about the prohibition of the use of the death penalty in international law is whether or not *jus cogens* (or for that matter international custom) is applicable to a state's punitive response to a violation of domestic law, traditionally an area viewed well within the domestic jurisdiction of the state. The question needing to be answered is: can *jus cogens* be applied to 'unilateral actions of states'?[6] Or to pose the question in a different form: is the death penalty an issue that has 'overriding interests' or reflects the 'values of the international community of states'?

As Hannikainen (1988, p. 4) points out:

There is virtually no disagreement that the *purpose* of international peremptory law is to protect *overriding interests and values of the international* community of States (emphasis added). Present-day writers have frequently stated that peremptory norms protect vital interests and values of the international community of States, not the interests of some certain individual States. Mexico stated at the Vienna Conference on the Law of Treaties in 1968 that rules of *jus cogens* are derived from principles which the legal conscience of mankind deems absolutely essential to coexistence in the international community at a given stage of the community's historical development.

As he (Hannikainen, 1988, p. 5) further notes, in citing the *Barcelona Traction Case* of 1970:

... there exist obligations of States towards the international community, that these obligations are the concern of all States, and that in the protection of these obligations *all* States can be held to have a *legal interest* (emphasis added). It is the task of the international community of States as a whole, and at present primarily of the UN, to supervise the observance of obligations towards the international community of States and to react to instances of violations. All States should be recognized as having a legal interest in the vindication of obligations towards the international community of States.

Thus he (*ibid.*, p. 6) concludes there is a fifth criterion for *jus cogens*:

---

6 See Meron, 1986, p. 19: 'Another question crucial to international human rights is whether the concept of *jus cogens* applies only to the law of treaties or whether it extends to other fields of international law, including the unilateral acts of states, rather than from international agreements. The non-treaty aspect of the problem is far more important than the treaty aspect. Even scholars who reserve *jus cogens* to treaty law tend to agree with the elementary proposition that international public order, public order of the international community and international public policy do not allow individual states to violate such norms as they are prohibited from violating jointly with other states.'

5. Peremptory obligations are owed by all States and other subjects of international law to the international community of States.

Therefore, is it appropriate to discuss the possibility of the prohibition of the state use of capital punishment becoming *jus cogens*? Perhaps the closest example of what is viewed as a peremptory norm and worthy of comparison with the death penalty is the international prohibition on slavery. Here, arguably, is an accepted international prohibition on the domestic action of states by the international community. Yet even slavery, as contrary to human liberty as it is, was not quickly or easily condemned by international law.

Hannikainen (1988, p. 77) points out:

The prohibition of slavery advanced more slowly than the prohibition of the slave trade. In 1855, Umpire Bates of the American-British Claims Commission stated in the Creole Case that slavery, however odious and contrary to the principles of justice and humanity, could be established by law in any country. Having been established in many States, it could not be contrary to international law.

None the less, over the course of time the slavery prohibition was seen to develop into an international peremptory norm (*ibid.*, p. 79):

The prohibition of slavery gained increasing international legal significance when the last Latin American States, where slavery *had* been lawful, finally prohibited it. In the 1890s it could be said that slavery had been generally prohibited and even criminalized in the laws of the members of the society of States. The society of States had proved successful in the use of political pressure to have individual States prohibit slavery.

While it is still debatable whether the practice of state–accepted slavery was abolished in the nineteenth century due to its violating international law or as a result of states 'voluntarily' choosing to abolish the institution, it is clear that state–condoned slavery is not now acceptable or widely practised by the international community in the twentieth century.

As Hannikainen (1988, pp. 446, 447) also notes, 'It appears without a doubt that universal customary norms have emerged prohibiting States from legitimizing or encouraging slavery and the slave trade' and that the prohibitions 'are peremptory norms in contemporary international law'. The process that altered the status of state-legitimized slavery was long but steady. The evidence supporting the above conclusion is considerable, and includes among other factors: the *Slavery Convention of 1926* (over 100 parties), the *Supplementary Convention on the Abolition of Slavery, the Slave Trade and Institutions and Practices Similar to Slavery of 1956* (over 100 parties), whose Articles 5 and 6 prohibit slavery and make it a criminal offence, Article 13 of the 1958 *Geneva Convention on the High Seas*, Article 99 of the 1982 *UN Convention on the Law of the Seas* ('prohibiting and punishing the transit of slaves'), Article 4 of the

Universal Declaration of Human Rights ('No one shall be held in slavery or servitude; slavery and the slave trade shall be prohibited in all their forms'), and the conclusion of the International Law Commission (ILC) that the obligations of States not to legitimize slavery and the slave trade are peremptory (Hannikainen, 1988, pp. 444-447).

Taking Hannikainen's and Meron's discussion, it would seem possible that international morality can ultimately be seen as *jus cogens*.[7] The prohibition of slavery may be the classical example, (although similar arguments can be made against apartheid, torture and genocide) and may provide guidance as to the methodology. According to Hannikainen (1988, p. 354),

International efforts to combat the international slave trade reached in the 19th century a magnitude that constituted relevant evidence of the urgent concern of the society of States. Since the slave trade between any two States did not as such violate the individual rights or direct legal interests of third States, the obligations to refrain from the practices of slavery and the slave trade tended to develop towards the society of States, out of elementary consideration of humanity.

Even prior to the Second World War, the trend was clear. The Slavery Convention prior to the war was ratified by over 44 states (with notable exceptions — Persia, Argentina, Brazil and Colombia). Article 22 of the Covenant of the League of Nations prohibited the slave trade by mandatory states (those states exercising authority and control over other territories), and the actions of the League were directed at the suppression of the slave trade, even closing membership to the community of states to those states not recognizing 'the urgent need to suppress the slave trade to eliminate slavery'.[8]

Could a similar set of events be now evolving that will bring an eventual end to capital punishment? While it may be premature to conclude that its prohibition is an emerging universal peremptory norm, evidence may suggest that it is emerging at a greater pace in some geopolitical regions. If it is, is there a distinction on an East-West basis? The remainder of this chapter will review some of this evidence and see if any conclusions can be drawn.

---

[7] See Tomuschat, 1986: 'Ethical considerations also have a strong impact on the concept of *jus cogens* which has been recognized in Arts. 53 and 64 of the Vienna Convention on the Law of Treaties (1969). Although no substantive definition was given by the drafters, who only described its legal effects, it is obvious that in order to identify those norms "from which no derogation is permitted", recourse must be had to value judgment sustained both by legal arguments as well as ethical reasoning. Without a perfect coincidence of law and morality, no norm could be held to possess the specific quality of *jus cogens*.'

[8] Hannikainen, 1988, pp. 138-9. He notes that Ethiopia's request for membership in the League was questioned in regard to its practice of slavery.

3. The prohibition of capital punishment and international documents

Before considering these questions, a preliminary question must be addressed; whether the rights contained within international declarations and treaties, albeit not prohibiting the death penalty, allow for the ultimate creation of a norm that prohibits the death penalty? In other words, did the drafters of the various human rights instruments envision an 'expansive' interpretation that would permit the eventual prohibition of the use of execution by nation states?

This kind of reasoning was used by the United States Supreme Court in prohibiting punishments that were permissible at the time of the drafting of the US Eighth Amendment. By concluding that the drafters of that prohibition had envisioned evolving standards, it permitted the Court to conclude that punishments originally permitted were later to be viewed as 'cruel and unusual' and, hence, unconstitutional, *Weems v. United States* 217 US 349 (1910). Similarly, it is worth considering if the same kind of logic was envisioned by the original drafters of the pertinent international documents guaranteeing human rights.

The two rights that conceivably prohibit the use of capital punishment are the 'right to life' and the 'prohibition of cruel, inhuman and degrading treatment'. Peripheral and yet significant in discussing the death penalty is 'due process' and, as is clear from the *Roach and Pinkerton* decision, 'equal justice'.

In his report (1987), Marc J. Bossuyt, Special Rapporteur of the Sub-Commission on the Prevention of Discrimination and the Protection of Minorities, makes an important contribution to understanding the role of international documents in the status of the death penalty in international law. Although he makes no reference to the Universal Declaration of Human Rights, it should be noted that 'the right to life' (Article 3: Everyone has the right to life, liberty and the security of person), and 'the cruel, inhuman and degrading punishment' prohibitions (Article 5: No one shall be subjected to torture or to cruel, inhuman or degrading treatment or punishment), make no clear statement as to the abolition of the death penalty as an international norm. Bossuyt does give evidence that a review of the drafters' intentions for the International Covenant on Civil and Political Rights provides some insights on the status of the death penalty. He notes in a summary of the drafters' views that, among other conclusions, Article 6 according to Bossuyt 'imposes strict conditions on the execution of the death penalty':

The requirement of gravity: 'only for the most serious crimes';
The requirements of legality and non-retroactivity: 'in accordance with the law in force at the time of the commission of the crime';
The requirement of conformity with the Covenant and the Genocide

Convention: 'not contrary to the provisions of the present Covenant and to the Convention on the Prevention and Punishment of the Crime of Genocide'. The requirement of 'a final judgment rendered by a competent court'.

Article 6, paragraph 4, favours non-execution of the death penalty by stating that 'amnesty, pardon or commutation of the sentence of death may be granted in all cases'.

Article 6, paragraph 5, excludes two categories of persons from the imposition of the death penalty: persons below 18 years of age and pregnant women.

Furthermore, in a significant statement, he claims the drafters, in Article 6, paragraph 6, express clearly a strong presumption in favour of the abolition of the death penalty by stating that 'Nothing in this article shall be invoked to delay or to prevent the abolition of capital punishment by any State party to the present Covenant.'

He also notes, in supporting this conclusion, that the text of Article 6, paragraph 6, was adopted by 54 votes to 4 with 1 abstention and that it was included 'to avoid the impression that the Covenant sanctioned capital punishment' (Bossuyt, 1987, p. 3). This evidence arguably supports a conclusion that the International Covenant was written in a fashion that would permit the retention of the death penalty by ratifying states, but that there was a clear preference for its eventual prohibition.[9] To further buttress this conclusion, Bossuyt (1987, p. 6) cites the General Comments adopted on 27 July 1982 by the Human Rights Committee where they stated:

While it follows from article 6(2) to (6) that States parties are not obliged to abolish the death penalty totally, they are obliged to limit its use and, in particular, to abolish it for other than the 'most serious crimes'. Accordingly, they ought to consider reviewing their criminal laws in this light and, in any event, are obliged to restrict the application of the death penalty to the 'most serious crimes'. *The article also refers generally to abolition in terms which strongly suggest (paragraphs 2(2) and (6)) that abolition is desirable. The Committee concludes that all measures of abolition should be considered as progress in the enjoyment of the right to life within the meaning of article 40, and should as such be reported to the Committee* (emphasis added). The Committee notes that a number of States have already abolished the death penalty or suspended its application. Nevertheless, States' report show that progress made towards abolishing or limiting the application of the death penalty is quite inadequate.

Along similar lines, the UN Economic and Social Council, in adopting *Safeguards Guaranteeing Protection of the Rights of those Facing the Death Penalty* (1984), did so on the understanding that they would not be invoked to delay or to prevent the abolition of capital punishment (*Report of the Secretary-General*, 1988). These

---

[9] In contrast, it is certainly supportable that this phrase represents a compromise between 'retentionist' and 'abolitionist' states and does not reflect a presumption for or against the death penalty.

safeguards (included in the appendix) add evidence to the conclusions that there is a universal movement to restrict the use of the
death penalty in those states that accept it. Among its provisions are:
'Capital punishment may be imposed only for the most serious
crimes', '[it] may be imposed only for a crime for which the death
penalty is prescribed by law', as well as others which set forth
additional safeguards.[10]

The provisions of the European Convention on Human Rights
similarly provide safeguards but present some different conclusions
from the International Covenant for the ultimate elimination of the
death penalty.

Article 2, paragraph 1, of the European Convention clearly permits
the imposition of the death penalty:

Everyone's right to life shall be protected by law. No one shall be deprived of
his life intentionally save in the execution of a sentence of a court following
his conviction of a crime for which this penalty is provided by law.

As has been discussed, the logic found in the *Soering* Case relies
partly on Article 2, paragraph 1, and seems to prohibit an eventual
judicial interpretation of the European Convention that would
abolish capital punishment. This obstacle to a jurisprudential evolution, leading to the ultimate prohibition of the death penalty,
necessitates an additional treaty device to abolish capital punishment: Protocol No. 6 to the European Convention on Human Rights.
This Protocol (ironically, which led to the Court's conclusion in
Soering) could be viewed as a major step, at minimum in the regional
prohibition of capital punishment, and will be discussed later in the
chapter.

Article 1 of the American Declaration on the Rights and Duties of
Man (see *supra*) provides no support for a conclusion that the death
penalty is prohibited by international law. On the other hand, the
American Convention on Human Rights does provide some language
that suggests the possibility of an eventual regional prohibition of
capital punishment. For example Article 4, paragraph 2, reads:

In countries that have not abolished the death penalty, it may be imposed
only for the most serious crimes and pursuant to a final judgment rendered
by a competent court and in accordance with a law establishing such
punishment, enacted prior to the commission of the crime. The application of
such punishment shall not be extended to crimes to which it does not
presently apply.

Bossuyt (1987, p. 14) demonstrates the significance of this provision

---

[10] For a review of the results of a questionnaire sent to states by the Crime Prevention
and Criminal Justice Branch of the UN Offices at Vienna (1987) indicating
adherence to these safeguards, see Hood, 1989, pp. 57–83.

when he brings to our attention the advisory opinion of the Inter-American Court on Human Rights (8 September 1983). In that decision[11] the Court concluded by a unanimous vote that the convention imposes an absolute prohibition on the extension of the death penalty and that, consequently, the Government of a State Party cannot apply the death penalty to crimes for which penalty was not previously provided for under its domestic law (Bossuyt, 1987, p. 14).

Thus, Article 4, as interpreted by the Inter-American Court, serves to block the extension of the death penalty and ban its growth by ratifying states. Perhaps of equal significance is paragraph 3 which seems to make the decision to abolish the death penalty irreversible on the part of ratifying states; thus arguably making the prohibition of capital punishment a progressive goal of the Inter-American system: 'The death penalty shall not be re-established in States that have abolished it.' This provision conceivably could serve to ensure that abolitionist states are bound to their decision and would facilitate an eventual region-wide prohibition on the use of capital punishment.

The American Convention also provides strong evidence to indicate that some use of the death penalty may be emerging as prohibitive of customary law. Its Article 4, paragraph 4, prohibits the infliction of capital punishment 'for political offences or related common crimes' and its Article 4, paragraph 5, bans its use for 'persons who, at the time the crime was committed, were under 18 years of age or over 70 years of age, nor shall it be applied to pregnant women.'

Further evincing how Article 4 appears to allow for progressive steps in the regional elimination of capital punishment is the decision of the Inter-American Commission of 1984 (63rd session), in which it decided, in accordance with the spirit of Article 4 of the American Convention on Human Rights and the *universal trend* to eliminate the death penalty, to call on all countries in the Americas to abolish the death penalty (Bossuyt, 1987, p. 14).

Obviously such a statement, albeit not binding on states, adds weight to the proposition that the death penalty is evolving into a prohibition of international law. Of course adherence to such a decision as evinced by the alteration of domestic law is the ultimate test. Nonetheless, the Inter-American Commission's decision is supportive of a position that a death penalty prohibition may now be emerging.

One additional note regarding international human rights treaties (although not directly relevant to an East-West analysis) providing evidence of an eventual prohibition of capital punishment is found in Article 4 of the African Charter on Human and Peoples' Rights. This

---

[11] I/A Court H.R., Restrictions to the Death Penalty (Arts. 4 (2) and 4 (4) American Convention on Human Rights), Advisory Opinion OC-3/83 of 8 September 1983. Series A, no. 3.

international treaty, adopted by the Organization of African Unity in 1981 (entered into force on 21 October 1986), provides some interesting language that may have some relevance for a discussion on the legality of the death penalty. Article 4 reads:

Human beings are inviolable. Every human being shall be entitled to respect for his life and the integrity of his person. No one may be arbitrarily deprived of his life.

Although the African Charter makes no reference to the death penalty, and although the practice of African states support a retentionist view of capital punishment, the use of the word 'inviolable' invites the possibility of an interpretation in support of an abolitionist position. *Inviolability*, as defined by Black's Law Dictionary (1983), is 'the attribute of being secured against violation'. Therefore, when the first phrase of Article 4 is read alone, 'Human beings are inviolable', it is possible to conclude that capital punishment under all circumstances is prohibited. On the other hand, when the first phrase is coupled with the last; 'No one may be arbitrarily deprived of his life' a different conclusion must be drawn. This inconsistency in language certainly invites discussion and debate. The African Commission, now formed, and in operation in Banjul, the Gambia, is empowered to interpret the Charter, and it is conceivable that the Commission will have the opportunity to review the full meaning of Article 4.

4. The shifting winds of abolition — the West

4.1 State practice — the West

In order to determine if the prohibition of capital punishment is 'emerging' as customary international law and/or *jus cogens*, it is essential to assess whether the prohibition is becoming accepted by the international *community of states as a whole* (see *supra*). A review of state practice as evidence of state acceptance or rejection of capital punishment is therefore critical for this analysis (Hood, 1989). For the purposes of this chapter, the analysis will attempt to decipher the trends via an East-West perspective. What is East-West in an era of great political change is a difficult question. For the purposes of this chapter, however, 'West' is Western Europe, the US, Canada, Australia, New Zealand, Japan, the Inter-American System of Human Rights and the European System of Human Rights. The 'East' refers to the members of the Warsaw Pact, and European socialist-marxist states.

Unquestionably, the domestic practice of the United States of America is a major obstacle to any conclusion that the Western winds are directed towards abolition. On the contrary, recent judicial rulings and political events indicate that the US winds are predominantly aimed at 'retention' if not 'expansion' of the use of capital punishment. Since the US Supreme Court's interpretation in *Gregg v. Georgia*, 448 US 153, 96 S.Ct. 2909 (1976), where it concluded 'the punishment of death does not invariably violate the Constitution', some states have reintroduced the death penalty, within permissible federal guidelines.

At present, only fourteen of the fifty states do not have the death penalty as an official sanction (Alaska, Delaware, Hawaii, Iowa, Kansas, Maine, Mass., Michigan, Minn., New York, North Dakota, Rhode Island, W. Virginia, Wisconsin, *The New York Times*, 19 June, 1989), and 1989 nearly saw the overturning of the Governor's veto of capital punishment in New York (Orlin, 1990).

As for the number of death sentences carried out, the US trend is not towards abolition. Of the states that have the death penalty, only three have not implemented it (New Hampshire, South Dakota and Vermont) and as the *New York Times* Chart (Figure 6.1) indicates, the use of capital punishment appears with some fluctuation as a prevalent practice.[12]

The Supreme Court case-law has permitted if not facilitated this trend. Although the Court did limit the use of executions to those aged 15 and up, *Thomas v. Oklahoma* — US —, 108 S.Ct. 2687 (1988), other decisions have permitted the use of capital punishment. As already noted, in *Penry v. Lynaugh* — US —, 109 S.Ct. 2934, 106 L.Ed. 2d. 256 (1989), the Court permitted the execution of a mentally retarded man (with an IQ of 60 and who functioned at the level of a six-year-old) and, in *Stanford v. Kentucky* — US —, 109 S.Ct. 2969 (1989), the Court found no violation of the Eighth Amendment prohibition of 'cruel and unusual punishment' in executing criminals who were 16 years old when they committed their crimes.

As for the trends among other Western states, a primary source is the records of the International Covenant on Civil and Political Rights' Human Rights Committee and the questions and responses to the state reports they review.[13]

For example, Japan's statement to the Human Rights Committee is interesting and is perhaps representative of the retentionist position:

The representative of Japan informed the Committee that the Legislative Council, one of the advisory bodies to the Minister of Justice, had recently

---

[12] *The New York Times*, 19 June 1989. See also *New York Times*, 27 February 1990, p. A16, for more recent update as to the number of death row inmates in the United States and the number of executions as of July 1989 (source: NAACP Legal Defense Fund). As of July 1989, the NAACP Legal Defense and Educational Fund, Inc., noted that there are fifteen jurisdictions without capital punishment statutes: Alaska, District of Columbia, Hawaii, Iowa, Kansas, Maine, Massachusetts, Michigan, Minnesota, New York, North Dakota, Rhode Island, Vermont, West Virginia and Wisconsin (NAACP Legal Defense and Educational Fund, Inc. Memorandum, 1989).

[13] Bossuyt, 1987, p. 4. See, also, *Report of the Secretary-General*, 1988, summarizing 'the progress made towards the preparation of a study on the question of the death penalty and new contributions of criminal science to the matter'.

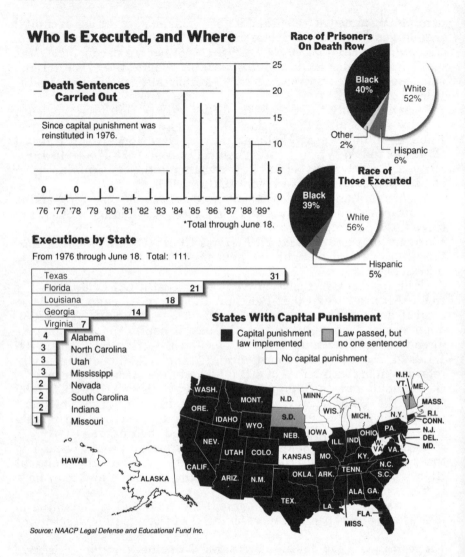

Figure 6.1.   Who is executed, and where

studied the question of capital punishment and had concluded *that its abolition would be unwarranted in view of the continued commission of brutal crimes and the fact that a large majority of Japanese people favoured the retention of the death penalty* (A/37/40, paragraph 82) (emphasis added).[14]

---

[14] Bossuyt, 1987, p. 5. *The Report of the Secretary-General*, 1988, reports that a Japanese advisory organ in a report to the Ministry of Justice 'recommended the number of capital offences should be reduced' (p. 17). See *infra* for more information regarding the Japanese position.

Four statements representative of the abolitionist position are those of Australia, Norway, Spain and Sweden:

Australia:
The representative of Australia informed the Committee that the last instance of the implementation of the death penalty in Australia had been in 1967, just six years before its abolishment in all areas of Commonwealth jurisdiction, including the Northern Territory; that although there was still a theoretical possibility of its being imposed in some States for some crimes, which was a survival of the colonial régime, the possibility was purely theoretical and that legislation was not to be prepared to provide for the severing of most of Australia's remaining links with its colonial past (A/38/40, para. 164).

Norway:
The representative of Norway stated that the abolition of the death penalty had deeply split public opinion in his country. In Parliament the division had been determined by political considerations and the abolitionists had only just carried the day (A/36/40, para. 339).

Spain:
The representative of Spain said that the death penalty had been abolished in Spain, except as provided in military criminal law applicable in time of war. Since the Penal Code reform in 1983, the death penalty had also been abolished for the crime of genocide (A/40/40, para. 483).

Sweden:
The representative of Sweden stressed that the death penalty had been abolished in Sweden long ago, the last execution having taken place in 1911. In various United Nations and other bodies, Sweden had striven to promote the gradual abolition of the death penalty and would continue to do so despite seemingly stiffening resistance (A/41/40, para. 119).

Another source indicating the trend towards capital punishment is the Secretary-General's reports made in accordance with Economic and Social Council resolution 1745 (LIV) (16 May 1973) Regarding the Status of Capital Punishment Among Member States. The third report (issued in 1985) covers the period of 1979–83. It showed that there were 19 retentionist states from North Africa and the Middle East, 43 from Africa south of the Sahara, 23 from Asia and the Pacific, and in the Western group only the United States (in part) and Liechtenstein are retentionists.[15]

As for the abolitionist states, 29 were abolitionist states by law and included, from the West: Austria, Denmark, Finland, France, Federal Republic of Germany, Holy See, Iceland, Luxembourg, Monaco, Netherlands, Norway, Portugal, Sweden. Of the 12 countries who have retained the death penalty only for exceptional crimes, several are from the West: Canada, Israel, Italy, San Marino, Spain, Switzer-

---

[15] Bossuyt, 1987, pp. 19–20. Liechtenstein has not had an execution since 1785 according to Amnesty International.

land, and the United Kingdom. (According to information provided by Amnesty International, Argentina, Cyprus, El Salvador, Fiji, Monaco, New Zealand and Peru also belong to this category. According to Amnesty International, Nepal is retentionist.)

Of the two states who by custom (for 40 years) have not used the death penalty, one is European: Belgium. Furthermore, among the nine states who are *de facto* abolitionist (for the past 10 years no execution) are Cyprus, Greece, Ireland and New Zealand (Bossuyt, 1987, pp. 19–21).

Perhaps the most interesting list (prepared by Amnesty International) indicating a shift in the wind towards abolition are those states which have recently taken actions limiting or eliminating the death penalty.

The following states have abolished the death penalty in recent years (1975–87);

1975: *Mexico* abolished the death penalty for ordinary offences.

1976: *Canada* abolished the death penalty for ordinary offences.

1977: *Portugal* abolished the death penalty for all offences.

1978: *Spain*: abolished the death penalty for ordinary offences; *Denmark* abolished the death penalty for all offences.

1979: *Luxembourg, Nicaragua and Norway* abolished the death penalty for all offences; *Brazil* and *Fiji* abolished the death penalty for ordinary offences.

1980: *Peru* abolished the death penalty for ordinary offences.

1981: *France* abolished the death penalty for all offences.

1982: *The Netherlands* abolished the death penalty for all offences.

1983: *Cyprus and El Salvador* abolished the death penalty for ordinary offences.

1984: *Argentina and Australia* abolished the death penalty for ordinary offences.

1985: *Australia* abolished the death penalty for all offences.

1987: *Haiti and the Philippines* abolished the death penalty for all offences.[16]

The list seems to indicate a clear direction for Western European states towards abolition, and perhaps the creation of a regional norm for abolition. This is a claim that Amnesty International made before the European Court of Human Rights in the *Soering* Case. In their comments they concluded:

---

[16] Bossuyt, 1987, pp. 20–1. *The Report of the Secretary General*, 1988, p. 17, states: 'Official initiatives or plans to abolish the death penalty are reported by *Jamaica* and *the Republic of Korea*. In the Republic of Korea, a Special Committee for the Reform of the Criminal Code, established in the Ministry of Justice, has been discussing the abolition of the death penalty. In Jamaica, where only murder is liable to capital punishment, the Government appointed a Committee in 1979 to consider possible changes in the law and the penal system required by the abolition of capital punishment. The Committee's report is being considered by the relevant authorities. In Cyprus, this question is being studied by the Ministry of Justice.

There is a virtual consensus in Western European legal systems that the death penalty is, under current circumstances, no longer consistent with regional standards of justice and human rights.[17]

To support this claim, among other arguments, Amnesty proposed this proposition:

It is submitted that Western European regional standards of penal policy have now so far evolved that what was once an exception to general norms protecting the right to life and, perhaps, the right not to be subjected to torture or inhuman or degrading treatment or punishment must now be held to constitute an anachronism in Western Europe, no longer worthy of restricting the full scope of the basic norms. This approach is consistent with the above modest statement of the minimum requirement of general international law (Amnesty International, 1989b, p. 4).

Supporting Amnesty's conclusion was the fact that all member states in the Council of Europe, either *de jure* or *de facto* (Belgium, Greece and Ireland), have abolished the death penalty for peacetime or ordinary offences; the only exception is Turkey. Furthermore, although retaining the death penalty, Turkey has had no executions since 1984.[18] President Evran openly proclaimed that he is opposed to the death penalty, and Turkey has a strong abolitionist movement. (This led Amnesty to conclude: 'It may be that Turkey should be understood as being in the process of joining the ranks of abolitionist states.)[19]

Amnesty also noted (in its comments submitted in the *Soering* Case) that 'only in the United Kingdom is the possibility of reintroduction of the penalty ever formally debated in the legislature, . . . the results of such debates are that preserving abolition repeatedly prevails over reintroduction by considerable margins'.[20]

---

[17] Amnesty International — 1989b, p. 6. It should be noted that although this claim was rejected by the court its advocacy should have some weight in indicating the possible future trend of the status of capital punishment in Western Europe.

[18] For a list of the crimes for which Turkey imposes capital punishment, see the *Report of the Secretary General*, 1988, p. 28.

[19] A poll cited by Hood, 1989, p. 10, reported that six out of ten Turks are against the death penalty. For a discussion of some additional effort to abolish capital punishment in Turkey, see Amnesty International, 1989c, which also includes a full list of abolitionist and retentionist countries as of April 1989.

[20] Amnesty International, *op.cit.*, note 19, pp. 5-6. As Roger Hood (1989, p. 10) noted: 'In June 1988, the eighteenth attempt in the British parliament to reintroduce capital punishment for some classes of murder was defeated by 341 votes to 218'. The United Kingdom's position as to its reasons for not supporting the Second Optional Protocol to the International Covenant on Civil and Political Rights may be equally relevant to its decision not to ratify Protocol No. 6 to the European Convention. The delegate from the United Kingdom to the Third Committee of the UN General Assembly, Mr Raven, made the following statement: 'It was difficult to achieve unanimity on such a complex moral issue, and successive British Governments had taken the view that the decision whether or not to abolish or reintroduce it should be left to individual Members of Parliament voting according to their own consciences. The United Kingdom therefore would not take on an international obligation on the abolition of the death penalty' (UN doc. A/C3/44/SR.52, 22 November 1989, p. 6).

Although the European Court of Human Rights rejected Amnesty's argument, is it conceivable that future events could alter the Court's conclusion? Perhaps movements via regional international organizations could lead to a reversal of the Court's opinion.

4.2 Regional trends and actions — the West

As has been discussed, clearly the European Court of Human Rights decision in *Soering* has implications for the international and regional legality of the death penalty. The Court none the less rejected Amnesty's argument that the death penalty is *per se* violative of Article 3 of the European Convention:

The Convention is to be read as a whole and Article 3 should therefore be construed in harmony with the provisions of Article 2 (see, *mutatis mutandis,* the *Klass and Others* judgment of 6 September 1978, Series A no. 28, p. 31, paragraph 68). On this basis Article 3 evidently cannot have been intended by the drafters of the Convention to include a general prohibition of the death penalty since that would nullify the clear wording of Article 2 paragraph 1 (1/1989/161/217, paragraph 103).

However, it did conclude that the US (Virginian) application of the death penalty violated the Convention due to the long and cruel wait the Court labelled 'the death row syndrome'. In deciding *Soering*, the Court not only made a judgment regarding the status of US law that would ban the extradition of a Federal Republic of Germany citizen from the UK to the US, but proclaimed a norm for the European system. Thus, *Soering* serves as a confirmation that certain applications of capital punishment by Western Europe States would be contrary to the Convention even if Article 2, paragraph 1 permits states to have the death penalty. It also arguably supports the conclusion that Western winds are in the clear direction of abolition.

Additional evidence that the West is moving in the direction of abolition is the 17 January 1986 resolution of the European Parliament, which described the death penalty as a cruel and inhuman form of punishment and a violation of the right to life, even where strict legal procedures are applied (Amnesty International, 1989b, p. 11). This resolution certainly adds weight to the abolitionist argument that the death penalty is contrary to the regional norms of Western Europe.

Perhaps the most significant evidential fact is the drafting and coming into force of Protocol No. 6 to the European Convention on Human Rights. The relevant provisions of this Protocol, which effectively ban the use of the death penalty in peace time, read as follows:

Article 1
The death penalty shall be abolished. No one shall be condemned to such
ıenalty or executed.

Article 2
A State may make provision in its law for the death penalty in respect of acts committed in time of war or of imminent threat of war; such penalty shall be applied only in the instances laid down in the law and in accordance with its provisions. The State shall communicate to the Secretary-General of the Council of Europe the relevant provisions of that law.

At present there are fifteen Council of Europe members which have ratified the Protocol (see Table 6.1).[21]

It can be argued that Protocol No. 6 could become the central vehicle by which the norm prohibiting capital punishment could develop in Europe. Given the experience of the Council of Europe, and the history of the growth and the eventual acceptance by all its Member States of the European Convention on Human Rights and its machinery, it is conceivable that within time a similar trend could be repeated in regard to the abolition of the death penalty. The fact that several states, for example Hungary and Poland, have recently expressed their intentions to join the Council and the European Rights System, only strengthens the potential for the growth in the number of European abolitionist states. Although on the one hand, the existence of the Protocol gave support to the Court's position that it was unable to declare jurisprudentially that the European Convention prohibited the death penalty (as Amnesty had argued), on the other hand, the Protocol may serve as an approach to broaden the abolitionist ranks and spread the norm beyond its present numbers.

As noted earlier, the European System is not the only regional system that has an impact on the international status of capital punishment. The Inter-American system with its Commissions' opinion in *Roach and Pinkerton*, along with the strong language of the American Convention, adds credibility to the view that the abolitionist position is growing in regions other than Europe. The advisory opinion of 8 September 1983 of the Inter-American Court of Human Rights further supports this contention. As noted earlier, this opinion, sought by the Inter-American Commission, confirmed unanimously that there is an absolute prohibition on the extension of the death penalty and consequently, the government of a State Party

---

[21] Council of Europe, *Chart of Signatures and Ratifications: Protocol 6 to the Human Rights Convention Concerning the Abolition of the Death Penalty* (3 January 1989; information on status of signatures and ratifications as of February 1990 provided by the Council of Europe). Finland ratified the European Convention together with its Protocol No. 6 on 4 May 1990. During times of peace, the death penalty has not been used in Finland for 140 years. Until 1950 it could, in theory, have been used as punishment for three crimes, but in practice those sentences were always pardoned. Since 1950, the law explicitly prohibits the use of the death penalty during peacetime (Anttila, 1967) and since 1972 capital punishment is prohibited during wartime as well. Amnesty reports that the last execution for an ordinary offence was in 1826 (1989c).

Table 6.1.   Council of Europe members which have ratified the Protocol

| *Signatory states*: | Belgium, Greece |
| *Contracting states*: | Austria, Denmark, Federal Republic of Germany, Finland, France, Iceland, Italy, Luxembourg, Netherlands, Norway, Portugal, San Marino, Spain, Sweden, Switzerland |

OPENING FOR SIGNATURE		*ENTRY INTO FORCE*	
Place: Strasbourg		Conditions:	
		5 Ratifications	
Date: 28/04/83		Date: 01/03/85	
Member states	Date of signature	Date of ratification	Date of entry into force
Austria	28/04/83	05/01/84	01/03/85
Belgium	28/04/83	—	—
Cyprus	—	—	—
Denmark	28/04/83	01/12/83	01/03/85
Finland	05/05/89	04/05/90	01/06/90
France	28/04/83	17/02/86	01/03/86
F.R. Germany	28/04/83	05/07/89	01/08/89
Greece	02/05/83	—	—
Iceland	24/04/85	22/05/87	01/06/87
Ireland	—	—	—
Italy	21/10/83	29/12/88	01/01/89
Liechtenstein	—	—	—
Luxembourg	28/04/83	19/02/85	01/03/85
Malta	—	—	—
Netherlands	28/04/83	25/04/86	01/05/86
Norway	28/04/83	25/10/88	01/11/88
Portugal	28/04/83	02/10/86	01/11/86
San Marino	01/03/89	23/03/89	01/04/89
Spain	28/04/83	14/01/85	01/03/85
Sweden	28/04/83	09/02/84	01/03/85
Switzerland	28/04/83	13/10/87	01/11/87
Turkey	—	—	—
United Kingdom	—	—	—

cannot apply the death penalty to crimes for which such a penalty was not previously provided under its domestic law (Bossuyt, 1987, Appendix II, p. 69). In addition to the Court's making a contribution to the non-extension of the death penalty, it argued for increased protection when the death penalty is used:

Thus, three types of limitations can be seen to be applicable to State Parties which have not abolished the death penalty. First, the imposition or application of this sanction is subject to certain procedural requirements whose compliance must be strictly observed and reviewed. Second, the application of the death penalty must be limited to the most serious common crimes not related to political offences. Finally, certain considerations involving the person of the defendant, which may bar the imposition or application of the death penalty, must be taken into account.

These conclusions were consistent with the Court's interpretative approach to the Convention and capital punishment (Bossuyt, 1987, pp. 68–9).

On this entire subject, the Convention adopts an approach that is clearly incremental in character. That is, without going so far as to abolish the death penalty, the Convention imposes restrictions designed to delimit strictly its application of the penalty to bring about its gradual disappearance.

Therefore arguably the adoption of the Convention, and not the Court's interpretation could encourage the eventual elimination of the death penalty in the Western hemisphere. Of course the position of the United States Government towards the Convention is detrimental to that trend. Although the US Senate has not ratified the Convention, it was signed by President Carter (December 1977). At the time, the US Government proposed reservations to Articles 4 and 5 as follows:

Article 4 deals with the right to life generally, and includes provisions on capital punishment. Many of the provisions of Article 4 are not in accord with United States law and policy, or deal with matters in which the law is unsettled. The Senate may wish to enter a reservation as follows: 'United States adherence to Article 4 is subject to the Constitution and other laws of the United States.'
  (Article (5), (p)aragraph 5 requires that minors subject to criminal proceedings are to be separated from adults and brought before specialized tribunals as speedily as possible. (. . .) With respect to paragraph (5), the law reserves the right to try minors as adults in certain cases and there is no present intent to revise these laws. The following statement is recommended:
  'The United States (. . .) with respect to paragraph (5), reserves the right in appropriate cases to subject minors to procedures and penalties applicable to adults.'

Although the Commission ultimately found the United States death penalty violative of the American Declaration on Human Rights,[22] on Equal Protection grounds, it was these reservations in fact that were the evidentiary support of the Commission's logic in *Roach and Pinkerton*, that the US was not in violation of the Declaration because of international custom or *jus cogens* banning the execution of 18 year olds.

Since the United States has protested the norm, it would not be applicable to the United States should it be held to exist. For a norm of customary

---

[22] The American Declaration of Human Rights is a non-binding document of the OAS, as opposed to the American Convention, which is a multilateral treaty binding on the ratifying states. See Buergenthal, 1988.

international law to be binding on a State which has protested the norm, it must have acquired the status of *jus cogens*.

Furthermore, the Commission did accept the US position regarding the non-existence of an international norm establishing 18 to be the minimum age for imposition of the death penalty.

The Commission is convinced by the U.S. Government's argument that there does not now exist a norm of customary international law establishing 18 to be the minimum age for imposition of the death penalty. Nonetheless, in light of the increasing numbers of States which are ratifying the American Convention on Human Rights and the United Nations Covenant on Civil and Political Rights, and modifying their domestic legislation in conformity with these instruments, *the norm is emerging*. As mentioned above, thirteen states and the U.S. capital have abolished the death penalty entirely and nine retentionist states have abolished it for offenders under the age of 18.[23]

Hence, it is apparent that if the American Convention were to be ratified by the US Senate, it would still not alter the international legal status of the death penalty within the hemisphere as long as the ratification is accompanied by reservations similar to or the same as the ones proposed in 1977. None the less, it can be argued that these steps (*Roach and Pinkerton* and the *Advisory Opinion*) are progressive, in that they contribute to bringing about an alteration in the status of capital punishment in international law and particularly in the Americas. After all, in the nineteenth century, the US practice of governmentally protected and sanctioned slavery was held to be legal in international law:

... in the *Le Louis* case (1817) W. Scott of the British High Court of Admiralty held that the slave trade was accepted both in the practice and law of civilized States and by courts in interpreting the law of nations. In 1825 the U.S. Supreme Court held in the *Antelope* case that the slave trade was not prohibited by international law. After that date, statements affirming the legality of the slave trade became rare (Hannikainen, 1988, pp. 76–7).

Arguably, if the prohibition of slavery, once accepted as permissible in international law, became *jus cogens*, why not ultimately the prohibition of the death penalty?

5. The shifting winds of abolition — the East

5.1 State practice

The trend towards abolition of the death penalty is not confined to Western Europe, but is now developing into a European-wide trend. It

---

[23] *Annual Report of the Inter-American Commission on Human Rights*, 1986–1987, pp. 147–93. (*Roach and Pinkerton* case: No. 9647).

is impossible, however, given the scope of this topic, to provide a nation by nation survey of the domestic status of capital punishment in Eastern Europe. None the less, the inclusion of information on the law and practice of some of these states may be useful. Once again a sample of statements of Eastern European nations before the Human Rights Committee is a vital source in attempting to understand these nations' positions *vis-à-vis* the death penalty. But while recent events may have made those statements somewhat obsolete, a comparison of these statements with more recent events (although at this point sketchy and in flux), may demonstrate a shift in wind direction away from a 'retentionist' position and towards an 'abolitionist' position.

Just to provide some examples, in July 1986, Hungary made the following statement to the Human Rights Committee (*Report of the Human Rights Committee*, GAOR 41st session, Supplement No. 40 (A/41-/40), 1986, p. 86, para. 388):

The representative of Hungary informed the Committee that the Criminal Code prescribed the death penalty as an exceptional measure for only a few offences of particular gravity, offences against the State, including armed conspiracy, sedition, sabotage, treason and espionage — none of which had been committed in Hungary in the previous decade; offences against humanity, including genocide and war crimes; offences against the person, including homicide when committed with premeditation, out of greed with particular cruelty or by a confirmed offender; offences against public order, including acts of terrorism or the hijacking of an aircraft when they caused death; and military offences. In the past 10 years, the death penalty had been enforced in 25 cases.

This statement can be characterized as a classical retentionist position. Yet Amnesty International reports, as recently as November 1989, that a Hungarian Non-Governmental Organization has been created, the League for the Abolition of the Death Penalty, whose intention is to persuade Parliament and the public to alter Hungary's position on the death penalty.

In fact, on 1 July 1989, the Hungarian Parliament, in response to a proposal from the Minister of Justice for an alteration of the Penal Code, 'abolished the death penalty for crimes against the state.' Also according to an Amnesty report, '(in Hungary) no executions can be carried out while the constitutional position of the Chairman of the Presidential Council, who is responsible for ratifying death sentences, is being reviewed'.[24]

Similarly, Amnesty reports that the Director of the Institute of Law of the Czechoslovakian Academy of Sciences informed Amnesty that

---

[24] Amnesty International, 1989a, pp. 1–2. See also, Hood, 1989, p. 11, where he reports on a memorandum from Prof. Dr Joseph Vigh of the Department of Criminology, Faculty of Law, Eötvös Lorand University, Budapest, stating that 'Hungary abolished the death penalty for offences against property in 1971 and for economic offences in 1979'.

its Institute is working towards abolition. In light of a Czechoslovakian statement to the Human Rights Committee, it seems as though an indigenous pressure group is beginning to address the death penalty issue in that country. It should also be noted that in 1962 Czechoslovakia reduced the number of capital offences from 80 to 23 and the authorities are considering reducing the number even further (*Report of the Secretary-General*, 1988, p. 17).

There are additional indications of breezes of change in Eastern Europe. According to Amnesty International:

In *Yugoslavia* it was announced in April 1988 that the Federal Assembly would consider changes to the Federal Criminal Code to reduce the number of capital offences, and the Federal Secretary of Justice . . ., has reportedly publicly expressed his support for abolition . . . . In the Yugoslav republic of Slovenia, where there have reportedly been no executions since 1957, the President of the Supreme Court of Slovenia announced in March 1988 that the death penalty would soon be abolished in the republic.[25]

While these examples provide evidence of breezes in Eastern Europe, there also exist some winds aimed at total abolition of the death penalty. The most impressive example is the German Democratic Republic. In its earlier statements to the Human Rights Committee it noted 'that the death penalty had not been abolished in the German Democratic Republic because the Government regarded it as an effective weapon against racialism, fascism and war criminals' (Bossuyt, 1987, p. 61f.). In a statement made in July 1984 the representative of the German Democratic Republic noted that 'nothing was more important than peace and all means should be used to achieve it, even the death penalty'. He emphasized, on the other hand, that the death penalty was applicable only to a very few crimes and that in practice, since the first periodic report submitted by the German Democratic Republic, 'there had been no cases of death sentences either imposed or executed' (*Report of the Human Rights Committee*, GAOR 39th session, Supplement No. 40 (A/39/40), p. 95, para. 492).

Yet on 17 July 1987, the German Democratic Republic 'abolished the death penalty for all crimes' (Amnesty International, *op.cit.* note

---

[25] Amnesty International, *op.cit.*, note 23, p. 2f. For a summary of the capital offences in Yugoslavia see *Report of the Secretary General*, 1988, p. 33. It should be noted that Yugoslavia, in its earlier statement to the Human Rights Committee, explained that while the number of offences subject to the death penalty seemed high, these were quite exceptional cases related to exceptional situations endangering the internal or external security of the State (Bossuyt, 1987, p. 67). In her explanation of the Yugoslav vote on the Third Committee's resolution adopting the Second Optional Protocol to the International Covenant on Civil and Political Rights (1989), Ms Ilic said that her delegation had voted in favour of the resolution. Her own country still had the death penalty but used it very rarely, and death sentences were usually commuted. *A discussion of its abolition was currently under way in Yugoslavia* (emphasis added) (UN doc. A/C.3/44/SR.52, p. 6).

23, p. 2). H. Eichler, the Secretary of the Council of State of the GDR, explaining the rationale of this decision provided the following logic (*GDR Committee for Human Rights Bulletin*, vol. 3, no. 2 (1987):

The GDR has lived up to its national and international responsibility concerning the consistent punishment of Nazi and war crimes and the eradication of the roots of fascism and militarism.

The GDR will continue to fulfil this commitment under international law without having to resort to the death penalty. This has been confirmed by its experience gained in recent years in the penal jurisdiction of the courts of the German Democratic Republic.

As a result of the successful development of its socialist society, the GDR has stable political, economic and social foundations guaranteeing a high degree of public order and security as an essential precondition for the safety and well-being of its citizens. The prevention of and the fight against crime have become a concern of society as a whole.

Therefore, the crime rate has fallen steadily so that the GDR today is one of the world's countries with the lowest crime rate. The majority of the crimes committed in the GDR are of lesser gravity. Felonious homicides and murders and other dangerous crimes of violence have for years had a minor share in criminal offences.

Acting in line with this changed scope and pattern of crime and mindful of the humanist nature of socialist society, GDR courts have not imposed a death penalty for a number of years.

The criminal law of the German Democratic Republic offers all the necessary legal conditions to ensure the all-round protection of socialist society and its citizens from criminal acts without having to resort to this type of punishment.

The application of criminal responsibility serves to protect socialism, its citizens and their rights as well as to educate criminal offenders in a spirit of respect for the law and of a responsible behaviour in society; it is neither vengeance nor an act of reprisal by the State against criminal offenders.

The abolition of the death penalty in the German Democratic Republic is in keeping with the recommendations of the United Nations aiming at the abolition of the death penalty on a global scale.

The German Democratic Republic is thereby stating its position that mankind is entitled to a life in peace and human dignity and that human rights must be protected in their entirety.

Polish sources have informed me that there is serious discussion in Parliament about the elimination or limitation of capital punishment. Some confirmation of this report is provided by Amnesty; an official of the Minister of Justice has proposed establishing a five-year moratorium on executions during which time the penal code would be reviewed.[26] According to recent information, a draft prepared by the Committee for the Reform of Criminal Law called for by the Ministry of Justice and published in February 1989 did not call

---

[26] Amnesty International, 1989a, p. 2. See also Hood, 1989, p. 13, reports that 'in 1987, the Polish Ministry of Justice appointed a new Commission on the Reform of the Penal Law, which will consider the subject (of abolition).'

for the abolition of the death penalty but sought its reduction. New reports prepared by the Committee sought by Mr. A. Bentkowski, the new Minister of Justice, calls for the abolition of the death penalty and its replacement with life sentences in cases of 'qualified murder'. In 1989 Polish courts did not apply the death penalty but three defendants were sentenced to death. They were not executed. The Senate Committee of Human Rights and Legality strongly supports the abolition of the death penalty.[27]

In the wake of the fall of the Ceausescu regime and his execution, the Romanian provisional government issued decrees ending the death penalty (*The New York Times*, 2 January 1990, p. 1). Subsequently, there was an announcement that the abolition decision was to be reconsidered in light of public support for capital punishment, and that the matter would be put to a national referendum. This decision has in turn been reversed, and the question has not yet been decided. It is likely that the death penalty will be a concern of the new regime and its constitutional and legal reforms (*The Independent*, 19 January 1990).

Finally, there seems to be some significant movement towards abolition in the Soviet Union. In another Amnesty summary[28] it was reported that *Izvestija* published new principles of criminal law which were due to be adopted in March 1989. These principles will be the model for anticipated alterations to the criminal law of all the fifteen Soviet Republics. Amnesty reports that '. . . they retain the death penalty as exceptional punishment but reduce its scope from 18 peacetime offences to six. These are: state treason, espionage, terrorist acts, sabotage, intentional homicide with aggravating circumstances, and rape of a minor . . .'

Furthermore, there are other restrictions on the death penalty which add support to the argument that certain applications of the death penalty are 'emerging' as contrary to international law. As evidence of this trend, the Soviet Union currently prohibits the execution of those under 18 years old, but the new proposals would exempt anyone over the age of 60 when the sentence is passed.[29] Obviously, if these steps are enacted, as expected, they, along with

---

[27] Information provided by Dr. (Senator) Alice Grześkowiak, Professor of Criminal Law, at the Faculty of Nicolaus Copernicus University of Torun, Poland, who also serves as Chairman of the Senate Constitutional Committee.

[28] Amnesty International, 1989d.

[29] *Report of the Secretary General*, 1988, p. 17, states: 'In the Byelorussian SSR, the Ukrainian SSR and the Union of Soviet Socialist Republics, revisions of the respective criminal codes are reported to be under way. In the course of these revisions, consideration is being given to limiting the number of offences liable to capital punishment and to the abolition of this penalty for some particular types of crime.' Hood, 1989, pp. 15-16, in his review of the Soviet trend concluded: 'All these indications, reflecting the policies of *Glasnost* and *Perestroika*, suggest that the Soviet Union is moving steadily towards restricting the use of the death penalty and possibly towards total abolition.'

the other events in Eastern Europe lead to the conclusion that the winds of change are clearly in the direction of abolition.

In its report Amnesty International (*op.cit.*, note 23, p. 3) concluded its remarks on a similar note of optimism: 'It is in these circumstances that we can hope with increasing confidence that the day when Europe, East and West, will be free from the death penalty may not be far off.'

6. Global shifting winds

Efforts to limit or eliminate the death penalty are not restricted to state or regional actions. On the contrary, there is evidence indicating that universal efforts are affecting the legal standing of capital punishment in international law.

6.1 The CSCE process

Breaching the East-West political divide is the CSCE (Helsinki) process (see chapter in this volume by Jan Helgesen). Its human rights accomplishments extend to a number of critical issues. As a process, its distinct advantage is that it includes the participation of the two superpowers, the Soviet Union and the United States (as well as states from diverse political traditions), an advantage not available through the operations of the Human Rights Committee, due to the non-ratification of the International Covenant on Civil and Political Rights by the United States. The Helsinki Final Act — although not a treaty and therefore not having the same force in international law as Protocol No. 6 of the European Convention on Human Rights or the Second Optional Protocol of the Political Covenant — has served an important function in the progressive realization of human rights.

Representatives of the participating states have recently 'reaffirmed their resolve fully to implement, unilaterally, bilaterally and multilaterally, all the provisions of the Final Act and of the other CSCE documents'.[30]

---

[30] *Concluding Document of the Vienna Meeting 1986 of Representatives of the Participating States of the Conference on Security and Co-operation in Europe. Held on the Basis of the Provisions of the Final Act Relating to the Follow-up to the Conference*, (1989), p. 3. The representatives of the participating States of the Conference on Security and Co-operation in Europe (CSCE) were Austria, Belgium, Bulgaria, Canada, Cyprus, Czechoslovakia, Denmark, Finland, France, the German Democratic Republic, the Federal Republic of Germany, Greece, the Holy See, Hungary, Iceland, Ireland, Italy, Liechtenstein, Luxembourg, Malta, Monaco, the Netherlands, Norway, Poland, Portugal, Romania, San Marino, Spain, Sweden, Switzerland, Turkey, the Union of Soviet Socialist Republics, the United Kingdom, the United States of America and Yugoslavia.

The 1986–89 meeting produced a set of principles, and for the first time the participating states made reference to the death penalty. Its substance is interesting, as it seems to summarize the present status of the death penalty and to hold out the possibility of elimination or limitation of capital punishment:

(24) With regard to the question of capital punishment, the participating States note that capital punishment has been abolished in a number of them. In participating States where capital punishment has not been abolished, sentence of death may be imposed only for the most serious crimes in accordance with the law in force at the time of the commission of the crime and not contrary to their international commitments. This question will be kept under consideration. In this context, the participating States will co-operate within relevant international organizations (Principle 24, p. 10).

6.2 United Nations efforts

As already noted, there is considerable evidence indicating there is within the language of International Covenant on Civil and Political Rights 'a preference for the eventual prohibition of the death penalty', but it also permits ratifying states to retain capital punishment (see above). None the less, efforts at the United Nations have been directed at altering this position. These multilateral efforts are critical to an analysis of the likelihood of a death penalty prohibition becoming customary international law and/or *jus cogens*. For just as the slavery conventions, with their strict prohibitions and their near universal acceptance, altered the status and acceptability of slavery and the slave trade in international law and the community of nations, so does the possibility exist ultimately to eliminate the death penalty via the process of widely accepting multilateral treaties.[31] The most significant United Nations effort to date is the drafting of a Second Optional Protocol to the International Covenant on Civil and Political Rights. Bossuyt in his report (1987, p. 24) has written:

At the initiative of the Federal Republic of Germany a debate has taken place in several United Nations organs leading to the appointment by the Economic and Social Council of a Special Rapporteur of the Sub-Commission on the Prevention of Discrimination and the Protection of Minorities entrusted with the preparation of an analysis concerning the proposition to elaborate a second optional protocol aiming at the abolition of the death penalty. Views on this proposition have been expressed by Governments in written form at the request and orally at the Third Committee of the General Assembly and at the Commission on Human Rights. This proposition was also discussed in

---

[31] A similar and more recent comparison can be made with genocide. See, for example, Hannikainen, 1988, pp. 456–66. The prohibition against genocide is peremptory in principle but, unfortunately, international efforts to limit genocidal actions have not been effective.

the Sub-Commission on the Prevention of Discrimination and the Protection of Minorities.

In the process of developing the Second Optional Protocol, on 15 December 1980, the General Assembly (Decision 35/437) requested the Secretary-General to transmit to states for their comments the draft text of the Second Optional Protocol to the International Covenant on Civil and Political Rights. This protocol had been prepared by Austria, Costa Rica, the Dominican Republic, the Federal Republic of Germany, Italy, Portugal and Sweden. Bossuyt reports that in the state comments the replies were almost evenly divided between retentionist (17) and abolitionist positions (18), with an additional note of support for the protocol from Australia.

Among the comments on the Protocol submitted by the retentionists were the following:

Japan (28 July 1981) — 'the majority of the Japanese citizens support retention of the death penalty as a just punishment for criminals who have committed particularly heinous crimes and regard it as an effective deterrent to such crimes' (UN doc. A/36/441, p. 11, reprinted CN.4/Sub. 2/1987/20, p. 25).[32]

United States of America (25 June 1981) — 'would have no reason to object if other countries wanted to adopt and accede to the draft protocol' (A/36/441, p. 20, reprinted E/CN.4/Sub. 2/1987/20, p. 26).

Among the comments on the Protocol submitted by the abolitionists were the following:

United Kingdom (11 August 1981) — 'stressed that the issues surrounding capital punishment are diverse and complex and that diametrically opposed views are held by people whose moral integrity and respect for those rights cannot be called into question' (A/36/441, pp. 18–19, reprinted E/CN.4/Sub. 2/1987/20, p. 26).

Belgium and Switzerland (23 July 1982 and 11 August 1981) — expressed a preference for keeping the possibility of providing capital punishment for military crimes in time of war (*ibid.*, p. 26).

Finland, the Netherlands, Norway, Sweden, Italy, Portugal, Denmark and Greece supported the draft Protocol while *Austria* (18 June 1982) emphasized the optional nature of the Protocol and thought the effort should not be limited to the regional level (*ibid.*, p. 26).

The *Federal Republic of Germany* (15 June 1982) — concluded its remarks with: 'Such an instrument would act as a signal for the future and give a

---

[32] Japan also reported to the Human Rights Committee: 'As a result of strict regulations, the number of executions had decreased in recent years and that during the period 1975–80, only 14 persons had been executed' (Bossuyt, 1987, p. 62).

fresh impulse and thrust to the discussion, with the ultimate objective of abolishing capital punishment world wide' (ibid., p. 26).

In 1982, the debate in the Third Committee (draft resolution A/C.3/ 37/L.60/Rev. 1) revealed other state positions regarding capital punishment. Among those states in favour of abolition of the death penalty were the following:

Canada: 'there was no doubt the United Nations would be honouring human dignity by enshrining the principle of the abolition of the death penalty in an international instrument' (UN doc. A/C.3/36/SR.31, para. 9).

Finland, also speaking on behalf of Denmark, Iceland, Norway and Sweden: 'every effort should be made to limit the imposition of the death penalty and to formulate international norms so that more and more countries would refrain from using the death penalty. The proposal being considered is one possible way of promoting the attainment of that objective' (A/C.3/36/SR.29, para. 9).

The Netherlands: 'since, the death penalty might contain elements of cruel, inhuman or degrading treatment, it might also violate article 7 of the International Covenant on Civil and Political Rights' (A/C.3/36/SR. 27, paras. 26–31).

Some other countries in favour of abolition were: Australia, Belgium, Cyprus, Greece, Ireland, Israel, Luxembourg, New Zealand, Spain, Turkey. Among those who voted against the resolution were: Bahrain, Burundi, Guinea, Iran, Iraq, Jordan, Kuwait, Lebanon, Libya, Malaysia, Oman, Nigeria, Philippines, Qatar, Saudi Arabia, Sierra Leone, Singapore, Somalia, Syria, Sudan, United Arab Emirates, Yemen.

The Resolution passed by 52 votes to 23, with 53 abstentions (Bossuyt, 1987, p. 27): a vote which at that point (1982) could be construed as indicating a trend, albeit not an overwhelming one towards a universal abolitionist position. Considering, however, the votes of the European nations (both the 'yes' votes of Western and the abstentions of Eastern European states) and some of the recent events in Eastern Europe, it may be possible to conclude that the velocity of the trend has since strengthened, especially in Europe.

This 1982 vote led to additional moves towards a Second Optional Protocol, with discussions by the UN Commission on Human Rights and the UN Sub-Commission on the Prevention of Discrimination and the Protection of Minorities, the passage of Resolution 1985/46 of 14 march 1985 — and ultimately the drafting and adoption of a Second Optional Protocol, prepared by the Special Rapporteur.

Its Article 1, which reflects an almost absolute abolitionist position, reads as follows:

1.   No one within the jurisdiction of a State party to the present Optional Protocol shall be executed.

2. Each State party shall take all necessary measures to abolish the death penalty within its jurisdiction.

Its Article 2 also limits reservations in a very narrow fashion, permitting the death penalty only in wartime and under very limited conditions:

1. No reservation is admissible to the present Protocol except for a reservation made at the time of ratification or accession that provides for the application of the death penalty in time of war pursuant to a conviction for a most serious crime of a military nature committed during wartime.
2. The State party making such a reservation shall at the time of ratification or accession communicate to the Secretary-General of the United Nations the relevant provisions of its national legislation applicable during wartime.
3. The State party having made such a reservation shall notify the Secretary-General of the United Nations of any beginning or ending of a state of war applicable to its territory.

The Protocol also calls for the expansion of the Covenant's reporting system to include 'information on the measures they have adopted to give effect to the Protocol' (Article 3), as well as provisions providing for individual complaints (Articles 4 and 5).

Undoubtedly, the Second Optional Protocol represents a progressive step in the development of an international norm outlawing the death penalty.

In November 1989, the Third Committee's recommendation to the General Assembly to open for signature, ratification and accession the Second Optional Protocol to the International Covenant on Civil and Political Rights Aiming at the Abolition of the Death Penalty, by a vote of 55 to 28, with 45 abstentions, most certainly indicated a pattern of support for the Protocol (UN doc. A/44/824, draft resolution a/C.3/44/L.42, 6 December 1989). Significantly, not one European state voted against the resolution, from either the East or the West, indicating strong support for an abolitionist position and for the international establishment of universal agreements to ban capital punishment in that geopolitical region, thus further supporting the conclusion that the abolitionist position is 'emerging' as a regional norm in Europe. The only two Western votes in opposition were Japan and the United States (despite the US government's 1981 statement that, 'it had no reason to object if other countries wanted to adopt and accede to the draft protocol' (*supra*).)

Among the support for the retentionist position, and voting 'no', were states strongly influenced by Islamic law (although there were two Islamic states that abstained, Algeria and Libyan Arab Jamahiriya). There were also a number of other African and Asian states that were opposed to abolition, including Nigeria, Tanzania, China and Japan.

A sample of summary statements from states opposed to the protocol reflect the Islamic position:

Mr. Galal (*Egypt*): First, it confused human rights concepts with the concept of criminal justice, which required that the criminal be punished. Second, the right to life was sacred, but it should not be distorted by upholding the criminal's right to life and ignoring the victim's equal right to life. That would simply encourage criminals. Third, if the countries which advocated the protocol regarded it as optional, they should keep it to themselves and not impose it on the international community. Fourth, his delegation considered it more important to accede to the Convention on the Prevention and Punishment of the Crime of Genocide and the International Convention on the Suppression and Punishment of the Crime of Apartheid than to defend the rights of criminals. Fifth, the draft protocol represented a racist, imperialist idea which certain countries were seeking to impose on the 115 countries which still had the death penalty. Lastly, if, as the sponsors claimed, the draft resolution was not binding on the international community, his delegation wondered what was the point of it. Such a claim challenged the validity of resolutions adopted by the General Assembly (UN doc. A/C.3/44/SR.52, pp. 2-3).

Mr. Ziada (*Iraq*): The draft resolution . . . ran counter to the democratic process. Less than one third of United Nations Member States had abolished the death penalty, which meant that the vast majority maintained it. If the draft resolution was adopted, that would mean either that many countries were hypocritical or that they had succumbed to pressure. That would be an extremely undemocratic approach for a Committee which was supposed to defend human rights, democracy and self-determination (A/C.3/44/SR.52, p. 3).

Mr. Al-Saud (*Saudi Arabia*): Abolition of the death penalty was contrary to the principles of his country's religion as enshrined in the Koran. It was also a violation of the right to life, which was guaranteed by the laws of his country. The death penalty aimed at protecting human rights and was a sanction against anyone who tried to take away human life. Statistics showed that crime had fallen in countries which maintained the death penalty, and its abolition could therefore lead to an increase in the number of crimes and victims. Legal systems which abolished the death penalty were not really protecting the lives of others. He suggested that the draft resolution should be set aside (A/C.3/44/SR.52, pp. 3-4).

Mr. Alaie (*Islamic Republic of Iran*): Under Islamic law, the destruction of even one human being who had not committed an offence was tantamount to the destruction of a whole society. Capital punishment was by no means a violation of human rights, nor did its absolute rejection signify respect for the value of the human person (A/C.3/44/SR.52, p. 4).

Ms. Tukan (*Jordan*): According to the Muslim religion, the right to life was sacred and no individual or society had the right to take life away. On religious grounds, therefore, her delegation could not support the abolition of the death penalty (A/C.3/44/SR.52, p. 4).

Mrs. Warzazi (*Morocco*): The draft resolution was addressed to those countries that had already abolished the death penalty, albeit without consulting their populations, and that those countries obviously did not need such an international instrument for themselves. The optional protocol was intended only to exert pressure on other countries to repeal laws designed to protect people. Morocco had not applied the death penalty for a long time . . . (A/C.3/44/SR.52, pp. 4–5).

China's and Japan's 'no' votes were explained as follows:

Ms. Gao Yanping (*China*): While the desire to abolish the death penalty was commendable, it would be impossible to abolish it throughout the world at the present time. The majority of countries maintained the death penalty and even if the draft protocol were adopted and implemented, abolition would not be universal. Supporters of the draft resolution claimed that it did not impose an international obligation or any pressure on other countries, yet it was clear from its final paragraph that further follow-up measures, including pressure on other countries, were likely to follow its adoption. China still imposed the death penalty, the relevant regulations being reflected in the Secretary-General's report in document A/44/592 (A/C.3/44/SR.52, p. 4).

Mr. Ito (*Japan*): The abolition of the death penalty had to be studied very carefully and in the context of the policies and domestic circumstances of each particular State. An international agreement should be universally applicable and it was pointless therefore to have one that would apply only to a limited number of States, views on the death penalty being evenly divided. It would be more appropriate to await the outcome of the debate on that issue currently under way in the Commission on Human Rights (A/C.3/44/SR.52, p. 7).

Algeria's abstention is interesting to note and perhaps reflects some shared objections to the Protocol as a device to universalize the abolition of the death penalty:

Miss Aiouaze (*Algeria*): International legal instruments adopted by the United Nations must reflect the concerns of all Member States if they were to be universal. It was clear, however, that universal action on the proposed optional protocol now before the Committee was impossible. The sponsors of the draft resolution had known that the abolition of capital punishment was highly controversial and that a large number of Member States had resolutely opposed it during the drafting of the optional protocol. More thought should have been given to the advisability of producing a legal instrument which obviously could not win the support of the entire international community. The lack of support could be attributed to the fact that the proposed instrument had taken the form of a protocol of the International Covenant on Civil and Political Rights, thereby appearing to establish a link between capital punishment, which was provided for in the criminal law of many Member States, and one of the human rights enunciated in the Covenant. Such a linkage would in fact go against article 6 of the Covenant. Despite her country's serious reservations on the advisability of the proposed action, her delegation noted that the proposed protocol was optional and would therefore abstain in the vote on the draft resolution (A/C.3/44/ SR.52, p. 3).

The consideration and voting pattern on the Resolution in the full General Assembly (15 December 1989) nearly mirrored the process in the Third Committee (with a marginal increase of 4 votes in favour of the Protocol): 59 yes, 26 no and 48 abstentions.[33]

States voting 'yes' in the General Assembly but 'no' in the Third Committee were: Dominican Republic, Grenada, Paraguay, St Kitts-Nevis, Saint Lucia, St Vincent and the Grenadines. Senegal shifted its vote from 'no' to 'abstention'. Cameroon went from an 'abstention' to a 'no vote'.

The Protocol was opened for signature in spring 1990 (with 10 ratifications needed for it to enter into force).

The impact of the Protocol on international law is still uncertain and will be dependent on the number and nature of ratifying states. None the less, the very existence of the Protocol had precipitated a healthy UN debate revealing states' attitudes towards capital punishment. The voting pattern in the Third Committee and the General Assembly may give some indication as to the support the Second Optional Protocol will receive in the community of nations. If its ratifications parallel the vote in the General Assembly, it is fair to conclude that the positions of the Islamic states, the United States, Japan and China are major stumbling blocks for the conclusion that the abolition of the death penalty is 'emerging' as a universal norm. On the other hand, if the support at the United Nations by European states (both East and West) translates into ratifications, it may be

---

[33] UN doc. Item 98 A/44/824, Resolution 44/128 UN General Assembly 44th Session, Meeting No. 82 (15 December 1989).
    In favour: Argentina, Australia, Austria, Belgium, Bolivia, Brazil, Bulgaria, Byelor-ussian SSR, Canada, Cape Verde, Columbia, Costa Rica, Cyprus, Czechoslovakia, Democratic Kampuchea, Denmark, Dominican Rep., Ecuador, El Salvador, Finland, France, Germany (Democratic Republic of), Germany (Federal Republic of), Greece, Grenada, Guatemala, Haiti, Honduras, Hungary, Iceland, Ireland, Italy, Lux-embourg, Malta, Mexico, Mongolia, Nepal, Netherlands, New Zealand, Norway, Panama, Paraguay, Peru, Philippines, Poland, Portugal, St Kitts-Nevis, Saint Lucia, St Vincent-Gren, Samoa, Spain, Sweden, Togo, Ukrainian SSR, USSR, United Kingdom, Uruguay, Venezuela, Yugoslavia.
    Against: Afghanistan, Bahrain, Bangladesh, Cameroon, China, Djibouti, Egypt, Indonesia, Iran (Islamic Republic of), Iraq, Japan, Jordan, Kuwait, Maldives, Morocco, Nigeria, Oman, Pakistan, Qatar, Saudi Arabia, Sierra Leone, Somalia, Syrian Arab Republic, United Republic of Tanzania, United States, Yemen.
    Abstaining: Algeria, Antigua-Barbuda, Bahamas, Barbados, Bhutan, Botswana, Brunei Dar-Salam, Burkina Faso, Burundi, Chile, Congo, Côte d'Ivoire, Cuba, Dem Yemen, Dominica, Ethiopia, Fiji, Gambia, Ghana, Guinea, Guyana, India, Israel, Jamaica, Kenya, Lebanon, Lesotho, Liberia, Libyan Arab Jamahiriya, Madagascar, Malawi, Mali, Mauritius, Mozambique, Myanmar, Romania, Rwanda, Senegal, Singapore, Solomon Islands, Sri Lanka, Suriname, Trinidad-Tobago, Turkey, Uganda, Vanuatu, Zambia, Zimbabwe.

fair to conclude that the abolitionist position has been significantly strengthened.

Finally, given the broad support for the UN General Assembly Resolution, in addition to European support, it is clear that the winds of abolition are growing in intensity.

7. Summary and conclusions

This chapter has addressed the questions surrounding the legality of capital punishment in international law. Although capital punishment is not prohibited by international law and its abolition has not taken on the characteristics of customary international law or *jus cogens*, its application has been limited.

This view is supported by provisions of the International Covenant on Civil and Political Rights, the judgments of the European Court on Human Rights, and the opinions of the Inter-American Commission on Human Rights, as well as by other international bodies, instruments, judgments and opinions.

The trends towards abolition have been assessed. Some conclusions drawn were:

1. The application and permissible use of capital punishment with international law has been limited and safeguards imposed.
2. There is an increasing trend among Western European states to abolish the death penalty, highlighted by the acceptance of Protocol No. 6 to the European Convention on Human Rights.
3. A similar trend, limiting or abolishing capital punishment, is beginning to develop with some intensity in Eastern Europe.
4. The Inter-American system has made some progressive steps towards abolition but the 'retentionist' (perhaps 'expansionist') position of the United States is a significant obstacle to the creation of a hemispheric regional norm.
5. The drafting and passage of the Second Optional Protocol may be a significant step for an ultimate global prohibition of capital punishment, in the same manner as the Slavery Conventions brought about the eventual international prohibition of slavery. Its passage by the Third Committee and the General Assembly in 1989 is a further step in the elimination of capital punishment. But it is premature to determine the impact of the Protocol until states begin to ratify it. The objections of the Islamic and other retentionist states, e.g. the United States, China, Japan, will be a considerable obstacle to the process.

Bibliography

Amnesty International, 1987. *United States of America. The Death Penalty.* London: Amnesty International Publications.

Amnesty International, 1989a. *Abolition of the Death Penalty in Eastern Europe.*

Amnesty International, 1989b. *Comments Submitted to the European Court of Human Rights on the Soering Case* (1/1989/161/214).

Amnesty International, 1989c. *When the State kills . . . the Death Penalty: a Human Rights Issue.* New York: Amnesty International USA.

Amnesty International, 1989d. *USSR: New Principles of Criminal Law,* Pamphlet EUR 46/03/89.

Annual Report of the Inter-American Commission on Human Rights 1986–1987.

Anttila, Inkeri, 1967. *The Death Penalty in Finland 1967.* New York: Columbia.

Black, Henry Campbell, 1983. *Black's Law Dictionary,* abridged 5th edition. St Paul: West Publishing Co.

Bossuyt, Marc J., 1987. *Analysis Concerning the Proposition to Elaborate a Second Optional Protocol to the International Covenant on Civil and Political Rights Aiming at the Abolition of the Death Penalty,* E/CN.4/Sub.2/1987/20. New York: United Nations.

Brownlie, Ian, 1979. *Principles of Public International Law,* 3rd edition. Oxford: Clarendon Press.

Buergenthal, Thomas, 1988. *International Human Rights in a Nutshell.* St Paul: West Publishing Co.

Concluding Document of the Vienna Meeting 1986 of Representatives of the Conference on Security and Co-operation in Europe. Held on the Basis of the Provisions of the Final Act Relating to the Follow-up to the Conference, 1989.

GDR Committee for Human Rights Bulletin, 1987, vol. 3, no. 2.

Hannikainen, Lauri, 1988. *Peremptory Norms (Jus Cogens) in International Law: Historical Development, Criteria, Present Status.* Helsinki: Finnish Lawyers' Publishing Company.

Hood, Roger, 1989. *The Death Penalty: A World-wide Perspective (A Report to the United Nations Committee on Crime Prevention and Control).* Oxford: Clarendon Press.

Meron, Theodor, 1986. 'On a Hierarchy of Human Rights', *American Journal of International Law,* vol. 80, no. 1.

Meron, Theodor, 1987. 'The Geneva Conventions as Customary Law', *American Journal of International Law,* vol. 81, no. 2.

NAACP Legal Defense and Educational Fund (LDF) Memorandum: *Death Row, U.S.A.,* July 1989.

Orlin, Theodore S., 1990. 'Human Rights' Law in American Domestic Law. A Focus on One Example: the Death Penalty in America', in Allan Rosas (ed.), *International Human Rights Norms in Domestic Law: The Cases of Finland and Poland.* Helsinki: Finnish Lawyers' Publishing Co.

Report of the UN Secretary-General to the Committee on Crime Prevention and Control: Implementation of the United Nations Safeguards Guaranteeing Protection of the Rights of those Facing Death Penalty, 1988 (UN doc. E/AC.57/1988/9).

Tomuschat, Christian, 1986. 'Ethos, Ethics and Morality in International Relations', *Encyclopedia on Public International Law,* Instalment 9, International Relations and Cooperation in General: Diplomacy and Consular Relations. Amsterdam: North-Holland.

Weil, Prosper, 1983. 'Towards Relative Normativity in International Law', *American Journal of International Law*, vol. 77, no. 3.

For further reading, see:
United Nations Social Defence Research Institute, 1988. *The Death Penalty: a Bibliographic Research*, Publication 32. Rome: UNSDRI.

7 The Right to Work

Christian Tomuschat

1. Introduction

All human communities depend for their existence on the work done by their members. Rarely, however, is this simple fact expressed as cogently as in the Italian Constitution of 1948 which states in its very first Article, paragraph 1:

Italy is a democratic Republic founded on labour.

Obviously, this provision is not meant to serve only as a factual description. By stressing that labour constitutes the basis of the life of the Italian State, the framers of the Constitution intended to set forth a guideline to be followed by all branches of government in discharging their functions. Thus, interestingly enough, work has become the centrepiece of the constitutional order of a so-called 'capitalist' state or a state that abstains from directly controlling all economic activities and instead leaves the allocation of means of production to market forces. Drawing the ultimate conclusion from this basic assumption, the Italian Constitution furthermore recognizes the right to work of everyone and proclaims that the Republic shall create the conditions that make this right effective (Article 4, paragraph 1).

The example of the Italian Constitution may suffice to show that the right to work should not be considered a specific and exclusive feature of states under a specific type of political constitution. There is no strict division based on political criteria. In East and West, in North and South the right to work has won broad and almost overwhelming recognition. In particular, the right to work is set forth in a number of international instruments that have been accepted by states from all of the regions of the world. However, some fundamental differences can be perceived as to the precise legal meaning of a right to work. What is its scope and content? In particular: does the right to work imply a right of everyone to be given employment whenever he or she is unable to find such employment on his or her own?

It should not be overlooked that a right to work denotes only one aspect of the overall position of an individual in his or her working environment. Once a person has found employment, the other features — working hours, trade union rights, holidays, maternity leave, etc. — tend to become the main focus of interest. In this respect, the right to work may be viewed as a cluster of rights of which a claimright to be provided with work in case of unemployment constitutes just one element. However, it is precisely this type of social entitlement which has given rise to fundamental controversies between East and West. Until recently it has been maintained that only a socialist state is in a position fully to guarantee employment for everyone, whereas market economies must necessarily fail in this endeavour (Kunz, 1989; Thiel, 1987). On the other hand, it has also been argued that to guarantee a right to work would amount to such massive interference with the rights of others that no valid justification could be found under the liberal regime of a Western democracy (Rath, 1974; Barth, 1976; Schwerdtner, 1977). Among authors from the Federal Republic of Germany and from the German Democratic Republic, the controversy about where the opportunity to work is better secured, has been particularly lively (Golla and Rodenbach, 1986; Kunz, 1988). To ascertain the correctness of such assertions shall be the main objective of the following discussion, although the relatedness of the right to work proper with the surrounding satellite rights will not be forgotten.

2. Legal bases of the right to work

The political consensus surrounding and supporting the right to work has produced numerous legal enactments on the national as well as on the international level. Although many of these provisions are well known, it may none the less be helpful to give a brief account of the main rules which today determine the legal position (see also Sieghart, 1983, p. 214ff.; Kartashkin, 1982, p. 115).

2.1 International instruments

It is the International Labour Organisation (ILO) which, since its establishment in 1919, has aimed at promoting and improving conditions of work for dependent workers. The central ideas underlying the ILO are set forth with particular vigour in the preamble of its Constitution which even establishes a link between social justice and world peace. However, a right to work is not mentioned anywhere in the Constitution of the ILO or in any of the conventions drafted and concluded under its auspices. *Convention No. 122 of 1964 Concerning Employment Policy* is limited to requiring States Parties to formulate and carry out policies suited to promote full employment for everyone. The first legal document on a world-wide scale in which a right to work is openly proclaimed is the *Universal Declaration of Human Rights* (Declaration), adopted by the UN General Assembly on 10

December 1948, more than 40 years ago. Article 23, paragraph 1, of the Declaration reads as follows:

Everyone has the right to work, to free choice of employment, to just and favourable conditions of work and to protection against unemployment.

In spite of many attempts in policy statements (Proclamation of Teheran, 1968, paragraph 2) as well as in legal doctrine to attribute a binding legal character to the Declaration as such,[1] the arguments adduced to support this conclusion are not entirely convincing. One cannot fail to note, first of all, that the two International Covenants of 1966 have remained distinctly below the level of legal guarantees set by the Declaration. Neither the 'right to seek and to enjoy in other countries asylum from persecution' (Article 14, paragraph 1), nor the 'right to a nationality' (Article 15, paragraph 1) or the 'right to own property' (Article 17, paragraph 1) are mentioned in the International Covenant on Civil and Political Rights. Furthermore, in spite of their impressive territorial scope of application, the two Covenants, which embody the substance of the Declaration in legally binding terms, today have been ratified by only slightly more than half of all the states existing at the present time. Under these circumstances, one has some difficulty in arguing that there is a universal *opinio juris* concerning each and every one of the rights laid down in the Declaration. On the other hand, there is no doubt that at least some of its elements have become part and parcel of the corpus of general international law. The right to life and the prohibition against torture do belong to these core elements. No such unequivocal conclusion is possible with regard to the right to work (scepticism expressed by Kühnhardt, 1987, p. 331). None the less, this uncertainty about the legal status of the Declaration cannot detract from the fact that its impact on domestic legal systems can hardly be overrated. Wherever a national Constitution is drawn up today, drafters automatically turn to the Declaration for guidance. At the international level, the competent political bodies of the UN, in particular the Commission on Human Rights, consistently rely on the Declaration to assess the performance of a given state in the field of human rights. To some extent, therefore, it has become irrelevant whether the right to work as proclaimed in Article 23 has become a true right within the meaning of international law.

At the level of a treaty law, the right to work has found its most prominent expression in the *International Covenant on Economic, Social and Cultural Rights* (Economic Covenant). Article 6, paragraph 1, of the Covenant states:

The States Parties of the present Covenant recognize the right to work, which

---

[1]   See, for instance, Carrillo Salcedo (1985, pp. 306-7); Sieghart (1986, pp. 64-5; a more cautious approach is favoured by Buergenthal (1988, pp. 29-33).

includes the right of everyone to the opportunity to gain his living by work which he freely chooses or accepts, and will take appropriate steps to safeguard this right.

In paragraph 2 of Article 6, measures are defined which states are required to take with a view to achieving the full realization of the right to work. These measures correspond closely to the policies and strategies that States Parties to the ILO Convention No. 122 concerning Employment Policy have undertaken to pursue. However, a shift of emphasis cannot be overlooked. Whereas under Article 6 of the Economic Covenant the obligations incumbent upon states are an elaboration on the right to work, the ILO Convention refers to the right to work only in its preambular part and confines itself to enunciating, in its operative part, the obligation of member states to take steps in order to guarantee 'that there is work for all who are available for and seeking work' (Article 1, paragraph 2(a)).

At the *regional level*, Western European nations have agreed upon economic and social rights in the *European Social Charter* of 1961. Although Article 1 in Part II of this instrument is concerned with rights relating to labour, a right to work is not explicitly recognized. In a rather ambiguous fashion, obligations of the States Parties are set forth 'with a view to ensuring the effective exercise of the right to work'. This formula must be read in connection with the propositions in Part I, which succinctly summarize the substance of Part II. In connection with labour, Part I mentions that 'everyone shall have the opportunity to earn his living in an occupation freely entered upon' (paragraph 1) and that 'all workers have the right to just conditions of work' (paragraph 2). Non-discrimination concerning the right to engage in a gainful activity is laid down in paragraph 18 to the benefit of nationals of other Contracting Parties, subject, however, to 'restrictions based on cogent economic or social reasons', a provision which corresponds to the undertaking in Article 18, paragraph 3, of Part II to 'liberalize' the regulations governing the employment of foreign workers. A right to work proper, however, does not figure in the Charter. In fact, in drawing up this instrument, the governments concerned wanted at all costs to avoid granting a true right to work. This is also evident from a number of other provisions of the Charter. Pursuant to the introductory words of Part I, the guarantees enshrined therein have the legal nature of policy aims. The characterization is confirmed by the interpretive understanding concerning Part III, specified in the Appendix of the Charter, according to which the Charter contains

legal obligations of an international character, the application of which is submitted solely to the supervision provided for in Part IV thereof.

In other words, it was the intention of the drafters not to allow individuals to invoke the substance of the Charter. Even if a country has enacted a law of approval, the provisions of the Charter, so it was assumed, are not translated into directly applicable domestic law. However, since ways and means of implementation are left to the sovereign discretion of each country individually, different solutions could evolve in practice.[2] In fact, in the Netherlands, for instance, cautious steps have been taken to attribute a self-executing effect at least to certain rights under the Charter (right to strike, Part II, Article 6, paragraph 4, see Betten and Jaspers, 1988, pp. 132-5). In general, the reluctance of the drafters has greatly hampered effective implementation of the Charter. A further shortcoming is its cumbersome and lengthy monitoring procedure. For that reason, the Charter has barely been able to leave a clear imprint on economic and social life in Western Europe.

A much greater impact must be attributed to the *Treaty Establishing the European Economic Community* (EEC Treaty) provisions on the freedom of movement of migrant workers. The EEC Treaty does not talk of a right to work. But it confers on every Community citizen the right to work everywhere within the entire territory of the twelve member states without any discrimination on grounds of nationality (Article 48). Thus, chances of finding employment are greatly enhanced. The initiative lies with the private individual. It is left to him to explore the labour market and to find out where conditions are best suited for the qualifications which he can offer a possible employer. Even among unemployed people, many would not even think of availing themselves of the opportunities provided to them by the freedom of movement under Article 48 of the EEC Treaty, because moving to a foreign country would mean leaving familiar surroundings. None the less, it cannot be denied that an open international labour market is a clear benefit for the job–seeker who is courageous enough to cope with a loss of his *Heimat*. The recent Declaration of Fundamental Rights and Freedoms, adopted by the European Parliament on 12 April 1989 (*Bulletin of the European Communities* 4-1989, p. 118), does not mention a right to work either. But it emphasizes all those aspects which are connected with freedom to work (Article 12):

1. Everyone shall have the right to choose freely an occupation and a place of work and to pursue freely that occupation.
. . .

3. No one shall be arbitrarily deprived of their work and no one shall be forced to take up specific work.

On the American continents, the right to work appears in the *American Declaration of the Rights and Duties of Man* of 1948, which

---

[2] The self-executing character of a rule of international law within the framework of domestic law can therefore only be determined by the latter, see Tomuschat (1983, pp. 807-11); for a contrary view see Jiménez de Aréchaga (1989, pp. 411-12).

was adopted even before the UN General Assembly approved the Universal Declaration of Human Rights. With great caution, Article XIV, paragraph 1, states:

Every person has the right to work, under proper conditions, and to follow his vocation freely, in so far as existing conditions of employment permit.

No specific guarantees of an economic and social character were, however, included in the *American Convention on Human Rights* of 1969. Quite deliberately, the drafters confined themselves to drawing up a general clause concerning economic and social rights (Article 26). This lacuna was closed only recently. On 14 November 1988, the States Parties to the American Convention adopted an *Additional Protocol on Human Rights in the Area of Economic, Social and Cultural Rights*. Article 6, paragraph 1, of this Protocol provides:

Everyone has the right to work, which includes the opportunity to secure the means for living a dignified and decent existence by performing a freely elected or accepted lawful activity.

In paragraph 2 of this Article it is specified that states are under an obligation to take general measures with a view to making the right to work fully effective. In particular, they shall strive for full employment.

The drafters of the *African Charter on Human and Peoples' Rights* of 1981 were not inhibited by any of the hesitations that ostensibly marked the drafting process in Western Europe as well as in the Americas. In a somewhat summary, though categorical, fashion, Article 15 sets forth:

Every individual shall have the right to work under equitable and satisfactory conditions, and shall receive equal pay for equal work.

Since the Charter entered into force only late in 1986, little can yet be known about its real impact.

2.2 National law

The right to work has also found its way into numerous national constitutions.

As early as the end of the eighteenth century, there were calls for proclaiming a right to work at a constitutional level.[3] During the French Revolution, the responsibility of the community for the

---

[3] For a short history of the right to work see Henning (1983, p. 31ff.); Kuczynski (1978); Kunz (1989, *passim*); Ramm (1983, p. 65ff); Schminck-Gustavus (1978); Tomuschat (1985, p. 47ff.).

destiny of unemployed people was emphasized in the Constitution of
1793 in the following terms (Article 21):

Les secours publics sont une dette sacrée. La société doit la subsistance aux
citoyens malheureux, soit en leur procurant du travail, soit en assurant les
moyens d'exister à ceux qui sont hors d'état de travailler.

However, this Constitution never entered into force and was quickly
forgotten. It would certainly be wrong to conclude, though, that the
bourgeoisie which had won its political battle against the European
monarchies did not care at all for the proletariat. This assumption
certainly has some truth to it. No one has described the sufferings of
the majority of the population more emphatically than Friedrich
Engels in his classical work *'Die Lage der arbeitenden Klasse in
England'* of 1845. It was this antagonism between the many poor and
the few rich that led to the publication of the Communist Manifesto
by Marx and Engels in 1848. It should not be overlooked, on the other
hand, that the governmental mechanisms of the eighteenth century
were hardly able to direct and control the economy in such a way as
to ensure employment for everyone. In spite of their powerful military
machinery, the European states still had to leave the development of
their economies essentially to the autonomous play of market forces.
Economics had not yet reached a sufficient level of sophistication to
enable governments to make systematic and comprehensive
interventions. Thus, to proclaim a right to work for everyone would
have been utterly illusionary and deceptive at the time.

Consequently, although the 'social question' had become ever more
acute during the nineteenth century, the courage to commit the state
formally by setting forth a right to work was found only in the
twentieth century. The first Soviet Constitution of 1918 still confined
itself to stating in fairly crude terms that 'he who does not work,
neither shall he eat'. It was in the Constitution of 1936 that the right
to work appeared for the first time (Article 118). After the Second
World War, many other states followed suit. The right to work
became a standard element of the constitutions of all Eastern
European states. It is now contained, for instance, in Article 40 of the
Constitution of the Soviet Union and in Article 24 of the Constitution
of the German Democratic Republic. Also in Western Europe many
nations abandoned their original inhibitions. The first one to move
ahead was the Weimar Constitution of the German Empire of 1919,
which provided (Article 136, paragraph 2) that 'every German shall
be given the opportunity to earn his living by economic work'. The
aftermath of the world economic crisis in the years from 1929 to 1933
made a mockery of this guarantee. After that, the Irish Constitution
of 1937 laid down a number of 'directive principles of social policy'
(Article 45), mentioning among these in the first place the principle
(2) (i)

that the citizens (all of whom, men and women equally, have the right to an adequate means of livelihood) may through their occupations find the means of making reasonable provision for their domestic needs.

It was explained at the same time that this provision was only intended for the general guidance of Parliament and could not be invoked before any court (Article 45, paragraph 1). Increased boldness was shown immediately after the war by the drafters of the French Constitution of 1946. They proclaimed in the preamble of this Constitution a number of political, economic and social principles 'comme particulièrement nécessaires à notre temps', stating *inter alia*

chacun a le devoir de travailler et le droit d'obtenir un emploi.

Since the preamble of the present Constitution of 1958 refers back to the preamble of the earlier Constitution, this proposition is still part and parcel of positive law in force in France at the present time.

With the entry into force of the Italian Constitution of 1948, a split began between a cautious approach, followed by states in the Northern part of Western Europe, and a more optimistic vision, adopted by states in Southern Europe which felt fewer scruples in setting forth an individual right to work in clear and straightforward language. Starting from the premise that fundamental rights laid down in the Basic Law should be enforceable rights directly binding upon the three branches of government (Article 1, paragraph 3), the drafters of this new constitutional instrument of the Western part of Germany felt that they should generally abstain from guaranteeing social entitlements. Apparently, no such reservations had been entertained when the Italian Constitution was drawn up. The Danish Constitution of 1953, although not evading the issue, carefully avoids speaking of a right of citizens when it states in Article 75, paragraph 1, that

in order to advance the public weal efforts should be made to afford work to every able-bodied citizen on terms that will secure his existence.

Similarly, the Norwegian Constitution (Article 110 as amended in 1954), the Swedish Constitution of 1975/76 as well as the new Dutch Constitution of 1983 (Article 19) are limited to stating broad policy goals which can in no way be understood as endowing the individual with any subjective rights. In contrast, Finland in 1972 amended Article 6, paragraph 2, of its Constitution by a new second sentence. The entire paragraph now reads:

The labour of the citizens shall be under the special protection of the State. Unless otherwise decreed, the State shall, when necessary, provide a citizen of Finland with an opportunity to be gainfully employed.

In spite of this wording, the Constitutional Committee of the Finnish

Parliament ruled in 1980 that the employment clause, whose legally binding force was not in doubt, could not be relied upon to file a suit against the state.[4] In any event, the text of the Finnish Constitution is close to the most recent Constitutions of the Mediterranean countries Portugal (1976, Article 59) and Spain (1978, Article 35), which frame the right to work as a true individual right. Less explicit is Article 22 of the Greek Constitution of 1976, whose precise legal meaning has not yet been clarified.

3. Social significance of a right to work

To many, the importance of the right to work seems so evident that in most legal discussions no need is felt to focus attention on the policy reasons underlying its formal recognition. Not all of these reasons are easily detectable, though. Consequently, it seems worthwhile to inquire into the social foundations of the right to work.

A good place to start is with the famous words from the Bible:

In the sweat of thy face shalt thou eat bread (Genesis 3, 19).

Condensed into one short sentence, these words provide a clear reference to labour as the means of ensuring man's existence, his survival in a world that does not provide him with a natural habitat.[5] Today, the main function of work is still to generate the necessary means of subsistence. In societies where inherited fortunes either do not exist at all or are generally fairly modest, few if any people can simply live on the revenues accruing to them from such assets. Normally, in order to earn a living, a person must work. To be sure, many developed societies, including almost all of the Western states, have developed social welfare systems. It is generally felt that it is the responsibility of the community not to let anybody starve. The International Covenant on Economic, Social and Cultural Rights embodies these ideas in Articles 9 and 11. It must be acknowledged, however, that such welfare schemes are invariably established at rather low levels. Whoever depends on general welfare programmes certainly receives coverage of basic needs, but cannot pretend to anything that goes beyond minimum levels. Therefore, the guarantee of the right to work can be considered a guarantee designed to ensure, through one's own efforts, the material conditions for a meaningful life in human dignity.

A second element goes far beyond the basic aspect of ensuring the material existence of a person. Human beings exist as much by themselves as through the activities which they perform in society.

---

[4]   For an extensive review of the provision see Karapuu and Rosas (1988, p. 38ff.).
[5]   This is the starting point of Locke's reasoning on the relationship between labour and property (1690, book II, Chapter V).

Man shapes his identity by dealing with his environment and looking for adequate responses to the many challenges confronting him in his daily life. Whoever is denied the opportunity to work lacks important possibilities to broaden his or her experience of the world. It is through work that a human being defines and develops his or her specific personality, gains an insight into the mechanisms of society and thus also learns how to participate fully in the life of the nation.[6] Any praise of work as being the distinctive feature of man must go hand in hand with a word of caution, however. Those who are not able to work, the mentally insane, the disabled, the elderly and the aged, neither lose their human dignity nor can be considered less valuable members of society. One may simply conclude that whoever is able to work enjoys a great privilege which should be made full use of for his or her personal benefit as well as for the benefit of the communities to which he or she belongs.

Lastly, social recognition depends to a great extent on a person's social involvement in performing useful work. Unemployed people are frequently looked at with some mistrust, even if being out of job is not attributable to any faulty behaviour on their part. Although the use of employment as a measure of social appreciation may be an aberration of the industrialized societies of our epoch, this pattern none the less cannot be denied. It also explains why work is given such high priority in the hierarchy of values upheld today.

4. Legal significance of the right to work

In order not to become the victim of political pitfalls, one should be extremely clear about the possible meaning and scope of a right to work. As was already shown in the beginning, it can by no means be considered a peculiar and exclusive feature of socialist societies. On closer examination it emerges that similarities and parallels between Eastern and Western societies are much larger than is usually assumed in ideologically inspired writings from the two 'camps'.

4.1 The right to choose and to perform work without hindrance

The right to work is a truly ambiguous concept according to its textual configuration. On the one hand, it denotes the right of everyone to use his or her abilities in order to do work without interference. One may call this aspect the active element of the right to work or simply the freedom to work. In the German language, one often speaks of a *Recht zur Arbeit*. Article 6 of the Economic

---

[6] For a recent apology of work from a socialist viewpoint see Campbell (1983, p. 171ff.). See also Baruzzi (1983, p. 35ff.).

Covenant clearly encompasses this dimension of the right to work in stating that everyone shall have the opportunity to gain a living by work 'which he freely chooses or accepts'. Or to put it differently: the individual is guaranteed the right not only to secure his or her livelihood as an employed worker, but also to pursue economic activities as a self-employed person. Additionally, the right to work can be understood as a right to be provided with work, to be given a job by an employer. It is this last aspect that normally attracts primary attention in legal writings.

In the first place, the right to work requires states not to prevent human beings from working. Normally, of course, no government is interested in establishing such prohibitions. The wealth and the well-being of a nation have their foundations in the labour which its citizens are able to perform. But legal impediments may derive from discriminatory practices (see *infra* 4.2) or affect the individual as a consequence of regimes which combine the right to work with a duty to work. In many socialist states, there existed in the past penal laws making 'parasitism' a punishable offence. Freely chosen activities as a writer, a painter or a poet were not recognized as 'true' work, so that the persons concerned were placed under a constant threat of prosecution and imprisonment. Rightly, therefore, the ILO Committee of Experts has consistently condemned such punitive practices,[7] which now seem to have terminated. The right to work, according to all relevant international texts, is to be understood as a right to perform the specific type of professional activity which the individual determines by his own free will. Thus, the scope of the right to work and that of the prohibition of forced or compulsory labour overlap in an important way.

In many countries, legislation enacted with a view to protecting women (prohibition of night work or of work requiring great physical strength) may turn out to be detrimental to them. No serious objections can be levelled against well-considered restrictions which conform to unchallengeable medical findings. Concern for the health of women should not be used as a pretext, however, to create and defend labour monopolies for men. Protection may degenerate quite easily into discrimination.

The freedom to work and to ensure one's livelihood through gainful activity as a self-employed person constitutes an important component of the right to work. Statistically, it may appear be be a right of only secondary rank. In the Federal Republic of Germany, for instance, roughly one–tenth of the active population makes up the group of self-employed persons. One may assume that the situation is largely the same in other Western Europe states. In spite of these

---

[7]   See for instance International Labour Conference, 70th Session 1984, Report III (part 4 A), Report of Committee of Experts on the Application of Conventions and Recommendations, p. 97ff.).

modest figures, the freedom to work on one's own behalf constitutes an important guarantee of personal independence and autonomy. It protects everyone against dependence on the will — and, maybe also the whims, the fancies, and the prejudices — of potential employers. Any person who has the necessary qualifications can in the last resort attempt to establish his or her own business. Thus, freedom to work assumes also a political function. It belongs to those checks that restrain the power of the state in the economy.

No lengthy elaboration is needed to show that this specific dimension of the right to work is more effective in the free market economies of the West than in the centrally planned economies of socialist states. In economies subject to bureaucratic planning procedures, there is normally little room for private initiative; at least, this has been the situation in the past. One certainly cannot deny that the International Covenant on Economic, Social and Cultural Rights does not curtail the right of states to organize their economies as they see fit, either opting for a market economy, or establishing a system that puts means of production into the hands of the state, or a combination of the two systems. Freedom to work is limited from the very outset by the peculiarities of either system. The fact that the freedom to work in a self-employed capacity has so little breathing space in socialist systems can by no means be called an infringement of Article 6 of the Economic Covenant. But it remains that market economies, which pre-suppose and encourage private economic activities, provide a much better framework for rendering the freedom to work effective.

4.2 A right to be provided with work?

Does the right to work, understood as a social entitlement mean that an individual has an enforceable right to be given a job corresponding to his or her specific qualifications, or simply any job? The Economic Covenant is very clear in this respect. It does not recognize such a right, neither in its modest nor in its full-fledged form. The obligations undertaken by states in ratifying the Covenant are defined in Article 6, paragraph 2. According to this provision, states are required to take steps of a general nature for the promotion and fostering of conditions that permit the realization of full employment. States are not obliged *vis-à-vis* the individual. Work for everyone is stated as a goal that states must strive for by all reasonable means. Thus used, the notion of a right to work to express a binding commitment for states is a somewhat bold way of beautifying a modest, but by no means insignificant, legal proposition. In fact, even if governments are not obligated to attain a specific result, they are still required to promote the objective of full employment by engaging their best endeavours.[8] A policy which would openly acknowledge that it does not care for the destiny of the unemployed would run counter to the obligation enshrined in Article 6, paragraph 2, of the Economic Covenant. 'Thatcherism' as a political ideology may have come close to the fatal brink. In actual terms, however, the British Government has always maintained that it was striving for full employment as one of its main policy goals (*Case Law on the European Social Charter*, 1982, p. 2).

It is this weakness of the right to work as a social entitlement that has led critics of economic and social rights to challenge its nature as true human rights. Maurice Cranston is one of the most eloquent representatives of this sceptical school of legal thought. To his mind, human rights are only those rights that may be derived directly from the dignity of man, of which everyone — and not only a specific class of individuals — is a holder and which everyone may enforce through the courts (Cranston, 1973, p. 66ff.). His reasoning is biased, however, in that his criticism centres mainly on the right of 'periodic holidays with pay', which Article 7 (d) of the Economic Covenant solemnly proclaims, and which was inspired by a mood of boundless optimism that has long since left us and is now considered simply an expression of naiveté. In order to buttress better his position, Cranston should have dealt with the right of work as the centrepiece of economic and social rights that cannot be 'killed' by a few sarcastic observations. As has been shown, there is a direct link between the basic concept of human dignity and the right to work. Thus, the right to work, to employ the words of Cranston (1973, p. 68) himself, is 'something of which no one may be deprived without a grave affront to justice'.

Among Western states that have included the right to work in their Constitutions, not a single one views this guarantee as conferring on an individual the right to be provided with employment. They all follow the lines of Article 6 of the Economic Covenant, interpreting the 'right to work' as committing the entire machinery of the state to deploy its best efforts for securing full employment. A 1957 judgment of the Italian Constitutional Court[9] held that the constitutional guarantee of the right to work amounted to a recognition at the constitutional level of the social importance of labour, intended to induce the competent legislative bodies to take all appropriate action. In a later judgment of 1965[10] it was added that the right to work gave neither a right to be afforded with a position nor a right to preserve

---

[8]　See the 'Limburg Principles', which were adopted by a private expert meeting convened under the auspices of the International Commission of Jurists in June 1986, *The Review of the International Commission of Jurists*, vol. 37 (1986, p. 43, §§ 16–24).

[9]　*Corte costituzionale*, judgment of 16 January 1957. *Raccolta ufficiale*, vol. 2 (1957), p. 21 (27).

[10]　*Corte costituzionale*, judgment of 26 May 1965, *Raccolta ufficiale*, vol. 21 (1965), p. 397 (403).

one's employment. Nowhere has constitutional jurisprudence interpreted the right to work as a right to be given a job. Indeed, such a construction would have necessitated implementing legislation. Such legislation seems to exist only in Finland and Sweden, which do not recognize the right to work as a true enforceable right. In both countries, municipalities are under an obligation to set up labour schemes for unemployed young people under 25 years of age and people already out of work for periods (Finland) or for unemployed youths between 18 and 20 (Sweden). Obviously, at the local level only limited types of jobs can be created. It has been reported from Sweden that teams are formed and that work is carried out that normally would not be performed (Källström, 1988, p. 103). One is thus far from the idea of providing employment specifically tailored to the wishes and qualifications of the persons concerned.

In examining the relevant rules enacted in socialist states by way of ordinary legislation, one finds that the legal position is not entirely dissimilar. According to official comments on the ways and means by which the right to work becomes effective, the individual exercises his or her right by concluding a work contract.[11] In other words, it is necessary to find an employer who is prepared to accept, and pay for, his or her services. The individual cannot resort to a formalized mechanism if no offer is made. Apparently, until now socialist systems have proceeded from the assumption that their economies are likely to produce enough job opportunities, directed as they are by a centralized bureaucracy that cares more intensely about the fate of job–seekers than does a capitalist system. In addition, protection against dismissal has been pushed to a high level of effectiveness.[12] Whoever has been able to join the labour force can normally feel safeguarded against the threat of losing his or her job. Against this background, one may find it understandable that in socialist countries no comprehensive system of assistance for dealing with cases of unemployment has been established. Also legal writers in the West that have analysed the operation of the socialist economic systems have concluded that it is 'easy' for a socialist state to safeguard the right to work of its citizens because it controls all means of production.[13]

Comparisons between the rates of joblessness in the East and the West are often referred to as evidence that the key element is the comprehensive control of the economy by the socialist state. In fact, in many Western states the percentage of unemployment remains at frightening levels, sometimes surpassing even a threshold of 10 per cent. By contrast, socialist states have until recently reported that they had reached full employment or quasi-full employment. At the

---

[11] See *Arbeitsrecht von A-Z*, entry *'Recht auf Arbeit'* (1987, p. 292); Lohmann (1987, p. 29).
[12] See, for instance §§ 54 *et seq.* of the Labour Code of the German Democratic Republic.
[13] Däubler (1978, p. 170); Riedel (1986, pp. 48, 138); Westen (1983, p. 135).

present juncture, however, many illusions have been put to rest. Open discussion has begun in socialist states on whether it might be necessary to allow at least a modest degree of unemployment in order to facilitate a process of modernization in which workers can move among sectors of the economy, and some first measures in this direction have been taken. Additionally, it has been disclosed that in some parts of the Soviet Union there exists widespread unemployment with millions of people vainly looking for a job.[14] Concerning free market economies, on the other hand, one cannot fail to observe that there are a number of countries in which unemployment is virtually non-existent. Luxembourg, Sweden, and Switzerland may be counted as belonging to this privileged group of countries. Furthermore, closer scrutiny of statistical data from countries where unemployment rates have reached high levels and seem to remain at stable plateaus often shows that unemployment does not constitute a general phenomenon. In many sectors, demand cannot be satisfied, whereas unqualified labour in particular finds hardly any job opportunities. It has thus become misleading just to compare general figures without a detailed breakdown. One should therefore take a fresh look at the factual circumstances that condition the success or the failure of full employment policies.

4.3 Non-discrimination

A largely unexplored element of the right to work is the element of non-discrimination by which it, like any other human right, is characterized. The International Covenant on Economic, Social and Cultural Rights explicitly confers the right to work on 'everyone', and it is clear from Article 2, paragraph 3, that in fact the Covenant simply means what it says. Generally, the right to work is not confined to nationals, but rather, its benefits are also bestowed upon aliens. Only developing countries are exempted from the obligations to extend the right to non-nationals. In addition, the usual non-discrimination clause applies. Any discrimination as to race, colour, sex, language, religion, political or other opinion, national or social origin, property, birth or other status is forbidden (Article 2, paragraph 2). In addition, it should be noted that the jurisprudence of the Human Rights Committee has interpreted Article 26 of the International Covenant on Civil and Political Rights (equal protection of the law and non-discrimination) as extending also to rights of an economic and social character.[15] Discrimination is also banned

---

[14] Report in *Frankfurter Allgemeine Zeitung*, 23 November 1989, with quotations from Soviet periodicals.
[15] Views of 9 April 1987 in case *Zwaan-de Vries*, communication 182/1984 [Eleventh] Report of the Human Rights Committee, GAOR 42nd session (UN doc. A/42/40), p. 160.

under Article 1 of the ILO Convention (No. 111) concerning Discrimination in Respect of Employment and Occupation. Special emphasis has been placed in the International Convention on the Elimination of All Forms of Racial Discrimination of 1965 (Article 5 (e) (i)) as well as in the Convention on the Elimination of All Forms of Discrimination against Women of 1979 (Article 11) on committing States Parties to combat and do away with any kind of discrimination in employment. Finally, the Concluding Document of the 1989 Vienna CSCE Conference also stresses (principle 13.7) that the enjoyment of all human rights and fundamental freedoms shall be ensured to everyone 'without distinction of any kind', listing the forbidden grounds of discrimination by literally reproducing the words employed by the two Covenants of 1966.

Although the Economic Covenant generally contains only promotional obligations, this characterization is not true of all its stipulations. The prohibition of discrimination is a case in point. Although states are not placed under a strict obligation fully to realize all the aims listed in the provisions of the Covenant as individual rights, they must refrain from practising any kind of forbidden discrimination if and when they take measures for the fulfilment of their duties. The rationale underlying the 'soft' character of the bulk of these duties does not apply here. States may not have the financial means to set up a mechanism of social security; but they are always in a position to refrain from discriminatory practices.[16]

The ways in which the right to work has been affected in the past through methods of discrimination are well known. In socialist countries, in the first decade after the Second World War, members of the former elites and their descendants generally suffered invidious treatment on a massive scale. In particular, children from such families were denied access to institutions of higher education.[17] At no such time has it been uncommon for political dissidents to be dismissed from their jobs on pretexts that hardly anyone believed. In Czechoslovakia, sanctions against opponents of the regime were particularly harsh after a dissident movement dared to raise its head in 1977 ('Charter 77'). For many years, the present foreign minister, Jiri Dienstbier, had to work as a stoker.[18] It is another sad fact that people applying for authorization to leave their country have often suffered similar fates, immediately losing their jobs but having to wait for months or even years before being granted the requested emigration visas. Such punitive action is simply inconsistent with

---

[16] Rightly emphasized in the 13 April 1973 Explanatory Report of the Federal Government concerning the Economic Covenant, *Bundesrats-Drucksache* 305/73, p. 17, and confirmed by the Limburg Principles (note 8), §§ 22, 35.

[17] For a personal report by a victim see *Bonner General-Anzeiger*, 27 December 1989, p. 31.

[18] *Frankfurter Allgemeine Zeitung*, 14 December 1989, p. 16.

the non-discrimination clauses of the Economic Covenant. Standards applied by bodies of the ILO are sometimes so strict that even the Federal Republic of Germany was found to be in breach of its obligations under ILO Convention No. 111 concerning Discrimination in Respect of Employment and Occupation in generally preventing members of extremist parties, including the communist party, from having access to public service.[19]

Even more generally, some of the practices in which Western states have engaged and are still engaging are legally doubtful at best. The Covenant does not specify the relationship that is required between the enjoyment of the rights it sets forth and the nature of a person's stay in any of the Contracting Parties' territories. It would seem reasonable to assume that most of the rights presuppose a stable right of sojourn in the country concerned. No foreign traveller in transit through an airport can expect to be covered by social security (Article 9). Nor can a short sojourn by a tourist trigger the enjoyment of all the rights of the Covenant. But in the case of a more extended stay in the territory of a Contracting Party, at some point a threshold is reached beyond which this state cannot go on denying the benefits of the Covenant to a non-national. One can only note the fact that the potential of the Economic Covenant has not yet been discovered by the legal community. It would appear that almost all countries take it for granted that they have retained full powers to regulate the economic activity of aliens within their borders as they see fit. This prevailing view does not seem to be in harmony with the requirements of Article 6 of the Economic Covenant, read in conjunction with the non-discrimination clauses of Article 2. To be sure, in contradistinction to the Treaty Establishing the European Economic Community, the Economic Covenant does not enjoin states to open their borders to citizens from other Contracting Parties. Once they are legally established, however, the wording of Article 6, paragraph 1, applies, according to which 'everyone' shall have the opportunity to gain his or her living by work.

The legal position is different under the European Social Charter. The Charter uses fairly guarded wording in referring to the right to engage in a gainful occupation in the territory of another contracting state. It simply provides that the regulations governing the employment of foreign workers shall be liberalized. Thus, from the very outset a clear distinction is drawn between nationals and aliens.

---

[19] Report of the Commission of Inquiry appointed under Article 26 of the Constitution of the International Labour Organisation to examine the observance of the Discrimination (Employment and Occupation) Convention, 1958 (No. 111) by the Federal Republic of Germany, of 26 November 1986, 5 December 1986, 3 February 1987, ILO doc. GB.235/4/7, commented upon by Manin (1988). The European Court of Human Rights did not examine the merits of two applications which had been submitted to it in this respect: *Glasenapp and Kosiek* cases, judgments of 28 August 1986, Publ. E.C.H.R., Series A, vols. 104 and 105 (1986).

Such a distinction is not recognized by the Economic Covenant, so that one can only argue about whether its prohibition of discrimination against aliens is to be understood strictly or whether, on reasonable grounds, some restrictions are permitted.[20]

A particularly delicate case in point is provided by the case of asylum-seekers. In the Federal Republic of Germany, for example, the right of asylum is granted by Article 16, paragraph 2, of the Basic Law to any person persecuted on political grounds. Asylum-seekers also have a right to pursue their alleged right of asylum by all available judicial remedies, eventually taking their case to the Constitutional Court. These procedures may be extremely time-consuming. People may have to wait for years until they obtain a definitive determination regarding their applications. During all this time (up to five years), they are prohibited from working, based on the rationale that there should be no incentive for abusive applications. Thus *Wohltat wird zur Plage*: the seemingly grandiose gesture of providing a right of asylum and additionally the right to take judicial remedies become a trap for the asylum-seeker, whose capacities to lead an active and productive life may easily disintegrate through a passivity lasting several years. Is the right to work not also intended to safeguard the autonomy and potential self-reliance of a human being?[21] It seems clear that in any event a period of five years exceeds any reasonable limits. Only extremely strong and exceptional characters would be able to keep their working capacity intact during such a long time. Arguments to the effect that the stay of an asylum-seeker is only of a factual nature or that it is only semi-legal miss the relevant point, namely that an individual, irrespective of the legal status of his or her stay in the country concerned, inevitably suffers heavy damage by being forcibly kept away from the labour market for a good part of his or her life.[22]

5. Factual background of the right to work

There is hardly any field of legal research where the reader has experiences as frustrating as those connected with studies devoted to the right to work. Many books and articles take a narrow dogmatic look at the relevant issues and hardly take into account concrete

---

[20] See Explanatory Report (note 16), p. 18; Schiedermair and Wollenschläger (1989, section 3 B, points 4–6); Zuleeg (1974, p. 328).

[21] The relevant jurisprudence in the Federal Republic of Germany has never referred, in this connection, to Article 6 of the Economic Covenant.

[22] In a resolution of 12 March 1987, operative paragraph 1(p), the European Parliament has requested that access to the labour market be given to asylum-seekers after the expiry of six months, *Official Journal of the European Communities*, 1987, C99, p. 167.

facts.[23] Indeed, until recently the right to work was one of the preferred battlegrounds of the ideological struggle between East and West. Authors from Eastern Europe generally attempted to demonstrate the superiority of the socialist system which, they claimed, was able to provide full job security. Recent events in Eastern Europe have cast many doubts on such contentions. It has emerged that even centrally planned states are no almighty leviathans. It has also become clear that many citizens of these countries would much prefer to work and earn their wages in Western societies. Thus, the time seems to have come for a more sober analysis of the different elements that either promote or hamper full employment. In particular, one should simply acknowledge that every employer, be he part of a socialist or a market economy, holds power because he may hire a person — or else may refuse to do so or dismiss a worker. This dichotomy can never be overcome. But legislation may usefully limit the powers of the employer, making him accountable or conferring specific rights of participation on trade unions. It is in the light of these considerations that in the following sections a few issues will be highlighted that are specifically topical for the right to work.

5.1 Employment and education policies

Employment policies cannot be detached from education policies. In Western countries, it is essentially left to high school graduates to choose the areas in which they wish to study or to undergo vocational training, provided they possess the requisite qualifications. States dispose of few, if any, instruments capable of channelling applicants to fields where society needs a fresh supply of labour. This situation is disliked by governments. Thus, very recently it was suggested in the Federal Republic of Germany that the number of places available in medical schools should be reduced to curtail the excessive output of young doctors every year. Such planning in order to adjust supply and demand of the national community constitutes a novel idea, however. Until now, it was usually felt that students should have a right to enrol themselves in whatever discipline they might choose. The *numerus clausus* regulations of the past, some of which still exist at the present time, have not been justified by an alleged necessity to restrict the number of admissions to the number needed to replace the retiring members of a given profession. Instead they were simply considered a transitional measure dictated by a shortage in teaching

---

[23] See Kuczynski (1978, p. 27): 'No one would dream of saying that a stone has the right to fall to the ground when it has been thrown up into the air because it is acting in accordance with the law of gravity; likewise, one ought not to speak of a right to work under socialism because in accordance with the laws of this system, there is work for all.' As little helpful is the article by Thiel (1987).

capacities, given an excessive number of applications.[24] It must be admitted that these official explanations are not free of ambiguity. In providing funds to universities, state parliaments and ministerial departments in the Federal Republic of Germany have always taken into account, *inter alia*, forecasts concerning community requirements. None the less, they have never been given the power to enforce a policy of matching demand for admission to educational establishments with forecasts of replacement figures.

In socialist countries, the picture seems to be different. According to information whose accuracy has not been challenged, each institution of education or vocational training accepts no more than the contingent of students or trainees that, according to prognostic assessments, will be needed on the labour market once the education is completed.[25] Thus, job security is to a great extent secured through expectations of the probable evolution of the labour market. Such calculations may prove to be erroneous. But at least they effectively prevent a situation whereby tens of thousands of young people are educated and trained for activities that they will never in their lives be able to perform.

This basic discrepancy may not be overlooked in comparing labour statistics from the East and West. Long ago, in the Federal Republic of Germany it was observed that very few teachers would be required during the 1980s and 1990s, due to the dramatically low birth rate of the country. In spite of this basic fact, which was publicized throughout the media, thousands of students chose to acquire a degree as teachers. Many of these former students are now unemployed. It is hard to see how a state can cope with this type of situation. If no teachers are needed, no teachers can be hired. To do otherwise would amount to a waste of public money that the public in a democratic society would not condone.

5.2 The interrelationship between national economies and the international economic situation

The second element to be borne in mind is the high degree of dependence of Western economies on the development of world markets. The member states of the European Economic Community and of the European Free Trade Association have widely opened their doors to foreign imports. They themselves do not produce goods just for closed national markets, but act within the framework of a larger European or even the world market. Economic repercussions

---

[24] *Bundesverfassungsgericht*, judgment of 18 July 1972, *Entscheidungen des Bundesverfassungsgerichts*, vol. 33, p. 303 (329ff.).

[25] Article 24 of the GDR Constitution makes the right to employment subject to 'social requirements'. On this basis, a regulation on professional guidance (*Berufsberatung und Berufslenkung*) was enacted in 1955, see Kunz (1989, p. 80).

from these markets beyond national frontiers are manifold and essentially uncontrollable. Yet, it is only through these transnational connections that Western economies have been able to reach the level of material well-being that now seems to have become their sign of distinction. Therefore, governments cannot simply turn around and adopt a totally different orientation of their economic systems, even less so since no better alternative is in sight. Competition in markets beyond national boundaries exposes industries to rapid changes. From day to day, adjustments have to be made. No sector can rest on its laurels. Branches that lose an edge of competitiveness are quickly squeezed out of the market, with all the related hardships for employment. Steel and coal industries, for instance, were much in demand 20 years ago, but have lost most of their workforce during the last two decades. Workers that were made redundant had to be absorbed by other more successful sectors. It is hard to believe that any state–controlled system can do better and relieve the economy and its workforce of the heavy burden of this constant adjustment, which necessarily entails periods of unemployment for many.

5.3 Limits of state power

It is a matter of common knowledge that most states, in particular states in the Third World, still lack the technical capacity to control the economies of their countries. Industrialized nations, by enacting appropriate legislation and establishing complex administrative systems involving injunctions and prohibitions, could *à la rigueur* push everyone into occupation, even against any economic logic, where no real need exists to increase levels of employment. Third World governments in many regions of the globe are satisfied if they merely succeed in keeping their countries together. Difficult processes of nation-building would be made impossible or would be gravely compromised by excessive demands on potential private employers. In agrarian societies, such a class of employers is simply lacking. For these reasons alone, many governments are utterly unable to undertake a guarantee of full employment. Even the Soviet Union has not succeeded in securing full employment in a number of peripheral areas, especially in the Central Asian Republics.

5.4 Modernization of the economy

During the last decade, in particular, Western economies to a greater extent than socialist systems have undergone rapid changes. In general, economic structures have become more complex due to the introduction of modern techniques of data processing. The rise of information systems has made it possible to construct machines that discharge functions formerly performed by human workers, and accordingly the demand for unskilled labour has tremendously decreased. In almost all professions, even at the lowest levels, some solid knowledge about machines and their handling is necessary. Whoever is able to do no more than take a shovel and dig a hole can hardly have any hope these days of finding employment. By the same token, unfortunately, chances for handicapped individuals have also plummeted dramatically.

5.5 Demand for work

Lastly, it should not be overlooked that the demand for work is not a stable factor. In modern societies deeply marked by individualism, families have shrunk in size — if they exist at all. As both a premise and a consequence of this development, the wish to engage in a gainful occupation has become almost universal. There is hardly anyone who does not look for a paid job. In general, the rate of housewives in the overall population is constantly declining. Thus, the pressures on the labour market tend to become stronger, thereby rendering more difficult the task of governments to secure employment for all.

6. Satellite rights

If an individual right to be given employment according to one's capabilities and specifications largely belongs to a sphere of utopian and wishful thinking, this does not mean that governments lack the power to provide individuals with work. In fact, many types of measures can be instituted for the purpose of promoting and fostering real enjoyment of the pledge expressed by setting forth a right to work. Leaving aside all policies and strategies designed to stimulate growth in general, only those steps that directly affect the individual will be considered.

6.1 Vocational training

A basic deficiency of many economies is that demand is not matched by supply. First of all, at the present time, one can generally note a definite lack of qualified labour, whereas unskilled workers are too numerous in the face of shrinking demand. This is probably true of Western as well as socialist economic systems. A specific feature of Western systems, however, seems to be the fact that many youths choose professions in which they are not needed. Although in most instances such erroneous choices could have been avoided by the victims themselves, states should not leave young people alone in their efforts to acquire the qualifications that markets require.

Rightly, therefore, the Economic Covenant stresses (Article 6, paragraph 2) that steps to be taken by states shall include 'technical and vocational guidance and training programmes'. Similarly, ILO Convention No. 122 concerning Employment Policy states that there should be 'the fullest possible opportunity for each worker to qualify for . . . a job for which he is well suited' (Article 1, paragraph 2, (c)).[26] Many states can boast impressive accomplishments in this regard. It would require a detailed examination to assess the pros and cons of such schemes in order to make recommendations if shortcomings can be found. It is only by raising the level of education that mankind can hope effectively to deal with the many challenges which are already confronting it and which will become even more dramatic in the future.

6.2 Protection against dismissal from work

It may also be inferred from the right to work that workers should enjoy protection against arbitrary dismissals at short notice. Dismissals cannot be avoided altogether. Systems that totally hinder dismissals or make them practically impossible generally suffer serious economic drawbacks. Absolute or quasi-absolute protection favours the *beati possidentes* ('work owners') and operates to the detriment of youths; enterprises are prevented from adjusting to changing circumstances. Thus, in many socialist countries, there may have been overprotection in the past. Enterprises could not even make redundant workers who openly demonstrated their laziness and did not comply with any rules of labour discipline. But no one should have to face unemployment from one moment to the next. Reasonable periods are required to defer the dates at which a notice of dismissal may take effect. Workers must be able to look during that time for a new job. An employer who has hired someone assumes responsibility for the employee by and through the act of hiring. He cannot legitimately claim that he should be free unconditionally to rid himself of a worker whose services he no longer needs. Therefore, the obligation to give prior notice well ahead cannot be considered an excessive burden to him. In this respect, the law of the United States seems to be marred by inherent flaws. It is clear, too, that the elderly need specific protection against dismissal from work. Care must also be taken to secure that dismissals which have become economically necessary are not conducted in a way that infringes the principles of equality and non-discrimination.[27] Legally accepted grounds for dismissal should always be work-related. Lastly, to deny a worker the

---

[26] See also the Human Resources Development Convention (No. 142), and Recommendation (No. 150), adopted by the ILO in 1975.

[27] See also the Termination of Employment Recommendation (No. 119), adopted by the ILO in 1963.

usual protection because he does not belong to a specific trade union would also appear to amount to an infringement of the right to work. In *Young, James and Webster*, the European Court of Human Rights held that pressure either to join a trade union or to accept dismissal from employment resulted in a violation of Article 11 of the European Convention on Human Rights.[28] Since the right to work does not figure in the European Convention, the aspects which are relevant in the present context could not be dealt with by the Court.

Since employment is such an essential element of anyone's situation as an individual and as a member of society, judicial protection is imperative in all instances of dismissal. A person who has been dismissed from a job should always have the right to appeal the decision of his or her employer before an impartial tribunal, in accordance with the requirements laid down in Article 14, paragraph 1, of the International Covenant on Civil and Political Rights.

6.3 Unemployment insurance

All states should be required to establish schemes of assistance for unemployed individuals. If one takes the view that unemployment is at least inevitable as a transitional phenomenon, then a jobless person appears as a victim who makes a sacrifice for the common good, and thus enables the market forces to shift manpower to those sectors of the economy where actual requirements exist. No one should be excessively frightened by such periods of redundancy. Only if an individual is sufficiently supported by the community can that individual without too much external pressure look for a new job commensurate with his or her skills. In Western systems, all of which have created such schemes, the additional question arises of how long a person should be entitled to unemployment benefits before having to rely on general social assistance programmes. Another issue is what kind of job an individual must be considered duty-bound to accept in order to evade exclusion from such benefits. In Scandinavian countries, the main problems have been connected with offers of work in places located high up in the north. A more general difficulty has to be dealt with in all instances where a person is required to take a down-graded job that ranks far below his or her level of knowledge and skills. Here, the relevant international documents do not provide concrete solutions. It must be left to the practice of the relevant international monitoring bodies to strike a reasonable balance between the interests of the unemployed and the interests of the community. It is obvious that excessive rigour may eventually lead to a violation of the prohibition of forced or compulsory labour.

---

[28] Judgment of 13 August 1981, Publ. E.C.H.R., Series A, vol. 44 (1981), p. 26, paragraph 65.

6.4 Handicapped and uneducated persons

The weakest group among job-seekers is handicapped individuals. The more sophisticated and economic system becomes, the more difficult it becomes to integrate these people into the labour process. Mentally retarded or brain damaged persons, in particular, can only work in fairly simple jobs where they must be placed under constant supervision. A precise cost-benefit analysis rarely speaks to their advantage. Notwithstanding its frailty, this group must not be left alone to cope with its problems. A truly civilized society, whose members do not invoke human rights solely for their direct benefit, but which takes seriously the basic premise that human rights derive from human dignity, may be measured by its preparedness effectively to assist handicapped people in their efforts to become and to remain, to the greatest extent possible, autonomous and self-reliant members of society, on a par with all other citizens.[29] Unfortunately, the group needing such protection and assistance from the community must be expected to grow in all countries. As has been pointed out in this section, the complexity of modern work processes requires a labour force whose skills and qualifications should be constantly increasing. But a large part of the population cannot hope to reach high levels of intellectual sophistication. Here, governments must assume a subsidiary function. Even if one takes the view that, in general, the play of market forces is better suited to promote economic well-being for all, such basic assumptions must not prevent governments from taking steps with a view to integrating those for whose services the market has no demand into the economic life of the country. There is always room for improving community services in modern societies, whose social network is damaged by so many holes.

7. Conclusions

The introduction of the right to work is not a magic formula for solving the problems encountered in labour markets. A high degree of

---

[29] The Community Charter of the Fundamental Social Rights of Workers, adopted by the Heads of State and Government of eleven member states of the European Community on 8 and 9 December 1989, states in this respect (Article 26, paragraph 1):

All disabled persons, whatever the origin and nature of their disablement, must be entitled to additional concrete measures aimed at improving their social and professional integration.

A much more straightforward provision had been contained in the preliminary draft, adopted by the Commission of the European Communities on 30 May 1989, Bull. EC 5-1989, p. 116:

Measures shall be taken to ensure the fullest possible integration of disabled persons into working life, in particular where vocational training, occupational reintegration, and readaptation and social integration are concerned, by means of improving accessibility, mobility, means of transport and housing.

realism is necessary in assessing its inherent qualities. But it would be an obvious exaggeration to contend that it is totally devoid of any concrete legal meaning. Some aspects of the right to work can be characterized as strict rules, namely the freedom to work and the prohibition against discrimination, including equality for aliens. For the most part, however, the right to work embodies policy objectives. First and foremost, governments are required to conceive and carry out full employment policies, whose success is highly volatile. Some aspects, though, should in any event be made the object of detailed regulation, namely vocational training, protection against dismissal, schemes of unemployment benefits and specific protection schemes for handicapped persons. To that extent also, effective remedies should be available.

Bibliography

Arbeitsrecht von A-Z, 1987. Berlin: Staatsverlag der DDR.

Barth, Dieter, 1976. *Recht auf Arbeit*. Köln: Deutscher Instituts-Verlag.

Baruzzi, Arno, 1983. *Recht auf Arbeit und Beruf?* Freiburg/München: Karl Alber.

Betten, Lammy and Theun Jaspers, 1988. 'The Netherlands', in A.Ph.C.M. Jaspers and L. Betten (eds), *25 years European Social Charter*. Deventer *et al.*: Kluwer.

Buergenthal, Thomas, 1988. *International Human Rights in a Nutshell*. St Paul, Minn.: West Publishing Co.

Campbell, Tom, 1983. *The Left and rights. A conceptual analysis of the idea of socialist rights*. London *et al.*: Routledge & Kegan Paul.

Carrillo Salscedo, Juan, 1985. 'Human Rights, Universal Declaration (1948)', in Rudolf Bernhardt (ed.), *Encyclopedia of Public International Law*, vol. 8. Amsterdam/New York/Oxford: North Holland.

Case Law of the European Social Charter, 1982. Strasbourg: Council of Europe.

Cranston, Maurice, 1973. *What are Human Rights?* London: The Bodley Head.

Däubler, Wolfgang, 1978. 'Recht auf Arbeit verfassungswidrig?', in Udo Achten, *Recht auf Arbeit — eine politische Herausforderung*. Neuwied/Darmstadt: Luchterhand.

Engels, Friedrich, 1845. *Die Lage der arbeitenden Klasse in England*, (ed.), dtv Bibliothek. München, 1973: Deutscher Taschenbuch Verlag.

Golla, Joachim and Hermann Josef Rodenbach, 1986. 'Friedenssicherung und Menschenrechte. Zur Menschenrechtsdiskussion in der DDR', *Deutschland-Archiv*, vol. 19.

Henning, Hansjoachim, 1983. 'Sozio-ökonomische Hintergründe der Realisierungsversuche des Rechts auf Arbeit', in Hans Ryffel and Johannes Schwartländer (eds), *Das Recht des Menschen auf Arbeit*. Kehl/Strassburg: Engel.

Jiménez de Aréchaga, Eduardo, 1989. 'Self-Executing Provisions of International Law', in *Staat und Völkerrechtsordnung. Festschrift für Karl Doehring*. Berlin *et al.*: Springer-Verlag.

Källström, Kent, 1988. 'Sweden', in A.Ph.C.M. Jaspers and L. Betten (eds), *25 years European Social Charter*.

Karapuu, Heikki and Allan Rosas, 1988. 'The Juridical Force of Economic, Social and Cultural Rights — Some Finnish Examples', *Mennesker og Rettigheter* — Nordic Journal on Human Rights, vol. 6, no. 4.

Kartashkin, Vladimir, 1982. 'Economic, Social and Cultural Rights', in Karel Vasek and Philip Alston (eds), *The International Dimensions of Human Rights*, vol. 1. Westport, Connecticut: Greenwood Press; and Paris: Unesco.

Kuczynski, Jürgen, 1978. 'The Human Right to Work', *GDR Committee for Human Rights Bulletin*, no. 1.

Kühnhardt, Ludger, 1987. *Die Universalität der Menschenrechte*. München: Günther Olzog.

Kunz, Frithjof, 1988. 'Ideologischer Streit und Dialog zum Menschenrecht auf Arbeit', *Staat und Recht*, vol. 37.

Kunz, Frithjof, 1989. *Des Menschen Recht auf Arbeit*. Berlin: Staatsverlag der DDR.

Locke, John, 1690. *Two Treatises of Civil Government*, (ed.), Everyman's Library, no. 751. London, 1966: Dente; and New York: Dutton.

Lohmann, Ulrich, 1987. *Das Arbeitsrecht der DDR*. Berlin: Berlin Verlag Arno Spitz.

Manin, Aleth, 1988. 'La commission d'enquête de l'O.I.T. instituée pour examiner l'observation de la Convention 111 par la République fédérale d'Allemagne: de nouveaux enseignements, *Annuaire français de droit international*, vol. 34.

Ramm, Thilo, 1983. 'Das Recht auf Arbeit und die Gesellschaftsordnung', in Hans Ryffel and Johannes Schwartländer (eds), *Das Recht des Menschen auf Arbeit*. Kehl/Strassburg: Engel.

Rath, Michael, 1974. *Die Garantie des Rechts auf Arbeit*. Göttingen: Otto Schwartz.

Riedel, Eibe H., 1986. *Theorie der Menschenrechtsstandards*. Berlin: Duncker & Humblot.

Schiedermair, Rudolf and Michael Wollenschläger, 1985. *Handbuch des Ausländer-rechts der Bundesrepublik Deutschland*. Frankfurt am Main (looseleaf).

Schminck-Gustavus, Christoph, U., 1978. 'Recht auf Arbeit — Zur Geschichte einer konkreten Utopie', in Udo Achten, *Recht auf Arbeit — eine politische Herausforderung*. Neuwied/Darmstadt: Luchtenhand.

Schwerdtner, Peter, 1977. 'Die Garantie des Rechts auf Arbeit — Ein Weg zur Knechtschaft? ' *Zeitschrift für Arbeitsrecht*, vol. 8.

Sieghart, Paul, 1983. *The International Law of Human Rights*. Oxford: Clarendon Press.

Sieghart, Paul, 1986. *The Lawful Rights of Mankind*. Oxford/New York: Oxford University Press.

Thiel, Wera, 1987. 'On the Human Right to Work in the GDR', *GDR Committee for Human Rights Bulletin*, vol. 13, no. 2.

Tomuschat, Christian, 1983. 'Zur Rechtswirkung der von der Europäischen Gemeinschaft abgeschlossenen Verträge in der Gemeinschaftsordnung', in *Rechtsvergleichung, Europarecht und Staatenintegration. Gedächtnisschrift für Léontin-Jean Constantinesco*. Köln *et al.*: Carl Heymans Verlag KG.

Tomuschat, Christian, 1985. 'Recht auf Arbeit — Rechtsvergleichende Aspekte', in Jost Pietzcker, Herbert Fenn, Christian Tomuschat and Bernd

Baron von Maydell, *Recht auf Arbeit*. Bonn: Bouvier Verlag Herbert Grundmann.

Westen, Klaus, 1983. 'Das Recht auf Arbeit in den Prämissen sozialistischer Verfassungen', in Hans Ryffel and Johannes Schwartländer (eds), *Das Recht des Menschen auf Arbeit*. Kehl/Strassburg: Engel.

Zuleeg, Manfred, 1974. 'Der internationale Pakt über wirtschaftliche, soziale und kulturelle Recht, *Recht der Arbeit*, vol. 27.

8 National Minorities and International Law

I.P. Blischenko and A.H. Abashidze

The international protection of national minorities has for some time attracted the attention of the international community. In spite of the difficulties met in attempting to solve this problem, the experience acquired by states prior to the formation of the League of Nations, as well as within the League of Nations itself and later within the United Nations and its functional organs, shows that it is possible for states to co-operate in developing principles and joint activities directed at the protection of national minorities on the basis of generally recognized international law. In addition to these endeavours, the drawing-up of general principles of international protection based on the principle of non-interference in internal affairs of states could help to reduce the tensions that often arise in multi-national states and assist the government of such states in solving the problem of providing equal rights and opportunities for all nationalities and peoples in that state and preventing the tendency towards separatism and disunity.

The above–mentioned problem directly concerns, among others, the European continent, which has set the objective of creating a common European home. It is comforting that, at present, an unprecedented programme of concrete measures aimed at international co-operation is evolving. This may be the first essential step in concretizing the idea of a common European home.

The idea of a common European home is based on new European thinking, operating not on the basis of categories of international or inter-bloc contradictions, but on notions of the unity of common human values and common European values, which must become the corner–stone for building the projected home. Naturally, such an approach calls for the conscious participation of all 33 European countries, the United States and Canada, all of which are equally interested in regulating international problems in their countries through national as well as international legal methods. By right, the initiative for international co-operation in the area of protection of national minorities belongs to the European continent. Among the earliest international agreements containing provisions on national minorities, one can single out the following: the Westphalian Peace Treaty, 1648; the Paris Peace Treaty, 1856; the St Stephen Peace Agreement, 1878; and the Berlin Congress Act, 1878.

Even though in some instances, these and similar agreements led to positive results (for example in relation to the Balkan peoples), unfortunately, the true aim of posing as well as solving the problem of protection of national minorities, was to satisfy the urge of the great European powers to weaken their opponents and, as such, ensure their domination in the international area. The claim of protecting national minorities served the great European powers as a means of direct interference in the internal affairs of other states. And more so because such practices were of a limited, unsystematic and inconsistent character, focusing, as a rule, on very small states, and most often those which had been conquered. It did not apply to colonial peoples.

There were many shortcomings in the practice of protection of national minorities during the above-mentioned period. Even if the role of guarantor of the rights of national minorities in accordance with the above-mentioned agreements was delegated to a number of states, the duty to ensure the observance of the terms of these agreements was exercised by these states individually. The right to interpret the obligations taken by states in relation to their national minorities was given to each state guarantor separately. This in turn led to the weakening of the guaranty; legal and organizational mechanisms to check the progress of the state's fulfilment of its obligations were omitted from these instruments as were enforcement mechanisms in cases where states did not fulfil their obligations.

Even though the League of Nations system of protection of national minorities provided for a mechanism for presenting petitions on violations of the rights of national minorities, the conditions for the League's accepting these petitions, its procedure for collecting information on violations of the terms of the various agreements and the political interests of the great European powers, who acted as guarantors of the implementation of international agreements on national minorities through their participation in the Council of the League of Nations, predominated over legal arguments, thereby nullifying the rights of national minorities.

The experience acquired by the League of Nations in the sphere of protection of national minorities could be usefully and creatively applied today by European states acting on the basis of existing generally recognized principles and norms of international law.

Post-war Europe has accumulated a good deal of experience in balancing the interests at stake when addressing minority rights questions. For example, one can name the decisions of the Potsdam Conference, the Moscow Treaty between the Soviet Union and the Federal Republic of Germany, 1970, and the agreement on establishing relations between the Council of Mutual Economic Assistance (CMEA) and the European Economic Community. In this regard, it would not be an exaggeration to recognize the uniqueness of the Helsinki Final Act, which lay the foundation for a Common European process. This process, which addresses a wide spectrum of questions on inter-state relations, is now on the threshold of a qualitatively new stage. It is making a transition from providing a forum for making recommendations to actively taking decisions, in particular in regard to the building of mechanisms for humanitarian co-operation. In this connection, the Helsinki process constitutes the optimal foundation for erecting a common European home.

The guarantee of maintaining relations of goodwill in implementing the humanitarian aspect of the European process is based on a triad which comprises the following (Amirjanov and Cherkasov, 1988, p. 34):

(a) the duty of states to provide maximum suitable conditions for their citizens to realize their rights;
(b) the co-operation of states in the realization of human rights, based on corresponding international agreements;
(c) the exchange of accumulated experience in this sphere.

The creation of a common European mechanism for humanitarian co-operation would provide a useful framework for addressing the above–mentioned problems and regulating the activities of the necessary international apparatus. To some extent, this mechanism is already in place: the member-countries of the CSCE (Conference on Security and Co-operation in Europe) are pursuing such projects at both governmental and doctrinal levels.

It is impossible, however, to create any type of stable common European legal order without solving international problems, while taking into consideration the common interests of all states and enlisting their co-operation and support. It is quite clear that, first and foremost, it is necessary to work out a Code of International Co-operation on humanitarian problems, the foundation of which could be formed by the following principles (Blischenko, 1988, p. 114):

1. respect for the rights of peoples and nationalities to self–determination, in structuring their fate as the people themselves desire, without external influence;
2. mutual security;
3. co-operation of all states in solving global problems, irrespective of their socio-economic systems;
4. co-operation of states in spreading the ideas of peace and disarmament and respect for human rights and basic freedoms;
5. dissemination of objective information with the aim of increasing its standard, facilitating the mutual acquaintance of peoples with each others' way of life and strengthening trust and mutual understanding.
6. obligations of states to promote co-operation among parties, social movements and public figures in the fields of science and culture, mass media, the development of tourism, and the widening of contacts between people and organizations;
7. prohibition of any type of discrimination against peoples and nationalities, genocide, apartheid, and the propagation of fascism.

Although concrete decisions on humanitarian problems may be taken by each state, taking into consideration the peculiarities which exist in that given state, the main demand is that consideration be taken of obligations arising out of regional or universal treaties, since international humanitarian problems affect the interests, rights and freedoms of peoples of other states (Kolosov, 1988).

Since the beginning of the European process and the adoption of the Helsinki Final Act, the question arises as to what provisions in this document relate to the question of national minorities. The answer can be found in the seventh principle of the Declaration on Principles, which is entitled, 'Respect for Human Rights and Fundamental Freedoms, Including the Freedom of Thought, Conscience, Religion or Belief.' CSCE states on whose territories there are national minorities must respect the right of persons belonging to such minorities to equality before the law and must provide them with all opportunities for the actual utilization of their rights and fundamental freedoms.

The inclusion of the term 'national minorities' in the above-mentioned principle, as compared to its exclusion from Article 27 of the International Covenant on Civil and Political Rights, is important both in itself and in relation to the interpretation of the term. It is well known that within the framework of the UN Sub-Commission on the Prevention of Discrimination and the Protection of Minorities, whose sphere of activity is limited by the minorities listed in Article 27 of the International Covenant on Civil and Political Rights, there have been different interpretations of that Article. An assertion which was included in one report of the working-group of the Sub-Commission states that, because Article 27 of the Covenant refers to persons belonging to ethnic, religious and linguistic minorities, the activities of the Sub-Commission do not encompass persons belonging to national minorities and therefore a proposed Declaration of the Rights of Persons Belonging to Minorities, on which the Sub-Commission was working, should include provisions specifically referring to national minorities. As a result of such an interpretation, the term 'national minority' was placed in brackets in the draft Declaration on the Rights of Minorities.

The direct mention of national minorities in the Helsinki Final Act precludes such narrow interpretations in the future.

When studying the problems of national minorities, one ought to keep in mind the fact that these problems have specific features and therefore must be separated from other problems of a humanitarian character. Such an approach will allow for a comprehensive analysis of these problems and reflect their importance to the creation of a common European home.

Unfortunately, the provisions of the Helsinki Final Act on national minorities, as well as the provisions of other international agreements on human rights developed under the auspices of the UN, show a predominant tendency towards protection of the human

rights of individuals belonging to national minorities, while under-
estimating the collective character of the right. This can lead to
unpleasant consequences.

International protection of human rights at present does not take
into account and does not provide for the protection of the collective
rights of minorities, since it only provides a mechanism for the
protection of individual human rights, including the protection of the
rights of persons belonging to national minorities.

Hence, there arises the necessity that either the existing norms of
international law concerning national minorities be complemented
by new norms regulating the collective rights of national minorities
in conjunction with the nationalities' right to self-determination, or
that a concept be developed allowing for an optimal combination of
both the individual and collective approach in protecting the rights of
national minorities.

In defining violations of the rights of national minorities, it is
necessary to consider not only the criteria of the massive character of
the violation, but also the gravity of such a violation. Experience
shows that a flagrant violation of the rights of national minorities is
always predetermined by the gravity of the violation. Violations of
the rights of national minorities, in most cases, are massive and
serious in character since the discrimination is directed primarily
against the collective rights of national minorities.

The question arises as to which national minorities fall under
international protection and consequently what are the criteria by
which states define such national minorities. Here the approaches
may be different and depend entirely on the will of the Contracting
States. One of the criteria may be the existence of discrimination
against national minorities as compared to the rest of the population
of a given country. For the purposes of defining such discrimination,
an international organ of independent experts may be established.
The powers of such an organ can be defined by the Contracting
States. One of the criteria for defining discrimination could be
discrimination of such a degree that it creates a real threat to peace
and security in circumstances where the problem directly affects the
interests of other states. This feature of discrimination would limit
the scope of the definition of 'national minority' only to those groups
of the population that are subject to limitations of rights and
freedoms. In reality, there are national minorities that are not subject
to discrimination. Thus, the above–mentioned approach is justified
by the fact that those national minorities which are not subject to
discrimination do not fall under international protection, since the
necessity for such protection does not exist.

Another approach may be to list in supplement to a given agreement on the international protection of national minorities, those
minorities that should enjoy such protection. Such an approach has
an advantage over that mentioned above, since, from the inception,
the possibility of interference in internal affairs is removed and even

those national minorities which are not discriminated against may be included in the list. Any such list should include, first of all, national minorities that live on territories of two or more European states.

We cannot agree with those scientists who consider that the definition of national minority must contain an element of settlement. In accordance with this position, national minorities who do not live compactly in a given country could not exercise the right to self-determination, which is a wrong view. The fact is that any demand by national minorities, in the final analysis, is a demand to create democratic conditions to promote the free development of these minorities. This is characteristic of all minorities irrespective of how they live, compactly or not. The difference in approach to these minorities should only be in the manner in which they realize their demands and on the concrete situation in a given country. For example, if a minority lives compactly, it may demand the formation of a state within the country. If a minority does not live compactly, then it could demand the establishment of such legal organizational mechanisms at the state or local level as would provide for their free development.

In both cases, the demands of national minorities are based on the rights of peoples and nations to self-determination. Although the criteria of settlement, historical attachment to land and so forth, are taken into account by the minorities when defining the form in which they will exercise their right to self-determination, one cannot violate the right of any people to self-determination.

It is necessary to examine the question of the prevention of discrimination and protection of minorities in the context of preventive measures, with the aim of avoiding the violations of the rights of national minorities.

The words 'prevention' and 'protection' encompass almost all aspects of the problem of national minorities. The Sub-Commission on the Prevention of Discrimination and the Protection of Minorities, in a document on 'the importance of terminologies relating to the eradication of discrimination and the protection of minorities', stated that 'the prevention of discrimination' signifies the removal of any measures denying equal rights to individual or groups of persons. These conclusions of the Sub-Commission are not comprehensive in character, since the 'prevention of discrimination' includes not only the act of removing any measures denying individuals or groups of persons equal rights, but also includes other positive acts, for example, the observance, respect and extension by states of the rights of national minorities. All such actions a state takes unilaterally, in fulfilling its international obligations or for other reasons, constitute measures to prevent discrimination against national minorities.

In this regard, one may suggest the development and exercising of preventive measures under the control of an international organization, with the aim of observing the principle of the international protection of human rights and the avoidance of violations of the rights of national minorities. Such an approach is not an attempt to change the concept of guarantee to the concept of preventive measures. In this case, the two concepts are intertwined, to the benefit of the guarantee concept. Furthermore, these measures cannot be considered as interference in internal affairs, since they are exercised willingly by individual states, on their own territory, in accordance with international treaties to which they are parties.

It is not rare in international legal literature to find the assertion that, because some national minorities need international protection and thus demand special rights, they cannot be considered as equals as the rights they demand are additional to those enjoyed by majority groups. It is clear, however, that special and additional rights for the protection of national minorities are necessary to ensure their protection in discriminatory conditions. Why do we call these rights special and additional? We can use an example to explain: in many countries, constitutions contain provisions on the rights of all nationalities and peoples to preserve and develop their native language. At the same time, however, in practice there are many instances in which national minorities do not even have the opportunity to establish a school which is conducted in their native language. In this connection, there arises a necessity and duty of the state to implement additional measures to assist in establishing such schools. If this is considered an additional duty by the state, then for the national minorities these are additional rights in accordance with fundamental law of the country. These additional rights, in order not to be evaluated as special privileges for national minorities in relation to the rest of the population of the country must stipulate that it is necessary to adopt special measures to provide national minorities and persons belonging to them an equal opportunity to exercise their human rights and fundamental freedoms, as is required by international law. This should not be looked upon as an exceptional privilege, since such special attention is necessary until such time as the objective for which it was introduced has been achieved.

In practice, unfortunately, one can encounter states in Europe which do not recognize the presence of national minorities on their territories, even when they have been living there for centuries. Such an attitude cannot help solve the problem, and in many cases it has been transformed into a problem of religious minorities or has created grounds for the appearance of underground nationalist movements.

The fact that France, for example, in its reservation to Article 27 of the International Covenant on Civil and Political Rights, declared the Article inapplicable to France (doc. CCPR/C/2/Rev. 2, 12 May 1989, p. 18), did not eradicate the problem of the Corsicans or the Bretons.

For a number of European states, the question of the so-called indigenous population still stands (e.g. Norway, Sweden, Finland, and the Soviet Union). It would seem that the recognition of indigenous populations as national minorities may assist in providing their right to a special community. The problem of national minorities is tied in with the appearance of a large number of immigrant workers on the territories of European states. Of course this question has its own significance, but in cases where these immigrant workers have lived on the territories of these states for a long time and represent a compact national minority, and more so if they have become citizens of these states, then the question arises as to the provision of their rights. This question must receive due attention.

At present, the external policies of the majority of European states show that they have begun to examine critically their own views of the world and the trends in European development, and to consider how their national interests can be provided for in modern conditions. It becomes quite evident, that in the course of such a re-examination, European states have turned to a wider view of a unified, interconnected and interdependent world and have considered the character of international relations in such a world.

Taking into consideration these very points, the Minister of Foreign Affairs of the Soviet Union has emphasized that 'there are two interconnected levels of new political thinking . . . internal and international' (in an interview, *Izvestija*, 17 February 1988). New political thinking in international relations suggests the consolidation of principles, which must predetermine the relations between states: the priority of common human values over national, class and ideological values, freedom of choice derived from the sovereign equality of peoples, and so forth. At the same time, new thinking must, in particular, base itself on the idea of the global character of the problems of human rights. In practice, this calls for the rejection of confrontation in favour of co-operation and interaction, de-ideologization of inter-state relations and the recognition of the general and universal character of human rights and international standards in the humanitarian sphere.

The disbalance in socio-political and cultural development within a country creates conditions whereby national minorities strive for strong autonomy. This thesis is applicable to any country, irrespective of its socio-economic system. To illustrate this point we shall examine the example of Belgium, where the Flemish inhabit the northern part of the country and at present constitute about 51 per cent of the population of the country, and the French inhabit the southern part of the country and constitute about 32 per cent of the population. Because a common state language does not exist in Belgium, there have been many problems in establishing a Belgian federation. During the 1960s, there occurred a sharp increase in conflicts between the two major language groups. In order to regularize relations between them, Belgium, in 1963, divided itself into four linguistic regions: Flemish, French, German and the Brussels district. Although the Brussels district is situated in the Flemish region, French is predominant and Brussels has a bilingual status. These recent efforts by the Belgian Government did not yield the desired results. In the eight Flemish communities where the minority speaks French, the French-speakers have the right and opportunity to turn to institutions, conduct official correspondence and receive documents in French. However, in other areas, these rights are in many ways limited. For example, in order to occupy an official post, French-speakers in these communities must take a Flemish language examination.

There is a different type of problem in the Brussels region, where the French-speakers are predominant. The Flemish-speakers constitute only 20 per cent of the population, but the rights of this minority are carefully protected. In all institutions, official correspondence and documentation, and in oral messages, the right to use both languages is guaranteed. Brussels has French and Flemish schools to which parents can send their children according to their choice. The police, postal and council workers have to be able to speak both languages. Even though the Brussels experience is one of the most democratic and progressive, it nevertheless appears to be privileged if you look at it from the point of view of the French-speakers living in Flemish-speaking parts of Belgium.

Although the problem of national minorities should be approached independently from the remaining problems of a humanitarian character, it does not mean that they are not interconnected. In relation to this, it should be noted that the problem of national minorities is of a complex character. This means that solving the problems of national minorities automatically means the solving of other problems of a humanitarian nature.

For example, the provision of rights of national minorities brings about a decrease in the number of refugees. On the other hand, the simplification of travel procedures automatically nullifies many demands of national minorities. At this point we can draw the conclusion that co-operation between states in all humanitarian areas can be gained only on the basis of mutual co-operation.

The principle of President Wilson in relation to national minorities would have had real success if the Western powers had supported and recognized in time the principle that the newly formed Soviet state called for: the universal and compulsory principle of the right of peoples and nationalities to self-determination. The absence of the principle of the rights of peoples and nationalities to self-determination gave rise to the fact that no international treaties before the end of the Second World War provided for the protection of national minorities and their rights, but only the rights of separate individuals of the same national origin. In other words, the collective rights of national minorities were denied.

In Soviet literature, one may often encounter assertions that countries with different socio-economic systems encounter different problems when attempting to solve the nationalities question and therefore they must solve them differently. However, even where different mistakes have been made through the legal enforcement of the inequality of national minorities in the formation of national or administrative territorial units, the problems facing national minorities are basically the same in socialist and capitalist countries.

The experience of the various functional organs of the United Nations working on minorities questions shows that universal regulation of these questions has not yielded the desired results. This is partially exacerbated by the fact that, first of all, the problems of all minorities, national, ethnic, linguistic and religious, are examined together, which means it is only those problems which are characteristic of all minorities that are considered. Therefore, specific problems of individual types of minorities are ignored and thus the universal approach ignores many specific problems of national minorities of separate regions. For example, if in Arab countries, religious minorities struggle to be considered as such, many groups of the indigenous population of the United States refuse to be considered as minorities. Also, within the framework of separate regions, some national minorities are at the same time presented as religious minorities, and therefore their demands differ from the demands of those national minorities which profess the same religion as the majority population of that country.

Given the above problems and the fact that at the regional level it is perhaps most possible to consider all the demands and characteristic features of all national minorities, regional international co-operation of states seems to represent the optimal model for the protection of national minorities.

As is well known, the European Convention on Human Rights and the European Commission and Court of Human Rights do not provide for the protection of national minorities as a community of people. In this light, it is necessary to take into consideration the following facts: each region in the world is faced with different problems of national minorities. In some regions, problems of ethnic minorities predominate, in others linguistic minorities coincide with national minorities and in still others religious minorities are at the same time national minorities.

Taking into consideration the above, it is arguable that regional co-operation among states, through participation in the CSCE process, is the optimal model for co-operation in protecting national minorities. Such co-operation does not contravene the universal approach to that question within the framework of the UN. On the contrary, it will speed up the process of creating the mechanisms for protecting national minorities within the framework of the UN and undoubtedly influence change in the various approaches to that question taken by the Sub-Commission for the Prevention of Discrimination and Protection of Minorities and the UN Commission on Human Rights.

It is worth noting here that religious organizations working in the field of human rights have contributed to progress in modern international relations. This, however, has not occurred through any dependence on the UN Charter, which, among all the various regional agreements, mentions only agreements relating to the support of international peace and security. On the other hand, the UN Charter does not question the legality of establishing regional organizations for developing co-operation between states in economic, social, humanitarian and other areas (see the decisions of Sub-Commission III/4/A at the San Francisco Conference 1945, *Documents of the United Nations Conference on International Organizations*, vol. 12, pp. 833, 857–8).

Thus, in the UN Charter one can find provisions legalizing the possibility of establishing regional systems in the area of human rights. It follows that the activities of any regional organization must be based on the principles of the UN Charter and, in particular, on the demands to be met by regional agreements in Chapter VIII of the UN Charter to promote the development of peaceful and friendly relations between states.

In almost all human rights agreements adopted within the framework of the UN, the importance of solving problems of a humanitarian nature with the aim of strengthening general peace and security, is emphasized. For example, in the Preamble of the International Covenant on Economic, Social and Cultural Rights, it is mentioned that in accordance with the principles declared by the UN Charter, states must recognize the honour inherent in all members of the human family and the principle that their inviolable rights are the basis for freedom, justice and universal peace.

The question of the necessity of establishing a regional system on human rights protection was examined by the UN Commission on Human Rights. The Commission set up a special Working Group to study the question of establishing regional commissions on human rights. Its report to the 24th Session of the UN Commission on Human Rights made clear that the members of the group held different opinions and so could not make recommendations on the necessity of establishing such regional commissions. Some of the members of the Working Group contended that the development of co-operation between states in the sphere of human rights is better accomplished on the universal level. Some voiced the opinion that the establishment of regional commissions was premature and unnecessary. Some emphasized that the main responsibility for observing human rights and freedoms rests on the states themselves, and that they are supposed to take any necessary internal measures to that end. One should not think of establishing new organs, but about the full and effective use of the internal mechanisms existing within the framework of the UN. The Commission also noted, however, that any initiatives to establish regional commissions on human rights, including the definition of their powers and functions must evolve not from the UN or from any group of states, but from a definite region.

Western Europe took such an initiative but, even so, the European Convention contains only some of the rights and freedoms provided for in the Universal Declaration of Human Rights and the International Covenants. The European Convention does not mention some of the basic rights listed in the Covenant on Civil and Political Rights, such as the right of peoples to self-determination, equality of all before the law and the right to equal protection of the law without any discrimination. Nor does it protect the right of ethnic, religious or linguistic minorities to conduct their own culture or religion or to use their mother tongue. Moreover, any state, when ratifying the Convention, may make reservations to any of the various substantive provisions (Article 64). The European Convention does not prohibit propaganda for war, or for national, racial or religious hatred. Neither were these rights secured in the European Social Charter, adopted in 1961 by member states of the Council of Europe.

Although Western European countries recognize the limited nature of the rights and freedoms expressed in the European Convention, they view the European Convention's establishment of a mechanism for its implementation as a way of solving the problem. An analysis of the work of the European Commission and Court of Human Rights shows that this mechanism could have achieved considerable results if it were operating on the basis of a more perfected international agreement on human rights. Such an agreement can be worked out only if all the countries in the region participate and only if the experience and demands of the modern world, peoples, and states are taken into consideration.

In the process of building a common European home and defining a common legal ground, it becomes possible to create an all-European regional organization with one of its functions being the protection of national minorities. Such protection must be based on a special international agreement among European states, taking into consideration the experience of both the West and the East. The following provisions could be included in such a convention:

1. The principle of self-determination, which is understood as the right of every national minority to equal conditions of existence and development to those enjoyed by the nationality constituting the majority in a given country.
2. The obligation of neighbouring states to conclude agreements providing for the rights of national minorities in those cases when the national minority of one country, by reason of ethnic origin, is connected to the national majority of the other country. This is of great importance because many states, in their constitutional provisions, take upon themselves the responsibility of protecting the interests of their compatriots wherever they live (see, for example, Section 6, paragraph 3, of the Hungarian Constitution).

3. The establishment of the possibility of rendering collective humanitarian assistance in cases of serious violation of the rights of national minorities, especially when such violations not only create tension between states, but threaten international peace. This relates to the question of the interrelationship between internal competence and interference in internal affairs. In conditions of an interdependent and interconnected world, this interrelationship must be examined in favour of active interference by the international community in cases of genocide, systematic and massive violations of human rights, racial discrimination and the preparation for aggression, that is, in cases where international crimes are committed. To this end, it is necessary to work out a corresponding mechanism with an inquiry committee endowed with the right of on-the-spot inspection.

4. The provision of freedom of relations between national minorities and freedom of movement, including also provisions on the use of these freedoms with the objective of developing a given national minority, while promoting friendly and neighbourly relations between countries.

5. The examination of appeals, from both individual persons who consider their rights to have been violated because they belong to a national minority and from the national minority collectively. In this case, we speak of an international court procedure which could be based on the experience gained by Western Europe.

These basic provisions do not in any way take up the role and responsibility of governments in observing the rights of national minorities or in implementing appropriate national legislation, but the establishment of a common legal ground unites the efforts of all European countries in providing and realizing the rights of national minorities in the interests of the development of mankind and friendly relations between states.

Bibliography

AMIRDZANOV M., CERKASOV, O. ETAZI OBSCEEVROPEJSKOGO DOMA. MEZDUNARODNAJA ZIZN 1988-Nr. 11, S.34. (Amirjanov, M. and O. Cherkasov, 1988. 'The Floors of Common European Home', *International life*, no. 11. Moscow: International Relations).

BLISCENKO, I. P. NA PUTI K SOZDANIJU NOVOGO MEZDUNARODNOGO PRAVOPORJADKA. SOVETSKOV GOSUDARSTVO I PRAVO Nr. 4, STR. 114 (Blischenko, I.P., 1988. 'On the Way of the Creation of a New International Law Order', *Soviet State and Law*, no. 4. Moscow: Nauka).

KOLOSOV, JU. M. KNOVOMU ETAPU MEZDUNARODNOGO SOTRUDNICESTVA V GUMANITARNOJ OBLASTI./SOVETSKOE GOSUDARSTVO I PRAVO Nr. 21 1988. (Kolosov, U.M., 1988. 'A New Stage of International Cooperation in Humanitarian Issues', *Soviet State and Law*, no. 21. Moscow: Nauka).

Report of the Working Group on the Rights of Persons Belonging to National, Ethnic, Religious and Linguistic Minorities (UN doc. E/CN.4/1990/71, 5 March 1990).

9 Right to Peace, Right to Development, Right to a Healthy Environment: Part of the Solution or Part of the Problem?

Gábor Kardos

1. Introduction

There is a widely shared view today of world problems endangering the existence of mankind: their solutions are interrelated and their implementation needs solidarity both on the national and international scenes. Because of the globalization of human activities we must find the institutional means to this solidarity (Mavi, 1987-88). The vital questions of mankind — to a large extent due to well-developed telecommunication and mass communication systems — have become truly international issues. We can receive information nearly all over the world within minutes. The constant flow of news well illustrates the structural problems the world is facing. World-wide publicity, made possible by technological development, has been proven to have influenced the development of international relations in more than one way. This influence is not in all cases positive, since for example it incites international terrorism; however, by way of 'live' symbols it also makes possible intimate encounters with global problems. Another important factor that contributes to keeping global problems on the agenda is the universal network of international organizations.

This is by and large common ground, but it does not mean that everybody accepts the same solution for these problems or at least that part of the solution relates to the 'third generation of human rights' or the concept of 'peoples' rights'.

When the notion of 'third generation rights' was introduced in the scientific analysis of human rights (a prominent representative of this initiative was Karel Vasak), the ongoing dispute around the issue of development of human rights received a new dimension. Earlier, one simply spoke of an increased catalogue of human rights or of various categories of human rights, whereas now the use of the term 'generations' is becoming more common. Why are the terms 'catalogues' or categories no longer appropriate for the description of a new phenomenon? As Stephen P. Marks writes (1985, p. 504):

The answer is simply that the former terms ('catalogues' or 'categories') are static, whereas the concept of human rights in international law and politics is eminently dynamic — as is law in general, of course . . . Although the natural law tradition is closely linked with the proclamation of human rights, the history of human rights, both national and international, clearly reveals that the formation and the very existence of rights vary over time.

However, no matter how true it may be that the existence and the contents of human rights vary over time, still the term 'generations' is more an expression of the fact that, as Philip Alston (1982, p. 316) put it:

Just as a child replaces his or her parent as the family standard-bearer, application of the concept of generation to human rights implies that one generation gives away to and is replaced by, the next, even though it may carry on some of the characteristics of its ancestors.

So even the term 'generation' is very questionable.

There is much criticism in the international literature which highlights the weaknesses of the concept of peoples' rights. 'Peoples' are not 'real actors' on the international scene, so 'it would be most inopportunate generally to substitute peoples for States in international law', wrote Christian Tomuschat (1986, p. 354). According to Paul Sieghart (1983, p. 368) this kind of conceptualization is dangerous:

. . . abstract concepts have in the past only too often presented great dangers to the enjoyment by individuals of their human rights and fundamental freedoms. Some of the worst violations of those rights have been perpetrated in the service of some inspiring abstraction, such as 'the one true faith', 'the state' (including, as a recent example, *'das Reich'*), 'the economy' (including 'a strong dollar/or pound') and indeed 'the masses'. A 'people' is no less an abstraction than the individuals who compose it. If any of the individual rights and freedoms protected by modern international human rights law ever came to be regarded as subservient to the rights of a 'people' . . . there would be a very real risk that legitimacy might be claimed on such a ground for grave violations of the human rights of individuals.

On the ground of legal purism, which is one of the most important values of theory-building, the existence of this concept can easily be doubted. There is no universal treaty which includes this concept, and the content of the rights belonging to it is uncertain. But the concept of peoples' rights is built into the African Charter of Human and Peoples' Rights, and it is recognized by certain significant UN Declarations. And although, as stated by one of the members of the working group during the discussion over this chapter, it is easier to find arguments against the concept than in favour of it, the debate is going on because of the importance of the values standing behind the rights belonging to it. Actually, this concept opened the Pandora's Box of the theory of international law, both in the context of North-

South issues (especially the right to development) and East-West issues (especially right to peace).

The common element of the criticism against the rights belonging to the 'third generation' or to the concept of 'peoples' rights' is the fear that the rights of the individual and the precise nature of international human rights law are prejudiced. On the following pages, I will examine certain specific rights, the right to peace, the right to development and the right to a healthy environment as *complex* (human, peoples' and, if it seems to be justified, state) rights. This approach provides certain benefits in accordance with the values protected by the above-mentioned criticism, but because it is not possible to elaborate a general concept, the outcome of this anlysis is fragmented and produces more questions than answers. Thus, B.G. Ramcharan's (1987, p. 9) question concerning peoples' rights remains valid: 'Has the notion of peoples' rights much more to offer than a political idea or a legal fiction?'

In this chapter, the main emphasis is not UN General Assembly declarations. From the point of view of sources, the most that can be established about these declarations is that they are *para-droit, pre-droit, droit-vert* or *normes sauvages*. However, by using these terms we risk setting our foot on the path of what was once called by a French international lawyer the 'pathology of the international normativity system' (Weil, 1983, pp. 413, 415), where, by accepting such notions we are 'blurring the normativity threshold' of international law. True, international law 'does not come out of social nothingness' (Abi-Saab, 1980, p. 162), but it is present in United Nations resolutions and declarations only to the extent they can be traced in any of the traditional sources of international law. So they do not really impose limits on *de lege ferenda* speculations.

2. The right to peace

War is absurd. Moreover, it is immoral. Finally, it doesn't pay (Tromp, 1987).

2.1 War and peace

Throughout history, and especially in times of war, the partisans of peace have hoped that their humanist dream will become reality for eternity. There were, and still are, some who believe that development will make wars impossible. Such views have developed in response to the production of new weapons capable of causing levels of destruction earlier thought to be impossible. In the Middle Ages, for example, it was believed that the invention of the crossbow would prevent all further wars. Others thought that the changing structure of inter-state relations, for example mutual interdependence, is irreconcilable with war. Based on this idea, a representative of the neo-realist school of international relations has demonstrated that those states that fought against one another during the First World War were each others' leading economic partners before the war (Waltz, 1979, pp. 158-9). Establishing ways to prevent the eruption of war is another approach to the ideal of securing lasting peace. Kant (1985, p. 9), for example, believed that regular armies should, with time, be completely disbanded, because they represent a constant threat to other states. Following the First World War, many shared the view that the establishment of a collective security system would be able to deter a potential aggressor, and that the setting-up of a Permanent International Court of Justice to pass judgement on the basis of international law principles, would with time replace arbitrary action. After the Second World War, the illusion that the new world organization would be able to prevent new wars lasted for no longer than the 'honeymoon' period of the United Nations; however, the UN Charter did pronounce the prohibition by international law of the use of force. This is the first *general prohibition*, the violations of which are well recorded. With these two principles, the non-use of force and the peaceful settlement of disputes, international law was entrusted with its most difficult task: finding a solution to the problem of the peaceful coexistence of states. The realization of these two objectives presuppose especially intensive international co-operation, considered unimaginable in an earlier era (Herczegh, 1982, p. 134). Today, a world war could lead to a global nuclear catastrophe. Arthur Larson (1962, p. 341) writes:

Rousseau, in his book on education called *Emile* wrote:
'The best way to teach Emile not to fall out of the window is to let him fall out. Unfortunately the defect of the system is that the pupil may not survive to profit by his experience. The world has been learning about international relations for centuries by a process of periodically falling out of the window. The injuries have been severe, but never quite fatal. But we all know that one more fall will be our last.'

Nuclear weapons have changed more than just human thinking. The possibility of a nuclear war has changed the face of possibly the most personal human relation: death. It has fundamentally upset and transformed this emotional experience, since for millions a nuclear war may mean that their often inhuman life will thus be stripped even of the prospect of a 'human' death.

There is no death so alienating as dying in nuclear war. People attach hopes and wishes to the way they die. The quality of death is seen as an important aspect of life. Death stripped of anything personal and particular to the individual dying is a source of anxiety. To be left totally to the mercy of the irreversible without any personal note breeds feelings of horror. The prospect embodied in nuclear war, of death among millions, is therefore a vision unpleasant to the extreme. It would mean collective and standardized death.

Short of identity, special features, uniqueness and meaning it holds the prospect of destruction rather than death in any human sense (Lider, 1979, p. 343).

In the Northern part of the world, in the shadow of deterrence exist enormous stockpiles of a destructive potential that have not been put to use *en masse* for more than 40 years. This is the 'baroque arsenal', i.e. an increasingly complex and expensive collection of military hardware, which is becoming more and more difficult to handle and requires spare parts by the thousands (Kaldor, 1983). At the same time, Third World countries have also doubled their share of military spending since the early sixties, and have become structural parts of the global arms race culture and the world military order (Kaldor, 1983, p. 97). In the countries of the Third World, these weapons are used. Most of the 140–150 wars since 1945 were, or still are, fought in these states, some of them with 'near nuclear weapons' (Klare, 1983, pp. 438–44). The consequences of these wars, even if only the economic consequences, are disastrous. Since 1945, 16 million people have died as casualties of wars. The 1.5 million dollars spent each minute by the governments of the world on armaments (Ferencz and Keyes, 1988, p. 12) is an essential condition for the above.

Be it scenarios conceived in the imagination of 'nuclear theologians' or local wars fought by conventional weaponry, one thing is certain: 'the *final* solution should be nothing but the total abandonment of war, as a social phenomenon. To reach a condition in which there is no preparation, no expectation, no chance of war, i.e., stable peace' (Boulding, 1978). To realize this objective, the focus of thinking must shift from war to peace. 'For every thousand pages published on the causes of war, there is less than one page directly on causes of peace' (Blainey, 1983, p. 3). 'An international system should be established that — based on the experiences of peaceful conflict resolution — would channel conflict situations in a way that the use of force, war — as a means of resolution — would be excluded in practice. However, the culture of peaceful conflict resolution will develop and become general practice only in the case of a radical change of international relations and the realization of the inseparable elements of the necessary new, *democratic and demilitarized world order* (Szentes, 1987).

In other words, in contrast to negative peace, signifying merely the absence of open violence, positive peace is attained. It is equally obvious that, in the spirit of the Kantian approach, together with the elimination of the structural causes of wars and violence, the means to these should also be eliminated. That is why such importance is attached to those principles and strategies that contain a possible solution to the present 'security dilemma' (Wheeler and Booth, 1987) and are directed towards an alternative security system, for example de-nuclearization, widening arms control, general and complete disarmament, unilateral disarmament, demilitarizing governing processes, non-violence, and holding leaders accountable for crimes of states (the Nuremberg obligation) (Weston *et al.*, 1980, pp. 1106–7).

At the same time, we should remember Ali Mazrui's (1967, as quoted by Bull, 1977, p. 97) warning: 'the importance of peace is, in the ultimate analysis, *derivative*. Taken to its deepest roots, peace is important because "the dignity and worth of the human person" are important' (emphasis in original).

2.2 Law of peace

If we accept that 'before there is an attempt to postulate a "right to" there is a development of a "law of" ' (Marks, 1985, p. 507), then we shouldn't find the right to peace as especially problematic, since international law with the exclusion of some of its components, is the 'law of peace', that is, it regulates the peaceful co-operation of states. However, the above is only a necessary, but not sufficient condition. It is equally true that international law itself is a factor of peace. 'Law is, essentially, an order for the promotion of peace', pointed out Kelsen (1942, as quoted by Rumpf, 1984, p. 32). This statement, however, naturally does not clarify all the interrelationships. Peace has become the most important value; what does this signify from the point of view of international law? How does international law reflect the prohibition of the direct use of force, the concepts of negative and positive peace?

The case of negative peace seems simpler, since the basic norm of the non-use of force stipulates the absence of direct violence between states. This, however, does not mean an absolute prohibition, since external armed intervention at the request and on behalf of a government, self-defence and liberation struggle serve as exceptions. The last of these signals the comeback of the just war concept (Rumpf, 1984, p. 442), as expressed in the Resolution on the Definition of Aggression, declaring as legal wars of

peoples under colonial and racist regimes or other form of alien domination to struggle for independence and receive support.

International humanitarian law and the international law of armed conflicts together signify the limits of open violence between states. International law may only impose a limit, but may not prohibit the direct use of force within a state. These limits are as follows: Article 4 of the International Covenant on Civil and Political Rights (non-derogable rights) and regulations concerning non-international armed conflicts contained in common Article 3 of the 1949 Geneva Conventions and Additional Protocol II of 1977. As Denise Plattner (1988, p. 10) writes:

Mezzo-soprano is a voice of half-way between soprano and contralto. The part it has to sing is reputedly the most difficult of all, but also the most delicate and expressive. In international humanitarian law, internal armed conflicts occupy a similarly intermediate and special place between international armed conflicts and internal disturbances. Like the mezzo-soprano's art, they are naturally subject to contradictory attractions — upward and downward attractions, so to speak.

According to Helmut Rumpf (1984, p. 437), negative peace between states

is tantamount to a stabilization of the status quo especially as regards national boundaries, while positive peace should give a chance to peaceful change.

Within international law, the concept of negative peace signifies a prohibition to change the status quo in a violent way, rather than the stabilization of the status quo. It is, however, unquestionable that we thus deprive change of its most dynamic and at the same time most devastating instrument. However, in the shadow of nuclear weapons there is no other choice. The only exclusion is the liberation struggle. Consequently, as an exception, there is a violent way to establish the state of positive peace. Nevertheless, the most important procedural issue related to positive peace is finding the balance between the need for stability and the dynamics of peaceful change. It is especially difficult to trace the concept of positive peace from present day universal international law; however, the observed principle of respect for human rights is most certainly a good example. Negative peace opens the possibility, but does not necessarily lead to the increasingly comprehensive practice of human rights, which is a vital issue of social emancipation within individual states. The latter is a necessary, but not sufficient, condition of democratic co-operation to replace structural inter-state dependencies.

2.3 Approaches to the right to peace

The concept of the right to negative peace may be significant from both practical and theoretical aspects. In this case, practice means the peace-keeping activity of the public, while theory relates to international law. According to Katarina Tomasevski (1982, p. 43):

The conception of peace as a human right would undoubtedly help in raising public awareness that everyone has a stake in peace-keeping, widening support for disarmament policy.

How the right to peace helps in raising public awareness is well illustrated by the following quotation from page 2 of the *PlanetHood* volume: 'Proclamation! I hereby assert: I have the right to live in a peaceful world free from the threat of death by nuclear war' (Ferencz and Keyes, 1988, p. 2).

As far as the theoretical significance of the concept is concerned, it lies mostly in the establishment of a *linkage* between the rights and the responsibilities of the subjects of international law, since the right to peace can be mentioned 'as an example of the linkage between human rights and peace.' However, the right to peace

forms a link between the principles of international law to peaceful coexistence of States belonging to differing social systems, the fundamental rights of peoples to self-determination and the basic right of each individual to life (Graefrath, 1985, p. 79).

Since the right to positive peace is a concept significantly more difficult to grasp, its practical mobilizing power is much smaller. In this respect, however, the argumentation used in relation to the right to development, which refers to the hopeless situation of the majority of Third World countries, may have a mobilizing effect. At the same time, it is obvious that the right to positive peace may also establish an intellectual *linkage*, for example between *international law and the future of mankind*. However, for the purposes of this chapter, in all further references to potential subjects of the right to peace, the notion of peace will be used in its negative sense.

In related literature, there are various approaches to the individual's right to peace. The right was first recognized by the Declaration on the Preparation of Societies for Life in Peace, adopted by the UN General Assembly on 15 December 1978 (resolution 33/73). Different approaches give different interpretations of the contents of the right to peace of the individual, varying according to what elements they find especially important. The right to peace lends special legitimation to an 'active social work towards shaping peaceful attitudes and public opinion favouring peace' (Lopatka, 1980, p. 366). Others are of the opinion that the right to peace also covers resistance against the implementation of government policies based on the use of force (Bilder, 1980, p. 387).

Of the views that give a radical interpretation of the right to peace of the individual, the position held by Asbjørn Eide is especially worth examining. According to Eide, the individual may resist military service if the military preparations of his country exceed the level necessary for defence. Moreover, he is obliged to refuse the order if it calls for participation in an act of aggression or unlawful intervention and if it has been qualified accordingly by the Security Council of the United Nations. If however, it is the General Assembly that makes a similar decision, the individual is free to decide whether or not he will obey the order (Eide, 1980b, as quoted by Lopatka, 1980, p. 366). Such a radical approach, however, is unrealistic. In a world where the drafting of a covenant that would include the individual responsibility of the politicians of the aggressor state is only a hope for the future, placing the burden of decision-making on the shoulders of the individual is hardly the right thing to do, since if the Security Council is unable to come to a decision, the individuals themselves would have to decide to take a stand against the national war machine. The sufficiency of a given level of defence is an issue that even military experts find it difficult to agree upon. Historical evidence demonstrates that not once has refusal to follow an order prevented an act of aggression. There still remains the question of how this idea could be formulated in terms of an international agreement or a simple UN General Assembly declaration and whether it is at all possible to establish links between the competence of the individual, the citizen, the Security Council or the General Assembly. By widening the scope of the political possibilities of the individual as such to nearly utopian extremes, the whole concept seems strongly influenced by *Sartrian* existentialism. The concept is more of a *radical utopia*, which in this case also fulfils the intellectual functions related to the phenomenon of human thinking.

Raising the issue of conscientious objection to military service represents a more realistic approach to the right of the individual to peace, since it has already been recognized by the domestic legal system of a number of states and the UN Commission on Human Rights has passed resolutions which call upon the states to refrain from the imprisonment of such persons and to introduce 'various forms of alternative service' (Resolution E/CN.4/1987 L 73). (It is worth noting in this context that the servicing of the 'baroque arsenal' requires a decreasing number of highly trained personnel and therefore provides the material basis for the possibility of conscientious objection to military service.)

As indicated already in the title of the Declaration on the Right of Peoples to Peace, adopted by the UN General Assembly on 12 November 1984 (resolution 39/11), peoples are also subjects of the right to peace.

The right to peace assists peoples to act on questions of war and peace. The history of the right to self-determination clearly shows that the *active subject* that has invoked this right has always been some sort of a liberation *organization*. The situation is similar in the case of the peoples' right to peace, since this right 'lends special legitimation to the worldwide peace movement' (Poeggel, 1982, p. 178). At this point, it may be of interest to recall Johan Galtung's (1988, p. 380) peace movement interpretation:

Perhaps the essence of the peace movement goes . . . back to the origins of the modern state. Perhaps it is a challenge to that vestige of feudalism, the right to exercise violence, vested in the leadership of the modern state as the successor to the feudal prince, who, in turn, exercised his power over life and death *gratia dei*.

Experts in international law represent strongly opposing views in relation to the issue of the necessity of 'peoples' rights. In the case of the peoples' right to peace according to Katarina Tomasevski (1982, p. 61), since 'security is being preserved by increasing capabilities of annihilation', 'all of humanity [is] a single helpless hostage'. Christian Tomuschat (1987, pp. 7–8), on the other hand, represents a different view when he writes:

To say that a people is against its government is tantamount to saying that dictatorship has emerged, which has suppressed the democratic rights of citizens ... As far as the domestic legal order is concerned ... rights of a people against its own government are simply inconceivable as long as the maxim 'Government of the people, by the people and for the people' is applied.

I believe that both views are somewhat exaggerated. The notion that humanity is a hostage of the arms race suggests that 'humanity' had no role whatsoever in the formation of such politics, which in turn implies that the democratic rights of citizens are nowhere valid. However, I believe that the quoted maxim is not invalidated by the fact that 'everywhere there are differences between governments and peoples' (Decree on Peace, 1987, p. 20), even if they are limited in their number and scope, or that the peoples (i.e. peace movements of the peoples in this case) impose demands upon their government as well as other governments. The origin of Tomuschat's (1987, p. 6) position lies in his belief that the peoples 'by definition ... constitute unorganized communities.' Consequently, he comes to the conclusion that 'it is difficult to see how ... the peoples promote this desirable aim', which is 'reasonable and balanced disarmament' (Tomuschat, 1987, p. 8). On the same basis, he also states that within the system of inter-state relations the peoples cannot play an active, independent role (1987, p. 6). Of course, should we accept peace organizations and movements as active subjects, this in itself is equal to the acknowledgment of the reality of their international activity, as, for example, is evinced by *Rainbow Warrior*. As Richard Falk (1987, p. 183) writes:

The Greenpeace provocation was to monitor and protest against French nuclear testing in the region of the Pacific Islands. Here, again, the statist refusal to desist from such testing which is harmful to health, environment and resources indicates the impotence of the established procedures of international society to challenge official French behaviour. Only a private transnational actor has been able to pose such a challenge. It operates within a framework of militant nonviolence, but it generates a violent style of reaction.

As far as the contents of the peoples' right to peace is concerned, it must include the demand for negative peace and its preconditions. Therefore, these are *demands* that either support or oppose the policy of a government or governments. These demands implicate that 'competent agencies examine the situation in all cases',[1] i.e. that decisions be considered and reconsidered. This is in fact every citizen's right. Citizens, however, need to act in a concerted way in order to articulate their demands.

3. Right to a healthy environment

There will clearly be enormous conflicts about whose rights and whose responsibilities are going to be put in. Matina Horner ('Agenda 2000', *The Christian Science Monitor*, 8–14 August, 1988, p. B6).

3.1 The effects of the abuse of the environment

Of those who identify international relations with power politics, most of those who specialize in other than the fields of international law often tend to see nothing but hysterical exaggerations behind the statements of scientists and activists concerned about the deterioration of the environment. As Richard Falk (1983, p. 13) says:

In the face of all evidence of disarray the realists turn away, occasionally pausing long enough to condemn those who take such issues seriously as 'alarmists', 'salvationists' or 'prophets of doom'.

However, the growing number of various phenomena, supported by various scientific sources — water and air pollution, atmospheric sulphur and carbon dioxide, ozone depletion, desertification, acid rain, global warming and so forth — have influenced the political life of states and international co-operation. Under the influence of ecology politics or political ecology if you like, social movements and political parties have been formed and international institutions established, for example the UN Environmental Programme. Today, environmental law is a part of both domestic law and the corpus of public international law.

Despite such achievements as the Ozone Agreement, no breakthrough has been achieved in the field of international co-operation and almost every day another disaster occurs. The use of natural resources in most cases *remains* at an unacceptably high 'social cost'. As Dan Tarlock and Pedro Tarak (1983, p. 85) write:

The continued use of watersheds, land resources, atmosphere as sinks for the

---

[1]   This is the wording used in the draft Protocol on the right to a healthy environment which was to be annexed to the European Convention on Human Rights.

disposal of human residuals results in unacceptable social costs, such as increased illness, crop losses, ecosystem disruption and creation of low level, long term health risks such as cancer.

Many of such social costs directly affect individuals and communities. This and the everyday encounters with the waste of natural resources have a mobilizing effect. Here also a 'new way of thinking', global thinking, is necessary.

What we need is a set of *environmental* accounts that take seriously the notion that resources and environment are a part of the productive stock of a society — just the way that the capital stock investment in a factory or an educational system are part of the productive future potential of the area (emphasis in original).

writes William C. Clark ('Agenda 2000', *The Christian Science Monitor*, 8-14 August, 1988, p. B5).

When examining the aims of the environmentalist social movements and the values behind related legal regulation, we encounter a post-material view, which places the quality of life above the growth of GNP, and, takes a long-term economic approach which wishes to ensure that future generations will also enjoy the benefits of natural resources. The legal defence of these values is often less effective than it could be, due to the weakness of internal legal regulation (the insufficient stringency of sanctions as is the case in Hungary, for example) as well as the often not sufficiently strict manner in which responsibilities deriving from relevant international agreements are established. The full development of international environmental law is hindered by the situation of the majority of the developing countries. Will the developed countries be willing to 'pay rent for those environmental resources they do not wish to see destroyed' ('Agenda 2000', *The Christian Science Monitor*, 8-14 August, 1988, p. B5)? This is one of the most vital issues of ecology; it is also a challenge to international environmental law.

3.2 Approaches to the right to a healthy environment

The right to a healthy environment, in a similar way as the right to peace, may naturally increase the awareness of the public in relation to this issue, since it lends legitimacy to those ecological movements that 'generate debate about environmental problems and their solution' (Tarlock and Tarack, 1983, p. 93) which include an interplay between cultural norms and the law. Christopher D. Stone (1988, p. 65) describes this process:

At some level of growth the groups complain that the practices they oppose deserve not only moral censure, but also legal relief. Activity focuses upon proposed legislation or upon a vivid legal test case. The agitation of law reform unites the movement behind a tangible and often dramatic agenda. Moreover, it affords the reformers an opportunity to educate the public (as well as themselves) as to their exact position. Public consciousness is advanced so that an idea which might originally have been dismissed with contempt or humour . . . that animals have rights — is received as a familiar and intelligible, if not yet compelling, alternative. The legal measures that result from this first stage will quite likely be less than what the advocates wanted. Nonetheless, even a token victory in a legislature or court authoritatively legitimates the advocates' concern. This initial legitimation strengthens and broadens support in the general culture, thereby advancing the prospects for a subsequent generation of proposals.

A vital aspect of the individual right to a healthy environment has for some time already been a part of sub-regional international law. The Convention on the Protection of the Environment, also known as the Nordic Environmental Convention, was concluded in 1972. This Convention, as pointed out by B. Johnson Theutenberg (1984, p. 240), declares:

Any individual who is affected or may be affected, by nuisance from harmful activities has the right to challenge the permissibility of such activities before appropriate court or administrative authority of that State, regardless of the fact the he is *not* a citizen of that State but of *another contracting State*. He has also a right of appeal against any decision (emphasis in original).

This must have been the solution that inspired the 'principle of equal right of hearing' which is included in the legally non-obligatory 'Principles concerning Transfrontier Pollution' adopted by the OECD countries in 1977. Another 1977 OECD recommendation calls upon its member states to introduce legal regulations that provide protection on an equal basis for persons inside and outside the polluting country. This would mean that those affected by pollution should have the right of access to legal and administrative procedure in the polluting country and they should have the right to obtain compensation for damage. The right, according to the recommendation, should also apply to those persons seeking the prevention of pollution from abroad and those who suffer from exposure to pollution. Consequently, the individual right to a healthy environment must already exist in the OECD countries.

The individual right to a healthy environment may in the future be extended to include the right to refuse to perform work harmful to the environment. However, the fact that no analogous solution has occurred in relation to the right of the individual to peace, i.e. the creation of a right to refuse to produce weapons for use by countries in a state of war, for example, indicates that this idea is for the time being utopian.

Environmental movements are the active subjects of the peoples' right to a healthy environment. These movements represent an *ecological ethos* (Falk, 1983, p. 264) of sorts. The essence of their activity is well reflected in a draft Protocol to the European Convention on Human Rights:

Article 1
(1) No one should be exposed to intolerable damage or threats to his health or to intolerable impairment of his well-being as a result of adverse changes in the natural conditions of life.
(2) An impairment of well-being may, however, be deemed to be tolerable if it is necessary for the maintenance and development of the economic conditions of the community and if there is no alternative way of making it possible to avoid this impairment.
Article 2
(1) If adverse changes in the natural conditions of life are likely to occur in his vital sphere as a result of the action of other parties, any individual is entitled to demand that the competent agencies examine the situation in all cases where Article 1 applies.
(2) Any individual acting under paragraph 1 shall, within a reasonable time, receive detailed information stating what measures — if any — have been taken to prevent those adverse changes.

Although neither the draft Protocol nor the annexed memorandum provide an answer to such questions as whether or not a state must pay damages for prior injuries (Gromley, 1976, p. 93), these documents nevertheless represent significant attempts to describe the ethos of ecology in legal terms.

4. Right to development

A *lucus a non lucendo* is an explanation by contraries ... Critics have maintained that the New International Economic Order is also a *lucus a non lucendo*. There is nothing new in it (they say), because all the proposals have been made before. It is not international, for much of it is about delinking and self-reliance. It is not economic, but about power and its distribution. And it is not an order, for some advocates of the NIED call for confrontation and conflict, while others wish to replace the magical order of the market by the chaos of bureaucratic controls. These critics, and the politicians and officials from the North engaged in the North-South negotiations are like an inverted Micawber: they always wait for something to turn down. Would it not be more constructive to meet inadequate or counterproductive proposals from the South by positive counter-proposals on the part of the Northern negotiators? (Paul Streeten, 1984, p. 5).

4.1 What kind of development?

Even after 'sustainable development', 'self-reliance' and a number of other development strategies, and even after the work, resolutions and documents of international organizations, and the thousands of pages of political declarations, books and studies such as the Brandt reports or the Brundtland report, the question asked by Mme Rajni Patel, an Indian social scientist, 'Whom are we trying to fool?', remains justified. Suffice it to cast an eye on some alarming statistical data on the situation in the Third World: each day 40,000 young children die unnecessarily of such easily curable diseases as diarrhoea. This means 20 million children die annually and another four times as many go to bed each night hungry or malnourished (Patel, 1988, p. 17).

Development, and especially economic development, has been in the focus of scientific research for quite a long period of time. Several decades ago the view that economic development should be seen as the linear consequence of various stages was generally accepted. Such an approach meant that interest centred around the way a given stage of development can be left and the next entered. In the light of contemporary theories, it seems that the most important issue is the evaluation of integration into the international economic system. There exist two opposing theories in this respect. According to the first, the key to economic growth is increasingly intensive participation in the system of international economic relations, while according to the second not only is the operation of this system the actual cause of underdevelopment, it is also responsible for the preservation of this situation. There exists a conciliatory view as well, according to which if a developing country follows a selective policy it may benefit from the positive effects transmitted by the industrialized states, without having to surrender itself to parallel negative forces. In other words, the solution is to avoid both absolute integration and total isolation (Streeten, 1977, pp. 4–5). But even such a seemingly simple recipe for economic growth holds out rather grim prospects. According to a calculation based on World Bank statistical data, it would take China 2990 and Mauritius 3224 years to reach the GNP per capita level of the most developed countries ('Agenda 2000', *The Christian Science Monitor*, 8–14 August, 1988, p. B7). Development, however, must not be identified with the growth of GNP, since it must also involve a radical change in the system of distribution. According to a World Bank estimate, a 2 per cent annual transfer of money from the upper classes to the bottom 40 per cent of the populations of the developing countries could successfully finance both the short-term and the long-term goals of development strategy over a 25-year period (Falk, 1983, p. 264). But this is not the only reason why economic growth should not be identified with development. As pointed out by Rodrigo Botero ('Agenda 2000', *The Christian Science Monitor*, 8–14 August, 1988, p. D7):

Lowering the infant mortality rate means much more to the ordinary man and woman of a developing country than obtaining an x percentage of growth in the GNP per capita, which to the majority of [those] people is an absolutely abstract and mysterious concept.

This remark leads to the recognition that 'the human person is the central subject of development' (Article 1, paragraph 1, of the UN Declaration on the Right to Development), consequently economic growth is merely an instrument and not an ultimate purpose. It follows that economic development must never serve as a justification for the violation of human rights. Development 'with a human face' must preserve the cultural identity of peoples and nations (Weeremantry, 1985, pp. 482–3).

Can development be accelerated internationally? There are some who believe that the solution lies in the action of the 'invisible hand of the free market', whereas others stress the necessity of a 'deliberate strategy'. One of the proponents of this latter view is Andrew Young (1985, pp. 443–4) who summoned as examples the New Deal, the rise of the American South and the success of the Marshall Plan, to argue that the developing world could serve as the only real market for the European Economic Community, the United States and Japan. Interstate solidarity, the belief in international social justice, or the colonialism-based moral obligation of the developed world to provide assistance all could serve as a basis for a deliberate strategy. However, this basis could also be the right of the developing countries to development.

4.2. A right of the developing states

The twentieth–century development of capitalist society led to profound changes in the domain of civil law, which regulates financial and personal relations. As a result of the class struggle, and in close correlation with the unfolding of the welfare state concept, social law and the obligation of the welfare state concept, social law and the obligation of the state to provide for its citizens (*Fürsorgepflicht*) (Eörsi, 1975, pp. 217-25) developed. This period also saw the unfolding of economic, social and cultural rights.

As a result of the growing self–awareness, the changes in historical power relations, and last, but not least, the fact that post-industrial capitalist development does not necessitate drawing foreign territories under its own sovereignty in legal terms, Third World states gained independence. Currently, the most significant scene of the class struggle has shifted to the North-South, centre-periphery relationship. The question now is, to what extent has international law become 'social law' as a result?

International law with 'social' features is actually what science since the mid-1970s has been calling the international law of development. The essence of the international law of development is the legal reflection of the material inequality of states. Oscar Schachter (1976, pp. 9-10) points out the most important element of this function:

What is striking about this conception is not so much its espousal by the large majority of poor and handicapped countries but the fact that it has been accepted — by and large — by the most affluent countries to whom the demands are addressed. The evidence for this can be found not only in the international resolutions with which the rich countries have concurred but also, and more convincingly, in the series of actions by them to grant assistance and preferences to those in the less-developed world, though it may well be the case that their actions fall short of meeting the actual requirements of many of the recipient countries, the scale and the duration of the response have been substantial enough to demonstrate the practical acceptance of a responsibility based on the entitlement of those in need.

The assistance to developing countries and the differential treatment offered may be considered a part of present day customary international law. This may be proven by the existence of official development assistance, the work of universal international financial institutions (International Monetary Fund, World Bank, International Development Association), the UN Development Programme, and, in the field of foreign trade, Article 36 of the General Agreement on Tariffs and Trade treaty (as a result of which reciprocity does not necessarily prevail between developing and developed countries), regulations for the transfer of technology in the UN Convention on the Law of the Sea, the Lomé Convention's Stabex mechanism, and so forth. *The essence of the right to development of states is, therefore, the right to a differential treatment and the right to demand development assistance.* Since states provide special assistance only to countries recognized as developing countries, the right to development is in fact only the right of the developing countries to development. According to Roland Y. Rich (1983, p. 327), the legal basis of the right to development of the developing states is clear since 'state practice largely confirms the *opinio iuris* in this area, or alternatively, the *opinio iuris* articulates the growing practice of states'. Schachter (1979, pp. 251-2) found a more sophisticated solution:

But it can be said that the expressions of responsibility by the Governments of rich countries, backed by continued grants have created a climate of opinion and expectations that tend to support their continuation and in that way, the line between voluntary and obligatory aid has begun to blur. It may still be possible for donors to cut down on aid or to introduce limitations of one kind or another but it has become much less likely that they will completely eliminate assistance.

If we suppose that one person in relation to another is granted a right to something, then this causes a substantial change in the interrelation of these two persons. Alexis de Tocqueville writes:

There is nothing which, generally speaking, elevates and sustains the human spirit more than the idea of rights. There is something great and virile in the idea of a right which removes from any request its suppliant character, and places the one who claims it on the same level as the one who grants it (de Tocqueville and Beaumont, 1968, as quoted by Minogue, 1978, p. 34).

De Tocqueville, however, believes that the above does not apply in the case of those demands that the poor impose on the rich, an analogous situation to the one discussed: 'But the right of the poor to obtain society's help is unique in that instead of elevating the heart of the man who exercises it, lowers him' (de Tocqueville and Beaumont, 1968, as quoted by Minogue, 1978, p. 34).

More than one hundred years later, Kenneth Boulding came to a different conclusion: 'If A gives B something without expecting anything in return the inference must be drawn that B is "part" of A, or that A and B together are part of a larger system of interests and organisations' (Boulding, 1965, as quoted by Bull, 1977, pp. 87-8).

In relation to the first opinion it may be worth adding that the practice of such a right hardly lowers the one who exercises it more than his actual material state. This is especially true in the international context. As far as Boulding's statement is concerned, it highlights an important communal function of the right to development of the developing states. This right is a strengthening bond of the international community.

The right of the developing countries to development can obviously promote the implementation of human rights, especially economic, social and cultural rights. As Pieter van Dijk (1984, p. 227) notes: 'the State must be enabled by other States . . . to implement human rights.' However, this does not mean that underdevelopment can be accepted as an excuse for the violation of civil and political rights. In fact, van Dijk (1984, p. 227) believes that the right to development entails an obligation in relation to the developing country as well, and that is the respect for human rights:

The meaning of the right to development . . . also entails an obligation. The obligation to pursue a policy aimed at using the available resources in such a way as to realize human rights to the fullest possible extent, according priority to those rights which are essential for an existence worthy of human dignity.

The source of this obligation is not so much the right to development but rather the principle of international law that declares the observance of human rights, as well as the legal obligations set forth in the two Covenants. This is especially true since despite the fact that some countries, the Netherlands for example, have linked the issues of human rights and development assistance, this solution should not be considered a rule of customary law.

The right to development raises problems that are linked to the struggle of the developing world for a new international economic order. When the developing countries demand the expansion of development assistance and differential treatment, they have the new international economic order in mind as the ultimate purpose. The problem of the right to development 'serves to highlight the need to create a new international order, in social and cultural as much as in economic terms' (Alston, 1980, p. 108).

5. Right to development as individual and peoples' right

The right to development of the individual is definitely a synthetic right. Concerning its contents there is no full agreement. According to one interpretation, the individual right to development 'is nothing but the aggregate of the rights recognized in the international covenants' (Abi-Saab, 1980, p. 163). Another approach finds that the individual right to development is an aggregate of the basic rights (right to life, right to adequate food, clothing and medical care) and the non-derogable rights of the International Covenant on Civil and Political Rights (Mestdagh, 1981, p. 50). The author of the above view, Karel de Vey Mestdagh believes that another element should be added: 'the minimum level of opportunities for individuals to participate in the development process' (1981, p. 50). The Declaration on the Right to Development does not highlight civil and political rights, but even the rights it includes are mentioned *inter alia*:

Article 8
1. States should undertake, at the national level, all necessary measures for the realization of the right to development and shall ensure, *inter alia*, equality of opportunity for all in their access to basic resources, education, health services, food, housing, employment and the fair distribution of income. Effective measures should be undertaken to ensure that women have an active role in the development process. Appropriate economic and social reforms should be made with a view to eradicating all social injustices.
2. States should encourage popular participation in all spheres as an important factor in development and in the full realization of all human rights.

Here, it may be interesting to refer to H.G. Wells' *The Rights of Man* (1940, p. 62). During the Second World War the famous writer prepared a manifesto, the Declaration of Rights, to answer the question, 'what are we fighting for?' It already included the right to development of the individual:

(1) That every man without distinction of race or colour is entitled to nourishment, housing, clothing, medical care and attention sufficient to realise his full possibilities of physical and mental development and to keep him in a state of health from his birth to death.

'To realise his full possibilities of physical and mental development' — it is the final message of the right to development of the individual, already stated almost 50 years ago.

As far as the peoples' right to development is concerned, the economists of development economics, the foreign office officials of development diplomacy or the bureaucracy of international organizations dealing with development can hardly be considered as development-oriented social movements. The Group of 77 has tried to act as the 'trade union' of the developing world. It seems, however, that the right of developing countries to development is the only basis on which relationships within this group of countries are practicable. There exist, however, organizations that protest against *maldevelopment* (a notion introduced by Asbjørn Eide, 1980a, p. 415), that try to prevent the destruction of traditional values and structures, although their number and influence is smaller than those of the peace and environment movements. For example, there exist town preservationist movements in Hungary as well. Such movements are the embodiment of community awareness and at the same time the active subjects of the peoples' right to development, or more precisely put, the right to protest against maldevelopment, the essence of which is the right to demand that governments reconsider poor decisions.

6. Conclusions

Of the right to peace, the right to a healthy environment and the right to development, the structure of the first two is fundamentally the same, while the last mentioned is different in that it is justified to limit the right to development to a finite group of countries: the developing countries. Whereas in relation to the right to development, a group of countries may demand a well-defined pattern of behaviour from the others — the right holders and duty bearers can be defined and distinguished — in the case of the right to peace and the right to a healthy environment all states are right holders and duty bearers with respect to the same obligations. Consequently, the rather doubtful notion of 'generations of rights' cannot be applied in this case, although the essence of this concept 'is nothing less than an attempt to transpose, synthesize and adapt contemporary global challenges to the human rights system' (Drzewicki, 1988, p. 46).

In response to global problems, as Rajni Kothari (1983, as quoted by Alger, 1988, p. 331) stated, 'grassroots movements and non-party formations' come 'from a deep stirring of consciousness and an intuitive awareness of crises that could conceivably be turned into a catalyst of new opportunities'. These new movements are trying to 'open alternative political spaces' (Kothari, 1983, as quoted by Alger, 1988, p. 331) and have actually done so.

The movements that first had their voice heard in Western Europe in the 1970s, as well as those which, since the second half of the 1980s, have begun to represent an increasingly influential force in

East European countries, prove the significance and dynamics of social action on these issues. Social autonomy has expanded to stop the arms race, and to prevent the destruction of the environment and traditional structures and values. But the voices can be heard from the Third World as well. These movements 'challenge traditional state prerogatives' (especially security policy) and 'simultaneously, development experts have been challenged by grassroots movements', wrote Chadwick Alger (1989, p. 6). Expressed in a different way by Richard Falk (1989, p. 58):

One central insight of popular movements over the last two decades has been the imperative need to supplement the international legal efforts by governments to uphold human rights with a quite distinctive conception of standards and procedures based on the right of peoples, championing claims on behalf of individuals and groups in relation to issues of peace, justice, basic human needs, and equitable development that are put forward outside the formal state-centred framework of international relations . . . To affirm the rights of peoples in an expression of legal, moral and political support on a transnational basis for popular struggles against various contemporary forms of oppression.

The concept of peoples' rights is in a 'in search of subjects' state (Marie, 1986, p. 201).

International law — with the exception of the individual — operates with formal subjects. When a health treaty is concluded, the negotiating parties are not the two states but two ministers of health, a central body of one state administration co-operates with its counterpart in another (Valki, 1981, p. 21). In the past, in the time of absolute monarchy, international law was a law of ruling persons at that time: the formal and the active subject coincided (Pound, 1923, p. 76). Today, the government acts in the name of the state. In case of international organizations that are subjects of international law, suffice it to mention their principal attribute: 'intergovernmental'. Their real danger in relation to peoples' rights, therefore, lies in the way they enable *governments* to act on the international scene behind a *new* mask. Such is the obvious intention of a number of developing countries which feel weak within the system of inter-state politics and believe that if they present themselves in the capacity of a 'people' as well, their voice will be better heard. The solution to the dilemma of subjectivity might be formal recognition of social movements.

The statement that global problems necessitate global co-operation does not have to exclude all active subjects other than governments. What is needed is a *complex* superstructure: intergovernmental (UN bodies, deep Seabed Authority) and inter-NGO, as Majid Rahnema (1986, p. 44) observed:

That link together the grass-roots movements of the South but also establish new forms of coalition between them and those of the North . . . To sum up, new ways and means are to be imagined, mainly to allow each different group to be informed, to learn about other human groups and cultures . . . to be open to differences, to learn from them . . . only a highly decentralized, non-bureaucratic, intercultural rather than international network of persons and groups respond to such needs.

The final aim is clear, and is already stated in the Universal Declaration of Human Rights. Article 28 says:

Everyone is entitled to a social and international order in which the rights and freedoms set forth in this Declaration can be fully realized.

Bibliography

Abi-Saab, Georges, 1980. 'The Legal Formulation of a Right to Development (Subjects and Content)', in René-Jean Dupuy (ed.), *The Right to Development at International Level*, Workshop, The Hague, 16–18 October 1979. Alphen aan den Rijn: Sijthoff-Noordhoff.

Alger, Chadwick, 1988. 'Perceiving, Analysing and Coping with the Local-Global Thing', *International Social Science Journal*, vol. 60, no. 3.

Alger, Chadwick, 1989. 'A Grassroots Approach to Life in Peace', *Peace Review*, vol. 1, no. 3.

Alston, Philip, 1980. 'The Right to Development at International Level', in René-Jean Dupuy (ed.), *The Right to Development at International Level*, Workshop, the Hague, 16–18 October 1979. Alphen aan den Rijn: Sijthoff-Noordhoff.

Alston, Philip, 1982. 'A Third Generation of Solidarity Rights: Progressive Development or Obfuscation of International Human Rights Law?', *Netherlands International Law Review*, vol. 29, no. 3.

Bilder, Richard, 1980. 'The Individual and the Right to Peace', *Bulletin of Peace Proposals*, vol. 11, no. 4.

Blainey, Geoffrey, 1983. *The Causes of War*. London: Macmillan.

Boulding, Kenneth E., 1965. 'The Concept of World Interest', in Bert F. Hoselitz (ed.), *Economics and the Idea of Mankind*. New York: Columbia University Press.

Boulding, Kenneth E., 1978. *Stable Peace*. Austin: The University of Texas Press.

Bull, Hedley, 1977. *A Study of Order in World Politics*. London: Macmillan.

'Decree on Peace, 1987', *GDR Committee for Human Rights Bulletin*, vol. 13, no. 1.

Dijk, Pieter van, 1984. 'The Right to Development and Human Rights: A Matter of Equality and Priority', in *Israel Yearbook on Human Rights*, vol. 14.

Drzewicki, Krysztof, 1988. 'The Rights of Solidarity as Human Rights: Some Methodological Aspects', *Mennesker og Rettigheter-Nordic Journal of Human Rights*, vol. 6, no. 4.

Eide, Asbjørn, 1980a. 'Maldevelopment and the "Rights to Development": A Critical Note With a Constructive Intent', in René-Jean Dupuy (ed.), *The Right to Development at International Level*, Workshop, the Hague, 16–18 October 1979. Alphen aan den Rijn: Sijthoff-Noordhoff.

Eide, Asbjørn, 1980b. *Towards a Declaration on Right to Peace*, a discussion paper presented to the III. Armand Hammer Conference, Warsaw, 3–6 July 1980.

Eörsi, Gyula, 1975. *Összehasonlíto polgári jog* (Comparative civil law). Budapest: Akadémiai.

Falk, Richard, 1983. *The End of World Order: Essays on Normative International Relations.* New York: Holmes and Meier.

Falk, Richard, 1987. 'The Global Promise of Social Movements: Explorations at the Edge of Time', *Alternatives*, vol. 12, no. 2.

Falk, Richard, 1989. 'United States Foreign Policy as an Obstacle to the Rights of Peoples', *Social Justice*, vol. 16, no. 1.

Ferencz, Benjamin B. and Ken Keyes, 1988. *Planethood: The Key to Your Survival and Prosperity.* Coos Bay, Oregon: Vision Books.

Galtung, Johan, 1988. 'The Peace Movement: An Exercise in Micro-Macro Linkages', *International Social Science Journal*, vol. 60, no. 3.

Graefrath, Bernhard, 1985. 'Priority to Right to Peace: On the 40th Anniversary of the United Nations', *GDR Committee for Human Rights Bulletin*, vol. 11, no. 2.

Gromley, Paul W., 1976. *Human Rights and the Environment: The Need for International Co-operation.* Leyden: Sijthoff.

Herczegh, Géza, 1982. 'Conditions of Effectivity in International Law', in Vanda Lamm (ed.), *Impact of International Organizations on Public Administration*, Conference held in Pilisszentkereszt, Hungary, 4–6 May 1982. Budapest: Complex Development Research Programme in Public Administration.

Johnson Theutenberg, B., 1985. 'The International Environmental Law: Some Basic Viewpoints', in René-Jean Dupuy (ed.), *The Future of the International Law of the Environment*, The Hague, 12–14 November 1984. Dordrecht: Martinus Nijhoff.

Kaldor, Mary, 1983. *The Baroque Arsenal.* London: Abacus.

Kant, Immanuel, 1985. *Az örök béke* (Zum ewigen Frieden). Budapest: Európa.

Kelson, Hans, 1942. *Law and Peace in International Relations.* Cambridge, Mass.: Harvard University Press.

Klare, Michael, 1983. 'New Arms Technology', issue 'The Conventional Weapons Fallacy', *The Nation*, 9 April.

Kothari, Rajni, 1983. 'Party and State in our Times: The Rise of Non-Party Political Formations', *Alternatives*, vol. 9, no. 4.

Larson, Arthur, 1962. 'The Role of Law in Building Peace', in Q. Wright, F.W. Evan and Deutsch (eds), *Preventing World War III.* New York: Simon and Schuster.

Lider, Julian, 1979. *On the Nature of War.* Farnborough, Hants: Saxon House.

Lopatka, Adam, 1980. 'The Right to Live in Peace as a Human Right', *Bulletin of Peace Proposals*, vol. 11, no. 4.

Marie, Jean-Bernhard, 1986. 'Relations Between Peoples' Rights and Human Rights: Semantic and Methodological Distinctions', *Human Rights Law Journal*, vol. 7, no. 2–4.

Marks, Stephan P., 1985. 'Emerging Human Rights: A New Generation for the 1980's', in R. Falk, F. Kratochwill and Sh. Mendlowitz (eds), *International Law.* Boulder/London: Westview.

Mavi, Viktor, 1987–88. 'Szolidaritási jogok avagy az emberi jogok harmadik nemzedéke' (Solidarity Rights or else the Third Generation of Human Rights), *Állam és Jogtudomány*, vol. 30, no. 1-2.

Mazrui, Ali, 1967. *Towards a Pax Africana*. London: Weidenfeld and Nicolson.

Mestdagh, Karel de Vey, 1981. 'Right to Development', *Netherlands International Law Review*, vol. 28, no. 1.

Minogue, K.R., 1978. 'Natural Rights, Ideology and the Game of Life', in E. Kamenka and Alice Erh-Soon Tay (eds), *Human Rights*. London: Edward Arnold.

Patel, Rajni, 1988. 'Interview', *Heti Világgazdaság*, 2 July.

Plattner, Denise, 1988. 'Internal Armed Conflicts, or Mezzo-Soprano's Art', *Dissemination*, no. 9.

Pound, Roscoe, 1923. 'Philosophical Theory and International Law', *Bibliotheca Visseriana*, vol. 1.

Poeggel, Walter, 1982. 'Human Rights and Peace', *Kansainoikeus — Ius Gentium*, vol. 4, no. 1-2.

Rahnema, Majid, 1986. 'Under the Banner of Development', *Development*, no. 1-2.

Ramcharan, B.G., 1987. 'Peoples' Rights and Minorities Rights', *Nordic Journal of International Law — Acta scandinavica juris gentium*, vol. 56, no. 1.

Rich, Roland Y., 1983. 'The Rights to Development as an Emerging Human Right', *Virginia Journal of International Law*, vol. 23 (1984) no. 2.

Rumpf, Helmut, 1984. 'The Concepts of Peace and War in International Relations', *German Yearbook of International Law*, vol. 27.

Schachter, Oscar, 1976. 'The Evolving International Law of Development', *Columbia Journal of Transnational Law*, vol. 15, no. 1.

Schachter, Oscar, 1979. 'Principles of International Social Justice', in Gabriel M. Wilner, *Jus et Societas: Essays in Tribute to Wolfgang Friedman*. The Hague: Nijhoff.

Sieghart, Paul, 1983. *The International Law of Human Rights*. Oxford: Clarendon Press.

Stone, Christopher, 1988. 'The Law as a Force in Shaping Cultural Norms Relating to War and the Environment', in Arthur H. Westing, *Cultural Norms, War and the Environment*. Oxford: Oxford University Press.

Streeten, Paul, 1977. 'L'évolution des théories relatives au développement économique', *Problémes Economiques*, no. 1546, 9 November.

Streeten, Paul, 1984. 'Interdependence: A North-South Perspective', *Development and Peace*, vol. 5, no. 1.

Szentes, Tamás, 1987. 'Real Emancipation and Peaceful Cooperation Aiming at a New Democratic World Order', *Bulletin of Peace Proposals*, vol. 18, no. 3.

Tarlock, Dan A. and Pedro Tarak, 1983. 'An Overview of Comparative Environmental Law', *Denver Journal of International Law and Policy*, vol. 13, no. 1.

Tocqueville, A. de and G. de Beaumont, 1968. *Tocqueville and Beaumont on Social Reform*. Edited and translated with an introduction by Seymour Drescher. New York: Harper & Row.

Tomasevski, Katarina, 1982. 'The Right to Peace', *Current Research on Peace and Violence*, vol. 5, no. 1.

Tomuschat, Christian, 1986. 'Rights of Peoples: Some Preliminary Observations', in Y. Hangartner and S. Treschsel (eds), *Völkerrecht im Dienste des Menschen: Festschrift für Hans Haug*. Bern: Verlag Paul Haupt.

Tomuschat, Christian, 1987. *The Rights of Peoples and Human Rights, their Relationship within the Context of Western Europe*, Unesco Symposium, Canberra, Australia, 24-28 August 1987.

Tromp, Hylke, 1987. *On Peace and Research*. A contribution to the discussions in working group VIII at the General Pugwash Conference, Gmunden am Traunsee, Austria, 1-6 September 1987.

Valki, László, 1981. *A nemzetközi jog sajátos társadalmi természete* (The particular social nature of international law). Budapest: Akadémiai.

Waltz, Kenneth N., 1979. *Theory of International Politics*. Reading, MA: Addison-Wesley.

Weeremantry, C.G., 1985. 'The Right to Development', *The Indian Journal of International Law*, vol. 25, no. 3-4.

Wells, H.G., 1940. *The Rights of Man*. Harmondsworth: Penguin.

Weil, Prosper, 1983. 'Towards Relative Normativity in International Law', *American Journal of International Law*, vol. 77, no. 3.

Weston, Burns H., Richard A. Falk and Anthony A. D'Amato, 1980. *International Law and World Order*. St Paul, Minn.: West Publishing Co.

Wheeler, Nicholas J. and Ken Booth, 1987. 'Beyond the Security Dilemma: Technology, Strategy and International Security', in Carl G. Jacobsen (ed.), *The Uncertain Course of New Weapons, Strategies and Mind-sets*. Oxford: Oxford University Press.

Young, Andrew, 1985. 'Human Right or Necessity?', *California Western International Law Journal*, vol. 15, no. 3.

10 Between Helsinkis — and Beyond? Human Rights in the CSCE (Conference on Security and Co-operation in Europe) Process

Jan Helgesen

1. Introduction: from the Prague spring to the Berlin fall

As the media have been reporting on recent events in Eastern Europe, each one more incredible than the last, this writer has been confronted with a fundamental problem: is it possible from now on to analyse and predict the evolution — or rather, the revolution — in Eastern Europe within a scientific paradigm? Or is it more honest to leave these matters to someone else — some clairvoyant with metaphysical skills? An experiment to test this hypothesis: let us assume that less than two years ago, in December 1988, a scientist in an article like this predicted that within the next year a Christian Solidarity leader would be the Prime Minister of Poland, that the Berlin Wall would fall down, that the playwright and novelist Vaclav Havel would be the president of Czechoslovakia and that President Ceauscescu should be brought before a martial court and executed. Would such a person have any scientific credibility at all? Certainly not. How then, is it scientifically credible to write an article in 1990 when the perspective leads into the future? One thing is to describe the different stages between the Helsinki Meeting in 1975 and the Helsinki Meeting in 1992 — 'between Helsinkis'. It is quite a different matter to pass well into the 1990s — and to predict the mainstreams of the East-West human rights process in the next decade — 'beyond Helsinki'. This article has a more modest aim: to describe and not to predict. It is tempting to guess, however.

Adding to the complications, a description of the past in times like these is of little interest when it comes to grasping the future. To paraphrase a famous sentence by the German J.H. von Kirchmann: revolutions are making whole libraries into waste paper. Under these circumstances there are few lessons to be learned from history. Beyond Helsinki is an era beyond a strict scientific analysis. We will all include our hopes, our imaginations, our concern and our deep emotions in that analysis.

In retrospect, nothing has happened in accordance with tradition. Not even the calendar is correct. The period between the Prague spring and the Berlin fall lasted for more than 20 years. And it was certainly not a hot summer, rather a chilly winter. As influential commentators in the West feared a new Tienanmen at Alexander-platz, they witnessed instead the fall of the Wall — the very symbol of a divided Europe. From now on, the words 'Berlin fall' have a double meaning. And from that moment we are approaching the human rights problem in a pan-European process with our hearts, our emotions as much as with our brains, our intellect.

The Helsinki process has been called a child of the Cold War. Viewed against its historical background, in its political context, this is a sound judgment. Viewed in terms of its political functions, the effects of this process, the statement is false. One could possibly argue that what was born as a Cold War baby has developed into a relatively harmonious, relaxed and self-confident teenager. The Helsinki process has contributed actively to the reduction of tensions between East and West, as we have witnessed during the last months (and more).

After the summit meeting at Malta between presidents Bush and Gorbachev (December 1989), the cold war has been declared dead. Does this mean that the Helsinki Process has reached the end, that the political resources in the CSCE regime are exhausted? Most observers do not believe that this is so. But this belongs to the uncertain future.

2. The background of the Final Act

The Second World War ended without a formal peace treaty. The new borders were drawn as a consequence of the *de facto* military situation on a given day. One cannot approach the CSCE process without keeping this fact in mind.

East and West have had different perceptions of the status quo in post-war Europe. The Warsaw Pact countries wished very strongly to have formal recognition of the *de facto* borders. Furthermore, they were interested in a broad discussion on security matters in Europe. Viewed from the West and from NATO, such a formal recognition of a divided Europe was most undesirable. The focus was turned on the two German states. The Federal Republic of Germany, as well as the other NATO countries, did not want to compromise on this point. The dream of a reunited Germany was vivid and strong in the 1950s.

Gradually, however, co-operation between the East and the West in different political areas started. Once more, the focus was on Germany. The new Chancellor, Willy Brandt, launched his 'Ostpolitik'. This resulted in a general agreement between the two German states as well as in bilateral agreements with the Soviet Union, Poland and Czechoslovakia. This pragmatic policy had broad support within the NATO alliance.

In the late 1960s, the Western group discussed extensively the preconditions which were to be met before they were willing to get down to the real negotiations. From the very beginning, it was clear that the concept 'Europe' must include, not only the European Continent, but the North American states — the USA and Canada — as well. Another important precondition was to put human rights problems on the agenda. The underlying idea was that one could not conceivably speak of reduced tension — both military and politically — if the peoples of Europe were not liberated and were not free to travel, to exchange views, and so forth. The Neutral and Non-Aligned (hereafter: NNA) states shared this basic approach, and gradually the East was forced to include this item on the future agenda.

As the real negotiations slowly came closer, the Finnish Government, through President Kekkonen, proposed to host a conference on security and co-operation in Europe. After many years of quiet diplomacy, the 35 states met in Helsinki 1972-73. That meeting was a preparatory meeting, an introduction to three stages of negotiations before the Final Act became a reality (Helsinki 1973, Geneva 1973-75 and Helsinki 1975).

The third stage of the conference was a short but politically very important event. The 35 participating states sent their heads of state or prime ministers to Helsinki for the adoption and signing of the Final Act (30 July-1 August 1975). Few had hoped for such a substantive document, that progress actually had been achieved in the different areas. On the other hand, it must be admitted that the national representatives, in their interventions, gave different priorities to different problems. Here is but one example: the NATO states emphasized very strongly the role of human rights and fundamental freedoms in a future Europe with less tension. The Warsaw Pact states put more emphasis on the importance of the principle of the inviolability of frontiers.

During the meeting of the signing of the Final Act, it was already possible to detect a tendency among the Warsaw Pact states to reduce the implications of the human rights provisions in the document, basically by passing by them in silence. To the extent they touched upon them at all, they made it clear that the human rights provisions would have to be implemented in the social and political framework of each and every country. The future strategy became evident: criticism of the human rights record of a country was claimed to be in contravention of other provisions in the Final Act: basically, the principle of non-intervention in domestic affairs. The media in the West reflected these early warnings to a very modest degree. On the contrary, they praised the victories gained by the Western powers and the Final Act of 1975 was interpreted as a breakthrough for the protection of human rights in our region.

These high public expectations partly explain the deep dissatisfaction or even distrust that made itself felt as the years passed after Helsinki. Some of the governments, having signed the agreement, failed seriously in their observation of its provisions. In 1990, it is easy to find many influential commentators on Eastern Europe or from Eastern Europe stating that these regimes committed themselves in Helsinki to obligations which they had no intention of honouring. This rather cynical statement formed the other extreme point of view. Between these extremes, one could find different kinds of realists, those who believed that the fight for human rights in pan-Europe would be long and arduous, but who on the other hand believed that the Eastern bloc had exposed itself to a kind of international criticism which gradually would have the effect of improving their record irrespective of the intention of the governments.

Viewed in retrospect, most of the experts, most of the observers, even most of the operators themselves were wrong. Described according to an extremely rationalized formula, during the first decade of the CSCE Process, there was very little progress in the human rights area. The Final Act was certainly not a 'Magna Carta' for Europe. During the second decade, human rights revolutions took place in Eastern Europe. The Final Act certainly had an impact on these revolutions.

Seen from the outside, it is of course extremely difficult to assess the different factors that produced the results we have been witnessing. Both internal and external forces have been instrumental in achieving the revolutionary changes. Among them, and probably among the more important ones, is the Final Act of Helsinki.

3. The Final Act of Helsinki

The technical concept used in the CSCE Process to group the problems and provisions into different parts of the Final Act of Helsinki is 'basket'. The document is divided into three 'baskets' (or four, if the provisions on the Follow-up to the conference is included). The first basket covers 'Questions relating to security in Europe'. The second basket relates to 'Co-operation in the field of economics, of science and technology and of the environment'. The third basket deals with 'Co-operation in humanitarian and other fields.' In addition, there are certain provisions on 'Questions relating to security and co-operation in the Mediterranean'. Finally, the document concludes with the very important agreement on 'Follow-up to the Conference'.

A key concept in the 1970s was *'détente'*. This word was supposed to reflect the main thrust of the CSCE Process as such. The correct interpretation of the concept is, admittedly, controversial. As the CSCE Process later on reached a stalemate, the positive value of the concept diminished. In 1975, post-war Europe was based on the necessity of détente and this is expressed clearly in the preamble. Détente was to be achieved through different ways and means, among them being the implementation of the human rights standards.

The Final Act opens (in the first basket) with a 'Declaration on principles guiding relations between participating states'. This idea is parallel to the UN (The 'Friendly relations declaration'), although this one is modelled at the European level and according to European problems.

The first principle is the idea of sovereign equality, respect for the rights inherent in sovereignty. This provision is important because as the Western and NNA countries gradually have raised their voices in criticism of the failure of the Eastern group to implement human rights, the latter group has reverted (also) to the first principle of the Declaration. They have stated that this principle explicitly recognizes 'the right of every State to juridical equality'. They have also pointed to the last sentence of the first paragraph: 'They will also respect each other's right freely to choose and develop its political, social, economic and cultural systems as well as its right to determine its laws and regulations.' In other words, this principle lays down equality between social systems. The idea behind this is that the CSCE Process should not become a fighting arena for differing social systems. As a matter of fact, this was exactly what happened during the early years. From time to time, the debate amounted to heavy ideological campaigns.

The first principle has been interpreted by the Warsaw Pact states so as to accept that international human rights standards must be implemented domestically within each state's own social, political and legal system. Seen from this perspective, the principle of sovereignty has served as a pretext for not implementing international human rights norms straight away. The principle of sovereignty has, especially in the CSCE context, been a kind of filter through which the international norms must be filtrated. This view has never been accepted by the Western or NNA groups, who present two lines of arguments. First, that international co-operation and international supervision, including criticism, of the protection of human rights in no way infringes the principle of sovereignty, but is rather a consequence of it. Second, that international human rights norms must precede domestic law in a possible conflict. The idea of international supervision in this area is null and void if domestic legislation were to represent a valid excuse for non-implementation of international norms. However, Eastern European states have gradually left their traditional positions on this question. At the next juncture of the CSCE Process, no state is likely to defend such an extreme point of view.

One of the most important principles in the whole catalogue, seen from the human rights perspective, is Principle VI, 'Non-intervention in internal affairs':

The participating States will refrain from any intervention, direct or indirect, individual or collective, in the internal or external affairs falling within the domestic jurisdiction of another participating State, regardless of their mutual relations.

They will accordingly refrain from any form of armed intervention or threat of such intervention against another participating State.

They will likewise in all circumstances refrain from any other act of military, or of political, economic or other coercion designed to subordinate to their own interest the exercise by another participating State of the rights inherent in its sovereignty and thus to secure advantages of any kind.

Accordingly, they will, inter alia, refrain from direct or indirect assistance to terrorist activities, or to subversive or other activities directed towards the violent overthrow of the regime of another participating State.

This principle has, practically speaking, constituted the first line of defence of Eastern European States against any kind of criticism on their human rights records. Seen from the angle of the Western and the NNA countries, this defence has represented an abuse of the sixth principle. From now on, it is hoped that this problem will have academic interest only. (see also discussion *infra*).

The seventh principle is the basis for the human rights concern in the Helsinki Process. Already in the title one gets an indication of this thrust: 'Respect for human rights and fundamental freedoms, including the freedom of thought, conscience, religion or belief.' The impression becomes even clearer in the text itself:

The participating States will respect human rights and fundamental freedoms, including the freedom of thought, conscience, religion or belief, for all without distinction as to race, sex, language or religion.

They will promote and encourage the effective exercise of civil, political, economic, social, cultural and other rights and freedoms all of which derive from the inherent dignity of the human person and are essential for his free and full development.

Within this framework the participating States will recognize and respect the freedom of the individual to profess and practise, alone or in community with others, religion or belief acting in accordance with the dictates of his own conscience.

The participating States on whose territory national minorities exist will respect the right of persons belonging to such minorities to equality before the law, will afford them the full opportunity for their actual enjoyment of human rights and fundamental freedoms and will, in this manner, protect their legitimate interests in this sphere.

The participating States recognize the universal significance of human rights and fundamental freedoms, respect for which is an essential factor for the peace, justice and well-being necessary to ensure the development of friendly relations and co-operation among themselves as among all States.

They will constantly respect these rights and freedoms in their mutual relations and will endeavour jointly and separately, including in co-operation with the United Nations, to promote universal and effective respect for them.

They confirm the right of the individual to know and act upon his rights and duties in this field.

In the field of human rights and fundamental freedoms, the participating States will act in conformity with the purposes and principles of the Charter of the United Nations and with the Universal Declaration of Human Rights. They will also fulfil their obligations as set forth in the international declarations and agreements in this field, including inter alia the International Covenants on Human Rights, by which they may be bound.

Civil and political rights are put in the forefront, with freedom of thought, conscience, religion or belief receiving particular emphasis. The text also makes references to the universal system under the auspices of the United Nations.

Principle VIII, 'Equal rights and self-determination of peoples', certainly has important connections to the human rights field.

The catalogue concludes with the tenth principle on 'Fulfilment in good faith of obligations under international law'. Of great interest seen from our point of view, is the second paragraph:

In exercising their sovereign rights, including the right to determine their laws and regulations, they will conform with their legal obligations under international law; they will furthermore pay due regard to and implement the provisions in the Final Act of the Conference on Security and Cooperation in Europe.

This must be viewed in connection with Principle I. In establishing and developing domestic political and legal systems, states must abide by international standards, including human rights norms, according to universal and regional conventions, declarations and the Final Act itself. This is a heavy counter argument against the approach taken by the Eastern European states in the past.

As the catalogue of the ten principles is about to be finished, the text brings a passage which has been referred to again and again in the subsequent years. It has turned out to be a corner–stone, or rather a stumbling–block, in the debates in the meetings on the implementation of the commitments in the Final Act:

All the principles set forth above are of primary significance and, accordingly, they will be equally and unreservedly applied, each of them being interpreted taking into account the others.

This provision has been used by all the groups of the CSCE. The Eastern European states have argued strongly that the implementation of the human rights principle (VII) must be 'interpreted taking into account' Principle I regarding the sovereignty of each state (including the right to decide on its political and legal system) and Principle VI regarding non-intervention in domestic affairs. They have, furthermore, claimed that the West has focused too heavily on the protection of human rights (Principle VII). In their view, it is not acceptable to hold that human rights should play such a predominant role in the co-operation between the European states. Principle VII has no higher value than the other nine principles.

The Western and NNA countries have normally taken the view

that they do not distort the balance among equally important principles by raising criticism in relation to Principle VII as well. Furthermore, as mentioned above, they do not accept the traditional Eastern interpretation of principles I and VI. Principle VII makes it abundantly clear that international concern for human rights is a legitimate subject in the international arena. Criticism could in no way constitute 'intervention' in the sense used in Principle VI. Nor is it acceptable, according to Principle I, that some states establish their domestic legislation in total disregard of international legal obligations and political commitments.

Along these lines, one may also refer to the immediately following paragraph in the Final Act:

The participating States express their determination fully to respect and apply these principles, as set forth in the present Declaration, in all aspects, to their mutual relations and cooperation in order to ensure to each participating State the benefits resulting from the respect and application of these principles by all.

In other words, it is a duty for all states to help promote the implementation of all ten principles by all other states.

The rest of the first basket is devoted to other aspects of security, military problems in particular. All these aspects represent various connotations of détente. From this fact flows the well-known position, taken by all the participating states, that any document, any result which is produced along the road must not only be substantive (that is make real progress), but also *balanced*. Moreover, and even more important, during the negotiations the linkage between the different aspects of security is apparent. There is an intimate relationship between problems relating to military security and problems relating to the promotion and protection of human rights. Such a relationship between incommensurable entities might well be disapproved of. Nevertheless, it remains true. In some periods, progress in one of these areas produced progress in the other, while in other periods stagnation in one area resulted in stagnation in the other. But this is not necessarily so. It is also worth noting that stagnation or a complete stalemate in one area (the military) might lead to concessions in the other (human rights), in order to reopen discussions and to regain momentum. The same is valid for the second basket questions, which we will not go into here.

The third basket must be approached with great attention. The relationship between Principle VII in the first basket and the third basket may be described in different ways. One accepted explanation is that the third basket spells out in great detail important aspects of the seventh principle. In other words, co-operation in humanitarian affairs is an implication of the human rights principle.

The concept 'humanitarian' is a familiar one in international law. Often, it connotes the protection of human beings in times of war. In terms of the CSCE process, the concept 'humanitarian' is to be determined by the rights and freedoms described in the text itself. The Final Act has defined its own area of humanitarian affairs. The tone is set in the preamble to the third basket, in a combined interpretation of the first and second paragraphs of that preamble:

The participating States,
Desiring to contribute to the strengthening of peace and understanding among peoples . . .
Conscious that increased cultural and educational exchanges, contacts between peoples and the solution of humanitarian problems will contribute to the attainment on these aims.

The third basket is subdivided into four main sections: (1) human contacts, (2) information, (3) culture and (4) education.

Compared to other international human rights instruments, the richness of the text is amazing. Critics will claim that the level of commitment is not too advanced. It is true that many of the provisions contain phrases like: 'the participating States will deal in a positive and humane spirit with. . .' or 'the participating States will examine favourably. . .'. On the other hand, the problem areas which the third basket is dealing with were — in 1975 — delicate. Some of them were very sensitive at that time. These areas had never been explored by human rights lawyers or diplomats. In this respect, also, some of the provisions in this part of the document are innovative.

The *human contacts* provisions are placed in its context when the preamble to this section opens with the following statement: 'The participating States, *considering* the development of contacts to be an important element in the strengthening of friendly relations and trust among peoples'.

Although the main proponents of these commitments, the Western group and the NNA countries, were concerned about human contacts in general, in all relations and aspects, the text focuses on certain aspects of human contact which seem to be of great importance as well as being easier to legitimize: contacts and meetings on the basis of family ties, reunification of families, marriage between citizens of different states, travel for personal or professional reasons (including representatives of religious denominations), improvement of conditions for tourism, meetings of young people, enhancement of sports contacts and among governmental and non-governmental institutions.

The rationale behind the section on *information* — a consequence of the freedom of expression in general — is the consciousness 'of the need for an ever wider knowledge and understanding of the various aspects of life in other participating States' and 'acknowledging the contribution of this process to the growth of confidence between peoples' (from the information preamble). The operative part of the text opens a wide range of different ways and means by which information may be transmitted and received. Access by the public to newspapers and periodicals printed in foreign countries is emphasized. The working conditions for journalists are offered particular attention. The states promise to 'examine in a favourable spirit and within a suitable and reasonable time scale requests from journalists for visas'. Of practical importance is the provision stating 'to increase the opportunities for journalists . . . to communicate personally with their sources. . .'.

The section on *cultural co-operation* is even more detailed. The text operates with expressions like 'promoting co-operation of translators', 'exchange of catalogue cards between libraries', to develop joint projects like 'performances given by soloists, instrumental ensembles, orchestras, choirs and other artistic groups, including those composed of amateurs. . .'.

At the end of this section, one finds a provision of significance to a problem which has always been intricate in the CSCE context, and which certainly will not diminish in the future: cultural exchange between national minorities or regional cultures. The CSCE states recognized that members of minorities have legitimate interests in this respect, and that co–operation between them should be permitted and facilitated.

The latter part of the third basket elaborates on co–operation in the field of *education*, setting forth a number of ways and means to exchange ideas and thoughts and to exchange persons (scientists, teachers, students and pupils). Programmes shall be established, at different educational levels. Also in the field of education, there is a specific reference to co–operation among national minorities or regional cultures.

After the substantive part of the document, the three baskets, there is a section on 'Follow-up to the Conference'.

The 'Follow-up' part of the Helsinki Final Act declares that the Helsinki Conference has initiated a multilateral process which should be continued, basically by two strategies. First, the states declare their willingness to implement the provisions agreed upon in the Final Act, unilaterally, bilaterally and multilaterally (and within the framework of other existing international organizations), and second, by consenting to 'organizing to these ends meetings among their representatives'.

This condensed sketch of a future 'supervisory machinery' has triggered off much activity, a series of meetings, involving small and large delegations. Seen from a practical point of view, the CSCE Process has developed into a nearly permanent regime, engaging diplomats on a full-time basis all year around, at the meetings and between them.

The agenda for the Follow-up meetings has, basically, been divided into two main parts. In the section on Follow-up, the states

Declare furthermore their resolve to continue the multilateral process initiated by the Conference:
(a) by proceeding to a thorough exchange of views both on implementation of the provisions of the Final Act and of the tasks defined by the Conference, as well as, in the context of the questions dealt with by the latter, on the deepening of their mutual relations, the improvement of security and the development of co-operation in Europe, and the development of the process of détente in the future.

Thus, the first task is to look back, to discuss what the states have done since the last meeting to implement what they have undertaken. The second task is to look forward, to explore new ideas and to develop new techniques in order to deepen their co–operation in the respective areas. The first part of the mandate has been given the name 'implementation debate'. There has been some fighting between the groups as to the allocation of time for the two main items. Generally speaking, the Eastern bloc has expressed its strong preference for a short implementation debate and for spending more time on the architecture of the future Europe. The Western group and the NNA countries have always insisted on having a thorough implementation debate. Their motive has of course been to secure ample time for criticism against failures of implementation. These attitudes have been particularly visible in the human rights sphere.

The Follow-up part is a significant feature of the whole CSCE Process, distinguishing it from other systems and processes in the international human rights sphere. The Helsinki Final Act establishes no supervisory machinery like most of the other human rights instruments do (groups, rapporteurs, commissions, committees, courts). In part this is because the Helsinki document is not a treaty. Therefore, one might argue that such a document could not really establish a sophisticated supervisory machinery.

This argument certainly carries great weight, but is not necessarily decisive. By establishing no formal supervisory body with wide competence to investigate alleged violations of human rights, the 35 states created instead a very flexible system. Over the course of time, this system has gradually and very slowly been refined. Additional elements have in recent years been integrated into the process, which look promising for the future (*infra*). However, seen also in retrospect, this modest and innocent procedural system — one even doubts whether the word 'system' is appropriate under these unstructured circumstances — has proved to be a powerful instrument. The CSCE procedural system has in my view proved more effective and more powerful than many of the other supervisory systems which are established according to various other conventions, resolutions and declarations.

4. From Helsinki to Vienna

The first Follow-up meeting took place in Belgrade in 1977. More than two years had passed since Helsinki, two years for which the expectations were so high, particularly in our area.

We shall not dwell too long on the Belgrade meeting. In the real world, outside the conference halls, the human rights situation had hardly improved since the summer of 1975. In some of the Eastern European states, there had been set-backs in the respect for human rights. The Final Act had triggered off different kinds of popular movements, more or less organized, to defend human rights. Some of the groups called themselves Helsinki watch groups (or Helsinki monitoring groups), inspired by the Final Act, to scrutinize the implementation measures taken by their own governments to honour Helsinki commitments. Many of these groups were heavily oppressed, their members were imprisoned or kept in mental hospitals.

The Belgrade meeting was a meeting of heavy confrontation and very strong criticism on the human rights records of Eastern states. The Warsaw Pact countries on their part presented their line of argumentation which became well known during the next decade: that such criticism was a flagrant violation of the principle of sovereignty (Principle I) and constituted an interference into domestic jurisdiction in contradiction of Principle VI. Furthermore, they presented their own interpretation of the human rights concept: that the West, in an unbalanced way, concentrated on civil and political rights only and disregarded completely socio-economic rights. They also tried to prove that the leading Western powers systematically violated social, economic and cultural rights. Of special concern to the Eastern European governments were the typical problems of the capitalist economy: unemployment, homelessness, people living below the poverty line and racial discrimination, both in the civil and political area as well as in the socio-economic area.

The media and public opinion in the West reacted very negatively to the developments in Belgrade. Building on the high expectations flowing from the prosperous days in Helsinki, editorial comments first disclosed total confusion in public opinion, and later a deep disappointment and feeling of anger. The human rights communities felt betrayed. Strong warnings were voiced: from now on, the only morally defensible way was to keep the flag flying high, to confront the communist regimes with their shortcomings and deficiencies.

Seen in retrospect, it was a stroke of luck that the Belgrade meeting did not collapse. If so, the whole CSCE Process might have broken down. The danger was probably not too apparent among the diplomats or governments in Belgrade, even though the climate was cold. They were even able to work out a Concluding Document. This required great efforts by the representatives from the three groups.

The NNA delegates in particular took on themselves a role which they later have played with great talent, that of go-between between the East and the West. In the concluding document from the Belgrade meeting the states recognized that 'the exchange of views constitutes in itself a valuable contribution towards the achievement of the aims set by the CSCE, although different views were expressed as to the degree of implementation of the Final Act reached so far.'

As far as new proposals for the future work was concerned, a lot of proposals relating to all three baskets were put on the table. The only proposal which the states were able to agree upon related to the Follow-up part. The 35 participating states wanted to give the CSCE Process a new chance. They decided to come together — for the second Follow-up meeting — in Madrid on 11 November 1980.

The general political climate in the East-West relations was even worse than two years before when the second meeting was convened in Madrid. The Soviet invasion of Afghanistan nearly one year before was a set-back for détente (although, strictly speaking, Afghanistan was outside the geographical scope of the Final Act). The invasion had had a series of repercussions, including the boycott by many countries of participation in the 1980 Summer Olympic Games in Moscow. The Olympic Games also created other political problems. Because the Soviet authorities were afraid of too close contact between visitors to Moscow (a great number of them being media people) and different political opposition groups, Helsinki watch groups and the like, many prominent dissidents were arrested. There were also other discouraging signs in the whole Eastern European bloc.

The delegations did meet, however. The implementation debate more or less followed the same pattern as in Belgrade. As far as the second point on the agenda was concerned, discussion on proposals was more constructive. In mid-1981, most people dared to believe that a Concluding Document was within reach. Then, in December 1981, martial law was imposed in Poland. This was a terrible blow to the entire process, a blow which could not be ignored. The Madrid Conference went into recession and the delegates left the city, leaving the CSCE Process at a crucial stage.

They returned after some eight months to continue the exercise. This was a sign of welcome for all those who wished to see the process as a living process. The participating governments realized that they had at least one interest in common, namely to keep the process going. On their table they had a text of compromise for a Concluding Document produced by the NNA states, which was finally adopted.

Looking back on the Concluding Document from Madrid, however, one may claim that the document is better than might have been expected under such circumstances. A lot of factors may explain why this was possible. Among them would be progress made in basket two, and in the military area. The document organizes a particular Conference on Confidence- and Security–building Measures and

Disarmament in Europe, in Stockholm. The Eastern Bloc had worked very hard to have such a conference arranged. The fact that they succeeded may explain why they were willing to make some concessions in the human rights sphere, to which we shall direct our attention.

The Madrid Document is much more concrete and contains more new ideas than did the Belgrade Document. One subject, which has always been dear to the Western group, is the freedom of religion. The Madrid Document reaffirms the commitment already expressed in the Final Act. But it adds details as well. The text declares that the states undertake to consult religious faiths, institutions and organizations involved in religious matters 'whenever necessary'. They also undertake [to] 'favourably consider' applications by religious communities to be given official status according to domestic legislation. One qualification is prominent in this text. The religious groups and organizations must act 'within the constitutional framework' of the state. In the view of many non-governmental organizations, this is a serious deficiency in the Madrid Document. On the other hand, one may find some trace of this restriction in the Final Act itself (*infra*).

Another problem buried in the text is a question of principle. When the aim is to fight for religious freedom, and if some restriction and caution is necessary, what is the right strategy: to fight for greater respect for the established congregations and groups or to fight for the 'underground church', the groups which are not registered? The Madrid Document focuses on the right to register, thereby paying more attention to and creating more respect for official churches.

The Madrid Concluding Document also has a specific provision on the equality between the sexes.

During the years in Madrid, the freedom of the trade unions was an important and very sensitive political issue. The situation in Poland and the new Solidarity movement were followed with great attention. The Madrid Document tries to accommodate more than one group of participating states. It states the right of workers 'freely to establish and join trade unions, the right of trade unions freely to exercise their activities and other rights as laid down in relevant international instruments.' On the other hand, 'these rights will be exercised in compliance with the law of the State and in conformity with the State's obligations under international law'. Problems are obviously inherent in this qualification of the freedom.

The Document makes important progress on the procedural front. First, there was consensus to arrange an expert meeting on human rights in Ottawa. Annexed to the Document is also, in a statement made by the Chairman, a text which invites the states to convene an expert meeting on human contacts in Bern.

Second, the Document also suggests that the states arrange bilateral meetings in order to discuss human rights problems which may exist between them. This idea is called 'human rights round tables'. Some states have used this opportunity.

These kinds of meetings, as well as others linked to the other areas of the Final Act, must be seen as a promising step. From now on, inter-sessional meetings between the regular Follow-up meetings are introduced. This is a decisive step towards a more formalized supervisory machinery.

Also in the third basket area, the Madrid Concluding Document contains changes. There is to be a strengthening of human contacts, i.e. by allowing reunification of families to a greater extent than before. Applications for emigration shall be handled more quickly. If the application is refused, this shall not influence the social position of the applicant or his family. Fees for the handling of such applications are to be gradually reduced. The Document also provides for better conditions for the dissemination of information. It contains provisions designed to facilitate further the working conditions of journalists, among other means by securing their right to establish personal contacts in the country in question. Finally, there are several formulations aimed at promoting increased co–operation within the cultural and educational fields.

According to the Madrid Document, the third Follow-up meeting should take place in Vienna (from 4 November 1986).

The expert meetings in Ottawa and Berne produced no Concluding Document. In the view of the media, these meetings were a failure since they ended without such documents. This is an assessment which was not shared by the experts themselves. In the open plenary sessions concluding the two meetings, most of them declared explicitly that the implementation debate and the discussion of new proposals had been constructive.

5. The Vienna meeting

When the third Follow-up meeting ended in January 1989, after more than two years of intensive negotiations, the event was once more greatly praised by statesmen, by the NGOs as well as by the media. All of a sudden one felt the same spirit as in Helsinki 15 years earlier. After more than a decade of disappointment, one now 'watched the turn of history'. What had really happened in Vienna?

Everyday life in Vienna brought mixed experiences. During the opening speeches, the Soviet foreign minister declared that human rights was a legitimate concern for the Soviet Government as well as for the Vienna Follow-up meeting. They had nothing to hide. The Soviet Government invited the CSCE states to convene in Moscow, to discuss further progress in the human rights sphere. On the other hand, some of the other Eastern European regimes chose a rather orthodox approach *vis-à-vis* the criticism expressed during the implementation debate. The argument relating to non-interference according to principle VI was hardly used at all, however. In general, the atmosphere of the implementation debate was better and more constructive than in previous meetings.

In relation to the other part of the mandate, this general positive attitude was reflected only to a modest degree in the proposals. The items were basically the same, and so were the approaches taken by the different groups. A much-used expression was: why has not glasnost reached Vienna? One of the most crucial problems was — now more than ever before — the question of limitations. The Eastern bloc wanted to include in the concluding text escape clauses, of a very open character. The Western group generally was negative towards such a move. In the end, one was able to take care of both points of view. Seen from the outside, these formulations are certainly not very elegant. They appear in different provisions of the Document. Some would also claim that they are too restrictive. This must be a task for the coming conferences, resolving the problems in a more satisfactory way (see also *infra*).

What then is the most important news of the Vienna Document, as far as human rights are concerned?

Freedom of religion is developed and specified on a number of points: a ban on discrimination on a religious basis, the right of religious communities to accept financial contributions for religious activities, the right of parents to teach their children about religious matters, the right to import religious literature freely. There are, however, certain restrictions applying to these rights, but they are not so radical as they were in the Madrid Document. One important point is that, in the future, national limitations regarding the right to freedom of religion must conform to international provisions on human rights.

The Document demands that the state shall protect the identity of national minorities and prepare the ground for such protection.

The Vienna Document also lays down a right which the Western states have fought for a long time to obtain, namely the right to leave one's own country and to return. There is, nevertheless, a limitation, inasmuch as the Document refers to accepted limitations of this right in international human rights instruments. It emphasizes, however, that these limitations are not to be abused.

The Document contains a provision on the protection of patients in psychiatric or other institutions. The states shall ensure human rights of patients.

When we next return to the third basket of the Document, the paragraph on human contacts commences by laying down the states' obligations to deal with all outstanding applications for family visits, family reunions, travelling and so forth within six months after the close of the Vienna meeting. It also states that, after that time, new applications shall be handled as quickly as possible, as a rule within one month.

The text also provides for rather extensive rights to family reunions, including relatives outside the nuclear family. Family reunions imply among other things family meetings, marriages, returning small children to their parents (where the family is split by national borders). Visits in connection with important family events are to be regarded as straightforward cases and should be decided as soon as possible, usually within three days. Visits designed to establish contacts shall be facilitated, by simplifying application procedures, gradually reducing obligations concerning foreign exchange, and similar means.

A controversial issue during a number of years has been the right to leave the country for persons who are in possession of classified information. According to the Vienna Concluding Document, the state shall on application assess the real need to keep the person back. The Document also mentions purely practical aspects connected with human contacts. Among other things, it has been decided to expand the Inter-Rail system throughout Europe, to make it easier for young people to meet. And in the future, mail and telecommunication systems shall be allowed more freedom to function than has been the case so far.

The next main paragraph of the third basket is concerned with information between the states. Radio transmissions are not to be disrupted by interference, modern technical appliances like cables and satellites are to be employed with a view to increasing the free exchange of all kinds of information. The working conditions of journalists are to be further improved, they shall *inter alia* be allowed to establish contact with private citizens in a foreign country in order to obtain information.

The next Follow-up meeting is scheduled to take place in Helsinki, commencing on 10 March 1992.

In the Vienna Concluding Document there is a section which is found neither in the Helsinki Agreement itself nor in the Madrid Document: 'Human dimension of the CSCE'. There are two main points. First, there is the establishment of a *Mechanism* of information and consultation in connection with problems of human rights. Second, three meetings on the human dimension are scheduled, both as to time and mandate (Paris 1989, Copenhagen 1990 and Moscow 1991). The three meetings are called '*the Conference*'.

The mandate of *the Conference* is to discuss the states' implementation of the human rights obligations in the CSCE documents, to assess experiences gained through the use of *the Mechanism*, and to submit new proposals designed to improve respect for human rights.

The Document describes the four aspects of *the Mechanism*. There is a right to communicate information and to ask for information on human rights problems to and from other states, it is possible to demand bilateral meetings with a view to discussing such issues, the cases may be brought before the meetings in Paris, Copenhagen and

Moscow, as well as before the Follow-up meeting in Helsinki (On *the Conference*, see *infra*).

The Mechanism and *the Conference* may possibly be the embryo of a more permanent institutionalized surveillance system under the aegis of the CSCE. It is true that their existence has not been guaranteed beyond the 1992 Helsinki Meeting, but on the other hand, their life spans have not been restricted to this period. The fate of *the Mechanism* and *the Conference* will be decided in Helsinki, and the outcome depends on factors we do not know enough about today.

The Vienna Document represents considerable progress as regards protection of human rights in Europe. However, there were also some shadows over the Document. It was to be regretted that at the end of the Vienna Meeting, Romania made a series of reservations regarding several of the important points mentioned above. The formal significance of these reservations is not quite clear, as Romania had been one of the states to adopt the Document (the resolution was unanimous). After the revolution in Romania in December 1989, the state has now withdrawn all reservations.

6. Some general problems

One basic principle underlying the whole exercise is the principle of consensus — which means that there is agreement on a particular point if no objections are raised. Most observers would claim that this was the only possible way of proceeding in post-war Europe. Critics, however, would emphasize that this principle has been hampering progress in the human rights sphere, that one should rather endeavour to reach a strong text with reservations from the states which could not go along. By doing so, one might be able to achieve two objectives: to improve the level of human rights protection in other countries, as well as to stigmatize publicly those states which are lagging behind.

From the early days, the CSCE Process has been regarded, by both insiders and outsiders, as a separate process, distinct from that of the Council of Europe or the United Nations, for instance. Although one might discover some references from the CSCE to the United Nations, comparatively few parallels have been drawn from the universal to the regional level. There are a lot of reasons that may explain this. Among the more substantial ones are that the CSCE Process is an East-West exercise, the North-South perspective is missing. Moreover, the CSCE Process involves military questions to a degree which is unknown in the United Nations. As a consequence, the European states, although they operate as individual states, remain so closely linked to the military alliances; the Warsaw Pact, NATO or the neutral or non-aligned status. One rarely sees the same kind of strict discipline in the United Nations.

In spite of this lack of systematic co-ordination, it is tempting in a theoretical analysis to try to compare, at least in a superficial way, the human rights protection in the CSCE Process and other international instruments.

If one focuses on Principle VII in the first basket, it goes without saying that the very condensed text of Principle VII cannot easily be compared with the more elaborate texts of the respective (legally binding) conventions or declarations of a non-legal character. The provision declaring the freedom of thought, conscience, religion or belief is less developed than its parallel in other instruments. Even the Universal Declaration of 1948 is more developed. On one point, however, the CSCE text is more explicit. It gives the national minorities actually existing on a state's territory certain guarantees — both in a specific and a general form — (equality before the law, full opportunity for the actual enjoyment of human rights). Compared to the International Covenant on Civil and Political Rights, Article 27, even this part of Principle VII seems rather modest.

Turning to the third basket, one discovers how the universal and regional instruments of a general character are lagging behind. Of course, one might find documents within the UN specialized agencies which may on certain points go beyond the CSCE level. In this article, we shall confine ourselves to dealing with the general instruments at the universal and regional levels.

Starting with the Human Contacts section of the third basket, it is worthwhile noting that the Final Act does not state (or restate) the general principle contained in Article 12 of the International Covenant on Civil and Political Rights on liberty of movement within a state's territory, nor the principle on the freedom to leave any country and to return to his own country (parallel provisions can be found in Article 2 in Additional Protocol No. 4 to the European Convention on Human Rights). On the other hand, the third basket takes certain steps which may be said to be somewhat further down the road. First, it picks up a problem which normally is not approached in human rights law in particular, but in public international law in general: the right to enter a country which is not one's own. On different occasions, the third basket commitments also challenge the immigration policy of the participating states (for instance meetings on the basis of family ties, reunification of families, marriage between citizens of different states). In spite of the fact that these kinds of travel open both the question of emigration and immigration (temporary or permanent), one cannot go to the other extreme point of view, namely that the CSCE documents place the right to leave any country and the right to enter a foreign country at the same level. This has been an increasingly problematic area during CSCE meetings. As the regulations concerning leaving a country gradually were relaxed by the Eastern European states, those states claimed that the Western states tightened their immigration policy. Leaving the empirical problems for the moment, the Western and NNA countries could legitimately claim that these two liberties were not parallel.

In the Vienna Concluding Document, there is an explicit reference to the freedom of movement and the right to leave any country and to enter one's own.

The provision (of the Final Act) on contacts between religious denominations and organizations deserves a more general reflection. The text has a specific limitation: '. . . religious faiths. . . , preaching with the constitutional framework of the participating States'. As will be recalled, such a limitation does not occur in the paragraph on religious freedom in the first basket, seventh principle. In the more operative third basket, the Eastern countries insisted on having such an explicit limitation. Such a limitation might *prima facie* seem both natural and legitimate. However, looking closer, one will realize that this innocent limitation clause is not so innocent after all. First, the limitation is unqualified, the constitution does not have to meet certain criteria which are common in human rights texts (for instance 'public order', 'health or morals', 'national security'). Second, the reference to constitutional law hides an important problem inherent in any kind of international human rights protection: the relationship of international standards and domestic standards. If the expression mentioned above is to be interpreted literally, the international human rights norms — be they political or legal — are subordinated to the domestic constitution. This argument is totally unsound, as it leads directly to the interrelationship between Principles I, VI and VII in the first basket (*supra*). The correct way to approach this question is to say that the domestic legislation, including the constitution, must be in harmony with international commitments. This is the quintessence of international concern with human rights; the problem is a general one in public international law and in human rights standard-setting in particular. This position, which was strongly advocated by the West and the NNA countries, is so self-evident that it needs no further justification. But in the subsequent CSCE work the problem had been introduced by this innocent reference to the domestic constitutional framework. And the problem remained, through Madrid to Vienna (see *supra*).

The next section, on 'Information' again raises many problems which lead beyond the already established human rights law. Both Article 19 of the International Covenant on Civil and Political Rights and Article 10 of the European Convention have certain provisions on freedom of expression, freedom to receive and impart information. The instruments operate on a much more abstract level than does the Final Act. Since the approach of the various instruments is so different, a more detailed comparison is not possible.

This is also true if one compares the provisions in the sections on culture and on education with their corresponding parallels in general human rights instruments (see, *inter alia*, The Universal Declaration Articles 26 and 27, the International Covenant on Economic, Social and Cultural Rights Articles 13-15, the European Convention, Protocol No. 1, Article 2). It is worth noting that their approaches are different not only regarding the level of abstraction. They are different also in the sense that while the other documents are concerned with the promotion and implementation of the agreed rights and freedoms at the national level through national measures, the Final Act focuses heavily on international contacts and co-operation between states and individuals. The CSCE Process creates a 'good' circle. The right to contact across frontiers is part of the human rights concept. By allowing these kinds of contacts, the states also promote and implement the other elements of the human rights concept. Above, we raised the problem of the relationship between Principle VII and the third basket. This is yet another way of interpreting this relationship.

We have already briefly touched upon the *status* of the different documents, or generally, the whole CSCE Process. The traditional way of approaching this question is that the norms are not legal norms, but political ones. The Final Act is not a treaty, it is a political document. The Western European group in particular has been very concerned that the document should have no higher status because of the provision relating to the borders of Europe. The other side of the coin is of course that the human rights norms have the same political status. To some states in the Western group this is a most satisfactory solution. Others would probably have liked to see this part of the whole process as legally binding upon the states.

This problem deserves to be analysed in a broader context than we are able to do in this article. Many questions may be raised to give a satisfactory answer. This would lead deeply into the problems of sources of international law. Suffice it to say that the fact that the Final Act is a statement of political intent, not a treaty, does not mean that the practical value of the document has been modest. On the contrary, many observers would claim that the CSCE Process has had greater effect on the human rights situation in pan-Europe than have the treaty-based systems.

7. Where does the CSCE road lead from here?

The answer to this question depends both on developments in the different Eastern European states and on developments in international relations, in particular between the two superpowers. It is crucial to remember the close interrelationship between the human rights area and the other areas in the Helsinki Process, an inter-relationship which we have been able to cover to a modest degree only. The future pan-European human rights system is not dependent solely on human rights considerations.

Before passing completely into uncertainty, let us briefly state recent events and events expected in the near future.

The first of the three meetings scheduled under the heading *'the Conference'* took place in Paris in May-June 1989.

The period between Vienna and Paris was short. One could not expect much development in the course of these months. The meeting nevertheless represented a constructive contribution in the new human rights dialogue between East and West. However, some states unfortunately demonstrated far less interest in active participation in the process. Bulgaria and Romania thus suffered severe criticism for their bad human rights records.

Attempts to arrive at a concluding document at the Paris Meeting failed, a fact that few will regret nowadays. Nor were the numerous proposals submitted for improvement of the respect for human rights in the CSCE area to no avail, as they will accompany the Process from Paris to Copenhagen and to Moscow, and finally to Helsinki for the Fourth Follow-up meeting.

The second meeting of the 'Conference on the human dimension' will take place in Copenhagen in June this year. This meeting will be a continuation of the Paris Meeting, and will in time be followed by the third meeting in Moscow (next year). The results of the 'Conference on human dimension' will be reported to the next main Follow-up meeting in Helsinki (1992). There, the 35 states will have to agree upon the future course of the Process.

New developments have brought a change in the schedule fixed in the Vienna Document. Towards the end of 1989, President Gorbachev launched the idea of staging a new summit meeting, which he called Helsinki II. His legitimation was that the very profound changes in Europe which are taking place in front of our eyes, needed to be considered at a particular conference. At this moment, it seems that his idea will materialize into a summit meeting between the leaders of the participating states in connection with the closing of the negotiations in Vienna on the reduction of conventional forces in Europe. The content of this meeting is obviously open so far, and so is the relationship between this meeting and the Follow-up meeting in Helsinki.

If we look into the crystal ball, many scenarios are discernible as far as a pan-European human rights system is concerned. First, the option certainly exists to pursue the CSCE Process, to develop further both the substantial norms and the supervisory system which already exists in an embryonic form. Second, many experts and politicians are looking to the Council of Europe, their intention being to extend the geographical scope of membership to cover the whole of Europe and to invite the Eastern European states to ratify the European Convention on Human Rights. One responsible scenario could be an integration of the CSCE Process and the Council of Europe. Even other scenarios may be the subject of consideration. The European Community is raising its profile in the area of human rights, a process which certainly will be continued and strengthened beyond 1992. At one stage, some Eastern European human rights idealists — and some governments — contemplated establishing a human rights convention for Eastern Europe. This idea must cer tainly be dead considering recent events. President Gorbachev has launched the idea of a 'Common European home', with a lot of rooms, among them is what he calls 'a single legal space' covering the whole of Europe. That surely refers to the legal structure at the domestic level, not at the international level. On the other hand, there is every reason to believe that the architecture of the single legal room at the domestic level will be strongly influenced by the international human rights system. The idea of a Common European home has already been brought into the CSCE and has been favourably received by most of the states.

Which, then, will be the decisive arguments and which scenario is most likely to be chosen among these and possibly others? This final question brings us back to the introductory part of the article. Here the guessing starts. My guess is that the CSCE Process will gain more strength and become even more instrumental in building Europe 'beyond Helsinki'.

Further reading

Bloed, A., and van Dijk, P. (eds), 1985. *Essays on Human Rights in the Helsinki Process*. Dordrecht: Martinus Nijhoff Publishers.

Human Rights and Religious Freedom in Europe for Peace and in the Spirit of Helsinki. Conference organized on 3-6 February 1988 in Venice by the Georgio Cini Foundation. Venice 1989: Marsilio Editori.

Maresca, John J., 1985. *To Helsinki. The Conference on Security and Cooperation in Europe, 1973-75*. Durham, NC and London: Duke University Press.

Symposium: Human Rights and the Helsinki Accord — A Five-Year Road to Madrid, *Vanderbilt Journal of Transnational Law*, Vol. 13 (1980), Nos. 2-3.

11 National Implementation of Human Rights
Roman Wieruszewski

1. Introduction

The international order is still a community of states. Human rights and freedoms are primarily realized through the state. Individuals can effectively enjoy human rights only when the state provides its citizens with appropriate remedies.

The question of the national implementation of human rights instruments is not free from problems, however. For instance: are national remedies governed by an internationally recognized standard? Can the realization of human rights be quantified and the results used to evaluate the performance of governments? When can we claim that remedies applied are 'effective'?

In Western Europe, there is, of course, also an international system of supervision and implementation. One of the main objectives of the European Convention for the Protection of Human Rights and Fundamental Freedoms (European Convention on Human Rights) is undoubtedly the achievement of an effective and uniform standard of protection. But many European states still stand outside this treaty regime. It is conceivable that in the future all Eastern and Central European states will become bound by the European Convention. The main obstacle is still a different understanding of human rights values. Until recently, these differences influenced not only the various states' approaches to the international implementation of human rights treaties but first and foremost the domestic effects of these treaties. How can these differences be overcome?

The CSCE Process creates a very important possibility for achieving a more uniform approach to the protection of human rights within the 35 participating states. The 'non-legal' aspects of the CSCE monitoring system should be considered an advantage. On the other hand, I share the opinion that the signatories to the CSCE documents should apply them as strictly as any formal treaty, despite their character as 'soft law' (Schachter, 1982, p. 126; Mullerson, 1989, pp. 509-12).

The present chapter will devote more space to national implementation mechanisms in Eastern and Central European countries than in the Western European ones. This approach is justified by the fact that it is the former region which is undergoing basic changes concerning practically speaking all aspects of social and political life. Needless to say, the functioning of the legal institutions has been significantly affected by this process. Some of the changes are still *in statu nascendi* and so the picture cannot be complete.

2. Domestic remedies and mechanisms from an international human rights perspective

2.1 The International Bill of Rights

Unlike many other international treaties, human rights treaties are primarily aimed at having an impact on the domestic legal systems of states. As a rule, the treaties themselves do not specify in a detailed manner how they should be implemented at the national level. It is nevertheless possible to formulate some general standards, based on the appropriate provision of the International Covenants on Human Rights of 1966. True, international legal instruments often contain principles and norms that are susceptible to different interpretations. But there is, on the other hand, a trend in international law in general, and international human rights law in particular, to bring about more precision in the application of the law.

The very idea of human rights as a legal concept is based, *inter alia*, on the principle *ubi jus ibi remedium* — where there is a right, there must be a remedy. This principle has already been expressed in the Universal Declaration of Human Rights. According to Article 8, 'everyone has the right to an effective remedy by the competent national tribunals for acts violating the fundamental rights granted him by the constitution or by law'. This obligation on the part of the state cannot be limited to access to judicial remedies in the strict sense. Nevertheless, judicial remedies constitute a *conditio sine qua non* for a system of effective remedies. They are a necessary but not a sufficient condition for a satisfactory national system of implementation.

The corresponding obligations of the States Parties to the 1966 International Covenant on Civil and Political Rights are formulated in a much broader sense. One would expect the domestic implementation provisions of the Covenant to be formulated with clarity and precision. Surprisingly enough, when the Covenant was being drafted there were proposals to abandon an explicit clause on national implementation measures. The reason given was that the requirement of domestic remedies was implicit in the general obligations of the States Parties to respect the Covenant. That view was rejected (Bossuyt, 1987, pp. 58–63) and the Covenant came to include Article 2, which provides for various national implementation measures.

According to Article 2, paragraph 1, of the Covenant, each State Party 'undertakes to respect and to ensure to all individuals within its territory and subject to its jurisdiction the rights recognized in the present Covenant. . .'.

It is an interesting question to consider the more precise nature of the obligations created by Article 2; whether they are so-called obligations of result or obligations of conduct. In the legal literature, it has been stressed — correctly, it is submitted — that, in principle, Article 2 leaves it to the States Parties concerned to choose their respective methods of implementation (Schachter, 1982, pp. 311–12; Nowak, 1989, p. 57). They are not obliged to incorporate the Covenant into their domestic legal systems. But according to Article 2, paragraph 2, they should 'adopt such legislative or other measures as may be necessary to give effect to the rights recognized' in the Covenant. Legislative steps alone are usually not sufficient. In one of its general comments, the Human Rights Committee (GAOR, 36th session, Supplement No. 40, A/36/40, Annex VII) stated the following:

(T)he implementation does not depend solely on constitutional or legislative measures, which in themselves are often not *per se* sufficient. The Committee considers it necessary to draw attention of States parties to the fact that the obligation under the Covenant is not confined to the respect for human rights, but that States parties have also undertaken to ensure the enjoyment of these rights to all individuals under their jurisdiction. This aspect calls for specific activities by the States parties to enable individuals to enjoy their rights.

It is thus not enough for the state to say that it respects and ensures the rights enshrined in the Covenant. It must also fulfil the obligation to use all necessary domestic means to give effect to these rights and to make good any violations.

This obligation may also call for preventive measures. The scope of such an obligation is not determined by the Covenant, however. The Human Rights Committee has, in considering an individual communication (no. 113/1981), pointed out that

The Covenant provides that a remedy shall be granted whenever a violation of one of the rights guaranteed by it has occurred; consequently, it does not generally prescribe preventive protection, but confines itself to requiring effective redress *ex post facto*.

As to the meaning of the phrase 'effective remedy', the question again arises as to whether judicial remedies are required. In the light of the preparatory work it is clear that this is not necessarily the case. The proper enforcement of the Covenant depends on whether the individual is granted effective protection against abuses. There should be adequate remedies, whether judicial or not; they should be made available to the individual; and they should be enforced by the competent authorities (Bossuyt, 1987, p. 58ff).

The Covenant certainly highlights the existence of judicial remedies. The Human Rights Committee has also stressed this aspect. Traditional socialist conceptions of human rights, on the other hand, never treated this category of remedies as the most important guarantee of the individual's rights. Oddly enough, the opposition against a strict judicial remedies clause was based not so much on political or ideological differences as on differences in legal traditions.

Among non-judicial remedies, the institution of the *ombudsman* stands out as an important mechanism. This was emphasized at a 1978 UN seminar on national and local institutions for the promotion and protection of human rights. The seminar put forward a set of guidelines for the functioning and structure of such institutions. It was recommended that the ombudsman should be authorized to receive complaints from individuals and groups concerning human rights violations; that they should possess independent fact-finding mechanisms for the investigation of complaints; and that they should provide appropriate remedies through conciliation and other means of redress.

It is a truism to say that different rights require different remedies. But it is important to stress that effective protection may require a combination of various measures. Article 2 of the International Covenant on Civil and Political Rights creates an 'obligation of result'. But it also seems to contain an 'obligation of conduct'. When a judicial remedy is lacking altogether, or when an administrative decision cannot be challenged before an independent body, or when the judiciary is not independent enough, a violation of the Covenant may be at hand.

With respect to the implementation provisions of the International Covenant on Economic, Social and Cultural Rights, it is important to keep in mind that these obligations are formulated differently from the corresponding provisions of the International Covenant on Civil and Political Rights (Alston and Quinn, 1987, p. 156f.; Simma, 1990). Article 2, paragraph 1, of the Economic Covenant obliges states to 'take steps' with a view to achieving progressively the full realization of the rights recognized in the Covenant. States should use 'all appropriate means, including particularly the adoption of legislative measures.' With respect to some specific rights, these measures are described in greater detail. For instance, Article 14, which regulates the question of compulsory and free education, provides for a two-year period during which a detailed plan of action for the progressive implementation of the principle of compulsory education, free of charge for all, should be worked out.

In regard to this Covenant, we can speak of promotional obligations. As a general rule, the provisions of the Covenant are not directly applicable. There are some exceptions to this rule, however, such as Article 8 on trade union rights. The domestic implementation of the Covenant on Economic, Social and Cultural Rights depends primarily on the resources available in a given state. In the light of Article 2, paragraph 1, it would seem to be very difficult to formulate objective criteria for evaluating the implementation methods used by a given state. Some hopes can be attached to the recently established Committee on Economic, Social and Cultural Rights, however (Alston, 1987, p. 332f.; Alston and Simma, 1987, p. 747f., Simma, 1990).

2.2. The CSCE Vienna Concluding Document

The question of the implementation of human rights norms should play an important role in the CSCE process. Only with the Vienna Concluding Document of 15 January 1989[1] has this question received sufficient attention, however. The outcome can be described as 'great progress as regards human rights' (Tretter, 1989, p. 259). As far as implementation measures are concerned, the progress made in Vienna is particularly conspicuous against the background of the Madrid Concluding Document of 1983. The latter document refers to the problem of implementation in a rather brief manner. In the section on 'Principles' the participating states 'stress their determination to promote and encourage the effective exercise of human rights and fundamental freedoms, all of which derive from the inherent dignity of the human person. . .'. They furthermore

stress their determination to develop their laws and regulations in the field of civil, political, economic, social, cultural and other rights and fundamental freedoms; they also emphasize their determination to ensure the effective exercise of these rights and freedoms.

In Madrid, it was not possible to draw up more detailed requirements concerning implementation methods. The substantial progress achieved since then has mainly been due to the evolution of the understanding of human rights which has taken place in the Eastern European countries. In Vienna, the participating states were able to draw the appropriate conclusions from their statement at Madrid, according to which human rights 'derive from the inherent dignity of the human person'. This means that ideological and political barriers should not prevent the formulation of international standards for domestic systems of human rights protection.

Principle 13 of the Vienna Concluding Document, which is contained in the section on 'Questions relating to security in Europe', lists a number of obligations relating to implementation methods. Paragraph 9 of Principle 13 lays down minimum standards with regard to the effective remedies that should be available to those who claim

---

[1] *Concluding Document of the Vienna Meeting 1986 of Representatives of the Participating States of the Conference on Security and Cooperation in Europe. Held on the Basis of the Provisions of the Final Act Relating to the Follow-up to the Conference.*

that their human rights and fundamental freedoms have been violated. In particular, the following remedies are listed:

— the right of the individual to appeal to executive, legislative, judicial or administrative organs;
— the right to a fair and public hearing within a reasonable time before an independent and impartial tribunal, including the right to present legal arguments and to be represented by legal counsel of one's own choice;
— the right to be promptly and officially informed of the decision taken on any appeal, including the legal grounds on which this decision was based. This information will be provided as a rule in writing and, in any event, in a way that will enable the individual to make effective use of further available remedies.

It can be argued that these standards go beyond the obligation of the States Parties to the International Covenant on Civil and Political Rights. The provision of Principle 13 (9) in particular constitute progress in comparison with Article 14 of the Covenant. On the other hand, one can argue that the standards of the Vienna Concluding Document do not have legal status since the Document is not a treaty. It is certainly beyond the scope of this chapter to discuss at length the question of the legal nature of the obligations contained in the CSCE documents. It should only be recalled that some authors are of the opinion that final acts of international conferences can create norms if they contain provisions which, according to the intentions of the parties, should have a normative character (see above).

Moreover, the significance of the above CSCE standards undoubtedly goes beyond their more or less disputable legal status. It is significant that the participating states agreed that every individual should have an effective judicial, administrative, legislative or executive remedy and that domestic remedies should be constructed so that they are in conformity with certain standards. The participating 35 states have assumed, if not a legal, then certainly a political responsibility for the enforcement of the standards agreed upon. It should also be pointed out that the states participating in the CSCE process are far more homogeneous than the totality of the states that adhere to the global human rights covenants. That is why it may be easier to compare and verify the application of the CSCE standards.

3. The legal position of the individual in Eastern Europe

The function of national implementation methods cannot be understood without taking into consideration the basic doctrinal concepts which govern the legal position of the individual in a given society. The Western concept of human rights is well known. What is more important, there are no fundamental changes in sight, in spite of the fact that some Western social scientists, in their search for an answer to contemporary Western problems, are questioning the principle of liberal individualism. In Eastern Europe, on the other hand, we are facing substantial changes in, if not a total rejection of, the traditional socialist concept of human rights (Wieruszewski, 1988, p. 27f.). It is now recognized that the socialist concept — based on the assumption that the accomplishment of the happiness of the individual is possible only by guaranteeing happiness for the whole of society — has failed to achieve its aims. Therefore, it should be a matter of interest to inject, against the background of traditional principles, some new elements into this concept.

Socialist theory traditionally rejected the natural law origin of citizens' rights and was unwilling to deduce them from either the nature of man or from the human mind. According to Marxist theory, these rights are the product of the socio-economic conditions of a given society. This theory rejected the idea that human rights reflect the relationship between society and the individual. Rather, it used to stress that the state is the origin and guarantor of these rights. The socialist concept, in its traditional form, claimed that only a socialist system is able to overcome the antagonism between the state and the citizen by eliminating the material basis for such an antagonism.

In reality, state ownership of the means of production creates a new basis for antagonistic relationships. In a socialist state, the processes of production and distribution are controlled by the state. The state is in charge of the national economy. Socialist doctrine emphasizes that this creates the necessary conditions for securing citizens' rights and that in a socialist society there is a unity and combination of public and private interests. But what happens when there is a conflict between the state and the citizens? The supposed conformity between public and private interests in no way precludes what has been called non-antagonistic conflicts of interest. In this case the public interest, which is represented and guarded by the state, has primacy. The socialist states did not accept the theory of separation of powers but have stuck to the concept of unity of powers with all its structural and functional consequences.

Socialist doctrine thus was not prepared to accept the concept of universally binding human values. Rather, it insisted that the meaning of human rights depended entirely on the socio-economic context. At the international level, we could speak only about 'co-operation', not about 'control', because the criteria for international control could not be evaluated objectively (Movchan, 1982; Chikvadze and Lukaszewa, 1986, p. 190f.; Graefrath, 1988, p. 29f.).

Today, this traditional approach is no longer accepted by a growing number of scholars from various Eastern European countries. There are at present considerable differences between the legal doctrines and policies of these countries. At this stage it is difficult to predict whether we are confronted with an evolution of the socialist concept of human rights or whether we are facing its decay.

The new elements include: (1) abandonment of the notion of the state as the source of individual rights; (2) acceptance of the binding character of universal values; (3) acceptance of various forms of international control mechanisms,[2] (4) recognition of the individual as a subject of international law.[3] At the domestic level, too, we can notice important changes, such as reducing state ownership of the means of production, limiting the role of the state and abolishing the leading position of the communist party.

4. Legislative measures

4.1. Application of human rights treaties in domestic legal systems

The application of international human rights treaties in domestic legal systems is an important factor in assessing the fulfilment of the obligations of State Parties. States are under no obligation to incorporate these treaties in their domestic law. An effective national protection of the rights and freedoms recognized under the Covenants does not depend on formal incorporation. These rights and freedoms must in substance be effectively ensured at the domestic level, irrespective of whether the Covenants themselves have the status of domestic law and, should they have such status, regardless of their place in the domestic legal hierarchy of norms.

On the other hand, even when the Covenants do not have the status of domestic law, individuals should not be prevented from

---

[2] Wiereszczetin and Mullerson, 1989, p. 10. Cf. Graefrath, 1988, p. 35, who defends the traditional approach, according to which states do not intend to reduce their sovereignty and to accept the international personality of the individual, when concluding human rights treaties.

[3] Glukhov, 1988, p. 39, writes:

> Soviet accession to the Optional Protocol (to the International Covenant on Civil and Political Rights) will enable us to discuss frankly concrete humanitarian problems and solve them on the basis of national legislation. The formidable barrier of prejudice and juggling with facts with regard to the actual state of affairs in human rights in this country is being torn down ... Consideration should also be given to an initiative of drafting a third optional protocol under which an international consultative body could be formed to receive complaints of human rights violations under the International Covenant on Economic, Social and Cultural Rights.

In a letter to the UN Secretary-General of February 1989, the Foreign Minister of the Soviet Union announced his country's acceptance of the compulsory jurisdiction of the International Court of Justice in respect of six international human rights conventions.

invoking their provisions in legal proceedings, with the understanding that there is a presumption of the prevailing legal force of the Covenants. That 'the Covenant would never become a living constitution of nations if the rights and freedoms it recognized could not be invoked in dealings with State authorities',[4] is a legitimate statement reflective of the nature of human rights treaties.

In Eastern European countries, human rights treaties do not as a rule have the status of an act of domestic law. In Poland, citizens cannot base their claims solely on the provisions of international conventions. Their provisions may, however, be invoked as a secondary source of law. In fact, the Constitutional Tribunal and the Supreme Administrative Court have cited human rights treaties, if only as persuasive argument (see, for example, the decision of the Constitutional Tribunal of 3 March 1987, *Europäische Grundrechte-Zeitschrift*, Heft 15/16 (22 September 1989), p. 362; see also Izdebski, 1987; Kulesza, 1985; Kedzia, 1987). The status of human rights treaties in the Polish legal system is not very clear. It can be expected that this problem will be solved by the new constitution.

The question is not only of legal but, perhaps predominantly, also of political significance. From a legalistic point of view, one could argue that in Poland, the Soviet Union, Czechoslovakia and Bulgaria, human rights treaties have been transformed into part of the domestic legal order and therefore can and should be directly applied. When reporting to the Human Rights Committee, representatives from these states have denied such a possibility.[5] Their statements have been based on a restrictive approach to the application of international treaties at the national level. This approach, again, was based on the socialist concept of human rights referred to above.

With the new understanding of human rights that has made headway recently, it can be expected that the negative attitude to the direct applicability of human rights treaties will also be changed. This does not imply, however, that there will be in the near future a wide acceptance of human rights provisions on the part of national judicial bodies. The experience of countries that have ratified the European Convention on Human Rights teaches us that it will take time before a judiciary is prepared to take cognizance of the importance of international norms (Drzemczewski, 1983). It is incumbent upon state authorities to try to facilitate such a process.

---

[4] Tomuschat, CCPR/C/SR.109, p. 11. See also a comprehensive study on implementation mechanisms by the same author: Tomuschat, 1985.

[5] Yugoslavia and Hungary have taken a different position. Yugoslavia informed the Human Rights Committee that the International Covenant on Civil and Political Rights has the legal effect of a federal statute and that accordingly its self-executing provisions can be directly applied (CCPR/C/1/Add. 23). Hungary, too, reported that the Covenant formed part of Hungarian domestic law and that its provisions can be invoked before the courts and state organs (CCPR/C/1/Add. 44).

As far as the other European CSCE countries are concerned, universal human rights conventions sometimes do not have the same status under domestic law as the European Convention. In Austria, for instance, Parliament has conferred constitutional law status upon the European Convention, while the International Covenant on Civil and Political Rights cannot be invoked before Austrian courts.[6] In the case of the Federal Republic of Germany, on the other hand, it can be assumed that the Covenant has the same legal status as the European Convention. Both conventions have been incorporated into domestic law and have, according to Article 59 of the German Basic Law, the status of federal law. The self-executing provisions of the Covenant can also be invoked before Belgian, Dutch, Finnish and French courts. Article 55 of the French Constitution states that treaties are superior to national laws.

Several other countries, such as Denmark, Iceland, Ireland, Malta, Norway, Sweden and the United Kingdom have not incorporated the International Covenant on Civil and Political Rights into their domestic legal systems. In these states, however, there exists a presumption that the judiciary should interpret municipal law so as to bring about compatibility with the state's international obligations.

As to the European Convention, it has been pointed out in the legal literature that its impact on national case-law has significantly increased over the years (Drzemczewski, 1987). A similar phenomenon can be observed, at least in some countries, with respect to the International Covenant on Civil and Political Rights. Nevertheless, the Covenant is still far from achieving the status of a 'living constitution of nations'.

4.2. *Constitutional protection*

There are different legal techniques to recognize and ensure individual rights and freedoms in domestic legal systems. The most common method is to include a bill of rights in the national constitution. There are different solutions as to how to determine the relationship between statutory laws and the constitution, especially regarding its provisions on the fundamental rights of the individual.

Eastern European states traditionally declared in their basic laws a broad range of citizens' rights and freedoms. Basing themselves on the model of the Soviet Constitution of 1936, these countries in their post-war constitutions put a strong emphasis on economic, social and cultural rights and citizens' duties. Political rights and individual freedoms were also taken into account, but several constitutions

---

[6] In ratifying the Covenant, Austria invoked a so-called reservation implementation clause, adopted in 1964. Treaties which have been ratified in this way have not been directly applicable before the courts.

stated that these rights should not be used against the will of the working class. A characteristic feature of these provisions was the emphasis on so-called material safeguards coupled with a lack of legal guarantees.

This situation started to change in the 1960s. The new stage in the constitutional protection of citizens' rights can be characterized as follows: (1) there was not one single model adopted in each and every country; (2) there was equal emphasis on all categories of rights; (3) citizens' duties were extensively regulated; (4) the new bills of rights included not only 'material safeguards' but also guarantees; (5) there were some general principles on the status of the individual as a member of the society (equality, interdependence between rights and duties, etc.). The importance of a bill of rights was stressed by placing it among the first chapters of the constitution. The subject of the rights proclaimed was the 'citizen'. The catalogue of rights covered, with a few exceptions, all internationally recognized rights. Among the exceptions were: the right to strike and the right to leave any country, including one's own. In line with the socialist concept of human rights referred to above, some Eastern European constitutions emphasized that individual rights cannot be used against the interest of the society or the state.[7]

It should be kept in mind that the Eastern European constitutions have not had a great impact on the legal status of the individual. Rather, this status has been regulated at the level of statutes and statutory orders. In Poland, for instance, the constitutional bill of rights has been in force since 1952, with cosmetic changes only. Yet, quite substantial changes have taken place over the last decades with regard to the legal regulation and especially enforcement of citizens' rights. The reason for the limited importance of constitutional bills of rights is the fact that constitutions have not served as a source of the subjective rights of the individual.[8] In fact, citizens could not base their claims against the state on constitutional bills of rights.[9] Judicial review of the constitutionality of legal acts was regarded as incompatible with the socialist legal system.

In Western European countries, constitutional bills of rights have a

---

[7] See, for example, Article 39 (2) of the Soviet Constitution, Article 19 (3) of the Constitution of the German Democratic Republic, Article 9 (2) of the Bulgarian Constitution and Articles 19 (1) and 34 of the Czechoslovak Constitution. The Polish Constitution previously contained the following provisions (Article 8): 'The laws of the Polish People's Republic shall express the interests and the will of the working people'. This Article, among others, was abolished on 28 December 1989. The newly enacted Article 1 states that 'Poland is a democratic state of law'. In Hungary, similar changes have been made during autumn 1989.

[8] The Constitution of the German Democratic Republic, however, stated already in its 1968 version (Article 105) that the Constitution was directly binding as law.

[9] Especially during the 1980s, several authors defended the concept of constitutional rights as subjective rights: Klenner, 1982, p. 136; Kartashkin, 1982, p. 632; Poppe, 1984, p. 181.

clear impact on the legal status of the individual. An interesting approach is to be found in France, where not only the Constitution of 1958, but also the 1789 Declaration on the Rights of Man and of the Citizen and the Preamble of the 1946 Constitution, taking also into account a decision of the Constitutional Council of 16 July 1971, are considered as having the rank of superior law. According to the doctrine of the separation of powers, French courts are not authorized to examine the constitutionality of acts of parliament. Under Article 61 of the Constitution, this competence belongs to the Constitutional Council. This body ensures that laws are in conformity with the 1789 Declaration as supplemented by the Preamble of the 1946 Constitution. These provisions are rather general and for this reason perhaps do not exert a strong influence on the legal status of the individual. In any case, and thanks to the activity of the Constitutional Council, the provisions serve as a 'French Bill of Rights'.

The Federal Republic of Germany is an example of a state where a constitutional bill of rights plays an important role as far as the legal status of the individual is concerned. The Basic Law of 1949 proclaims as an inviolable value 'the dignity of man'. It contains a comprehensive catalogue of individual rights which are granted partly as general human rights and partly as rights reserved for Germans. It is significant that, according to Article 1, paragraph 3, of the Basic Law, 'basic rights shall bind the legislature, the executive and the judiciary as directly enforceable law'. As a consequence, the Constitutional Court may decide whether particular legislative acts are compatible with the Constitution.

The legal system of Great Britain differs considerably from those mentioned above. There is no written constitution and thus no 'basic law'. The legal safeguards against violations of individual rights and freedoms are to be found in ordinary legislative acts and in case-law. Some British scholars and politicians are of the opinion that fundamental human rights are inadequately protected against governmental and administrative powers and that the enactment of a bill of rights could help to redress this situation (Fawcett, 1976; Zander, 1979; Campbell, 1980). The lack of a bill of rights may be one of the reasons for the relatively high number of individual complaints lodged against the United Kingdom with the Commission and the Court of Human Rights in Strasbourg.

In spite of its strong common law tradition, Canada, unlike the United Kingdom, adopted, in 1982, the Canadian Charter of Rights and Freedoms. The Charter replaced the Canadian Bill of Rights but, unlike its predecessor, was assigned the rank of constitutional law. The adoption of this instrument should be regarded as an important constitutional innovation. One of the biggest shortcomings of the Bill of Rights was its lack of effective remedies. In one of its judgments, the Canadian Supreme Court stated: 'You may have your rights infringed, but we cannot see what remedy we can give you'.[10] In order to avoid a comparable situation, the 1982 Charter contains an enforcement clause. Article 24, paragraph 1, provides: 'Anyone whose rights and freedoms, as guaranteed by this Charter, have been infringed or denied may apply to a court of competent jurisdiction to obtain such remedy as the court considers just and appropriate in the circumstances'. Thanks to this provision, the protection of the constitutional rights of Canadian citizens has been secured by the courts. Precisely because of this, many lawyers and politicians opposed the adoption of the Charter. They argued that it would be better to leave citizens' rights to the Parliament than to the judiciary.

4.3. Concluding remarks

The furtherance and observance of universal human rights standards should be seen as one of the most important elements within the CSCE process. In this context, the status of human rights treaties in general, and the International Covenant on Civil and Political Rights in particular, in domestic legal systems, serves as an important yardstick in evaluating the practice of states. The growing impact of human rights treaties on national legislation and jurisdiction is obvious, despite the fact that the substantive treaty provisions seldom are given the force of domestic law. As far as this aspect is concerned, we can expect a radical change of approach in the Eastern European states (Mullerson, 1989, pp. 494-9). International law can serve as an effective guarantee of individual rights and freedoms only when its norms enjoy the status of constitutional law and are directly applicable by courts, ordinary as well as constitutional ones. Up until now, these conditions have been fulfilled in a few countries only. More often than not constitutions contain a bill of rights.

The concept of constitutional protection of individual rights and freedoms is based on the need to impose certain barriers and limits on legislative, administrative and judicial authorities. When can constitutional provisions effectively perform such a function? It seems that at least the following conditions must be fulfilled: (1) the constitution should protect all basic rights, freedoms and duties of citizens; (2) the constitutional provisions should be as precise as possible; (3) any limitation clauses should be derived from the constitution itself; (4) the constitutional norms should establish subjective rights and they should be directly applicable before the courts, and (5) there should be judicial control of the constitutionality of legislative acts.

The legislative implementation of international human rights treaties should not be limited to the constitutional level. The follow-

---

[10] *Hogan v. The Queen* (1975), quoted from Tarnopolsky, 1983, p. 256. See also McWhinney, 1983, pp. 625-31.

ing observation made by the European Court of Human Rights has a bearing on universal human rights instruments as well: 'If a violation of one of those rights and freedoms is the result of non-observance of that obligation in the enactment of domestic legislation, the responsibility of the State for that violation is engaged'.[11]

Among states participating in the CSCE process, we can anticipate relatively rapid progress in overcoming the existing heterogeneity in value orientations. A developed system of the constitutional protection of individual rights can then be seen as one of the most important means to secure universally binding human rights standards.

5. National mechanisms

5.1. The Prokuratura

All Eastern European countries have had the Prokuratura system. This institution was supposed to serve as a guardian of citizens' rights. The underlying idea was to create an independent mediator. Therefore, the organs of the Prokuratura's office formed a separate branch within the system of state organs, together with the other main branches, that is, the organs of state power, the organs of state administration and the judiciary. The province of the Prokuratura was much wider than that of a public prosecutor. According to the constitutions of Eastern European countries, the primary function of the Prokurator's office was to safeguard and protect the lawful rights of citizens at all levels of administration. And so the Prokurator, unlike, for instance, a United States district attorney, whose task is to conduct proceedings against criminal suspects, was charged with the duty of achieving legality, not only on the part of the citizens but also on the part of the state, and not only in respect of criminal law but in respect of the legal system as a whole.

At the head of the Prokuratura was the Prokurator-General, who was appointed by, and responsible to, the legislative authorities or the head of state. The office was invested with supervisory powers over state organs, such as government ministries, state committees, enterprises and other state organs, local government bodies, co-operatives and other public organizations, officials and citizens.[12]

[11] Case of *Young, James and Webster*, judgment of 25 November 1980, Publ. E.C.H.R., Series A, vol. 44, p. 20.
[12] Article 164 of the Constitution of the Soviet Union. See also Article 112 of the Romanian Constitution, Article 133 of the Bulgarian Constitution, Article 97 of the Constitution of the German Democratic Republic. See further Articles 64 and 51, respectively, of the former versions of the Polish and Hungarian constitutions.

The supreme organs of the state, however, were exempted from his jurisdiction.

In order to obtain information about the conduct of public affairs, the Prokuratura was empowered to participate in meetings of local government bodies, to instruct superiors to control the activities of their subordinates, and even to participate in administrative proceedings that were still pending. When he participated in administrative proceedings, his task was to ensure that the procedure and the disposition of the case conformed to existing law. When a final decision had been rendered, he had the competence to ask a superior administrative organ to reopen the proceedings or, in certain circumstances, to bring about an amendment of the decision. If a matter was still subject to appeal, the Prokuratura could submit an appeal which had the same force of law as appeals submitted by the parties to the dispute. He could also make representations to the highest organs of state administration, which had to examine any objections voiced by him and to respond to them promptly.

Any citizen could lodge a complaint with the Prokuratura invoking infringement of his or her rights. The Prokuratura also had the right to institute disciplinary, administrative or criminal proceedings against a person guilty of breaches of the law.

One of the central duties of the Prokurator's office was the prevention of crime and the prosecution of criminals. Furthermore, it was expected to conduct preventive and educational activities. It should be stressed, on the other hand, that although the Prokuratura could establish violations of the law and of subjective rights, the institution was not empowered to impose sanctions, which power was left to the courts.

On the surface, the Prokuratura thus had formidable powers to guard citizens' rights. In reality, however, the Prokuratura was not a very active watchdog. On the contrary, the institution has drawn heavy criticism for providing inadequate protection. What were the main reasons for these failures? To explain this phenomenon, we should remember that the constitutions of the Eastern European countries imposed on the Prokuratura the task of protecting both public and private interests. As was indicated earlier, socialist doctrine did not recognize the possibility of antagonism between the interests. Unfortunately, real life did not support this expectation. When faced with conflicting interests, Prokurators as a rule defended the public rather than the individual interest. Let us also remind ourselves of the leading role of the Communist Party, which implied that the Party had a decisive influence over the policies and activities of all branches of government. The political and other ties between the Prokuratura and the state administration, especially at the local level, made the Prokurators unwilling to contest the decisions of local authorities. The Prokuratura may have had its accomplishments, but it was definitely far from being the strong shield against public disregard for citizens' rights that theory claimed it to be. Public opinion did not treat Prokurators as impartial mediators but rather as parts of the state machinery.

Within the present framework of restructuring the form of government of Eastern European countries, the Prokuratura will apparently undergo changes as to both its functions and status. In Poland, for instance, the Prokurator's office has been recently subordinated to the Ministry of Justice and its functions are now similar to those of Western European public prosecutors.

5.2. *Judicial remedies*

The importance of judicial remedies as one of the principal guarantees of human rights cannot be questioned. Events have revealed an interesting phenomenon, however: Eastern European countries are undertaking far-reaching changes in their respective legal systems, with the idea of strengthening the system of judicial protection. At the same time, legal doctrine in the West points out that judicial protection has its limits and that the rights of the individual are quite often better protected through other means.[13]

How should we interpret these contradictory tendencies from the point of view of protecting human rights? In fact, it is misleading to speak about a contradiction. The East and the West have different starting points. For a long time, judicial guarantees played only a limited role in the Eastern European states. 'Material guarantees' were considered to be the most important factor in the realization of human rights. Today, these states have to establish a balance between substantive guarantees and judicial remedies. In Western Europe, the situation is the reverse. In the West, judicial protection has reached a stage where its shortcomings become obvious. And so we witness a tendency to use quasi-judicial methods (Papier, 1989; see also Betterman, 1986).

It is not possible to deal with these tendencies at length here or to address the details of existing judicial remedies. In the following section, I shall have more to say about the new elements which are emerging with respect to the judicial protection of human rights in the Eastern European countries. Some comparisons with judicial remedies in the West are in order, however.

It is not possible to establish objectively which European country has the best judicial system, because judicial remedies constitute only one element in a system of guarantees. It is extremely difficult to isolate one such element and to measure its effectiveness. But there

---

[13] In the United States, for instance, there is the phenomenon that individuals try to avoid the judicial system because they find it inappropriate, costly, time-consuming and inaccessible. Widespread attempts are being made to offer alternatives whereby disputing parties can settle their differences by themselves. See *Mediation in the Justice System*, 1983.

are some criteria which can be used to assess judicial systems. The independence of the judiciary is one of the most important requirements. Judges and advocates should be free from governmental influence. This also requires that they be provided with adequate salaries and security of tenure. The independence and impartiality of the judiciary should be seen as a *condition sine qua non* of its effectiveness. But the accessibility of judicial remedies is also of great importance. The national legal system should provide for adequate legal aid to the poor and needy, especially in criminal cases and in cases of violations of human rights.

In countries with the common law system, judicial protection is essentially based on the power of the ordinary courts to review administrative acts. In these proceedings, the so-called prerogative writs play an important role. In addition, administrative acts can in Great Britain be challenged in a number of administrative tribunals or by using the public inquiry system. In these cases administrative organs act in a quasi-judicial capacity. Orders and decisions of these organs, too, can be challenged before the courts (Beloff, 1989, pp. 39–63).

There are no restrictions on a person's right of recourse to the courts and legal aid is generally available for those who cannot afford legal assistance. It should be remembered, however, that the powers of the British ordinary courts are considerably limited by the lack of a written constitution. Parliament is omnipotent, with absolute power to enact new laws and change existing ones. The courts do not recognize a higher legal order giving them powers to declare acts of Parliament null and void.

The situation in two other CSCE common law countries is different. Both in Canada and in the United States the protection of citizens' constitutional rights is entrusted to the courts. But while the United States Supreme Court quite often functions as a policy-maker in the field of civil liberties and human rights, the Canadian Supreme Court continues along more cautious lines.

A contrast to the common law system is offered by the French judicial system. In France, there exists a duality of judicial and administrative jurisdiction. The latter has been derived from the administrative machinery and is classified as a part of the executive branch. In spite of this classification, French administrative courts and the Conseil d'Etat enjoy the same independence as judicial bodies. In regard to individual rights and freedoms, the jurisdiction of the courts is divided in the following way: the administrative courts have jurisdiction with respect to administrative acts and transactions, the judicial courts have exclusive penal jurisdiction, while the civil courts are competent to deal with the relations between individuals. However, the judicial courts may, in exercising jurisdiction in penal matters, declare illegal an administrative act of a normative character which has been challenged by the defendant.

An individual who claims to be a victim of violations of his or her rights on the part of public authorities may apply to an administrative court for annulment of the act as *ultra vires*. The power of annulment vested in the Conseil d'Etat covers not only illegal administrative acts but also discretionary acts, if the Council of State finds that they are in violation of general principles of law.

A system of administrative courts also exists in the Federal Republic of Germany (for an interesting comparison between Germany and Switzerland, see Schmidt-Assmann, 1989, pp. 89–125). Administrative acts may be revised on the basis of an appeal to the administrative courts. The victim must first address a request to the administrative authorities. If the person concerned has suffered damage, however, he or she may sue the state or an entity of public law in the civil courts.

The legal system of the Federal Republic of Germany contains a further powerful judicial remedy, namely the constitutional complaint under Article 93, paragraph 1, of the Basic Law. An affected person who has exhausted all regular remedies, may lodge a complaint with the Constitutional Court claiming violation of any of the basic rights guaranteed by the Constitution. The importance of this remedy should not be overestimated, as it is used in exceptional circumstances only.

While judicial remedies in Eastern European countries were previously given only secondary importance, there is now growing public support for the proposition that an elaborated system of judicial remedies is essential for the adequate protection of citizens' rights and freedoms. Already in the 1960s, there was a trend in socialist doctrine to stress the importance of judicial remedies (see, for example, Sabo, 1966, p. 17). Periodic reports submitted by Eastern and Central European countries to the Human Rights Committee (under the International Covenant on Civil and Political Rights) have indicated that judicial remedies play an important function. But observers must ask whether a given legal system satisfies not only politicians and lawyers but most importantly the citizens themselves. In the public debate presently going on in this region, one of the most frequent demands concerns the reconstruction and strengthening of the judicial system. Without great risk of error, one can foresee that in the near future the basic concepts of the legal system will be revised. This is interesting from a legal philosophical point as well, but these problems go beyond the scope of this chapter and must be left aside.

A precondition of judicial reform is the popular demand to establish an independent judiciary. Independence should be seen as eliminating any direct political or administrative influence. As far as structural changes are concerned, the following have been proposed: (1) the establishment of general judicial control of the administration; (2) the creation of constitutional adjudicatory bodies, and (3) the establishment of an ombudsman institution.

As far as judicial control of the administration is concerned, considerable progress has been made during the last ten years (Kuss,

1988, pp. 510–52). The Eastern and Central European countries have gradually accepted the idea that administrative decisions can be submitted to impartial judicial review. The scope of this review and the institutional solutions adopted may be quite different. In two countries (Poland and Yugoslavia) there is a separate and specialized administrative judiciary. In Yugoslavia, however, ordinary courts, too, play a role in administrative cases. Federal administrative acts may be challenged in a federal court. In the republics and autonomous provinces, the situation varies. In Croatia and Bosnia-Hercegovina there are separate administrative courts, while in Serbia and the autonomous province of Vojvodina the district courts are competent to review the acts of local government and the Supreme Courts deal with acts of central administrative organs. In the rest of the country (Slovenia, Montenegro, Macedonia and Kossovo) the Supreme Courts also have administrative jurisdiction. It should be added that in Yugoslavia, acts issued by self-managing organizations and communities exercising public functions are subject to judicial control by labour courts.

In Poland, individuals can challenge administrative decisions before the Supreme Administrative Court. Poland has not adopted a general administrative appeal clause but has followed an enumeration system. The shortcomings of this system have been partly overcome by the application of a principle of extended competence, which means that in cases of doubt, there is a presumption speaking in favour of the competence of the Supreme Administrative Court. During the late 1980s, the jurisdiction of this Court was significantly broadened: it can now review, practically speaking, all administrative acts.

According to the Polish Administrative Procedure Act, administrative decisions in individual cases can be challenged as illegal if they belong to the defined sphere of state administration. Judging from its case-law, the Supreme Administrative Court seems to follow the following principles: (1) the principle of the protection of individual privacy against interferences on the part of the administration; (2) the principle of combating the 'overadministration' of individual and social life, and (3) the principle of protecting the rights of citizens against limitations imposed via statutes. The Supreme Administrative Court may also give a wide interpretation to the scope of its competence, sometimes even contrary to the letter but certainly in line with the spirit of applicable norms. In many cases the Court re-examines the merits of a case, acting as a judiciary *de novo*.

Elements of administrative jurisdiction have also been introduced in Romania and Bulgaria. Both countries have empowered the ordinary courts to exercise judicial control of the legality of administrative acts. In Bulgaria, a special chamber within each district court is competent to deal with such matters. When the decision appealed against has been issued, for instance, by a Minister or the head of a central administrative agency, the appeal is considered by the Supreme court. The Supreme Court also hears appeals against decisions that have been confirmed or amended by a Minister or a departmental head with ministerial rank. The Court is only concerned with the legality of the decision. When an administrative body refuses to issue a decision, the courts can compel it to do so, without providing specific instructions as to the content of the decision.

In Romania, administrative acts are subject to the jurisdiction of the ordinary courts — the lower courts in case of acts of local government and the district courts in case of acts of central government. Both Bulgaria and Romania have adopted a general appeal clause, with an enumeration of acts excluded from judicial control. The scope of this exclusion, however, is rather extensive, especially in Romania. Unlike the situation in Poland, the Bulgarian and Romanian courts have adopted a rather restrictive approach to the question of the scope of their powers.

In Hungary, the system of judicial control of the administration was considerably extended in 1981. A decree issued by the Council of Ministers contained a catalogue of administrative decisions which could be challenged before the courts. Taking into consideration that there is widespread support for judicial control, one can expect rapid changes in this respect.

In Czechoslovakia, judicial control has been limited to the following cases: (1) entry into the electoral registers; (2) the confinement of the mentally ill; (3) decisions in certain health insurance matters, and (4) decisions of social insurance bodies. In the first two cases, local courts have jurisdiction, while the third and fourth categories belong to the jurisdiction of the district courts.

The German Democratic Republic for a long time resisted the idea of judicial administrative proceedings. But on 14 December 1988, the People's Council passed a statute on the judicial review of administrative decisions, which was based on the principle of enumeration. The scope of judicial review is quite broad, however, covering such important questions as freedom of assembly and association, the right to travel abroad, the issuance of building permits, activities of private enterprises, education, house rentals and other similar matters. The procedural rules ensure the full participation of an affected individual in the court's proceedings. The system potentially serves as an important judicial control mechanism for the individual.

The Soviet Union has established a system of judicial control which, in many respects, differs from the above-mentioned systems. On 30 June 1987, the Supreme Soviet passed a law dealing with judicial appeal against unlawful acts which infringe citizens' rights. Under this Act, citizens can appeal to the ordinary courts whenever their subjective rights have been infringed. The remedy is not limited by subject matter. The peculiarity of the system is related to the fact that decisions of collective bodies cannot be challenged. The effectiveness of the remedy can also be seriously hampered by the fact that the courts do not have powers to annul decisions which they consider to be illegal.

With respect to Eastern European countries, it should be understood that, parallel to the court system, there exist systems of citizens' petitions and complaints and that the Prokuratura is still entrusted with the general supervision of the legality of actions. But in these cases the individual seeking redress is relegated to the status of a petitioner, without a right to participate effectively in the proceedings. It is not difficult to predict a further development of judicial control in this area. One probable element will be the introduction of constitutional review. Poland has already established a Constitutional Tribunal with powers to exercise control of the constitutionality of statutes and certain other normative acts. Recently, Hungary has followed that example. Legal doctrine in both countries is also in favour of granting the individual the right of constitutional complaint.

5.3. The ombudsman

The system of the ombudsman originated in Sweden. The idea behind this institution is to assist individuals when their rights have been violated by state or other public authorities. Today, ombudsman institutions under various names exist in more than 30 countries. The following list comprises the ombudsman institutions of the CSCE countries (source: Kubiak, 1989, pp. 269–72):

1. Sweden	1809	Justitieombudsman
2. Finland	1919	Eduskunnan oikeusasiamies-riksdagens justitieombudsman
3. Norway	1952	Ombudsmann for forsvaret
	1962	Stortingets ombudsmann for forvaltningen
4. Denmark	1954	Folketingets ombudsman
5. Federal Republic of Germany	1957	Wehrbeauftragter
	1974	Bürgerbeauftragter im Rheinland-Pfalz
6. United Kingdom	1967	Parliamentary Commissioner for Administration
	1969	Commissioner for Complaints in Northern Ireland
	1974	Commissioner for Local Administration in England and Wales
	1975	Commissioner for Local Administration in Scotland
7. Canada	1967	Ombudsman in Alberta and New

		Brunswick
	1968	Protecteur du Citoyen in Quebec
	1969	Ombudsman in Manitoba and Federal Commissioner of Official Languages
	1971	Ombudsman in New Scotland
	1972	Ombudsman in Saskatchewan
	1975	Ombudsman in Ontario and Newfoundland
	1979	Ombudsman in British Colombia
8. United States	1969	Ombudsman in Hawaii
	1971	Public Counsel in Nebraska
	1972	Citizens' Aide in Iowa
	1975	Ombudsman in Alaska
9. France	1973	Mèdiateur
10. Italy	1974	Difensore Civico in Liguria
	1975	" " " " " " Toscania
	1979	" " " " " " Campania
	1980	" " " " " " Lombardia
	1980	" " " " " " Umbria
	1981	" " " " " " Fruli–Venice
11. Portugal	1967	Provedor de Justica
12. Austria	1977	Volksanwaltschaft
13. Ireland	1978	Tanodbayan
14. Netherlands	1981	Nationale ombudsman
15. Spain	1981	Defensor del Pueblo
16. Poland	1987	Rzecznic Praw Obywatelskich
17. Hungary	1989	Emberi Jogok Bizottsaba

This list could be supplemented by a list of ombudsmen and so-called quasi-ombudsman institutions for special issues, such as the Health Service Commissioner, the Police Complaints Authority, the Data Protection Registrar and the Insurance Ombudsman Bureau in the United Kingdom. In Sweden, there are several similar offices, dealing with the freedom of the press, anti-monopoly activities, consumer protection, equality of women and the protection of immigrants. In Yugoslavia, there is the defender of self-government, but this institution cannot be classified as an ombudsman proper as it is not empowered to deal with individual complaints.

In spite of the differences, there are some basic elements which seem to be common to the offices of ombudsman. An ombudsman is an independent public official separated from the administrative and judicial authorities, answerable to parliament and quite often elected by them. An ombudsman performs a double function — protecting individual rights and informing parliament and public opinion about existing irregularities. An ombudsman acts quickly and in an informal manner and enjoys extensive powers to investigate individual complaints as well as grievances brought to his or her attention through the media. However, the ombudsman normally lacks the power to annul administrative acts (but may in some countries bring charges against civil servants).

The original Nordic model has been adopted and modified in the various countries. In some states the ombudsman functions only at the regional level. The independence of the ombudsman is secured by certain arrangements. For instance, the person holding the office is usually irremovable during the term of office, or at least a special procedure has to be followed to dismiss an ombudsman. The ombudsman as a rule enjoys some functional and jurisdictional immunity.

Why is the ombudsman institution so attractive that a number of countries have recently adopted it? The most important factor is perhaps the question of accessibility. The easy, quick and cheap access to an ombudsman is an advantage as compared to the rather slow and often costly court system. It is also important that the ombudsman, as a parliamentary organ, assumes an independent supervisory function in relation to the courts and the administration and thus supplements the more juridical mechanisms for the protection of citizens' rights.

Against this background, I shall present some features of the Polish ombudsman institution which began its activities on 1 January 1988. The Polish ombudsman has wide powers to deal with all complaints concerning political, civil, economic, social and cultural rights and freedoms. Like the Nordic ombudsmen, but contrary to the model adopted in some other countries, the Polish ombudsman has certain powers in relation to the administration of justice. For example, he or she can lodge an extraordinary appeal against a final court decision.

The present Ombudsman has established the following principles to guide her activities: (1) she refuses to act as an attorney, in the sense that she does not help provide for concrete services (apartments, cars, etc.); (2) she acts as a last resort, when all other means and procedures have been exhausted; (3) she deals primarily with problems of a general character, which are common to a group of people, and (4) she does not deal with problems that are beyond her capacity, such as housing or pollution (that is, problems which might be handled by an ombudsman in a better organized society than Poland).

The Polish ombudsman institution can no longer be viewed merely as an 'experiment'. The Ombudsman has established herself as a strong and useful instrument in guaranteeing citizens' rights and freedoms. She has gained respect among broad sectors of society and most remarkably among the state administration. She has successfully avoided politically sensitive questions in order to be able to solve many other socially important problems. The first

Ombudsman, Professor Ewa Letowska, deserves a good deal of credit for her performance.

6. Summary

The proceedings and Concluding Document of the 1986–89 Vienna Follow-up meeting of the CSCE countries proved unequivocally that, at least among the CSCE countries, there exists a possibility to achieve a common understanding as to the interpretation of the main values that underlie internationally recognized human rights. There are, of course, still substantial differences in the political and social structures of these countries which influence attitudes towards human rights. But one can observe an effort to overcome these differences so as to create favourable conditions for a more effective international system of human rights protection.

National implementation mechanisms still play a decisive role in human rights protection. International instruments are of a rather general nature when it comes to standards for national remedies. Nevertheless, some clear obligations on domestic implementation mechanisms ensue from the international instruments.

The requirements of the effectiveness of domestic remedies is crucial. In this respect, international instruments such as the International Covenant on Civil and Political Rights and the Vienna Concluding Document put an emphasis on judicial remedies. There now exists a consensus between the East and the West on the importance of judicial remedies.

With respect to the Eastern European countries, a seemingly rich system of non-judicial (petitions, complaints, activities of social and political organizations, etc.) and quasi-judicial (the Prokuratura) remedies proved to be neither effective nor adequate. In spite of the euphoric periodic reports submitted by these states to international bodies such as the Human Rights Committee, the individual was far too often powerless when confronted with bureaucratic state machinery. The current development of existing, and introduction of new, judicial remedies in the Eastern and Central European countries seem to adjust the domestic implementation system to the internationally required level. This tendency, of course, is to be welcomed. But at the same time it should be borne in mind that a given remedy system functions in a broader political setting. Without profound political changes, the process referred to above could not have taken place.

It is sometimes held that national implementation methods and mechanisms depend on the history, customs and political and social system of a given society. But if the idea of human rights is to be taken seriously, the influence of such factors should by no means undermine the main aim of national implementation systems — the protection of human rights values and not just conformity with the letter of a given human rights treaty.

In Europe, there today seems to be unqualified support for the goal of protecting the individual against overbearing wielders of public power. This goal is not always achieved, and probably never will be. But this does not mean that we should end our constant search for improved methods and new and better safeguards.

Bibliography

Alston, P. 1987. 'Out of the Abyss: The Challenges confronting the UN Committee on Economic, Social and Cultural Rights', *Human Rights Quarterly*, vol. 9.

Alston, P. and G. Quinn, 1987. 'The Nature and Scope of States Parties' Obligations under the International Covenant on Economic and Cultural Rights', *Human Rights Quarterly*, vol. 9.

Alston, P. and B. Simma, 1987. 'First Session of the UN Committee on Economic, Social and Cultural Rights, *American Journal of International Law*, vol. 82.

Beloff, M. 1989. 'Judicial Safeguards for Administrative Procedure: The United Kingdom', in F. Matscher (ed.), *Judicial Safeguards in Administrative Proceedings*. Kehl am Rhein: N.P. Engel Verlag.

Betterman, K.A., 1986. *Der totale Rechtsstaat*. Hamburg: Joachim Jungius-Gesellschaft der Wissenschaften, in Kommission beim Verlag Vandenhoeck & Ruprecht.

Bossuyt, M.J., 1987. *Guide to the 'Travaux Preparatoires' of the International Covenant on Civil and Political Rights*. Dordrecht: Martinus Nijhoff.

Campbell, C., 1980. *Do We Need a Bill of Rights?* Aldershot, Hants: Gower Publishing.

Chkikvadze, V. and E. Lukasheva, 1986. *Socjalistitheskaja koncepcja praw cheloveka*. Moskva: Nauka.

Drzemczewski, A., 1983. *European Human Rights Convention in Domestic Law*. Oxford: Clarendon Press.

Drzemczewski, A., 1987. 'The Growing Impact of the European Human Rights Convention upon National Case Law', *The Law Society's Gazette*, London, 25.02.1987.

Fawcett, J.E.S., 1976. 'A Bill of Rights for the United Kingdom', *Human Rights Review*, no. 1.

Glukhov, A., 1988. 'A Two-way Street', *International Affairs*, Moscow, July.

Graefrath, B., 1988. *Menschenrechte und internationale Kooperation: 10 Jahre Praxis des Internationalen Menschenrechtskomitee*. Berlin: Akademie-Verlag.

Izdebski, H., 1984. 'La jurisprudence de la Haute Cour Administration polonaise', *Revue internationale de droit compare*, no. 36.

Kartashkin, V., 1982. 'The Socialist Countries and Human Rights', in K. Vasak and P. Alston (eds), *The International Dimensions of Human Rights*. Westport: Greenwood & Unesco.

Kedzia, Z., 1987. 'Grundrechtsschutz in Polen im Lichte der Rechtssprechung des Hauptverwaltungsgerichtes, *Europäische Grundrechte-Zeitschrift*, no. 14.

Klenner, H., 1982. *Marxismus und Menschenrechte, Studium zur Rechtsphilosophie.* Berlin: Akademie-Verlag.

Kubiak, A., 1989. 'Rozwój instytucji ombudsmana w świecie', in L. Garlicki (ed.), *Rzecznik praw obywatelskich.* Warszawa: IWZZ.

Kulesza, M. (ed.), 1985. *Materialy do nauki prawa administracyjnego.* Warszawa: Wydawnictwa Uniwersytetu Warszawskiego.

Kuss, K.J., 1988. 'Judicial Review of Administrative Decisions in the Soviet Union and other East European Countries', *GYIL*, 31.

McWhinney, E., 1983. 'The Canada Act and the Constitution Act, 1982', *Jahrbuch des offentlichen Rechts der Gegenwart*, vol. 32.

Mediation in the Justice System, Conference Proceedings, 20–21 May 1982, American Bar Association.

Movchan, A., 1982. *Prawa cheloveka i mezhdunarodnyje otnoshenija.* Moskwa.

Mullerson, R., 1989. 'Sources of International Law: New Tendencies in Soviet Thinking', *American Journal of International Law*, vol. 83, no. 3.

Nowak, M., 1989. *Uno-Pakt über bürgerliche und politische Recht und Fakultativprotokoll. CCPR-Kommentar.* Kehl am Rhein: N.P. Engel Verlag.

Papier, H.J., 1989. 'Rechtsschutzgarantie gegen die öffentliche Gewalt', in Isensee, J. and Kirchhof, P. (eds), *Handbuch des Staatsrechts*, Bd. VI.

Poppe, E., 1984. *Staatsrecht der DDR*, 2nd edition. Berlin: Staatsverlag der DDR.

Sabo, I., 1966. 'Fundamental Questions Concerning the Theory and History of Citizens' Rights', in I. Sabo (ed.), *Socialist Concept of Human Rights.* Budapest: Akademiai Kiado.

Schachter, O., 1982. 'International Law in Theory and Practice', *178 Recueil des Cours.* Dordrecht: Martinus Nijhoff.

Schmidt-Assman, E., 1989. 'Verfahrensgarantien in Bereich des Öffentlichen Rechts: Darstellung der Rechtslage in der Bundesrepublik Deutschland mit vergleichenden Hinweisen auf die Bundesverwaltungsrechtspflege in der Schweiz im Blick auf Art. 6 Abs. 1 EMRK', in F. Matscher (ed.), *Judicial Safeguards in Administrative Proceedings.* Kehl am Rhein: N.P. Engel Verlag.

Simma, B., 1989. 'Der Ausschuss über wirtschaftliche, soziale und kulturelle Rechte: ein neues Menschenrechtsgremium der Vereinten Nationen, *Vereinten Nationen*, no. 6.

Tarnopolsky, A., 1983. 'The New Canadian Charter of Rights and Freedoms as Compared and Contrasted with the American Bill of Rights', *Human Rights Quarterly*, vol. 5, no. 1.

Tomuschat, Ch., 1985. 'National Implementation of International Standards on Human Rights', in *Canadian Human Rights Yearbook 1984–1985.*

Tretter, H., 1989. 'Human Rights in the Conference on Security and Cooperation in Europe (CSCE), Vienna 1989', *Human Rights Law Journal*, vol. 10.

Wiereszczetin, W. and R. Mullerson, 1989. 'Primat miezdunarodnowo prawa w mirowoj politikie', *Sowietskoje Gosudarstwo i Prawo*, no. 8.

Wieruszewski, R., 1988. 'The Evolution of the Socialist Concept of Human Rights', *Netherlands Quarterly of Human Rights (SIM Newsletter)*, vol. 6.

Wyrzykowski, M., 1983. *Sadownictwo administracyjne w PRL.* Warszawa.

Zander, M. 1979. *A Bill of Rights?*, 2nd edition. London: Kluwer Law Publishers.

12 Reporting and Complaint Systems in Universal Human Rights Treaties

Bernhard Graefrath

1. Place and function of implementation measures in international law

The scientific and technological developments after the Second World War, the growing influence of socialism and the process of decolonization have brought about major changes in international relations. Today we have a larger number and variety of states than ever before and, at the same time, we face a density of communication between peoples, individuals, groups and states all over the world which was unthinkable 50 years ago. The whole world is in a stage of transformation brought about by economic, scientific and technical developments and reflected in the growing awareness that our planet is small and that many human activities are producing far-reaching effects all over the world. Different forms of international co-operation in various fields have been developed and many international organizations have emerged. Despite many set-backs and brutal manifestations of old power politics, step-by-step an international legal order is developing which forms the framework of an international community of equally sovereign states. It is based on the system of the United Nations Charter and its principles, and has the difficult task of keeping pace with the social and legal changes in international relations in order to meet the challenges of scientific and technological progress and the global problems of our time.

New areas have been conquered by international law, such as space law, human rights, economic relations and environmental law. At the same time, old areas such as the law of the sea have undergone such a considerable change that a whole codex of rules is needed to explain what is meant today by the freedom of the sea.

As has often been stated, the main change in international law is reflected by the prohibition of the threat or use of force and the concomitant trend towards a principled orientation based on co-operation (Friedmann, 1964; Tunkin, 1983, p. 28; Cassese, 1986, p. 126). This change has led to a growing number of international organizations and multilateral treaties establishing rules which try to co-ordinate the activities of states in the main fields of international relations and to create a closer relationship between international and national law.

The change in international law is not limited to substantive rules.

It relates also to enforcement, or perhaps more correctly, to instrumental or procedural rules which are aimed at ensuring a state's compliance with international obligations. With the prohibition of force the arbitrary use of force has become illegal. Enforcement measures are justified only within a process of law and the use of armed force is restricted to self-defence, the rebuff of an armed attack. Developing the legal framework of ensuring compliance with international obligations has thus become all the more important. Furthermore, a general distinction is now made between international delicts and international crimes which entails different legal consequences (Spinedi, 1989, p. 7).

In addition to these developments, the extremely narrow understanding of enforcement has been overcome. Between compliance (state conduct in accordance with an international obligation) and the coerced enforcement of a violated right (measures to induce or compel compliance with an international obligation) a whole system of different 'supervisory mechanisms' (van Dijk, 1984), a 'legal framework of international supervision' (Chowdhury, 1986), has emerged in modern international law. The supervisory system is aimed at verifying, ensuring, promoting, enhancing or inducing observance by states of their international obligations (van Hoof and de Vey Mesdagh, 1984, p. 9; Cassese, 1986, p. 208).

While the term 'control' is normally used in connection with disarmament, in the field of human rights and general international law the term 'implementation measures' is quite common. These measures may have an informative function; they may be used to promote or enforce compliance and to correct wrongful conduct. They may also contribute to the progressive development, adjustment and specification of existing obligations, or to the avoidance or settlement of disputes or to the establishment of facts.[1] Implementation measures may be construed to satisfy all or only some of these functions: They may be of a general nature or depend on specific circumstances or cases. Their degree of institutionalization may reach from an *ad hoc* procedure to the foundation of a treaty organ or an international organization.

Agreement on specific implementation measures in multilateral treaties is an essential element in modern international law. It supplements relationships of reciprocity, may prevent disputes, adapt specific forms of compliance to different situations, and so forth. Implementation measures deserve our attention because they function as a kind of hybrid mechanism, combining elements of dispute avoidance with dispute settlement (Kirgis, 1989, p. 8; Fisher, 1981). They may serve as confidence building procedures and may

---

[1] We would not go so far as to specify a creative function which leads back from the observance of obligations to the legislative process, the creation ‚of rules and obligations or to pave the way in that direction: see, however, van Hoof and de Vey Mesdagh, 1984, p. 11; Chowdhury, 1986, p. 14.

make mutual exchanges of information and control of compliance possible without relying on charges of violation (Mohr, 1983, p. 61; *idem*, 1984, p. 22). They may be used in bilateral and in multilateral relationships. They are, in particular, applied to keep an ongoing process under review, as in disarmament treaties, or in traffic, transit, customs and environmental agreements.

Such measures are extremely important where observance of certain obligations is directed not so much at satisfying the claim of a given state but at serving the interests of the international community or all the parties of a given treaty, where the achievement of a common goal is at stake (Riphagen, 1983, p. 581; Sachariew, 1986, p. 76; *idem*, 1988, p. 281). In these circumstances, the implementation of an obligation is not related to a specifically affected state and thus neither is the right to apply enforcement measures in case of non-compliance left to the discretion of an individual State Party. Quite often implementation measures are specially framed to avoid or to make it impossible for one party to exercise a police function or to enforce its own understanding of compliance in relation to other States Parties. This is especially necessary when the obligation is of such a nature that it can only be fulfilled or violated in relation to all the other parties to the agreement. Such an approach is also useful when the obligation is one of result, leaving it to the state concerned to choose the ways and means of compliance. In such cases, specific implementation procedures are often construed to ensure compliance in forms and to the extent agreed upon by the States Parties. They take precedence over other measures, in particular over unilateral sanctions (Mohr, 1989, p. 343; Sachariew, 1988, p. 282). By such means, states co-ordinate their activities and try to exclude separate actions by one or another State Party which is not specifically affected.

It seems that, in general, these measures deal only with normal problems in the process of compliance. They are based on international co-operation and operate also within the realm of international delicts. However, they are not suited or intended to replace or hinder sanctions in cases of international crimes, such as apartheid, genocide or other mass violations 'of an international obligation of essential importance for safeguarding the human being' (Article 19, paragraph 3(c) of the ILC draft on State Responsibility).

2. Human rights standards and implementation measures

Agreed and often institutionalized implementation measures are a typical mechanism used by states in those human rights treaties which are not limited to the treatment of their own nationals by the other party (for example, in bilateral treaties on friendship, commerce and navigation) but instead set forth international human rights standards. The Covenant on Civil and Political Rights (Political Covenant), the Covenant on Economic, Social and Cultural

Rights (Economic Covenant), the Convention on the Elimination of All Forms of Racial Discrimination (Discrimination Convention), the Convention on the Elimination of All Forms of Discrimination against Women (Women's Convention), the Convention against Torture and Other Cruel, Inhuman or Degrading Treatment or Punishment (Torture Convention) are cases in point. But reference could be made to many others, as, for example, the Convention against Discrimination in Education, or the various ILO Conventions. The ILO system, however, is covered by the specific control mechanisms which are embodied in the ILO Constitution (Valticos, 1968, p. 311; *idem*, 1987, p. 505). All these conventions provide for specific implementation measures, mostly reporting and complaints procedures. They all set up treaty organs or use organs of international organizations in order to ensure a fair balance among the different States Parties in the fulfilment of the agreed review functions.

Universality is an important aspect of all these conventions. It necessarily implies taking into account that the agreed standards will be transformed and implemented within different legal systems and in countries with a great variety of backgrounds and traditions. Therefore any interpretation which identifies the international standard with a particular ideological concept or political system, whether western liberal, free market or socialist, would be a wrong interpretation.[2] In fact, all these conventions have been ratified by a considerable number of states. The Economic Covenant by 92 states, the Political Covenant by 87 states, the Discrimination Convention by 125 states, the Women's Convention by 94 states and the Torture Convention — despite the fact that it was adopted only in 1984 — has already been ratified by 33 states.

All these conventions establish rights and obligations among states. They are intended to strengthen peaceful and friendly relations among nations based on respect for the principle 'of equal rights and self-determination of peoples', as it is put in Article 55 of the UN Charter. However, the substantive obligations undertaken by the States Parties are tasks which have to be accomplished within the national legal orders. Ensuring international human rights standards is understood as an ongoing process in different legal systems. It develops depending on various factors which differ from country to country and from time to time. They are very much influenced by economic, political and other conditions.

The conventions do not try to and cannot establish a subjective right of the individual that would or could be realized or guaranteed by the international community. The state remains the source of the subjec-

---

[2]   This, however, is a very common approach in Western countries: see, for example, Donnelly, 1982, p. 303; Tentelen, 1985, p. 514; Jhabvala, 1985b, p. 485; Jhabvala, 1985a, p. 491; Kühnhardt, 1987; for the opposite view, see Klenner, 1982, p. 159; Graefrath, 1988a, p. 40; Alston, 1983, p. 60; Dicke, 1987, p. 422.

tive rights of the individual and the main resource for the means to implement them. Human rights treaties establish obligations for states to ensure the enjoyment of certain human rights within their jurisdiction. They are not, as such, the source of 'subjective' rights of the individual. A similar opinion has recently been expressed by F. Pocar, the Italian member in the Human Rights Committee. He stressed that despite the opinions expressed by part of the doctrine in favour of the direct relevance of international law to the legal rights or interests of private individuals, rather they are treated as objects of international rules, not being accorded an international legal personality. 'Therefore, we can talk about the international protection of human rights' only indirectly (Pocar, 1988, p. 65; see also Mohr, 1989, p. 345).

The conventions rely on the States Parties to guarantee the rights set forth in the international instrument. This has been clearly expressed by the Indian representative in the Third Committee of the General Assembly when the Covenants were finally polished in 1966. He made clear that the concept is based on the fundamental principle 'that States, and not any international body, were to continue to guarantee, ensure and protect the rights embodied in the Covenant' (UN doc. A/C.3/SR. 1430, paragraph 2). And the same has been stressed 20 years later by F. Jhabvala, when he stated:

One of the fundamental tenets of the international protection of human rights is that they have to be implemented domestically, through local institutions. The protection of human rights really rests therefore in domestic bodies and not in international bodies . . . (Jhabvala, 1984, p. 176).

The conventions therefore leave it to the States Parties to determine how and by what means they guarantee the rights set forth in the instrument within their legal systems. The international implementation measures which were established by the same treaties are aimed at promoting States Parties' national compliance with their obligations. They are designed for the mutual exchange of information, and to induce, promote and review national implementation but not to substitute for it. So, for example, the Women's Convention, when establishing the treaty organ, explicitly states that it meets 'for the purpose of considering the progress made in the implementation' of the Convention (Article 17; cf. Article 43 of the Convention on the Rights of the Child (Children's Convention)). These implementation measures often comprise different procedures which correspond to different stages of the process of compliance.

Although, in general, reporting procedures are obligatory, state and individual complaint procedures are most often optimal: they need special ratification or acceptance. The structure and the concrete procedures of the implementation systems are very closely linked to the substantive obligations set forth in the instrument concerned. They look similar but actually are different, and are specifically tailored to the requirements of the subject and the political possibilities.

The Women's Convention knows only a reporting procedure (Article 18).[3] The same is true for the Economic Covenant (Article 16), the Unesco Convention Against Discrimination in Education (Education Convention) (Article 7) and the Children's Convention (Article 44). The Political Covenant has an obligatory reporting procedure (Article 40), an optional state complaint procedure (Article 41) and an Optional Protocol which allows individuals to lodge complaints (communications) with the Human Rights Committee, the Political Covenant's organ.

The implementation measures of the Torture Convention are quite similar. It has an obligatory reporting procedure (Article 19) which, however, is different from the procedure under Article 40 of the Political Covenant, an optional state complaint procedure (Article 21) and an optional complaint procedure for individuals (Article 22).[4] But in addition, the Torture Convention provides for an inquiry procedure (Article 20), which can be set in motion when the Committee has 'reliable information which appears to it to contain well-founded indications that torture is being systematically practised in the territory of a State Party'. This procedure, however, may be excluded by reservation (Article 28).

The Discrimination Convention establishes an obligatory reporting procedure (Article 9) and an obligatory inter-state complaint procedure (Article 11). In addition, the Discrimination Convention has an optional complaint procedure for individuals or groups of individuals (Article 14) and a control function as to petitions from the inhabitants of Trust and Non-Self-Governing Territories (Article 15). It also enables States Parties to bring any dispute with respect to the interpretation or application of the convention not settled otherwise to the International Court of Justice (Article 22).

It is obvious that there exists a close relationship between the scope and contents of the substantive rights set forth in an instrument and its implementation mechanisms. When a convention relates to such basic rights as the prohibition of racial discrimination or torture, many states are ready to recognize far-reaching supervisory functions of an organ established under the treaty or with specific consent. But when the whole spectrum of human rights or social rights are concerned or affected, states in general are very reluctant to accept more than reporting procedures, because what are described as rights of the individual at the same time necessarily reflect very much the specific social, economic and political system of a society.

---

[3] It provides a general dispute/settlement procedure in Article 29 which may lead to the International Court of Justice if the dispute is not settled otherwise, a provision which provoked many reservations.

[4] It has in Article 30 the same general dispute/settlement procedure as the Women's Convention.

Based on the peoples' right to self-determination it is the basic right of each state 'freely to choose and develop its political, social, economic and cultural system.' In our world today, the limits of this freedom as determined by the international economic order cannot be overlooked or underestimated. But even under the pressure of international economic and financial constraints, states are not prepared to submit to a considerable or unpredictable extent to the censorship or control — let alone to injunctions — of other states or of international bodies which are clearly governed by a majority of members coming from another legal and social system.

It is therefore quite normal that negotiating implementation measures was always equally as important as determining the substantive rights which should be protected by a given instrument. The 'international legal framework' concerning the promotion and protection of human rights (UN resolution 41/155) which has emerged from the international human rights instruments is determined by the unity of both elements, the definition of state obligations in relation to human rights and the implementation measures applicable in that respect.

By agreeing on human rights standards, states did not simply transfer this subject from their domestic competence to the international level. They agreed on a standard which has to be vitalized, shaped and guaranteed within their legal systems to become subjective rights of the individual. And they accepted an international competence only to the extent defined by the agreements. This includes of course implementation measures. By concluding human rights treaties, states defined the scope, the procedure and the contents of international co-operation in this field (Graefrath, 1988b, p. 52; Mohr, 1989, p. 342).

This also strengthens and facilitates co–ordinated action to combat violations of human rights which are international crimes, such as slavery, genocide, apartheid and other large-scale systematic violations of 'basic rights of the human person' (*Barcelona Traction* Case, ICJ Report 1970, paragraph 34) or, as it has been put by the International Law Commission, serious breaches 'on a widespread scale of an international obligation of essential importance for safeguarding the human being' (Article 19, paragraph 3(ċ)). They are clearly matters of international concern, because they endanger international peace and security. There is, therefore, no doubt as to the competence of the United Nations and in particular the Security Council to deal with such matters. But this, of course, is quite different from international co-operation in the promotion of human rights as envisaged in Article 55 of the United Nations Charter and concretized by the international human rights instruments with which we are dealing.

Through treaties like the two human rights Covenants, states transformed the substance, that is ensuring human rights, just as little into a matter of international concern as with treaties on economic co-operation, which are also envisaged in Article 55. Accepting international obligations on human rights matters does not mean that states place ensuring human rights outside their sovereign control, nor allow others to apply sanctions whenever they unilaterally determine that rights set forth in a given instrument have been violated. Human rights treaties in general establish obligations of an 'integrated' structure which can be complied with or violated only in relation to all parties (Sachariew, 1988, p. 273).

The integrated content and structure of the obligation is certainly one of the main reasons why states felt it necessary to establish specific implementation measures which take precedence over the separate actions of individual states. They are also aimed at contributing to the avoidance of dispute, facilitating dispute settlements and ensuring a common standard.

Contrary to what again and again is contended (Verdross and Simma, 1984, p. 303; Henkin, 1977, p. 26), the existence of a treaty or an international obligation does not justify the conclusion that the whole matter is outside the jurisdiction of the states and has become a matter of international concern. The degree of internationalization depends on the content and extent of the obligations undertaken and the implementation measures agreed upon (Graefrath, 1988b, p. 36). Unfortunately, human rights have been quite often the subject of, or a pretext for, political interference which has been labelled 'sanction' but has had no legal justification at all. Suffice it to recall United States 'sanctions' against Nicaragua or Poland and on the other side its acquiescence to criminal policies in South Africa or Chile.

The agreed upon implementation measures in human rights instruments are of fundamental importance. They determine the degree, the means and the common international action or procedure states have agreed upon in this field. They therefore cannot be neglected or separated from the substantive provisions. This has been stated twice by the International Court of Justice; for the first time in 1970 in its *Barcelona Traction* decision (ICJ Report 1970, paragraphs 34 and 91) and again in its judgment in the case concerning 'Military and Para-military Activities in and Against Nicaragua' (ICJ Report 1986, paragraph 267):

When human rights are protected by international conventions, that protection takes the form of such arrangements for monitoring or ensuring respect for human rights as are provided for in the conventions themselves.

It is, therefore, worthwhile studying the scope of these implementation measures and their functioning in practice. They reflect existing law and the degree to which states have accepted international supervision on matters of human rights — without prejudice to the specific competences of states and the Security Council in case of international crimes.

All the human rights instruments which we consider here have created specific treaty organs to fulfil different functions in connection with the implementation measures of the respective conventions. These procedures are thereby institutionalized. They are in the hands of permanent bodies in order to ensure an objective approach. To avoid as much as possible any direct state interference, these treaty organs are mostly expert bodies: their members do not act as state representatives. While these treaty organs work closely together with the United Nations, they in general are independent bodies and cannot be treated as subsidiary bodies of UN organs.[5]

3. The reporting procedure

As already mentioned, the most common procedure in all instruments is the reporting procedure. We necessarily have to restrict ourselves to some important examples and main trends in this area. There are many reporting procedures not covered here, as, for example, the reporting procedures of the ILO, the Convention on the Suppression and Punishment of the Crime of Apartheid, the Convention related to the Status of Stateless Persons or the Convention against Discrimination in Education. As a typical example we will refer to the International Covenant on Civil and Political Rights.[6] While Article 2 of this Covenant states that

each State Party . . . undertakes to take the necessary steps, in accordance with its constitutional process and with the provisions of the present Covenant, to adopt such legislative or other measures as may be necessary to give effect to the rights recognized in the present Covenant.

Article 40 contains an obligation for the States Parties:

to submit reports on the measures they have adopted which give effect to the rights recognized herein and on the progress made in the enjoyment of these rights.

The same correlation between acknowledgment of national competence in implementing human rights standards by specific measures and an obligation to report on the measures taken, the progress made and the factors and difficulties affecting the fulfilment of the obligations also exists in other conventions.[7]

---

[5] The only exception is the Expert Committee on Economic, Social and Cultural Rights which is established as an expert body of the ECOSOC; cf. Alston, 1987.

[6] On the work of the Human Rights Committee see: Graefrath, 1988a; Nowak, 1980a, p. 532; Nowak, 1980b, p. 136; Nowak, 1984, p. 421; Jhabvala, 1984, p. 81; Fischer, 1982, p. 146; Movchan, 1982; Tomuschat, 1981, p. 141; Tomuschat, 1987, p. 157; Empell, 1987; Nowak, 1989.

[7] See Articles 2 and 16, Economic Covenant; Articles 2 and 16, Women's Convention; Articles 2 and 9, Discrimination Convention; Articles 2 and 19, Torture Convention; Articles 2 and 44, Children's Convention.

Normally, reports have to be submitted periodically, the initial reports within one or two years of the entry into force of the instrument for the State Party concerned and thereafter at four- or five-year intervals. The instruments are rather vague in describing the contents of state reports. While the two Covenants simply refer to the measures adopted, the Women's Convention refers explicitly to 'legislative, judicial, administrative or other measures.' As the practice of the Human Rights Committee and The Committee on the Elimination of Racial Discrimination shows, there is a general understanding that the term 'measures' does not simply refer to legislative measures but includes any measures taken or necessary in order to ensure respect for the rights or their implementation.

It is, therefore, necessary to go back to the substantive provisions of the instruments. Quite often they are not confined to a mere obligation of result but are very specific in describing measures deemed necessary to implement the obligation concerned. This is in particular true for the Convention against Discrimination in Education, the Women's Convention, the Education Convention, and the Economic Covenant. But such provisions can also be found in Article 20 of the Political Covenant and Articles 10 to 15 of the Torture Convention.

Originally, the Human Rights Commission's draft of the Covenant envisaged a quasi-judicial implementation system which was based on an inter-state complaint procedure which potentially could lead to the International Court of Justice. It was ten years later, in the General Assembly, that the system was totally changed (Schwelb, 1968, p. 827). This was the only way to get a general human rights convention which would be acceptable on a universal scale. In the final text, the reporting procedure became the most important and the only obligatory measure of implementation. It was clearly distinguished from any procedure which has a fact-finding, inquiry, mediation, conciliation or quasi-judicial function (for an opposite view, see Nowak, 1989, p. 541).

The reporting procedure consists of two elements. One is furnishing information and the other is the processing of the information and data submitted or received. While the first one is framed in terms of an obligation of the States Parties, the second one is determined both by the competence or the mandate given to the treaty organ by the respective international convention and by the co-operation of the States Parties.[8]

---

[8] The Economic Covenant does not provide for the establishment of a specific treaty organ. Reports are submitted to the ECOSOC. From 1979 to 1980, the ECOSOC considered state reports in a sessional working group, a procedure that turned out not to be very efficient. It therefore decided to establish a group of governmental experts and, since 1986, a group of non-governmental experts. This group, which held its first session in 1987, tries to follow closely the practice of the Human Rights Committee in studying state reports (UN doc. E/C.12/1987/5); cf. Alston & Simma, 1987, p. 747; Alston and Simma, 1988, p. 607; Mohr, 1988b, p. 100.

All treaty organs which have the function to study or consider the reports submitted have, following the practice of the Committee on the Elimination of Racial Discrimination (Heintze, 1987, p. 139), developed a dialogue with the State Party concerned.[9] This, in particular, means that a representative is invited to attend the Committee's meeting when his state's report is considered, in order to furnish additional information and to answer questions. This allows the Committee to elicit further information and to get necessary explanations. Members of the Committee may ask questions, make critical remarks, give their comments and opinions, or refer to different aspects of the report without the Committee as a whole expressing an opinion or decision about a given state's situation. Within the reporting procedure, treaty organs in general have to study reports, but do not have the function or competence to assess them:[10] this would presuppose a competence for fact-finding. They may, however, summarize their experience in considering state reports in the form of general comments, suggestions or recommendations.

3.1. Duty to furnish information

Furnishing information is a duty of the States Parties. The Committee, in its deliberations, has to rely on the information submitted by the State Party. Of course, states always tend to report only positive results and achievements. Difficulties or shortcomings, let alone violations of human rights which may have happened, or which have been dealt with by competent state organs and been remedied or have been in a process of being remedied were — as practice shows — very rarely mentioned in state reports. This of course, is regrettable, because it limits the efficiency of the reporting procedure. It has also often led to criticism by Committee members and provoked requests for additional information.

Obviously, many states have difficulty understanding that it is not only information about achievements but to the same extent information about problems and difficulties faced in the implementation of human rights standards, the failure of efforts or information about planned or envisaged measures which is of interest to other States Parties and the Committee. And it is this kind of information which can be extremely helpful in stimulating co-operation, mutual assist-

---

[9] On the practice of the Women's Committee see Oeser, 1988, p. 86; Galey, 1984, p. 475; Byrnes, 1989, p. 1.

[10] This was a highly controversial point in the beginning of the work of the Human Rights Committee and remains a difficult question today; cf. Graefrath, 1988b, p. 146; UN doc. A/35/40, paragraphs 370-383; see also recent discussions in the Economic Covenant Committee, UN doc. E/C/1989/SR.13, 22; for the opposite view see Nowak, 1989, p. 608.

ance, training programmes and so forth. It may also give hints how to avoid impasses and failures in ensuring the enjoyment of human rights without discrimination. It seems that, despite the cautious and prudent approach of the Human Rights Committee and other Committees such as the Education Committee and the Women's Committee, most states are very reluctant to furnish such information because they are afraid that it could be used against them for propaganda purposes, if not by the Committee, then by powerful press agencies that are in command of what is generally called public opinion.

Unfortunately, it is not difficult to find many examples where the discussion of state reports has been totally distorted by certain newspapers which gave false information or reproduced only negative details as news. In a way, the tendency to concentrate on shortcomings, violations or non-implementation is nourished also by lawyers who tend to understand or interpret the purpose of the reporting procedure as a fact-finding procedure to ascertain human rights violations. This impedes the effectiveness of the reporting procedure and limits its scope. It can very easily shift the emphasis of the reporting procedure from the level of mutual reporting of information and creating incentives to comply to accusing states of violations, conducting some kind of fact-finding or just engendering another form of a political dispute, thereby transforming the reporting procedure into a prelude for dispute settlement.

It is interesting enough to recognize that already very early on in the elaboration of the Covenant's implementation measures, the danger that a reporting procedure could be misused to trigger complaints or to be converted into a quasi-judicial process was clearly expressed by the British and French representatives in the Human Rights Commission. Both insisted on a clear-cut distinction between a reporting procedure on the one side and a complaint or inquiry procedure on the other side. So Mr Hoare stated:

There would be no point in studying them (State reports) unless the object was to verify that the legislation and practices of such State Party to the Covenant really conformed to the provisions of the Covenant. That would be tantamount to paving the way for complaints, and it would be most undesirable for the Commission on Human Rights to assume any such function. A study undertaken by the human rights committee would be equally pointless, unless it were intended that the committee should take note in advance of complaints and even take action upon, such deficiencies in legislation or practice as it discovered. That would be equally objectionable (UN doc. E/CN.4/SR.427, p. 12).

A quite similar reservation against a reporting procedure was raised by Mr Juvigny, the French representative. He was afraid that members of the Committee would face a difficult situation when they receive state reports although they were not to be judges, they would be in a quasi-judicial position and might be apt to prejudge that with which they should not concern themselves until a complaint was actually lodged. The reception of reports was an administrative rather than a quasi-judicial function (UN doc. E/CN.4/SR.428, p. 8).

While at that time objections were raised against mixing the reporting procedure with a fact-finding or a complaint procedure, later on, when the reporting procedure became the only obligatory procedure, all these arguments were forgotten and an effort was made to convert the reporting procedure into an *ex officio* inquiry mechanism (see, for example, McDonald, representative of Canada in A/C.3/SR.1426, paragraph 20).

In a way there were many attempts to revive the quasi-judicial approach which purposely was eliminated from the draft by the General Assembly. But the function and purpose of the reporting procedure is different and much broader. It will lose many of its constructive elements if it is changed and reduced to an inquiry procedure which states did not accept when ratifying or acceding to a given instrument.

The reporting procedure is based on the assumption that states are willing to implement their international obligations and that they are prepared to co-operate and to give the necessary information. To lay open the situation and to exchange information were considered to be helpful for others, by stimulating compliance, mutual understanding and the exchange of experiences in applying different means and procedures in the fulfilment of a common obligation.

Since information exchange is the heart and the purpose of the reporting procedure, the question necessarily arises how to get reliable information, what sources can be used and how to ensure the uniform provision of information. It is clear from most of the instruments that the information on which the Committee must base its consideration is the report submitted by the State Party. This may be supplemented by other official documents of the State Party, its laws, judicial decisions, statistics, reports to other bodies and by findings of United Nations bodies. Other sources, however, such as press reports or reports of NGOs or other international organizations, normally cannot be used as official documentation or information by the Committee. Such sources can be, and always are, of course, part of the background experts use in forming their opinions, questions and comments. They can, however, not be introduced into the procedure, and do not have the weight of evidence. Nevertheless, such information sometimes has been introduced directly, but this necessarily introduces the danger of changing the procedure into an investigative one. Inevitably, the first reaction in such a case is always to check the credibility or to verify the information used. This is already a far-reaching deviation from the reporting procedure, which brings not only the state but also the Committee into an awkward position and should be avoided (for the opposite view, see Nowak, 1989, p. 607). Such a procedure should be left to a political process such as that of the Conference on Security and Cooperation in Europe. It was, however, decided that the specific structure of the Economic Covenant should allow NGOs which have consultative status to present written statements (cf. Rules of Procedure, Rule 69 UN doc. E/1989/L.9, p. 119). The same is possible under the Torture Convention (cf. 62 of its Rules of Procedure, UN doc. A/43/46). Up to now there is not much practice which would allow an assessment of the extent to which this possibility has influenced the work of the respective Committees. Another aspect of the work of NGOs is the dissemination of information on human rights instruments and the work of treaty bodies. In that area, NGOs can successfully support the work of the committees and contribute to the implementation of the international conventions by making their principles and provisions widely known to the public at large. Specialized agencies such as the International Labour Organisation, the UN Educational and Cultural Organization, and the World Health Organization participate actively in the work of the Committee on Economic, Social and Cultural Rights.

If the information given by the State Party seems to be insufficient, which can easily be ascertained by asking questions, a Committee can ask for additional information. It may be given orally when the representative replies to questions, later on in a written supplementary report, or — what is quite often the case — when submitting the next periodic report. Attempts to press for additional information in writing and then reopening the discussion on the report have not been successful. They imply the danger of transforming the reporting procedure into an inquiry procedure which had not been accepted by the States Parties.[11]

All the Committees have developed guidelines regarding the contents and the form of reports (cf. the compilation in UN doc. A/40/600/Add.1). They are not binding upon States Parties, but are recommendations which aim to facilitate the work of the Committee and of the States Parties. The guidelines are to help ensure that state reports are submitted in a similar form, become compatible, and contain all the information necessary. They are structured according to the different instruments and stages in the reporting procedure. The Human Rights Committee and the Committee on Economic, Social and Cultural Rights distinguish between guidelines for initial and subsequent reports in order to avoid unnecessary duplication and to concentrate on or highlight specific items.

With the growing number of treaty bodies and the accumulation of

---

[11] However, Article 9, paragraph 1, of the Discrimination Convention entitles its Committee to request further information. Such an obligation on states cannot be introduced by a mere rule of procedure, cf. Rule 70, paragraph 2, of the Rules of Procedure of the Political Covenant.

reporting obligations, it has become more and more difficult for states to comply with the diverse and repetitive requests under different guidelines. Several proposals have therefore been made to harmonize and consolidate reporting guidelines (cf. paragraphs 46–53 of the Report of the Meeting of Chairpersons HRI/MC/1988/1). It is, however, not so easy to develop common guidelines or to condense reports due under different instruments to a general, all-embracing report which can be considered in its relevant parts by the respective bodies. So far, it seems possible only to harmonize the general parts of state reports which relate to land and people, the general political structure, the legal framework, information and publicity. This follows a Recommendation in the Report of the Meeting of Chairpersons of Human Rights Treaty Bodies (also published as UN doc. A/44/98, cf paragraph 79; cf. A/44/40, Annex VIII). It nevertheless remains questionable whether following this path will effectively ease the bureaucratic burden of States Parties and hinder a decline in the proper functioning of treaty bodies in regard to the reporting procedures.

3.2 The competence of the Committee

The second element of the reporting procedure, the processing of the information and data received through state reports, is determined by the mandate given to the treaty organ and the co-operation of the States Parties. Normally, the Committee has the duty

(a) to study, to consider or to examine state reports;
(b) to report on its activities.

The Human Rights Committee, before starting the discussion of state reports at its second meeting, had a preliminary exchange of views on both the procedures to be followed and the purposes of the consideration of state reports.

It was generally agreed that the main purpose of the consideration of reports should be to assist States Parties in the promotion and protection of the human rights recognized in this Covenant. The debates of the Committee on the reports of the States Parties should be conducted in a constructive spirit, taking fully into account the need to maintain and develop friendly relations among States (UN doc. A/32/44, paragraph 105).

It seems the experience of all Committees that this is the only way to develop and maintain a fruitful dialogue between the Committee and the State Party. The Committee on Economic, Social and Cultural Rights has tried to define in its first General Comment a variety of objectives that should be achieved by the reporting procedure. Among other points, this General Comment notes that the obligation to report should induce a state to undertake a comprehensive review with respect to its legislation, administrative rules, procedures and practices, to ensure the fullest possible conformity with the Covenant's requirements, to monitor the actual situation with respect to each of the rights, to facilitate the exchange of information among states, and to develop both a better understanding of the common problems faced by states and a fuller appreciation of the types of measures which might be taken to promote effective realization of each right contained in the Covenant (UN doc. E/1989/L.9, p. 97).

The results of a Committee's work in relation to the reporting procedure may lead to general comments, suggestions or general recommendations. From the practice of the Committee on the Elimination of Racial Discrimination, it is clear that the suggestions and general recommendations are not directed to a specific state but to all States Parties, and as such they are included in the annual report to the General Assembly (Discrimination Convention, Article 9). The same pattern is suggested in Article 40, paragraph 4, of the Political Covenant which says:

The Committee shall transmit its reports and such general comments as it may consider appropriate, to the States Parties.

However, there have been quite different interpretations of this provision, both in the literature (Graefrath, 1988b, p. 145; Empell, 1987, p. 101; Robertson, 1981, p. 350; Nowak, 1989, p. 608) and in the Human Rights Committee itself (cf. UN doc. A/36/40, paragraph 384). Many members wanted to interpret Article 40, paragraph 4, in such a way as to enable the Committee to establish a report on the human rights situation in each State Party and to direct specific comments to individual States Parties. To me, it is clear from the *travaux préparatoires* that, by introducing the word 'general' before comments and by not referring to the state 'concerned' but to States Parties in general, exactly this interpretation was to be precluded. The only unclear word in the paragraph is the word 'reports' in the plural. But since no other report than the annual report to the General Assembly is mentioned in this connection, no other reports could be meant. Otherwise the specific kind of report would have been thoroughly qualified as has been done in Articles 41 and 42 of the Political Covenant and in the Optional Protocol, where reports other than the annual report are dealt with. In such cases the reports are the result of an inquiry, fact-finding or conciliatory procedure.

To some extent, this interpretation of Article 40, paragraph 4, of the Political Covenant is confirmed on the one hand by the wording used in Article 21 of the Women's Convention and on the other hand by the purposely different wording of Article 19 of the Torture Convention. Article 21 of the Women's Convention provides that 'such suggestions and general recommendations shall be included in the report of the Committee', that is the annual report to the General Assembly.[12] In a clear deviation from this wording and the practice followed so far by all three other Committees, Article 19 of the Torture Convention not only provides that 'each (State) report shall be considered by the Committee' but also that it 'may make such general comments on the report as it may consider appropriate and shall forward these to the State Party concerned.' This, of course, is quite different wording from that of Article 40 of the Political Covenant (Nowak, 1988, p. 499). It reflects the meaning some would like to read into Article 40, paragraph 4.[13] But the difference in the texts clearly demonstrates that the Political Covenant does not intend this approach.

Whether the procedure foreseen in Article 19 of the Torture Convention, to comment on each state report, remains within the realm of a reporting procedure or will actually change it into an inquiry procedure remains to be seen. In any case it is true — as Nowak states — that

this provided an opportunity for the Committee (against Torture) to formulate its opinion on the compliance of each State Party with its obligations under the Convention (Nowak, 1987, p. 25).

A treaty organ, and in particular a group of non-governmental experts like the Committee on the Elimination of Racial Discrimination or the Human Rights Committee, cannot assume a fact-finding function by adopting procedural rules,[14] because each Committee's mandate is determined by its respective international instrument and is based on and results from an agreement among the States Parties. It cannot be changed or extended by an expert Committee. By adopting procedural rules, a Committee, a group of independent experts, cannot create obligations to which the States Parties have not agreed under the basic instrument. To amend a treaty remains a task and a competence of the states.

There have always been attempts within the Human Rights Committee and by representatives of states in the Third Committee of the General Assembly to encourage the Committee to expand its mandate.[15] The Committee was advised to stretch its reporting procedure into an inquiry procedure like the one practised by

---

[12] This wording is very similar to that of Article 9 of the Discrimination Convention.
[13] Nowak goes even further, saying that 'the Human Rights Committee may forward its own reports to each individual State Party as well as general comments to the States Parties in their entirety', cf. Nowak, 1987, p. 25.
[14] See Rule 70(3) Human Rights Committee, or Rule 66(A)(3) Discrimination Convention.
[15] See, for example, FRG, UN doc. A/C.3/38/SR.51, paragraphs 42, 45, 46; Italy, UN doc. A/C.3/37/SR.51, paragraph, 29; A/C.3/38/SR.51, paragraph 88; Canada, UN doc. A/C.3/37/SR.52, paragraph 47; A/C3/38/SR.15, paragraph 4 and SR.51, paragraph 69; Netherlands UN doc. A/C.3/36/SR.32, paragraph 6; cf. also Mohr, 1984, p. 23.

the International Labour Organisation, which is based on reporting but goes much further. The Committee has even been asked to perform tasks that are not explicitly forbidden by the Covenant. But, up to now, the Committee has been careful to act within its mandate, to keep close co-operation with States Parties, and not to be manoeuvred into confrontation. And this seems the only way for a treaty organ to preserve its impartiality and independence and to maintain and develop a fruitful dialogue with States Parties.

3.3 General comments and suggestions

An important instrument of the dialogue which exists in one form or another for all bodies established by human rights instruments is the possibility of making suggestions, general comments or recommendations. The wording differs slightly in each instrument. What is meant and practised is that the Committees filter the experience gained in discussing state reports, when drawing the attention of States Parties to certain problems, shortcomings or differences in implementing obligations. Thereby, they have a framework through which they may give their own opinions on the meaning and contents of convention provisions and procedures, and the way states fulfil their reporting obligations.[16]

Article 9 of the Racial Discrimination Convention and Article 21 of the Women's Convention provide that their Committees may make suggestions and general recommendations based on the examination of the reports and information received from the States Parties. Article 40, paragraph 4, of the Political Covenant says that the Human Rights Committee shall transmit 'such general comments as it may consider appropriate to the States Parties.'

Suggestions as well as comments and recommendations given by the Committees are not the outcome of a fact-finding or inquiry procedure. Neither are they the final statement in a judicial or quasi-judicial process, nor the result of an inquisitorial or adversarial procedure. They are the results of the reporting procedure and represent a generalization of the experience gained by the Committees in examining state reports. In this context, 'gained by the Committee' means the Committee as a whole. The strength of a suggestion, recommendation and general comment lies in its being adopted by consensus, thereby expressing the opinion of the Committee, not of individual members or a group of members. While the conventions and the rules of procedure normally stipulate that decisions by the Committees are to be taken by a majority vote, the Committees avoid voting and try to take their decisions by

---

[16] Only the general comments referred to in Article 19 of the Torture Convention are related to a state report. They are to be forwarded only to the State Party concerned.

consensus. This is a practice which has proved to be useful and to strengthen the authority of the statements or decisions made by the Committee.

In most of the Committees, it would be quite easy always to take decisions by the same majority against the same minority of two or three members who have a different position. But such a practice would only make it obvious that the decision taken reflects merely a majority view which does not have general support. That, of course, would deprive the Committee of its specific voice and generally recognized authority. It was not easy to convince members of the Human Rights Committee that working by consensus would pay off (Graefrath, 1988b, p. 131), but it has become a generally recognized working method in human rights bodies.[17] At the same time, it was extremely helpful in developing mutual understanding and co-operation among Committee members. When the Human Rights Committee started its work on general comments, it tried to explain their function. In an introduction to the first comments it stated:

The purpose of these general comments is to make this experience available for the benefit of all States Parties in order to promote their further implementation of the Covenant; to draw their attention to insufficiencies disclosed by a large number of reports; to suggest improvements in the reporting procedure and to stimulate the activities of these States and international organizations in the promotion and protection of human rights. These comments should also be of interest to other States, especially those preparing to become parties to the Covenant and thus strengthen the co-operation of all States in the universal promotion and protection of human rights.[18]

In its general comments, the Human Rights Committee has been quite cautious and prudent, when dealing with substantive provisions, not to change the contents States Parties agreed upon in the constituent instrument. Quite often the wording of certain provisions has been the outcome of difficult and lengthy negotiations. Normally the result has been a compromise formula which leaves room for discretion and individual application under different legal systems. Summarizing experience gained in discussing many state reports would be counterproductive if it were eventually to limit the scope or to destroy the inbuilt compromise of the Covenant itself. On the other hand, the Committee wanted to express its opinion on 'questions related to the application and the content of individual articles of the Covenant' (UN doc. A/39/40, p. 107).

It is true that the general comments adopted by the Human Rights

---

[17] See, for example, Economic Covenant, UN doc. E/C.12/1989/4 Annex III, Rule 46; Oeser, 1988, p. 90; Byrnes, 1989, p. 42.

[18] UN doc. A/36/40, p. 107. A very similar explanation has recently been given by the Economic Covenant Committee, cf. UN doc. E/1989/L.9, p. 96; cf. Nowak, 1989, p. 615.

Committee and published in its Annual Reports have received broad attention and support. They were widely welcomed and considered as authoritative opinion. And this they are indeed, since they have always been adopted by consensus, after thorough deliberation. Nevertheless, it has to be stressed that the Committee has no power to give authoritative interpretations of the Covenant (Tomuschat, 1983, paragraph 10). It therefore goes too far to say that the Committee's 'formal interpretative rulings yield a growing body of law' (Buergenthal, 1977, p. 207). The right to interpret the Covenant or any other international instrument, if not agreed otherwise, remains with the States Parties to that instrument. But because it can be so difficult for the States Parties to reach an agreed opinion, the weight of a unanimous opinion of a convention committee as a means of subsidiary interpretation should not be underestimated (cf. Nowak, 1989, p. 616).

It has happened several times that states have not agreed with a committee's comments. An example in point is the recommendation of the Committee on the Elimination of Racial Discrimination on reporting obligations in relation to Article 3, concerning apartheid (see Ansbach and Heintze, 1987, p. 135). Also general comment 14/23 of the Human Rights Committee, on the right to life, has been criticized by some Western states as being outside the mandate of the Committee. In that comment, the Committee voiced its concern

That the designing, testing, manufacture, possession and deployment of nuclear weapons are among the greatest threats to the right to life which confront mankind today. . .
Furthermore, the very existence and gravity of this threat generates a climate of suspicion and fear between States, which is in itself antagonistic to the promotion of universal respect for and observance of human rights and fundamental freedoms.

It was therefore of the opinion:

The production, testing, possession, deployment and use of nuclear weapons should be prohibited and recognized as crimes against humanity. The Committee called upon all States to take urgent steps . . . to rid the world of this menace.[19]

3.4 Too many reports?

The functioning of the reporting procedure, of course, firstly depends on the receipt of state reports and the ability of treaty bodies to consider them in time, to avoid a backlog in the discussion of

---

[19] UN doc. A/40/40, p. 162. Despite criticism, the Human Rights Committee has upheld its position in UN doc. A/40/40, paragraph 27.

submitted reports. The General Assembly has often reiterated the fundamental importance of reporting obligations under international human rights instruments and expressed concern over the increasing backlog of state reports and delays in consideration of reports by the treaty bodies (UN doc. GA resolution 41/171; 42/105; 43/115). Indeed, the growing number of reports and their steady refinement according to increasingly specific guidelines has placed a considerable burden on states and this burden will become even more onerous when additional instruments come into force. This sometimes makes it very difficult for states to prepare meaningful reports in time. It therefore happens quite often that even states which have an experienced and well-staffed administration face increasing problems in submitting their reports in a timely manner. Attempts have been made to harmonize and consolidate reporting guidelines with a view to assisting states in preparing more concise reports. Whether such efforts will succeed remains to be seen. Obviously, it is very difficult to harmonize guidelines and to streamline the consideration of reports because the substance under consideration in the various bodies is too different. It may, however, be useful to enhance co-ordination and information flow among the treaty bodies, to ratio-nalize reporting procedures and particularly to scrutinize periodic reports more intensively and expeditiously. It also seems to be reasonable, after having sent many reminders in vain, to consider multiple overdue reports in a consolidated form to avoid unnecessary repetition in periodic reports (a practice developed recently by the Committee on the Elimination of Racial Discrimination) and to stick to a rigid time economy, as, for example, has been introduced by the Committee on Economic, Social and Cultural Reports (UN doc. E/C.12/1989/SR.1; SR.2).

The problems concerning the effective functioning of the reporting procedures have been studied by the Netherlands Human Rights and Foreign Policy Advisory Committee (cf. UN doc. A/C.3/43/5, 5 October 1988). It summarized its study, saying:

The international procedures for monitoring compliance with the conven-tions are being threatened by stagnation, which is endangering the effective-ness of the whole system of supervision.

It came to the conclusion that the causes are largely to be found in the enormous backlog of periodic reports, the excessive burden placed on the various supervisory committees and financial problems. It has advanced several proposals to simplify reporting procedures and to improve the effective functioning of the various committees without requiring the amendment of the conventions.

The UN Human Rights Centre has also explored ways and means to rationalize reporting procedures. To this end, it supplies computer facilities and works to improve technical and advisory services. Since all this has to be seen in the light of a world-wide financial crisis, which is not at all limited to the United Nations system, it may be questionable whether the problems can be solved by technical and methodological means.

At the same time, it is very difficult to reduce the number of reports. It should be kept in mind that periodic reports allow for and ensure a permanent and ongoing exchange of information and review of developments. An essential element of reporting is to keep under review the progress made in the implementation of human rights. Indeed, the consideration of periodic reports is focused very much on this aspect. It has always been a main point in the introduction given by state representatives to their initial reports. This shows how unrealistic was the position of some Western states, who, at the time when the reporting procedure of the Political Covenant was proposed, held the view that there is nothing to report since states could only ratify the Covenant having taken all necessary measures to comply with their obligations under the Covenant (Nowak, 1989, p. 595).

In reality, the reporting procedure has shown that no state which can say that it has already implemented all its obligations under the Covenant, that there is nothing more to do to ensure the equal enjoyment of human rights and, hence, there is nothing to report. It is not only that all state reports demonstrate the extent to which ensuring human rights is an ongoing process, which cannot be isolated from the economic, political and international factors always influencing the situation of a given country, but it is also clear that the international instruments — the Political Covenant included — are themselves important tools assisting people to ensure and to implement international human rights standards and encouraging states to realize shortcomings and to take possible measures to overcome difficulties. As has been said in relation to the work of the Committee on the Elimination of Discrimination Against Women, it seems that the success and the efficiency of the reporting procedure in all treaty bodies depends on how they manage

to gain confidence of the States Parties, to encourage other States to accede to the Convention or ratify it and . . . to promote a policy geared to ensured equal rights for women in keeping with the obligation undertaken . . . (Oeser, 1988, p. 92).

This point certainly corresponds to the experience of other bodies and it is by no means limited to equal rights for women.

Despite the fact that many scholars criticize the reporting procedure as being too weak, or as not being an inquiry procedure similar to that used within the International Labour Organisation system, the reporting procedure has proved to be a very useful and effective step in reviewing the implementation of human rights instruments, in gathering meaningful information and in establishing a constructive public dialogue on a topic that hitherto has been considered as being exclusively a matter of domestic concern and that has suffered for a long time from being misused as a political weapon in international relations. The procedure has been established by the conventions as a reporting procedure. It has to be recognized as a particular method, well defined by its own characteristics and taking up its specific place within the system of implementation measures. Changing it into an inquiry procedure would destroy these characteristics and is outside the mandate of the treaty organs. It could be changed only through a new agreement between the States Parties to a given treaty.

It is an important step forward that international standards for human rights have been agreed upon and whose implementation can be reviewed in an ongoing dialogue between a State Party and an expert group established according to the respective instrument. This, of course, is not a procedure of fact-finding, decision-making or coercion. It is not a procedure or a means suited to fight serious violations of human rights. But it is a procedure to promote the implementation of international human rights standards and to foster awareness of human rights. It is an organized form of co-operation, an exchange of information in the human rights field. The procedure has proved to encourage implementation of international human rights standards, mutual respect for different systems, conditions and cultures and for different methods of guaranteeing human rights. It has also stimulated corrections and improvements which have become possible within the states concerned.

The reporting procedure has the advantage of being an automatic procedure which accompanies the process of implementation and which does not depend on suspicion or accusation of a breach of an international obligation. It therefore is neither a decision-making procedure which can be labelled as a means of dispute settlement nor a legal consequence that can be considered to belong to the sphere of state responsibility. It allows discussion at any time of any question that seems to be relevant to the realization of human rights set forth in a given instrument. It may stimulate international activities to assist states in their efforts to live up to international obligations. It may be used to pin-point problems and shortcomings in the process of implementation, without raising the accusation of non-compliance. It permits differentiation between an ongoing process of implementation and non-fulfilment or breach of an obligation. This, of course, is very important in the delicate sphere of ensuring the enjoyment of human rights, which remains a competence and a task of the state concerned.

There are numerous examples that states, as a result of or having been stimulated by the reporting procedure, have changed laws or practices, have created procedures and remedies and have spent more attention on the realization of human rights than before. This trend cannot be easily assessed in quantitative terms, but undoubtedly it already exists. It confirms that the reporting procedure is a specific implementation measure which has its own standing.

4. State-to-state complaint procedures

Not all major international rights instruments provide for inter-state complaint procedures. The Economic Covenant, Women's Convention and Children's Convention do not have such procedures. It has rightly been stated that, with the exception of International Labour Organisation procedures, 'the inter-state complaint is limited to addressing civil and political rights' (Leckie, 1988, p. 251). This is mainly a result of the old bourgeois concept which accepts only civil and political rights, that is rights which can be enforced by courts, as truly subjective rights and as human rights. Economic and social rights have been treated as programmatic or promotional rights.

In the draft Political Covenant originally prepared by the Human Rights Commission, the inter-state complaint procedure was conceived as a mandatory quasi-judicial procedure which was considered to be the main implementation measure which could lead to the International Court of Justice. But during final negotiations in the General Assembly, the whole system of implementation measures in the Political Covenant was changed, and the inter-state complaint procedure became only one of several measures. It was made optional, and stripped of its quasi-judicial elements, becoming a 'good office' and 'conciliatory' function. Nearly the same thing happened 25 years later, with Article 21 of the Torture Convention. Not only socialist, but most governments feared that a mandatory quasi-judicial complaint procedure would open the door to foreign interference. They therefore preferred an optional conciliation procedure. And practice shows that even this procedure is poorly accepted and not actually used.[20]

The place and function of inter-state procedures is quite different from that of reporting procedures. All complaint procedures are directed at specific supervision. They are not instruments of general review of an ongoing process, but always relate to a specific case based on an alleged violation. They start with an accusation and try to ascertain, to control and to remedy a specific breach of an international obligation.

In contrast to the individual complaint procedure contained in the Optional Protocol to the Political Covenant, it is not necessary for a state to claim to be the victim of the violation, although this may be the case if the rights of its nationals are affected. However, the procedure in general is conceived as a means to claim that an *erga omnes* obligation has been violated. The claimant acts on the basis of an *'actio popularis'*, in the interest of the common goal defined by the provisions of the treaty. Therefore, a state using the procedure, not

---

[20] See Schwelb, 1968, p. 827; Manov, 1986, p. 42; Kulishev, 1982, p. 101; Robertson, 1981, p. 332; Jhabvala, 1984, p. 85; Nowak, 1988, p. 510; Nowak, 1989, p. 625.

being especially affected, should be sure to act in the interest of all States Parties.

Furthermore, the basis for an inter-state complaint does not have to be an alleged violation of any of the rights set forth in the Covenant. It is sufficient that a state 'claims that another State Party is not fulfilling its obligation' under the Covenant (the same wording is found in the Torture Convention). This, of course, is considerably broader, as such a claim may encompass an accusation not to have enacted necessary laws, not to have fulfilled reporting obligations, and so forth. Though reference is made to the exhaustion of local remedies as a condition for the Committee to deal with a complaint within the state complaint procedure, the rule has a far more limited scope than in the individual complaint procedure. In cases which may be raised within an inter-state procedure, very often no domestic remedies may exist.

The inter-state complaint procedure is an institutionalized dispute settlement procedure. It is mandatory under the Convention against Racial Discrimination (Article 11 to 13) and in the International Labour Organisation system.[21] It is optional under the Political Covenant, the Torture Convention, and the Convention on Discrimination in Education.[22]

Inter-state complaint procedures have rarely been used at the universal level, and in only six cases within the International Labour Organisation system.[23] One of the reasons for its non-use undoubtedly is the fact that it is always loaded with political considerations and thus may lead to confrontations between states. It is not very well structured to de-politicize a conflict, to restrict it to specific legal aspects of a given situation.

Despite the fact that inter-state complaint procedures have some common features, as already pin-pointed by the term itself, they are quite different when it comes to details. This is obvious in relation to the International Labour Organisation, which has its own system and a unique structure. But it is also true in relation to such other instruments as the Political Covenant, Torture Convention, and the Racial Discrimination Convention.

If we compare the procedure of the Racial Discrimination Convention (Article 11) with that of the Political Covenant (Article 41) or the Torture Convention (Article 21), the main difference is that under the Racial Discrimination Convention the complaint procedure is mandatory. Every member state, by ratifying or acceding to the Convention, accepts this procedure. Nevertheless, the procedure has

---

[21] It is also mandatory under the European Convention on Human Rights and the African Charter on Human and Peoples' Rights.

[22] It is also optional under the American Convention on Human Rights: see Buergenthal, 1988, p. 155.

[23] Cf. Leckie, 1988, p. 277; Valticos, 1987, p. 505.

never been used. Attempts to apply it without a specific application by a member state have rightly been rejected (CERD/C/SR.507).

Under the Political Covenant and the Torture Convention, on the other hand, the procedure is optional; a specific declaration recognizing this procedure is necessary. Such a declaration so far has been made by only 23 States Parties to the Political Covenant and 12 States Parties to the Torture Convention. Up to now, the procedures have never been applied. Furthermore, a communication under the Racial Discrimination Convention may be brought directly to the attention of the Committee, so the Committee can be involved already from the beginning of the dispute. It may, however, deal with the communication only if after six months no solution has been found between the states concerned and the matter is again brought before the Committee. In such a case, the chairman of the Committee has the right to appoint an *ad hoc* conciliation commission. The commission submits a report 'on all questions of fact' (Article 13) and makes such 'recommendations as it may think proper for the amicable solution of the dispute.' Three months after communicating this report to the parties concerned, the chairman communicates the report and the declarations of the parties concerned to the other States Parties.

Under the Political Covenant and the Torture Convention, however, a communication can be referred to the appropriate Committee only six months after the dispute has not been settled by the States concerned. The Committee deals with such a complaint only after it has ascertained that local remedies have been exhausted. It makes available 'its good offices' with a view 'to a friendly solution'. Twelve months after receipt of the notice the Committee submits a report to the States Parties concerned. If a solution can be reached, the report is confined to a brief statement of the facts and the solution reached. If a solution cannot be reached, the report is confined to a brief statement of the facts with the submissions by the States Parties attached to the report. The Committee is not asked to make any proposals or findings.

Unlike under the Racial Discrimination Convention and the Torture Convention, an *ad hoc* conciliation commission can be established under the Political Covenant (Article 42) only with the prior consent of the States Parties concerned. Twelve months after having been seized of the matter, the Conciliation Commission submits a report to the chairman of the Committee for communication to the States Parties concerned, but not for publication. If the Commission is unable to complete its consideration, the report is confined to a brief statement of the status of its consideration. If an amicable solution is reached, the report is confined to a brief statement of the facts and the solution reached. If no solution is reached, the report embodies its findings of facts, its views on the possibilities of an amicable solution and the submissions made by the parties. The

States Parties notify the chairman within three months whether or not they accept the contents of the report.

I reproduce the detailed and technical looking provisions concerning the contents of reports in an inquiry procedure which only aims at a friendly conciliation in order to demonstrate how far-fetched it is to allege that, within the reporting procedure of Article 40, paragraph 4, of the Political Covenant, reports with detailed assessments of human rights situations in specific countries could have been intended.

As already mentioned, the inter-state procedures under the Racial Discrimination Convention and under the Political Covenant have never been used. This procedure is

Considered to be one of the most drastic and confrontational legal measures available to States . . . and in many of those cases where it has been used, has assisted in its politicization (Leckie, 1988, p. 254).

Inter-state procedures have been used several times within the closed system of the European Convention (Leckie, 1988, p. 271).[24] Within the International Labour Organisation, it has only recently awakened after a 40-year hibernation. Its revival came as a surprise even for the ILO staff. However, the procedure has been used only three times. It seems to be very optimistic to conclude under these circumstances that the inter-state complaint procedure has now reached an effective place among the other control procedures of the Organisation (Valticos, 1987, p. 515).

The inter-state complaint procedure can be used in different ways. It may fulfil a normal function as a settlement procedure in a dispute which is basically bilateral, for instance if the victims of a breach are nationals of the complaining state. It may be used on an *erga omnes* level like an *actio popularis*. This may have been the case in some of the complaints handled within the Western European system, but presupposes a relatively high degree of integration. The '*actio popularis*' model, however, opens the door for abusing this procedure, using it as a political weapon, applying it to exert pressure in order to reach a political goal in quite another field. In any case, it is built on an accusation and has a strong political background. It is often considered as an unfriendly act and states hesitate to use it. They normally prefer to apply more subtle diplomatic means.

It is very unlikely that a state will use this kind of procedure, if not to protect its own nationals or to accuse another state of grave and serious, widespread or systematic violations of human rights. It is politically too strong to be applied in isolated cases of human rights violations. As an instrument against serious or systematic violations of human rights, on the other hand, it is too slow and lacks sufficient

---

[24] Most of the Western European states have undertaken under Article 62 of the European Convention, not to make use of another complaint procedure *inter se*.

publicity. As a rule, all inter-state complaint procedures are confidential and some will never even reach the public, if they have not been brought to an amicable solution.

On the political level, the 1986 Vienna CSCE Meeting has created a flexible and easy-going information and complaint procedure in its concluding Document. Under the heading 'Human Dimension of the CSCE', the Document recommends using diplomatic channels on a bilateral basis and establishes a public forum for complaints at both Conferences on the Human Dimension and CSCE Follow-up Meetings, on an *'erga omnes* parties' level. Whether this will lead to new forms of co-operation in the promotion of human rights, or only serve as an institutionalized forum for mutual accusations between 'West' and 'East' and political pressure by NATO countries remains to be seen. Quite clearly, it is a political procedure which will not replace or supersede the inter-state complaint procedure established by human rights instruments.

5. Individual complaint procedures

In contrast to the inter-state procedure, individual complaint procedures today play an important role not only at the regional but also at the universal level. A large part of the work of the Human Rights Committee is devoted to the examination of individual complaints (communications) on violations 'of the rights set forth in the Covenant' in accordance with the Optional Protocol. Since the Committee started its work under the Optional Protocol, 371 communications concerning 28 countries have been submitted, of which 94 have been concluded by final views under Article 5, paragraph 4, of the Optional Protocol. Eighty-two have been declared inadmissible (UN doc. A/44/40, Chapter V, p. 138).

While the Political Covenant has been ratified by 87 states, its Optional Protocol is in force for only 45 states. This, nevertheless, is a remarkably high percentage, in particular if compared with the Racial Discrimination Convention. Out of 125 member states to the Discrimination Convention, only 12 accepted the Committee's competence to receive and consider individual communications under its Article 14. It was only in 1982 that this procedure became applicable, after 10 states had made the necessary declaration. It took nearly 20 years from the entry into force of the Convention to the adoption of an opinion on the first complaint. The Committee on the Elimination of Racial Discrimination considered its first case under Article 14 of the Convention only in 1984 (1/1984, adoption of Committee's opinion 10 August 1988, CERD/C/3-6/D/1/1984). Under the Convention against Torture, only 12 out of 33 states have ratified the individual complaint procedure provided for in Article 22.

Although the individual complaint procedure is confidential and is limited to civil and political rights, it is completely different from the reporting and the inter-state complaint procedure. It is the only procedure that can be initiated by an individual and that has no direct repercussions on the inter-state relationship of States Parties.[25]

It may be useful to underline some of the main differences between the various types of procedures. The individual complaint procedure is the only quasi-judicial procedure under the universal human rights instruments. It can be invoked only by individuals, or in case of Article 14 of the Discrimination Convention, by a group of individuals who claim to be the victim of a violation of a right set forth in the instrument for the benefit of individuals. The Human Rights Committee, in two recent admissibility decisions, has declared inadmissible communications where newspaper and printing companies claimed to be victims of human rights violations (UN doc. A/44/40, Chapter V,G,1, p. 141; communications nos. 360/1989 and 361/1989).

In an admissibility decision, the Human Rights Committee also held

The author, as an individual, cannot claim to be a victim of a violation of the right to self-determination enshrined in article 1 of the Covenant. Whereas the Optional Protocol provides a recourse procedure for individuals claiming that their rights have been violated, Article 1 of the Covenant deals with rights conferred upon peoples as such.

This view has been reaffirmed in another admissibility decision, where the Committee states:

That the Covenant recognizes and protects in most resolute terms a people's right of self-determination and its right to dispose of its natural resources, as an essential condition for the effective guarantee and observance of individual human rights and for the promotion and strengthening of those rights. However, the Committee observes ... that the author, as an individual, cannot claim under the Optional Protocol to be a victim of a violation of the right of self-determination enshrined in Article 1 of the Covenant which deals with rights conferred upon peoples, as such (UN doc. A/42/40, p. 106).

Within the individual complaint procedure, the competence of the Human Rights Committee is always limited to the isolated case of the complaining individual. It is, therefore, accidental what questions are brought before the Committee, and normally no general review of the human rights situation in the country concerned is possible.

---

[25] See Møse and Opsahl, 1981, p. 1; Nowak, 1980a, p. 537; Coussirat-Coustère, 1983, p. 510; de Zayas, Möller and Opsahl, 1985, p. 9; Nowak, 1988, p. 517; Nowak, 1989, p. 698. The decisions are published in the Annual Reports of the Human Rights Committee: UN doc. A/32-44/40; see also 'Human Rights Committee Selected Decision under the Optional Protocol', New York 1985 and 1989.

Individual complaint procedures necessarily presuppose the exhaustion of domestic remedies. This is one of the most important preconditions for an admissibility decision. The work of the Committee under the individual complaint procedure is not to offer 'good offices' or to recommend an 'amicable solution' of a dispute, but to give 'views' or an 'opinion' and to state whether or not the facts disclose violations of the Covenant or the Convention and to make appropriate suggestions or recommendations 'to the party concerned' (Article 14, paragraph 7(b) CERD).

The documents recording the outcome of the consideration of individual complaints, therefore, look quite different from reports under Article 41 of the Covenant or Article 13 of the Discrimination Convention. They are instead phrased like court decisions, stating the facts, describing the procedures followed, discussing the legal questions involved, and concluding with a statement as to whether or not there has been a violation. Such statements, however, are not made *vis-à-vis* another State Party and thus they cannot be equated with findings in procedures dealing with state responsibility. The Committee neither acts as a court between states nor acts as a judge between an individual and a state. It gives a legal opinion which is not binding, but stimulates States Parties to think anew and, if necessary, change their conduct. The specific features of this procedure have been described by the French representative in the Third Committee in the following words:

The Protocol would not empower the Human Rights Committee to act as a judge between States and individuals, but the Committee's role could be to express a different point of view from that held by States. The purpose of the communications procedures would be once again to direct a State's attention to a particularly serious matter involving the civil and political rights of an individual; at the request of an individual, the Human Rights Committee would ask that State to reopen the matter even if it had already been considered by the national courts (UN doc. A/C.3/SR.1441, paragraph 27).

The procedure aims at ensuring human rights and it therefore tries to persuade the state concerned because, ultimately, it is only the state that can guarantee the equal enjoyment of human rights.

Despite the fact that the Committee's views or opinions are not binding, they are powerful legal opinions which cannot easily be neglected by a state which has accepted the procedure and co-operated in the proceeding. It is the legal value of the decision which determines the strength of this procedure and its contribution to the promotion of human rights. Since the individual complaint procedure is in the hands of the same Committee that is responsible for the reporting procedure, the essence of a decision on an individual communication can find its way in a generalized form into the general comments which are occasionally issued by the Committee. That, indeed, has happened several times, and makes it possible to draw further advantages from a procedure which is otherwise limited to a particular individual case.

5.1. Some specific features and problems of individual complaint procedures

The individual complaint procedure under the Political Covenant was and is very controversial, as can be seen from the limited number of ratifications of the Optional Protocol. States are afraid that it puts the individual and the state on the same footing, which presupposes a supra-national legal order. To meet such concerns, the drafters of the Protocol were careful not to make the final views of the Human Rights Committee binding upon the States Parties. The individual complaint procedure had been eliminated from the draft Covenant in the General Assembly and was reintroduced in the form of an Optional Protocol at the last minute (UN doc. A/C.3/SR.1441). It is attached to the Covenant, and so only States Parties to the Covenant can become parties to the Protocol. It remains, however, a separate treaty, with its own provisions for ratification, reservations, amendments, and denunciation.

The main problem is not that such a procedure would or could change the structure of international law and make individuals subjects of international law, as is sometimes feared. The individual complaint procedure is not a legal mechanism which allows enforcement of rights of an individual under international law. It is an implementation measure agreed upon among states in order to review whether the state concerned has fulfilled its international obligations in relation to a specific individual case. It is, therefore, a measure to ensure compliance of a state with its international obligations. Its unique nature is that it is initiated by an individual and no other State Party is directly involved or has to forward accusations of non-compliance; no dispute between states has to be settled.

The standing of the individual depends on the ratification of the Covenant and of the Protocol by the state concerned. What is under review is a state's conduct within its jurisdiction. In reviewing communications under the Optional Protocol, two substantive questions arise:

(a) whether the right claimed to be violated is set forth in the Covenant;
(b) whether the internal legal regulation or the act complained of is or is not in conformity with the international obligation assumed by the State towards other States Parties.

The specific feature of this procedure is that it can be initiated only by the individual concerned. It does not lead to an international dispute between States Parties to the treaty, and thus it avoids confrontation and accusations between states. This is undoubtedly an advantage which distinguishes this procedure from the inter-state complaint procedure. It may very well be the reason why states more easily accept the individual than the inter-state complaint procedure.

However, if the procedure is taken seriously by the State Party, it may have far-reaching repercussions on its legal order. Normally, an individual communication can only be lodged after domestic remedies have been exhausted.[26] This quite often means that when a supreme or even a constitutional court has taken a decision finding an act lawful or constitutional and the individual still believes that he is a victim of a violation of any of the rights set forth in the Covenant, he may turn to the Committee. The state's act or conduct comes under supervision through the individual complaint procedure only when it has not been corrected within the internal legal system, and when the highest competent national authority has declared that the act complained of conforms to the applicable statutory or constitutional norms. The Committee's finding of a breach, therefore, very often may be tantamount to a statement that not only the conduct of an administrative organ in a particular case but even the law itself — despite being found constitutional — does not correspond to the state's international obligation. Such a decision may thus affect even the constitution itself.

It is the potential for interference with the constitutional process which makes it very difficult for many states to accept this procedure. It is interesting to recall that this was already clearly expressed in 1966 by the representative of India in the General Assembly. He rejected the proposed procedure because it

might disturb the constitutional and governmental system of States. In India the constitutional system provided for the supremacy of the judiciary, so that the review of legislation and judicial decisions could be carried out only by the supreme court; provision was also made for the review of administrative arrangements. It was impossible for his country to alter its constitutional system in order to accommodate the proposal (UN doc. A/C.3/SR.1436, paragraph 25).

To submit constitutional questions to an expert body, which often is composed of a majority rooted in another legal system, is something

---

[26] There is already a remarkable jurisprudence on the exhaustion of domestic remedies: see, for example, Gandhi, 1986, p. 232; Trindade, 1979, p. 734; de Zayas, Möller and Opsahl, 1985, p. 9; Møse and Opsahl, 1981, p. 1; Nowak, 1989, p. 749. For more recent decisions, see Annual Reports UN doc. A/43/40, p. 152; A/44/40, Chapter V, G., p. 141.

which states always will find difficult to do.[27] It is therefore indeed remarkable that so many states have ratified the Optional Protocol.[28] This is the more surprising since the rate of communications declared admissible is around 70 per cent, as compared with 4 per cent in the European Commission on Human Rights.

The filter of exhaustion of domestic remedies, therefore, is much more efficient in the West European system than in the practice of the Human Rights Committee. This is an interesting point — even if we assume that the inadmissibility rate in the Human Rights Committee is growing. It points to the fact that the strength of the national shield against international supervision depends very much on the functioning of an advanced system of judicial remedies within the national legal order. A state with a perfect system of domestic legal remedies can easily keep a case away from an individual international complaint procedure for 10–15 years without being found guilty of unduly delaying procedures. It is true that the Human Rights Committee can refuse to accept a state's plea that an individual has failed to exhaust domestic remedies if the applicable domestic procedures are unreasonably prolonged (Article 5, paragraph 2(b)). But this may mainly work against administrations which are inexperienced or make mistakes. There are cases where, during a period of five years' pre-trial detention or six years' court proceedings, domestic remedies were never exhausted.

It may very well be one of the positive incentives of this procedure that it stimulates the development and improvement of internal remedy systems which cannot be neglected by international supervisory bodies and — what is more important — will have a corrective and preventive effect against human rights violations. The first part of the Torture Convention may be interpreted as an agreement to establish efficient domestic safeguards and remedies in order to

---

[27] It may also happen that the Human Rights Committee interprets a provision much more broadly than does a State Party. This may not only cause problems of implementation but also heavy financial consequences, as occurred, for example, when the Human Rights Committee interpreted Article 26 of the Political Covenant to prohibit discrimination in law and in practice in any field regulated and protected by public authorities (cf. the first cases in UN doc. A/42/40 Annex VIII, B; A/42/40 Annex VIII, D); cf. Opsahl, 1988, p. 51; Graefrath, 1988b, p. 179; Tomuschat, 1989, p. 37; more recent cases in UN doc. A/43/40 p. 155; A/44/40, Chapter G, 2h, p. 146. These decisions provoked a serious discussion in the Netherlands' Government, which even considered whether it would be necessary to denounce the Covenant and afterwards to ratify it anew, making a reservation to protect the national legal system against unacceptable repercussions of the jurisprudence of the Human Rights Committee.

[28] To what extent this procedure can successfully be applied in connection with a socialist human rights concept remains to be seen. It could not be proved as long as the Stalinist system distorted and discredited socialist ideas, and the ratification of the Optional Protocol by states like Hungary and Poland is marked rather by a speedy transformation into a free-market economy than by the upholding and restructuring of socialist concepts.

prevent torture. Both the Political Covenant and the Discrimination Convention stress the general importance of national remedies as a condition for the admissibility of a complaint. In Article 2, paragraph 3, of the Political Covenant, States Parties undertake:

— that a person whose rights are violated shall have an effective remedy,
— that the right to a remedy shall be determined by competent judicial, administrative or legislative authorities or by any other competent authority provided for by the legal system,
— to ensure that remedies granted will be enforced.

Article 14, paragraph 2, of the Discrimination Convention even recommends creating a specific remedy against racial discrimination in addition to the normal national system of legal remedies. It suggests that a State Party should

establish or indicate a body within a national legal order which shall be competent to receive and consider petitions from individuals . . . who have exhausted other available local remedies.

It is only 'in the event of failure to obtain satisfaction from' such a body — if it exists — that 'the petitioner shall have the right to communicate the matter to the Committee within six months' (Article 14, paragraph 5). Despite this shelter, the Article 14 procedure has been accepted by only 12 States Parties to the Convention. It has not been applied in practice. Therefore, in the following discussion, we will rely on the procedure as applied by the Human Rights Committee, without going into the details of its jurisprudence.

5.2 Individual complaint procedures in the Human Rights Committee

The individual complaint procedure is a confidential procedure. Like the inter-state complaint procedure, the individual procedure is written only: no oral hearings are possible. Sometimes, it has been suggested that the Human Rights Committee be allowed to take oral evidence. But this would not only raise a lot of practical problems, it would also be a considerable change in the procedure as laid down in the Protocol itself. The Protocol explicitly limits the procedure to an evaluation of the written information before the Committee. When the Protocol was drafted, the fact that the 'proceedings were to be written and confidential' was considered to be a 'substantial precaution' (France, UN doc. A/C.3/SR.1438, paragraph 51; India, A/C.3/SR.1441, paragraph 31; Tunisia, A/C.3/SR.1441, paragraph 39/

40) against 'unwanted intrusions on State sovereignty' (Canada, UN doc. SR.1439, paragraph 47). Article 14, paragraph 6, of the Discrimination Convention stresses confidentiality and 'written explanations'.[29] Nevertheless, the Human Rights Committee decided from the beginning to publish both its final views in full and its decisions on inadmissibility, having substituted initials for the names of the victim and the author of the communication, in order to prevent biased quotations of parts of its decisions by the parties. As far as I know, there have never been any objections to this practice.

The consideration of communications under the Optional Protocol normally consists of three stages.

Communications concerning a State Party to the Protocol are received and registered by the Secretariat (Rule 78 of the Provisional Rules of Procedure). It may request necessary clarification or information from the author in regard to the applicability of the Protocol (Rule 80). The Secretariat prepares a list of communications and extended fact sheets which enable a working group of members of the Committee or a Special Rapporteur to prepare a recommendation on admissibility for the Committee.[30]

The Committee may declare a communication inadmissible without first obtaining information from the State Party concerned, but it may not declare a communication admissible unless the State Party has received the communication and has had an opportunity to make observations which are relevant to the question of admissibility (Rule 91). If the information before the Committee makes out a *prima facie* case,[31] and if the other admissibility conditions are fulfilled, the communication is declared admissible.

The decision on admissibility concludes the admissibility stage of the procedure and opens proceedings on the merits. The Committee normally requests, within six months, any necessary explanations from the State Party, giving the author an opportunity to comment on the observations received (Rule 93). If sufficient information is before the Committee, its final views are prepared in the form of a recommendation by a special rapporteur or a working group. The views are communicated to both the individual and the State Party concerned (Rule 94). Some time later they are released to the press

---

[29] See, however, Article 22 of the Torture Convention, which is less explicit, demanding only 'closed meetings when examining communications' (paragraph 6) and 'written explanations' (paragraph 3). It omits, however, the reference to 'written' information in paragraph 4, and provides for oral hearings under Article 21. In its rules of procedure, the Committee provides for hearing the author of the communication and the representative of the State Party concerned. Cf. Nowak, 1988, p. 523.

[30] In order to speed up the work, the Committee authorized the Working Group to decide even on admissibility if consensus existed; see UN doc. A/44/40, Chapter V,C, p. 139 and Annex IX, p. 179.

[31] The Committee has amended its Rule of Procedure 90b with the words 'sufficiently substantiated', to make clear that a claim is not just any allegation, but an allegation supported by a certain amount of substantiating evidence. See UN doc. A/44/40, Chapter V, G, 1c, p. 142.

and published in the annexes of the annual report. They are also published in a series entitled 'Selected Decisions'.

This general description of the procedure already makes clear that it takes much time to reach a decision. One year or more is needed to decide on admissibility and another one to two years for the decision on the merits. It is therefore not difficult to find examples where it has taken three to four years to reach a decision. It has even happened that final views have been adopted only four years after the decision on admissibility.

These delays in reaching a final decision point to one of the most serious shortcomings of this procedure. They impede its efficiency, a particularly serious matter if practical help for a victim of a human rights violation is at stake rather than the resolution of a legal question. In general, the delays are not caused by the Committee, despite the fact that it meets only three times a year. It takes time to get the necessary information and submissions from the State Party and the replies from the applicant. The material has to be processed and quite often translated into one of the working languages. The procedure, therefore, is slow.

But additional delays have been caused by States Parties which often could not manage to submit their explanations during the admissibility stage within eight weeks or to furnish their submissions on the merits within six or eight months. The Committee has had to apply a very flexible policy in extending time limits in order to ensure the co-operation of the parties and a well-founded decision. The situation may become even worse when the Committee is flooded with communications and itself faces a backlog in considering communications.[32] The time factor is all the more important since it should not be forgotten that an individual has to exhaust domestic remedies before he can go to the Human Rights Committee. The violation may, therefore, have happened eight or ten years prior to the Committee's expression of its views.

The views held by the Human Rights Committee, as by other Committees, are not binding on the State Party concerned. They are legal opinions. The State Party may accept that opinion or it may take another position. The situation may have changed or the matter settled, or other evidence which was not available to the Committee may lead to other results.[33] So, states have to give due consideration

---

[32] According to the most recent report, this stage has now been reached; cf. UN doc. A/44/40, Chapter V, p. 138.

[33] See, however, case No. 203/1986 in UN doc. A/44/40 Annex X, p. 200, where reference is made to Peruvian Law No. 23506 of 8 December 1982, which reads:

> Article 40. Any decision by an international body whose mandatory jurisdiction has been accepted by the Peruvian State requires no review or prior confirmation in order to become effective and enforceable. The Supreme Court of Justice of the Republic shall admit any decisions handed down by such an international body and order them to be enforced in accordance with current internal legislation and procedures concerning the enforcement of judgments.

to the Committee's opinion, but it is not a judgment of a court with which they have to comply. There is nothing similar to Article 59 of the Statute of the International Court of Justice in the Covenant or the Protocol. And, of course, there is no follow-up after the Committee has given its views.

No doubt it is important for the Committee to have some response, to get information about actions which may or may not have been taken by a State Party in response to the Committee's opinion, or whether the legal situation has been changed. But there is no follow-up procedure in the universal instruments, and this is not by chance. Even courts do not have means to enforce their judgments. There is no enforcement machinery under international law unless it is specifically agreed upon, as, for example, in certain international organizations and in case of a breach of the peace. States Parties to the Protocol are not under an obligation to comply with the views expressed by the Committee. They, therefore, are not obliged to report to the Human Rights Committee about what action, if any, they have taken in compliance with the opinion of the Committee. This may be regrettable but it is the legal situation,[34] and it may very well have been an important condition for many states to accept the individual complaint procedure. This is a specific procedure with many quasi-judicial aspects, but it cannot be equated with arbitration or the operation of an international judiciary.

Like the reporting procedure, the individual complaint procedure too is based on co-operation. Attempts in the Human Rights Committee to invent some kind of a follow-up procedure therefore must have failed. The most the Committee could do and actually has done, is to inform States Parties that it is interested in receiving information on any action taken 'pursuant to its views.' The Committee deliberately avoided the words 'in compliance with its views' because it was very well aware that states have not undertaken an obligation to so comply (UN doc. A/39/40, p. 126). Of course, any information states supply on their activities in relation to final views adopted by the Committee is welcome and useful, not only as far as the individual case is concerned, but also as an indication of the effectiveness of the Committee's work.

The attempts to invent a follow-up for the individual complaint procedure point to one of its principal limitations. It is framed like a national procedure of an administrative court but does not have the legal force, the practical facilities or the executive backing which are ordinary elements of a national legal order. It is simply unrealistic and contrary to the situation of our world today to believe that on a universal level the international protection of human rights in individual cases can be accomplished by judicial or quasi-judicial procedures.

---

[34] Cf. the discussion in CCP/C/SR.396; Graefrath, 1988b, p. 168.

Again, it was the Indian representative who pointed to these flaws in the proposed procedure. In the UN General Assembly, he noted that the procedure was

too weak to effectively ensure the protection of individuals; it authorized the individual to lodge a complaint but by way of remedy merely provided . . . for the committee to forward suggestions to the State Party concerned. If there was neither the willingness nor the authority at international level to take the necessary practical measures to protect the individual, it was preferable not to tackle the subject. Indeed, the new article (41 bis) was inconsistent with the system of implementation provided for in the Covenant, in which it had been consistently maintained that it would be the States Parties which were to guarantee, ensure and protect the rights embodied in the Covenant. Article 41 bis made an abrupt departure from that principle and pretended to make the international machinery the protector of the rights of the individual as against its own State. But such pretensions were fake since the international machinery lacked sanctions behind it. It would only raise false hopes and therefore frustrations in the mind of the individual (UN doc. A/C.3/SR.1440, paragraph 16).

The individual complaint procedure has a different place and function within a national legal order or within an integrated system such as the one established by the Council of Europe. But on the universal level, where none, or only a very limited hierarchical political and legal order, exists, it necessarily has a limited function.

Under these circumstances, its main role seems to lie in elaborating on the legal contents of an international human rights standard, its specific characteristics and its possibilities for adjustment. It is a means to exert a certain pressure on a state to adapt its laws and legal practice to the standard as interpreted by the group of experts serving on the Committee.

Another useful effect of the procedure is that it contributes to the demarcation of state conduct which amounts to a serious violation of human rights, whenever the individual complaint represents more than a single case. But to protect the affected individual, let alone guarantee its subjective rights, the procedure can do little. It starts too late, takes too much time, does not lead to binding results and lacks any effective enforcement. Even if the dialogue between the Committee and a State Party on an individual case is successful and leads to remedies and changes, it usually comes too late for the victim concerned. Nevertheless, it may be useful for other individuals who face similar problems but have not complained or could not do so. These are not flaws in the Committee's work: they are shortcomings which are inherent in the procedure, a procedure which mixes up invoking a violation of international law with enforcing subjective rights of an individual within a national legal order, while in fact lacking the power to do so.

6. Final remarks

Reporting and complaint procedures in universal international instruments on human rights are an essential means to ensure the identity and co-operation of States Parties in the 'legislative' and in the implementation processes of international human rights obligations. They reflect and correspond to the specific structure of these obligations and cannot be unilaterally replaced or substituted by other means.

Despite the fact that we still have a long way to go to reach universality of these instruments, they manifest one of the most important developments in international law. It therefore is highly regrettable that the work of treaty bodies in the field of human rights has already been seriously impeded by the global financial crisis. Unfortunately, we have to face the menace that with a continuing or even growing international debt crisis — which is by no means only a problem of developing countries — working conditions of treaty bodies may be adversely affected. We already have the experience that the work of the Racial Discrimination Committee, which depends on being financed by States Parties, has been severely hampered in recent years. Now Article 19 of the Torture Convention provides that States Parties to the Convention shall be responsible for expenses incurred by the United Nations in connection with the holding of meetings and the use of UN facilities. Knowing that conference services in the United Nations may cost $2000 a day and that the expenses for the Human Rights Committee are, on average, $1 million a year, states will have to consider whether they can afford the money in the hard currency they are expected to pay, having ratified or acceded to such Conventions.[35] It therefore did not come as a surprise that the German Democratic Republic, when ratifying the Torture Convention, declared that it could only pay for those of the Committee's activities which it recognized at ratification, that is, not for any of the optional procedures. This position has provoked an international debate.[36]

Irrespective of the legal questions involved, it seems obvious that it is only the state concerned that can decide whether it has or has not the money to finance all or only those procedures it has accepted. It does not make much sense to try to force a state to pay for expenses relating to procedures it has not accepted. It also seems impossible to persuade a responsible government to ratify a treaty if it is clear from the beginning that the state cannot afford the money necessary to

---

[35] The question of financing the Committee on the Rights of the Child could only reasonably be settled in the discussions on Article 43 of the Convention, at the 44th UN General Assembly. Up to the last minute, the US insisted on burdening the Convention with the same unworkable system as under the Convention Against Torture; cf. E/CN.4/1989/29, Article 43; A/C.3/44/L.44, Article 43.
[36] See Nowak, 1988, p. 495; Mohr, 1989, p. 345.

fulfil its financial obligations under the treaty. We even have to face a situation that states which thought they would be able to spend the money, later on realized that they could not pay their contribution. This may ultimately lead states to denounce treaties in order to avoid their debts growing year by year and their being harassed by unfriendly reminders.

It is not that states neglect their financial obligations, but that they are not in an economic position to pay for international conference services when they are not even able to meet the needs of their population. The future of the international implementation system of human rights treaties and its effective functioning, therefore, will very much depend on finding ways to reduce the implied financial burden on states. It will not be sufficient to simplify reporting methods.

The only general implementation procedure which is common to all universal instruments in the field of human rights is the reporting procedure. It succeeds in fulfilling its function as a permanent mechanism for exchanging information and at the same time providing a solid basis for a pertinent and fair dialogue on implementation, progress, problems and difficulties and specific national forms given to international human rights standards. This dialogue is independent of any accusation of violations and stimulates implementation and co-operation in the field of human rights. It promotes solidarity between the States Parties in fighting serious and systematic human rights violations.

While the inter-state complaint procedure envisaged in the instruments does not actually play any role in state practice, the individual complaint procedure has, to a certain extent, gained a place as far as civil and political rights are concerned. Thus, a new form of inquiry procedure, with quasi-judicial elements has emerged. It may lead to a finding of a violation, in regard to the complaining individual, but avoids invoking state responsibility. It cannot be equated with a dispute settlement procedure between states; it rather contributes to avoiding disputes between states. Although limited to individual cases in which alleged violations occurred long ago, it contributes to the legal interpretation and adjustment of international human rights standards and may persuade and encourage states to correct conduct which has been found not to be in conformity with obligations under a given international instrument.

The annual reports of the various Committees to the General Assembly testify to the vast international co-operation that has grown in the last decade in the field of human rights on a universal level. They have already become an important source for detailed information on the human rights situation of member states. It is, therefore, regrettable that not all states, and in particular not all states that have the money to do so, have ratified the universal instruments. These instruments have proved to be not only decisive standard setting documents, but also to function as a ground and a

tool for fruitful co-operation between states with different socio-
economic systems and different cultural and national traditions.

Bibliography

Alston, Philip, 1983. 'The Universal Declaration at 35: Western and Passé or
Alive and Universal', *The Review*, International Commission of Jurists, no.
31.
Alston, Philip, 1987. 'Out of the Abyss: The Challenges Confronting the New
Committee on Economic, Social and Cultural Rights', *Human Rights
Quarterly*, vol. 9, no. 3.
Alston, Philip and Bruno Simma, 1987. 'First Session of the UN Committee on
Economic, Social and Cultural Rights', *American Journal of International
Law*, vol. 81.
Alston, Philip and Bruno Simma, 1988. 'Second Session of the UN Committee
on Economic, Social and Cultural Rights', *American Journal of Interna-
tional Law*, vol. 82, no. 3.
Ansbach, Tatjana and Hans-Joachim Heintze, 1987. *Selbstbestimmung und
Verbot der Rassendiskriminierung im Völkerrecht.* Berlin: Staatsverlag.
Buergenthal, Thomas, 1977. 'Implementing the UN Racial Convention',
Texas International Law Journal, vol. 12.
Buergenthal, Thomas, 1988. *International Human Rights in a Nutshell.* St
Paul, Minn.: West Publishing Co.
Byrnes, Andrew, 1989. 'The "Other" Human Rights Treaty Body: The Work of
the Committee on the Elimination of Discrimination against Women', *Yale
Journal of International Law*, vol. 14, no. 1.
Cassese, Antonio, 1986. *International Law in a Divided World.* Oxford:
Clarendon Press.
Chowdhury, T.M.R., 1986. *Legal Framework of International Supervision.*
Stockholm: University of Stockholm.
Coussirat-Coustére, Vincent, 1983. 'L'adhésion de la France au Protocole
Facultatif se rapportant au Pacte International relatif aux Droits Civils et
Politique', *Annuaire Francais de Droit International*, vol. 24.
Dicke, Kurt, 1987. 'Rezension zu L. Kühnhardt, Die Universalität der Mens-
chenrechte', *German Yearbook of International Law*, vol. 30.
van Dijk, Pieter, 1984. *Supervisory Mechanisms in International Economic
Organizations.* The Hague: Kluwer Group.
Donelly, J., 1982. 'Human Rights and Human Dignity: An Analytic Critique of
Non-Western Conceptions of Human Rights', *American Political Science
Review*, vol. 76.
Empell, Hans-Michael, 1987. *Die Kompetenzen des UN-Menschenrechtsaus-
schusses im Staatenberichtsverfahren (Art. 40 des Internationalen Paktes
über bürgerliche und politische Rechte).* Frankfurt am Main: Lang.
Fischer, Doris, 1982. 'Reporting under the Covenant on Civil and Political
Rights: The First Five Years of the Human Rights Committee', *American
Journal of International Law*, vol. 76.
Fisher, Roger, 1981. *Improving Compliance with International Law.*
Charlottesville: University Press of Virginia.
Friedmann, Wolfgang, 1964. *The Changing Structure of International Law.*
New York: Feffer & Simons.
Galey, Margaret, 1984. 'International Enforcement of Women's Rights',
Human Rights Quarterly, vol. 6.

Gandhi, P.R., 1986. 'The Human Rights Committee and the Right of Individual Communication', *The British Year Book of International Law*, vol. 57.

Graefrath, Bernhard, 1988a. 'Human Rights and International Cooperation: 10 Years of Experience in the Human Rights Committee', *GDR Human Rights Bulletin*, vol. 14, no. 1.

Graefrath, Bernhard, 1988b. *Menschenrechte und internationale Kooperation: 10 Jahre Praxis des Internationalen Menschenrechtskomitees*. Berlin: Akademie-Verlag.

Heintze, Hans-Joachim, 1987. 'Schwerpunkte der Tätigkeit des Komitees für die Beseitigung der Rassendiskriminierung', *Probleme des Völkerrechts* 1987. Berlin: Akademie-Verlag.

Henkin, Louis, 1977. 'Human Rights and "Domestic Jurisdiction" ', in Thomas Buergenthal (ed.), *Human Rights, International Law and the Helsinki Accord*. Monclair, NJ: Allanheld, Osmun & Co.

van Hoof, G.J.H. and K. de Vey Mestdagh, 1984. 'Mechanisms of International Supervision', in Pieter van Dijk (ed.), *Supervisory Mechanisms in International Economic Organisations*. The Hague: Kluwer Group.

Jhabvala, Farrokh, 1984. 'The Practice of the Covenant's Human Rights Committee, 1976–82: Review of State Party Reports', *Human Rights Quarterly*, vol. 6.

Jhabvala, Farrokh, 1985a. 'The Soviet Bloc's View of the Implementation of Human Rights', *Human Rights Quarterly*, vol. 7.

Jhabvala, Farrokh, 1985b. 'Domestic Implementation of the Covenant on Civil and Political Rights', *Netherlands International Law Review*, vol. 32.

Kirgis, Frederic, 1989. 'Alternative Dispute Resolution in International Law', *Transnational Perspective*, vol. 15, no. 2.

Klenner, Hermann, 1982. *Marxismus und Menschenrechte, Studien zur Rechtsphilosophie*. Berlin: Akademie-Verlag.

Kühnhardt, Ludger, 1987. *Die Universalität der Menschenrechte*. München: Olzog.

Kulishev, L., 1982. 'International Protection of Civil and Political Human Rights', In *Mezdunarodno satrudnicestvo za zakrila na pravata na coveka*. Sofia.

Leckie, Scott, 1988. 'The Inter-State Complaint Procedure in International Human Rights Law: Hopeful Prospects or Wishful Thinking?', *Human Rights Quarterly*, vol. 10, no. 2.

Manov, B.G., 1986. *OON i sodejstvie osuscestvleniju soglasenij o pravach celoveka*. Moscow: Nauka.

Mohr, Manfred, 1983, 1984. 'Questions of Procedure under International Law in the Implementation of Human Rights Instruments', *GDR Human Rights Bulletin*, no. 1 (1983) and no. 2 (1984).

Mohr, Manfred, 1988a. 'Gewährleistung der Menschenrechte durch Völkerrecht', *Staat und Recht*, vol. 37.

Mohr, Manfred, 1988b. 'Procedural Problems Pertaining to the Work of the Committee on Economic, Social and Cultural Rights', *GDR Human Rights Bulletin*, vol. 14.

Mohr, Manfred, 1989. 'Internationale Kontrollmechanismen auf dem Gebiet der Menschenrechte: Möglichkeiten und Grenzen', *Neue Justiz*, vol. 43, no. 9.

Møse, Eric and Torkel Opsahl, 1981. 'The Optional Protocol to the International Covenant on Civil and Political Rights', *Santa Clara Law Review*, vol. 21.

Movchan, A.P., 1982. *Prava Celoveka i Mezdunarodnye Otnosenija*. Moscow.
Nowak, Manfred, 1980a. 'Die Durchsetzung des Internationalen Paktes über bürgerliche und politische Rechte, Bestandsaufnahme der ersten 10 Tagungen des UN-Ausschusses für Menschenrechte', *Europäische Grundrechte-Zeitschrift*, no. 20.
Nowak, Manfred, 1980b. 'The Effectiveness of the International Covenant on Civil and Political Rights: Stocktaking after the first eleven sessions of the UN-Human Rights Committee', *Human Rights Law Journal*, vol. 1.
Nowak, Manfred, 1984. 'UN-Human Rights Committee: Survey of Decisions'. *Human Rights Law Journal*, vol. 5.
Nowak, Manfred, 1987. 'Recent Developments in Combating Torture', *SIM, Newsletter*, no. 19.
Nowak, Manfred, 1988. 'The Implementation Functions of the UN Committee against Torture', in *Progress in the Spirit of Human Rights: Festschrift für Felix Ermacora*. Kehl am Rhein: Engel.
Nowak, Manfred, 1989. *UNO-Pakt über bürgerliche und politische Rechte und Fakultativprotokoll, CCPR-Kommentar*. Kehl am Rhein: Engel.
Oeser, Edith, 1988. 'Legal Questions in the Committee on the Elimination of Discrimination Against Women', *GDR Human Rights Bulletin*, vol. 14, no. 2.
Opsahl, Torkel, 1988. 'Equality in Human Rights Law, with Particular Reference to Article 26 of the International Covenant on Civil and Political Rights', in *Progress in the Spirit of Human Rights: Festschrift für Felix Ermacora*. Kehl am Rhein: Engel.
Pocar, Fausto, 1988. 'Considerations on the Legislative Function of the Universal Declaration of Human Rights in International Law', *Bulletin of Human Rights*, special issue.
Riphagen, Willem, 1983. 'State Responsibility: New Theories of Obligation in Interstate Relations', in R.St.J. Macdonald and Douglas M. Johnston (eds), *The Structure and Process of International Law: Essays in Legal Philosophy, Doctrine and Theory*. The Hague: Kluwer Group.
Robertson, A.H., 1981. 'The Implementation System: International Measures', in Louis Henkin (ed.), *The International Bill of Rights*. New York: Columbia University Press.
Sachariew, Kamen, 1986. *Die Rechtsstellung der betroffenen Staaten bei Verletzungen multilateraler Verträge: Fragen der Aktivlegitimation und der völkerrechtlich zugelassenen Rechtsfolgen*. Berlin: Akademie der Wissenschaften der DDR.
Sachariew, Kamen, 1988. 'State Responsibility for Multilateral Treaty Violations: Identifying the "Injured State" and its Legal Status', *Netherlands International Law Review*, vol. 35, issue 3.
Schwelb, Egon, 1968. 'Civil and Political Rights: The International Measures of Implementation', *American Journal of International Law*, vol. 62.
Spinedi, Marina, 1989. 'International Crimes of State: The Legislative History', in Joseph Weiler, Antonio Cassese and Marina Spinedi (eds), *International Crimes of State*. Berlin: de Gruyter.
Tentelen, A.D., 1985. 'The Unanswered Challenge of Relativism and the Consequences for Human Rights', *Human Rights Quarterly*, vol. 7.
Tomuschat, Christian, 1981. 'Ausschuss für Menschenrechte: Recht und Praxis', *Vereinte Nationen*, vol. 29.
Tomuschat, Christian, 1983. 'National implementation of international standards on human rights', in UN doc. HR/Geneva/1983/BP.3.

Tomuschat, Christian, 1987. 'Zehn Jahre Menschenrechtsausschuss: Versuch einer Bilanz', *Vereinte Nationen*, vol. 35, no. 5.

Tomuschat, Christian, 1989. 'Der Gleichheitsgrundsatz nach dem Internationalen Pakt über bürgerliche und politische Rechte', *Europäische Grundrechte-Zeitschrift*, vol. 16.

Trindade, A.A., Cançado, 1979. 'Exhaustion of Local Remedies under the UN Covenant on Civil and Political Rights and its Optional Protocol', *International and Comparative Law Quarterly*, vol. 28. no. 3.

Tunkin, G.I., 1983. *Pravo i Sila v Mezdunarodnoj Sisteme*. Moscow.

Valticos, Nicolas, 1968. 'Un Systeme de Controle International: La mise en Oeuvre des Conventions Internationales du Travail', *Recueil des Cours*, vol. 123.

Valticos, Nicolas, 1987. 'L'evolution du systeme de controle de L'Organisation Internationale du Travail', *International Law at the Time Of Its Codification*, vol. 2.

Verdross, Alfred and Bruno Simma, 1984. *Universelles Völkerrecht. Theorie und Praxis*. Berlin: Drucker and Humbolt.

de Zayas, Alfred, Jakob Möller and Torkel Opsahl, 1985. 'Application of the International Covenant on Civil and Political Rights under the Optional Protocol by the Human Rights Committee', *German Yearbook of International Law*, vol. 28.

13 CSCE State Adherence to Human Rights Conventions

Lauri Hannikainen

1. Introduction

Several chapters of this book analyse the human rights provision of various instruments of the Conference on Security and Co-operation in Europe (CSCE). Those provisions and the analyses of them are important to the clarification of the human rights standards of the economically and socially most advanced area of the world, the CSCE area. However, it seems possible to identify the content of only a limited number of human rights standards on the basis of CSCE instruments alone. This chapter endeavours to clarify CSCE human rights standards by using other sources, namely international human rights conventions. The purpose of this chapter is to contribute to the clarification of the acceptance of international human rights standards by the 35 states of the CSCE as follows:

1. to inform about the extent to which CSCE states have ratified major human rights conventions;
2. to clarify the areas in which reservations to human rights conventions denote disagreements among CSCE states;
3. to describe the extent to which CSCE states have consented to international monitoring, supervision and dispute settlement provided by human rights conventions.

This chapter is being written at a time when Eastern European socialist states are in the process of transforming themselves into parliamentary democracies or other forms of popular democracy and when the policy of glasnost is proceeding relatively well in the leading state of the Warsaw Pact, the Soviet Union. Since 1987, the rejection of orthodox socialism has been reflected in the changes in the patterns of attitudes of Warsaw Pact states towards human rights conventions. The 'first waves' of these changes are recorded in this chapter; they indicate the apparent direction of the changing patterns of Warsaw Pact states. One may assert with relative confidence that during the 1990s Eastern European states' appreciation of international human rights will grow and that their interpretations of the content of various human rights will become much more similar to those of the West than before the glasnost period.

2. Ratifications

Basic information regarding ratifications of major human rights conventions by CSCE states is given here in the form of two tables (Table 13.1 and 13.2). These tables record the ratifications of 26 human rights conventions by the CSCE states. The more detailed table — Table 13.1 — records the ratification or non-ratification of the listed conventions by every CSCE state. Table 13.2 classifies the information of Table 13.1 in terms of four groups of states; the main criterion of the grouping of the CSCE states here is their political affiliation, especially their affiliation with military blocs. The *four groups* of the CSCE states are the following:

1. the group of sixteen NATO states: Belgium, Canada, Denmark, France, the Federal Republic of Germany, Greece, Iceland, Italy, Luxembourg, the Netherlands, Norway, Portugal, Spain, Turkey, the United Kingdom, and the United States;
2. the group of seven Warsaw Pact states: Bulgaria, Czechoslovakia, the German Democratic Republic, Hungary, Poland, Romania, and the Soviet Union;
3. the group of eight neutral or non-aligned states: Austria, Cyprus, Finland, Ireland, Malta, Sweden, Switzerland, and Yugoslavia;
4. the group of four other states (mini-states): the Holy See, Liechtenstein, Monaco, and San Marino. These states participate in international intercourse to only a limited extent and have therefore ratified only a limited number of conventions.

In the list of conventions in Tables 13.1 and 13.2, only those human rights conventions are included which are open to all CSCE states and which appear to be of considerable importance to the contemporary socio-political situation in the CSCE area. The list includes both conventions formulating civil and political rights and conventions formulating economic, social and cultural rights. The pattern of ratifications and non-ratifications of the listed conventions reflects in an interesting way agreements or disagreements among CSCE states about human rights standards.

Tables 13.1 and 13.2 do not include any conventions concluded within the Council of Europe, because these conventions are open only to its member states and, in some cases, to states participating in the activities of the Council. However, since nearly all Western European states have assumed substantial human rights obligations under the conventions of the Council of Europe and since in the course of the 1990s many Eastern European states are expected to become members of the Council of Europe — thus increasing the significance of the conventions of the Council of Europe as sources of European human rights standards — Table 13.3 provides information on the ratifications of the major human rights conventions of the Council of Europe by the 23 member states.

Table 13.1   CSCE states: ratifications of principal human rights conventions (by state) (x = ratification, n = non-ratification)

	NATO states										
	Bel	Can	Den	Fra	FRG	Gre	Ice	Ita	Lux	Neth	Norw
1. Covenant on Economic, Social and Cultural Rights, 1966	x	x	x	x	x	x	x	x	x	x	x
2. Covenant on Civil and Political Rights, 1966	x	x	x	x	x	x	n	x	x	x	x
3. Convention on Racial Discrimination, 1965	x	x	x	x	x	x	x	x	x	x	x
4. ILO Convention Concerning Equal Remuneration, 1951	x	x	x	x	x	x	x	x	x	x	x
5. ILO Convention Concerning Discrimination in Employment and Occupations, 1958	x	x	x	x	x	x	x	x	n	x	x
6. Unesco Convention against Discrimination in Education, 1960	n	n	x	x	x	n	n	x	x	x	x
7. Convention on Discrimination against Women, 1979	x	x	x	x	x	x	x	x	n	n	x
8. Genocide Convention, 1948	x	x	x	x	x	x	x	x	x	x	x
9. Convention on Non-applicability of Statutory Limitations, 1968	n	n	n	n	n	n	n	n	n	n	n
10. Convention Against the Taking of Hostages, 1979	n	x	x	n	x	x	x	x	n	x	x
11. Torture Convention, 1984	n	x	x	x	n	x	n	x	x	x	x
12. ILO Convention Concerning Forced Labour, 1930	x	x	x	x	x	x	x	x	x	x	x
13. ILO Convention Concerning Abolition of Forced Labour, 1957	x	x	x	x	x	x	x	x	x	x	x
14. ILO Convention Concerning Freedom of Association, etc., 1948	x	x	x	x	x	x	x	x	x	x	x
15. ILO Convention Concerning the Right to Organize, 1949	x	n	x	x	x	x	x	x	x	n	x
16. ILO Convention Concerning Workers Representatives, 1971	n	n	x	x	x	n	n	x	x	x	x
17. Refugee Convention, 1951	x	x	x	x	x	x	x	x	x	x	x
18. Refugee Protocol, 1966	x	x	x	x	x	x	x	x	x	x	x
19. Convention on Stateless Persons 1954	x	n	x	x	x	x	n	x	x	x	x
20. Convention on the Reduction of Statelessness, 1961	n	x	x	n	x	n	n	n	n	x	x
21–24. Geneva Conventions on the Protection of War Victims, 1949	x	x	x	x	x	x	x	x	x	x	x
25. Additional Protocol I, 1977	x	n	x	n	n	x	x	x	x	x	x
26. Additional Protocol II, 1977	x	n	x	x	n	n	x	x	x	x	x
Total	20	19	25	22	22	20	20	24	21	23	25

					Warsaw Pact states							Neutral or non-aligned states								Other states			
Por	Spa	Tur	UK	USA	Bul	CZE	GDR	Hun	Pol	Rom	USSR	Aus	Cyp	Fin	Ire	Mal	Swe	Swi	Yug	Holy S	Liech	Mona	San M
x	x	n	x	n	x	x	x	x	x	x	x	x	x	x	x	n	x	n	x	n	n	n	x
x	x	n	x	n	x	x	x	x	x	x	x	x	x	x	x	x	n	x	n	x	n	n	x
x	x	n	x	n	x	x	x	x	x	x	x	x	x	x	x	n	x	x	n	x	x	n	n
x	x	x	x	n	x	x	x	x	x	x	x	x	x	x	x	x	n	x	x	x	n	x	x
x	x	x	n	n	x	x	x	x	x	x	x	x	x	x	x	n	x	x	x	x	n	n	x
x	x	n	x	n	x	x	x	x	x	x	x	n	x	x	n	x	x	n	x	n	n	n	n
x	x	x	x	n	x	x	x	x	x	x	x	x	x	x	x	n	x	n	x	n	n	n	n
n	x	x	x	x	x	x	x	x	x	x	x	x	x	x	n	x	n	x	n	x	n	x	n
n	n	n	n	n	x	x	x	x	x	x	x	n	n	n	n	n	n	x	n	x	n	n	n
x	x	x	x	x	x	x	x	x	n	n	x	x	x	n	x	n	n	x	x	x	n	n	n
x	x	x	x	n	x	x	x	x	x	n	x	n	x	n	x	n	n	x	x	n	n	n	n
x	x	n	x	n	x	x	n	x	x	x	x	x	x	x	x	x	x	x	n	x	n	n	n
x	x	x	x	n	n	n	n	n	n	x	n	n	x	n	x	x	x	x	x	n	n	n	n
x	x	n	x	n	x	x	x	x	x	x	x	x	x	x	x	x	x	x	x	x	n	n	x
x	x	x	x	n	x	x	x	x	x	x	x	x	x	x	x	x	x	x	n	x	n	n	x
x	x	n	x	n	x	n	n	x	x	x	x	n	x	n	x	n	x	n	x	n	n	n	n
x	x	x	x	x	n	n	n	x	n	n	n	x	x	x	x	x	x	x	x	x	x	x	n
x	x	x	x	x	n	n	n	x	n	n	n	x	x	x	x	x	x	x	x	x	x	x	n
n	n	n	x	n	n	n	n	n	n	n	n	n	n	x	n	x	n	x	x	n	n	n	n
n	n	n	x	n	n	n	n	n	n	x	n	x	n	x	n	n	n	n	n	n	n	n	n
x	x	x	x	x	x	x	x	x	x	x	x	x	x	x	x	x	x	x	x	x	x	x	x
n	x	n	n	n	x	n	n	x	n	n	x	x	x	x	n	x	x	x	x	n	x	n	n
n	x	n	n	n	x	n	n	x	n	n	x	x	n	x	n	x	x	n	x	x	x	n	n
20	23	14	22	7	20	18	18	23	19	17	20	23	19	24	19	14	25	16	23	9	8	7	10

Table 13.2 CSCE states: ratifications of principal human rights conventions (by groups of states)

	NATO states (16)	Warsaw Pact states (7)	Neutral or non-aligned states (8)	Other states (4)	Total by CSCE states (35)	Total by all states
1. Covenant on Economic, Social and Cultural Rights, 1966	14	7	6	1	28	94
2. Covenant on Civil and Political Rights, 1966	13	7	6	1	27	89
3. Convention on Racial Discrimination, 1965	14	7	6	1	28	128
4. ILO Convention Concerning Equal Remuneration, 1951	15	7	7	2	31	112
5. ILO Convention Concerning Discrimination in Employment and Occupations, 1958	13	7	7	1	28	111
6. Unesco Convention against Discrimination in Education, 1960	10	7	5	0	22	77
7. Convention on Discrimination against Women, 1979	13	7	6	0	26	101
8. Genocide Convention, 1948	15	7	6	1	29	102
9. Convention on Non-applicability of Statutory Limitations, 1968	0	7	1	0	8	31

Convention						
10. Convention Against the Taking of Hostages, 1979	13	5	5	0	23	59
11. Torture Convention, 1984	12	6	4	0	22	49
12. ILO Convention Concerning Forced Labour, 1930	14	6	8	0	28	130
13. ILO Convention Concerning Abolition of Forced Labour, 1957	15	1	7	0	23	107
14. ILO Convention Concerning Freedom of Association, etc., 1948	14	7	8	1	30	99
15. ILO Convention Concerning the Right to Organize, 1949	13	7	7	1	28	114
16. ILO Convention Concerning Workers Representatives, 1971	10	4	5	0	19	44
17. Refugee Convention, 1951	15	1	8	3	28	102
18. Refugee Protocol, 1966	16	1	8	2	27	103
19. Convention on Stateless Persons, 1954	10	0	5	0	15	36
20. Convention on the Reduction of Statelessness, 1961	6	0	3	0	9	15
21-24. Geneva Conventions on the Protection of War Victims, 1949	16	7	8	4	35	167
25. Additional Protocol I, 1977	9	3	7	2	21	92
26. Additional Protocol II, 1977	9	3	6	2	20	82

The list of conventions in Tables 13.1 and 13.2 includes the following kinds of conventions:

1. two comprehensive Covenants of 1966;
2. five conventions dealing with the prohibition of discrimination;
3. four conventions dealing with international crimes;
4. five conventions of the International Labour Organisation — ILO (others than those dealing with discrimination);
5. four Geneva Conventions of 1949 on the humanitarian protection of war victims (all four in one column) and the two Additional Protocols of 1977 to the Geneva Conventions. (These conventions form the nucleus of international humanitarian law.)

The following is a list of the conventions included in Tables 13.1 and 13.2. The list gives the official name of each convention, the source where the text of the convention concerned can be found, and the year of the instrument's entry into force.

1. International Covenant on Economic, Social and Cultural Rights, 1966. Entry into force, 1976.
2. International Covenant on Civil and Political Rights, 1966. Entry into force, 1976.
3. International Convention on the Elimination of All Forms of Racial Discrimination, 1965. Entry into force, 1969.
4. ILO Convention (No. 100) concerning Equal Remuneration for Men and Woman Workers for Work of Equal Value, 1951. Entry into force, 1953.
5. ILO Convention (No. 111) concerning Discrimination in Respect of Employment and Occupation, 1958. Entry into force, 1960.
6. Unesco Convention against Discrimination in Education, 1960. Entry into force, 1962.
7. Convention on the Elimination of All Forms of Discrimination against Women, 1979. Entry into force, 1981.
8. Convention on the Prevention and Punishment of the Crime of Genocide, 1948. Entry into force, 1951.
9. Convention on the Non-applicability of Statutory Limitations to War Crimes and Crimes against Humanity, 1968. Entry into force, 1970.
10. International Convention Against the Taking of Hostages, 1979. Entry into force, 1983.
11. Convention against Torture and Other Cruel, Inhuman or Degrading Treatment or Punishment, 1984. Entry into force, 1987.
12. ILO Convention (No. 29) concerning Forced Labour, 1930. Entry into force, 1932.

13. ILO Convention (No. 105) concerning the Abolition of Forced Labour, 1957. Entry into force, 1959.
14. ILO Convention (No. 87) concerning Freedom of Association and Protection of the Right to Organize, 1948. Entry into force, 1950.
15. ILO Convention (No. 98) concerning the Application of the Principles of the Right to Organize and Bargain Collectively, 1949. Entry into force, 1951.
16. ILO Convention (No. 135) concerning Protection and Facilities to be afforded to Workers' Representatives in the Undertaking, 1971. Entry into force, 1973.
17. Convention relating to the Status of Refugees, 1951. Entry into force, 1954.
18. Protocol relating to the Status of Refugees, 1966. Entry into force, 1967.
19. Convention relating to the Status of Stateless Persons, 1954. Entry into force, 1960.
20. Convention on the Reduction of Statelessness, 1961. Entry into force, 1975.
21–24 Geneva Convention for the Amelioration of the Condition of the Wounded and Sick in Armed Forces in the Field, 1949. Entry into force, 1950.
- Geneva Convention for the Amelioration of the Condition of Wounded, Sick and Shipwrecked Members of Armed Forces at Sea, 1949. Entry into force, 1950.
- Geneva Convention relative to the Treatment of Prisoners of War, 1949. Entry into force, 1950.
- Geneva Convention relative to the Protection of Civilian Persons in Time of War, 1949. Entry into force, 1950.
25. Protocol Additional to the Geneva Conventions of 12 August 1949 and relating to the Protection of Victims of International Armed Conflicts (Protocol I), 1977. Entry into force, 1978.
26. Protocol Additional to the Geneva Conventions of 12 August 1949 and relating to the Protection of Victims of Non-International Armed Conflicts (Protocol II), 1977. Entry into force, 1978.

Table 13.3 lists the following human rights instruments of the Council of Europe: the European Convention on Human Rights, those of its protocols that add human rights beyond those secured in the Convention, and the European Social Charter. Detailed information regarding those instruments is given in Table 13.3.

The dates of ratifications listed in the charts are as of 1 January 1990 with the exception of Finland, which ratified the European Convention on 4 May 1990.

Table 13.3 Council of Europe: ratifications of human rights instruments (by member state)

	Aus	Bel	Cyp	Den	Fin	Fra	FRG	Gre	Ice	Ire	Ita	Liech	Lux	Malta	Neth	Norw	Port	San M	Spa	Swe	Swi	Turk	UK	Total
European Convention on Human Rights, 1950. European Treaty Series, No. 5. (Entry into force, 1953)	x	x	x	x	x	x	x	x	x	x	x	x	x	x	x	x	x	x	x	x	x	x	x	23
Protocols to the European Convention																								
Protocol 1: Right to Property, Education and Free Elections (Entry into force, 1954)	x	x	x	x	x	x	x	x	x	x	x		x	x	x	x	x		x	x		x	x	20
Protocol 4: Freedom of Movement and Residence (Entry into force, 1968)	x		x	x	x	x	x	x	x	x	x		x		x	x	x	x		x				16
Protocol 6: Abolition of the Death Penalty (Entry into force, 1985)	x			x	x	x	x		x		x		x		x	x	x	x	x	x	x			15
Protocol 7: Prohibition of Expulsion of Aliens and Double Jeopardy, Rights of Criminal Appeal, Rights of Spouses (Entry into force, 1988)	x			x	x	x			x		x		x			x		x		x	x			11
European Social Charter, 1961. (Entry into force, 1965)	x	x	x	x		x	x	x	x	x				x	x	x		x		x			x	15
Total	6	3	4	6	5	6	5	4	6	4	5	1	5	3	5	6	4	5	3	6	3	2	3	

3. Observations on ratifications

CSCE states have a relatively good record of ratifications of the human rights conventions in Tables 13.1 and 13.2. Of the four groups of states, the NATO group and the neutral or non-aligned group have a ratification percentage of almost 80, and the Warsaw Pact group almost 75. (In calculating the number of ratifications and the percentage figures in Tables 13.1 and 13.2, the single column of the four Geneva Conventions of 1949 is counted as four ratifications.) In contrast, the fourth group, mini-states, has been passive in ratifying human rights conventions. However, due to the minor role of these mini-states in the international arena, their passivity in the ratification of human rights conventions hardly complicates the creation of human rights standards in the CSCE area.

The examination of ratifications by individual states in Table 13.1 shows that Scandinavian states have been the most active ratifiers among CSCE states. However, several other Western states have reached nearly as high a number of ratifications as have the Scandinavian states. This is also the case with Yugoslavia and the most active ratifier of the Warsaw Pact group, Hungary. In 1988–89, Hungary ratified several conventions.

It is surprising to note that the United States, which has been very active in human rights matters within the CSCE process, has ratified very few human rights conventions. It is also worth noting that Turkey, Switzerland and Malta have ratified only a limited number of conventions. However, these three European states have assumed many human rights obligations under conventions concluded within the Council of Europe.

Whereas most states of the Warsaw Pact may be expected to ratify more human rights conventions in the 1990s, the reluctance of the United States to ratify human rights conventions may be a signal indicating that it might be difficult to reach agreement on a number of human rights standards within the CSCE. There are also other states in the CSCE that may disagree with certain of the standards, for example, Turkey, the Soviet Union and the United Kingdom.

The International Covenant on Civil and Political Rights and the International Covenant on Economic, Social and Cultural Rights have been ratified by relatively many CSCE states. As regards those states which have not ratified the Covenant on Civil and Political Rights, nearly all of them have ratified the European Convention on Human Rights, which contains many provisions similar to those of the Covenant. From the perspective of ratifications, the only significant problem is the United States, which has not accepted international obligations corresponding to those laid down in the Covenant and in the European Convention.[1] On the other hand, the

---

[1] Of the other CSCE states, only two mini-states, the Holy See and Monaco remain outside both the Covenant and European Convention systems.

United States puts emphasis on the paramount importance of civil and political rights and respects them in practice, even though it does not agree with a number of formulations of civil and political rights in the Covenant (*American Journal of International Law*, vol. 72 (1978), pp. 620–31). Disagreements between the United States and the ratifiers of the Covenant and of the European Convention concerning the content of civil and political rights cannot be characterized as comprehensive and thorough. The chances of identifying many commonly acceptable standards appear to be relatively good, as was proved by the Vienna Follow-up Meeting of the CSCE.

As regards those CSCE states which have not ratified the Covenant on Economic, Social and Cultural Rights, a number of them have ratified the European Social Charter, the scope of which is the same as that of the Covenant. However, the United States, Switzerland and Turkey are bound by neither of these two conventions. These three states are very critical of economic, social and cultural rights as *legal* rights of individuals. Several other Western states are critical of economic and social rights as legal rights, and as the current economic problems of a number of Eastern European states complicate the realization of such rights, it appears that the identification of standards of economic and social rights in the CSCE area is a difficult task. On the other hand, there is no sharp distinction between, on the one hand, economic, social and cultural rights and, on the other hand, civil and political rights; for example, the 1979 Convention on the Elimination of All Forms of Discrimination against Women lays down obligations *vis-à-vis* both categories of human rights and many ILO conventions create strict obligations *vis-à-vis* economic and social rights.[2]

In Tables 13.1 and 13.2, nearly all ILO conventions and conventions dealing with the prohibition of discrimination have been ratified by relatively many CSCE states. However, the United States has not ratified any of them.

As regards the conventions dealing with international crimes, the Genocide Convention has been ratified by a great majority of the CSCE states. Also the Convention Against the Taking of Hostages (1979) and the Convention against Torture (1984) have been received fairly well; apparently these two conventions will receive some more ratifications from CSCE states in the early 1990s. It should also be noted that among those CSCE states which have not ratified the Convention Against the Taking of Hostages nearly all member states of the Council of Europe have assumed obligations against the taking of hostages in the 1977 European Convention on the Sup-

---

[2] Nieminen, 1990, pp. 467 et seq., and 489–91; Tomuschat, 1985, pp. 549–560; Sulkunen, 1988; Karapuu and Rosas, 1988; de Zayas *et al.*, 1989, pp. 447–9, and UNGA resolution 130/32 (1977).

pression of Terrorism,[3] and that torture and cruel, inhuman or degrading treatment or punishment are prohibited in absolute terms both by the Covenant on Civil and Political Rights and by the European Convention on Human Rights. It is evident that the prohibitions of genocide, the taking of hostages, torture and cruel treatment or punishment are norms of *jus cogens* in universal international law (Hannikainen, 1988, pp. 456–513).

The 1968 Convention on the Non-applicability of Statutory Limitations to War Crimes and Crimes Against Humanity has been ratified only by states with a socialist orientation, i.e. by the seven Warsaw Pact states and Yugoslavia. After their rejection of that convention, the members of the Council of Europe prepared in 1974 the European Convention on the Non-applicabiliy of Statutory Limitations to Crimes against Humanity, but this Convention has not entered into force as it has only been ratified by one country. Thus, it appears that CSCE states can reach only a very narrow agreement on the non-applicability of statutory limitations to international crimes.[4]

As regards the conventions concerning refugees and stateless persons, the group of Warsaw Pact states has abstained from ratification. However, Hungary became an exception in 1989, when it ratified the 1951 Refugee Convention and its 1966 Protocol. Almost all NATO states and neutral or non-aligned states have ratified the Refugee Convention and Protocol. On the other hand, the two conventions on stateless persons have received only limited support among CSCE states; clearly less than half of CSCE states have ratified them. None of the Warsaw Pact states have ratified these conventions on stateless persons.

It is to be hoped that in the 1990s Warsaw Pact states will take a more positive attitude towards the Refugee Convention and its Protocol. Politically this seems feasible, but economic difficulties in Warsaw Pact states may discourage ratification. Besides, in some Warsaw Pact states the government has had difficulties in controlling national tensions; the hostilities have forced many persons to flee either to another part of the state or abroad. In any case, it would be reasonable for Warsaw Pact states to assume more responsibility in relieving the world refugee problem.

All CSCE states have ratified the four 1949 Geneva Conventions on the protection of war victims. The Geneva Conventions, with their nearly universal ratification (167 states), form the basis of humanitarian law both in the universal context and in the context of the

---

[3] Thus, among CSCE states other than mini-states only Malta, Poland and Romania are outside both of these two conventions banning the taking of hostages. See Tupamäki, 1989.

[4] Furthermore, the Soviet Union, a party to the 1968 Convention, recently granted a general amnesty to all those guilty of crimes committed during the Second World War, including those guilty of war crimes and crimes against humanity.

CSCE. As regards the 1977 Additional Protocols, which endeavour to regulate modern warfare, more ratifications by CSCE states are needed. The Additional Protocols have received many ratifications in 1988–89; thus one may hope, and even expect, more ratifications in the near future. The Soviet Union and Hungary were the first Warsaw Pact states to ratify the Additional Protocols (in 1989); some other Warsaw Pact states may ratify the Additional Protocols soon. More ratifications are needed from NATO states. It is especially regrettable that leading NATO states have abstained from ratification.[5]

As regards Table 13.3 on ratification of major human rights conventions of the Council of Europe by its 23 member states, all member states have ratified the European Convention on Human Rights. One may note that nearly all NATO states (minus the United States and Canada) and neutral or non-aligned states (minus Yugoslavia) are members of the Council of Europe.

The European Convention on Human Rights is certainly the primary international source of human rights standards in Western Europe. One may note that as far as different civil and political rights are concerned, the European Convention does not add much to the Covenant on Civil and Political Rights. On the contrary, it guarantees a smaller number of rights than does the Covenant. However, from the perspective of the CSCE, it is significant that most of those CSCE states which have not ratified the Covenant have ratified the European Convention.

As regards the Protocols of the European Convention on Human Rights, only three member states have not ratified Protocol No. 1. This Protocol guarantees the right to own private property and the right to education. It also sets forth an obligation for states to arrange free elections by secret ballot at reasonable intervals. All three non-ratifying states, Spain, Switzerland and Liechtenstein, observe quite well the provisions of the Protocol in practice. During the 1990s the provisions of Protocol No. 1 will probably gain increasing significance in the CSCE area. Warsaw Pact states will pay increasing respect towards the right to own private property and it is likely that one of the basic values of the Council of Europe, parliamentary democracy with multi-party elections, will become the model also in Eastern Europe and, thus, in the entire CSCE area.[6] The standards of Protocol No. 1 go beyond those established in the Covenant on Civil and Political Rights.

Protocol No. 4 guarantees, *inter alia*, freedom of movement and residence and prohibits the expulsion of nationals and the collective expulsion of aliens. The prohibition of collective expulsion of aliens is

---

[5] Of the United States, the United Kingdom, France, and the Federal Republic of Germany, only France deposited a ratification, to Additional Protocol II in 1984.

[6] See the Final Document of the Bonn CSCE Conference on Economic Cooperation in Europe, April 1990.

important, because in many Western European states there are great numbers of migrant workers and there have been calls in these states for the expulsion of alien workers. A number of member states of the Council of Europe have not ratified Protocol No. 4, but they may none the less have obligations concerning the expulsion of alien/migrant workers arising from ratifications of Protocol No. 7, the Covenant on Civil and Political Rights, the 1977 European Convention on the Legal Status of Migrant Workers, or the European Social Charter. However, because of the danger of a rise in anti-alien sentiments in European states, it may be advisable for future CSCE meetings to consider the matter of the legal guarantees of aliens against expulsion. In the same context, the CSCE should be concerned with the expulsion of nationals representing minorities in violation of human rights conventions — a real problem especially in Bulgaria.

As regards Protocol No. 6 concerning the abolition of the death penalty, this subject matter is dealt with in Chapter 6 (Orlin) above.

Protocol No. 7 offers legal guarantees against the arbitrary expulsion of aliens, lists a number of legal guarantees to persons convicted or acquitted for a criminal offence and endeavours to ensure the equality of spouses, subjects to the interests of their children. Only about half the member states have ratified this Protocol.

Spain, Turkey, the United Kingdom and Malta have left several of the above-mentioned Protocols unratified. Of these states, Turkey and Malta are not parties to the Covenant on Civil and Political Rights.[7]

Conclusions

1. Because most CSCE states have ratified a great number of human rights conventions, these conventions form a good basis for identifying and creating CSCE human rights standards. However, more ratifications are needed.
2. It is likely that in the years to come Warsaw Pact states will ratify more human rights conventions and that they will observe their obligations under human rights conventions more faithfully.
3. The importance of the human rights instruments of the Council of Europe as sources of CSCE human rights standards is bound to grow and contribute to both the development and specification of CSCE human rights standards.
4. The United States should ratify more human rights conventions.

---

[7] Liechtenstein has ratified none of the four substantive Protocols. However, its record of assuming human rights obligations is better than the record of some other mini-states, such as the Holy See and Monaco which are neither members of the Council of Europe nor have ratified the Covenant on Civil and Political Rights. Liechtenstein has ratified the European Convention on Human Rights.

Other CSCE states should engage in a comprehensive dialogue
with the United States on the human rights standards within the
CSCE.

4. Reservations

Most of the conventions listed in Tables 13.1 to 13.3 either specifically
permit reservations or make no reference to this mechanism at all.
States have made reservations to conventions which are silent on the
matter. This practice corresponds to the prevailing rule, laid down in
Article 19 of the 1969 Vienna Convention on the Law of Treaties,
stipulating that when a treaty is silent on reservations, states are
entitled to formulate a reservation unless it is incompatible with the
object and purpose of the treaty (Horn, 1988, pp. 109–20, and Sinclair,
1983, pp. 61–3). On the other hand, the right to make reservations to
ILO conventions is very limited (*Official Bulletin of the International
Labour Organization*, 1951, pp. 274–312 and Valticos, 1979, p. 229)
and therefore reservations to ILO conventions will not be discussed
in this chapter.

It does not appear advisable to make a chart on reservations by
CSCE states to human rights conventions, because (1) it is not
always easy to say whether a state has made a real reservation or
just an interpretative declaration,[8] and (2) many reservations are
of minor significance in the context of the CSCE.

We are here concerned only with reservations to the limited number
of conventions which can be regarded as most important among
human rights conventions. In these conventions, we are concerned
only with reservations to those articles which formulate different
human rights; reservations refusing to submit to international supervision or to compulsory judicial settlement will be examined later in
the chapter.

Obligations of states under human rights conventions and, consequently, reservations to human rights conventions, do not have the
reciprocal character that characterizes many other kinds of international treaties.[9] This implies that a reservation by a State

---

[8]   According to Article 2 (1(d)) of the 1969 Vienna Convention on the Law of Treaties,
'reservation' means a unilateral statement, however phrased or named, made by a
state, signing, ratifying, accepting, approving or acceding to a treaty, whereby it
purports to exclude or modify the legal effect of certain provisions of the treaty in
their application to that state.

[9]   Statements to this effect have been made by the American Court of Human Rights in
its Advisory Opinion on The Effect of Reservations, OC-2/82, Series A, No. 2,
paragraphs 29–33; The European Court of Human Rights in the *Lawless* Case, Publ.
E.C.H.R., Series A, vol. 2, paragraph 239; the European Commission of Human
Rights admissibility decision on Application No. 788/60 (*Austria v. Italy*), *Yearbook
of the European Convention on Human Rights*, 1961, pp. 138 and 140; and the
International Court of Justice in its Advisory Opinion on the Reservations to the
Genocide Convention, *International Court of Justice; Reports of Judgments,
Advisory Opinions and Orders*, 1951, p. 23.

Party to a human right convention does not cause other States Parties to deny the treaty relationship between them and the reserving state. Indeed, Horn states in his study on reservations and interpretative declarations to conventions that human rights conventions belong to the group of conventions in relation to which other States Parties have rarely objected to reservations (Horn, 1988, pp. 189–90). However, objections are possible if a reservation is of such a character that it might be considered incompatible with the object and purpose of a treaty or if a reservation infringes, for one reason or another, the interests or values of other states. This matter will be considered further below, as will the following questions:

1. To which of the provisions of human rights conventions have substantial reservations been made by CSCE states, in particular, to which provisions have reservations been made by several or many states?
2. Have ratifying states later withdrawn their reservations?

Among those 26 CSCE states which have ratified the *International Covenant on Civil and Political Rights*, no Warsaw Pact states have made reservations. However, thirteen Western states have done so,[10] all having made at least three reservations and some having made as many as ten. These reserving states are among those states which have submitted their system of civil and political rights protection to international supervision.

The reservations to the Covenant formulated by Western states cover a number of provisions, the most common being the following:

(a) to Article 10 (2) and 10 (3), dictating that juvenile persons should be separated from adults in detention and in prison and accused persons should be segregated from convicted persons;
(b) to Article 14, ensuring adequate judicial guarantees to persons charged with crimes (the reservations to Article 14 are in general fairly narrow: they do not seriously jeopardize a fair trial);
(c) to Article 20 (1), prohibiting any propaganda for war. (The nine reserving CSCE states have referred to the paramount importance of freedom of expression. On the other hand, a number of other Western CSCE states have not made any reservations to Article 20 (1). The position of France is somewhat ambiguous, but its statement regarding Article 20 (1) appears to be more like an interpretative declaration than a reservation.)[11]

---

[10] Information regarding reservations, including the texts of reservations, to the conventions prepared within the framework of the UN can be found in the yearly publication 'Multilateral Treaties Deposited with the Secretary-General, Status as at 31 December (year)'.
[11] France stated that the term 'war' in Article 20 (1) 'is to be understood to mean war in contravention of international law and considers, in any case, that French legislation in this matter is adequate'.

Three states (Finland, the Netherlands, Norway) have withdrawn some of the reservations they had lodged when ratifying the Covenant. It is regrettable that most of the reserving states have not withdrawn any of their fairly numerous reservations.

None of the CSCE states has objected to any reservation to the Covenant made by another CSCE state.

There are so many reservations to the Political Covenant that it hardly is an exaggeration to conclude that the reservations gnaw away at several of the standards it creates.

CSCE states have made only a few reservations to the *International Covenant on Economic, Social and Cultural Rights*. The reason for the small number of reservations appears to be that many states understand the Covenant as an instrument laying down guidelines and programmatic obligations rather than strict legal obligations. Thus, many States Parties have not been concerned about inconsistencies between their domestic laws and the Covenant, at least if the inconsistencies have not been significant.

Warsaw Pact states have been the strongest advocates of the obligatory character of the Covenant; they have made no reservations.

Several Western states have made reservations to Article 4 of the *International Convention on the Elimination of All Forms of Racial Discrimination*, that Article prohibiting propaganda for racial discrimination. The reason for these reservations is the paramount importance of freedom of expression. Some reserving states have appealed in strong words for freedom of expression, some others have lodged comparatively narrow reservations. On the other hand, none of the Western states has made any reservations to Article 20 (2) of the Covenant on Civil and Political Rights, which prohibits any advocacy of national, racial or religious hatred that constitutes incitement to discrimination. The reason is that the prohibition in Article 20 (2) of the Covenant is more narrow than that in Article 4 of the Convention on Racial Discrimination.

Denmark has withdrawn one minor reservation.

None of the CSCE states has objected to any reservation to the Racial Discrimination Convention by another CSCE state.

Many Western states have made a limited number of reservations to the *Convention on the Elimination of All Forms of Discrimination Against Women*. Some five or six states have made reservations which appear to be based on the idea of traditional patriarchal relationship between men and women. A number of states have made reservations in favour of protective treatment of women. The absence of equality in the armed forces is the object of several reservations.

Two states (France, Ireland) have withdrawn some reservations.

None of the CSCE states has objected to any reservation to the Women's Convention by another CSCE state.

When the United States ratified the *Genocide Convention* in 1988, it made a reservation as follows: 'nothing in the Convention requires or authorizes legislation or other action by the United States of America prohibited by the Constitution of the United States as interpreted by the United States'. Eight Western States declared in December 1989 their objections to this reservation (UN doc. C.N.342.1989). Among them were the United Kingdom and Italy; furthermore, in March 1990 also the Federal Republic of Germany objected to the reservation (UN doc. C.N.12.1990). The message of the objections was, in the words of Denmark, Finland, Norway and Sweden, that 'this reservation is subject to the general principle of treaty interpretation according to which a party may not invoke the provisions of its internal law as justification for failure to perform a treaty'. The objections have a solid basis in international law, *inter alia*, Article 27 of the Vienna Convention on the Law of Treaties and several judgments of the Permanent Court of International Justice.[12] Wher-eas in practice the reservation of the United States hardly will lead to any violation of the Genocide Convention, the reservation is inconsistent with international law and should, thus, be withdrawn.

Western states have lodged only a few reservations to the *1949 Geneva Conventions on the protection of war victims*.[13] The United States and the Netherlands have made identical reservations to Article 68 (2) of Geneva Convention IV relative to the Protection of Civilian Persons in Time of War. The reservation is formulated in the following way:

[The State] reserves the right to impose the death penalty in accordance with the provisions of Article 68, paragraph 2, without regard whether the offences referred to therein are punishable by death under the law of the occupied territory at the time the occupation begins.

All the Warsaw Pact states have made virtually identical reservations to the Geneva Conventions. In regard to Article 12 of Geneva Convention III relative to the Treatment of Prisoners of War and Article 45 of Geneva Convention IV, the Warsaw Pact states do not consider it to be legal that a power which effects a transfer of prisoners of war or civilians is freed from its responsibility to apply the Conventions, even for the time during which such prisoners of war or civilians are in the custody of the power accepting them. In regard to Article 85 of Geneva Convention III, the Warsaw Pact states do not consider it to be legal that prisoners of war convicted of war crimes and crimes against humanity in accordance with the Nuremberg principles should enjoy the protection of the Convention.

---

[12] Reports of the Permanent Court of International Justice, the *Free Zones Case*, Ser. A/B, No. 46, p. 167 (1932), and the *Greco-Bulgarian Communities Case*, Ser. B, No. 17, p. 32 (1930). See also Brownlie, 1979, pp. 36–8.

[13] Information regarding the reservations, including the texts of reservations, to the 1949 Geneva Conventions and to their 1977 Additional Protocols can be found in Schindler and Toman, 1988, pp. 563–94 and 704–18.

In their view, such prisoners of war must be subject to the regulations in force in the detaining state for the execution of punishment.

When signing the Geneva Convention, several Western states made reservations. Most of these reservations were withdrawn either at the time of ratification or later.

The United States has objected to the reservations made by the Warsaw Pact states. However, the United States nevertheless accepts the treaty relationship between itself and the Warsaw Pact states, except as to the changes proposed by their reservations.

Several NATO states have made one very substantial reservation to *Additional Protocol I of the 1949 Geneva Conventions on the protection of war victims* upon their ratification or signing of the Additional Protocol. According to these states, Additional Protocol I applies only to the use of conventional weapons; its provisions do not apply to the use of nuclear weapons and other weapons of mass destruction (on the relevancy of this reservation in critical terms, see Hannikainen, 1988, pp. 615-21 and 680-86). Among the states expressing this view on signing the Protocol are two nuclear powers: the United States and the United Kingdom, neither of which has yet ratified the instrument.

Many of the Western states which have ratified Additional Protocol I have lodged reservations or interpretative declarations, in relation to Articles 51-58 and Article 75 in particular.

In 1989, the first Warsaw Pact states ratified the Additional Protocols: the Soviet Union, Hungary and Bulgaria. It is interesting to note that these states did not make any reservations to the Additional Protocols. This is especially significant in the case of the Soviet Union: this nuclear power did not state that Additional Protocol I would be applicable only to the use of conventional weapons. The Soviet Union's ratification of Additional Protocol I is an affirmative step and a positive offer to the nuclear powers of NATO.

CSCE states have lodged virtually no reservations to Additional Protocol II, which is much shorter than Additional Protocol I.

As far as we know, no reservations to the Additional Protocols have been withdrawn by the CSCE states and no party to the Additional Protocols has objected to the reservations by another party.

Western European states have made fewer reservations to the *European Convention on Human Rights* and to its four Protocols[14] than to the Covenant on Civil and Political Rights. This is due to the fact that whereas the Covenant is the product of three blocs of states

---

[14] Information regarding the reservations, including the texts of reservations, to the European Convention on Human Rights and to its Protocols can be found in 'European Convention on Human Rights', *Collected Texts*, Dordrecht, 1987: Nijhoff Publishers, pp. 76-99.

— Western, socialist and non-aligned (Third World) — the European Convention is entirely the product of Western thinking.

Many reservations have been made to the provisions dealing with the rights of persons who are deprived of their liberty by arrest or detention or who are charged with, or convicted of, a criminal offence (Articles 5 and 6 of the Convention and Articles 2–4 of Protocol No. 7; see also Frowein, 1988, pp. 194–5). These reservations gnaw away at the standards created by the Convention and by Protocol No. 7.

Several reservations have also been made to Article 2 of Protocol No. 1, according to which the state shall respect the right of parents to ensure such education and teaching in conformity with their own religious and philosophical convictions. Some of the reservations to this Article stress that the state does not consent to any 'unreasonable public expenditure' to guarantee the right of the parents.

There are also a number of reservations to several other provisions of the European Convention and its Protocols.

There have been declarations, which might be considered to have the character of objections, to one reservation, that of Portugal's in regard to Article 1 of Protocol No. 1. This Article guarantees the right to own private property, but also permits the expropriation of private property in the public interest and subject to the conditions provided for by law and by the general principles of international law. Portugal's reservation, referring to Article 82 of its Constitution, went so far as to state that expropriations of the property of large landowners, big property owners and entrepreneurs or shareholders may be subject to *no* compensation under the conditions laid down by Portuguese law. The Federal Republic of Germany, France and the United Kingdom declared that Portugal's reservation could not affect the general principle of international law which require prompt, adequate and effective compensation in respect of expropriation of foreign property (*Yearbook of the European Convention on Human Rights*, 1979, pp. 16–23, and Imbert, 1981, pp. 37–8). There has been a deep disagreement between Western states and socialist states on the contents of international law in regard to the question of compensation in respect of expropriation of foreign property. It remains to be seen whether the political changes in Eastern European states will lead to the approach of the Eastern European view to the Western view. As yet, it is difficult to identify a CSCE standard on this question.

In 1988, the European Court of Human Rights declared invalid a Swiss reservation to Article 6 of the European Convention, because the reservation was too vague and broad to satisfy the criteria which Article 64 of the Convention requires of reservations (*Belilos v. Switzerland*, E.C.H.R., Series A., vol. 132; see Bourgnignon, 1989). Article 64 stipulates that reservations of a general character shall not be permitted and that any reservation made shall contain a brief statement of the domestic law concerned. In the light of the judgment of the European Court, only reservations of limited and precise scope appear to be valid (MacDonald, 1988, p. 450; Cameron, 1988; Imbert, 1981, pp. 33-4). New members of the Council of Europe know that they can make only limited and precise reservations to the Convention and its Protocols.

Only a few reservations to the European Convention on Human Rights or to its four Protocols have been withdrawn later: Greece and Switzerland have both withdrawn one reservation. There have been fewer withdrawals of reservations than one might expect.

5. Observations on reservations

Our general assessment regarding reservations by CSCE states to the human rights conventions listed in Tables 13.1 to 13.3 is that Western states have made a considerable number of reservations. In the face of this fact it is advisable to remind Western states that in the course of time states should withdraw at least most of their reservations to human rights conventions. In the case of some conventions, many reservations have been withdrawn by Western states (the 1949 Geneva Conventions and the 1951 Refugee Convention), but in the case of many conventions only a very limited number of reservations have been withdrawn. Thus, the question of withdrawal of reservations to human rights conventions has to be given international attention.

Warsaw Pact states have made only a small number of reservations to human rights conventions. The problem of their performance of obligations under these conventions suggests, however, that Warsaw Pact states should perhaps have made more reservations. The virtual absence of reservations is at present a matter of considerable importance, when most Warsaw Pact states appear to be in the process of taking their human rights obligations much more seriously than before. Thus, when drafting new laws — and many new laws have been passed in recent years and apparently many more will be passed in the near future — Warsaw Pact states will have to pay serious attention to their numerous obligations under human rights conventions. It is also interesting to note that although Warsaw Pact states have been active in ratifying more human rights conventions in 1987-89, they have retained the tendency not to make reservations.

Only a limited number of reservations can be labelled outright as important in the CSCE context. One may regard as important at least the reservations (1) concerning the non-applicability of Additional Protocol I of the Geneva Conventions to the use of nuclear weapons and other weapons of mass destruction, (2) emphasizing the freedom of expression in the Covenant on Civil and Political Rights and in the Convention on Racial Discrimination, and (3) perpetuating ideas of traditional patriarchal relationships between men and women in the Convention on Discrimination Against Women.

As regards reservations concerning the non-applicability of Additional Protocol I to the use of nuclear weapons, even though this matter is of great concern from the perspective of human rights, e.g. the right to life, the reservations have been declared to be vital for the security interests of the reserving NATO states. Apparently only significant progress in disarmament might persuade the reserving NATO states to accept the applicability of Additional Protocol I to the use of nuclear weapons and other weapons of mass destruction.

As regards reservations to the obligation of states to prohibit by law any propaganda for war (Article 20 (1) of the Covenant on Civil and Political Rights), many Western states have thought that this categorical provision might unduly restrict the freedom of expression and that it is contrary to their constitutional, legal and traditional rules guaranteeing free speech (see Chapter 4 (Dimitrijevic) above). Would it not be sufficient for the purposes of Article 20 (1) that a party should prohibit any propaganda for aggressive war which is capable of influencing public opinion to favour aggressive war either in a crisis situation or in a situation where the threat of a crisis is evident? Thus, dangerous propaganda would be prohibited and the reserving states could hardly claim any more that the freedom of expression would be unduly restricted.

In one of the reserving states, Finland, a provision has been included in the new draft penal code criminalizing propaganda for aggressive war in an international political crisis involving Finland or in a situation where the threat of such a crisis is *immediate*, because in these situations propaganda for aggressive war *clearly* increases the danger of Finland's being drawn into war or into being the target of an act of war. The draft provision criminalizes both propaganda which calls upon another state to attack Finland and propaganda calling upon Finland to attack another state (*Rikoslain kokonaisuudistus II*, 1989, pp. 99–105 and 752). Whereas it is welcome that the draft provision criminalizes propaganda for aggressive war in both ways — another state's attack against Finland and a possible Finnish attack against another state — some of the criteria of the draft provision appear to be too restrictive. For example, it is too restrictive for the purposes of Article 20 (1) of the Covenant that the threat of a crisis must be immediate and that propaganda for aggressive war must clearly increase the danger of Finland's being drawn into war (Hannikainen, 1984, pp. 172–8). For the purpose of Article 20 (1), it would perhaps be sufficient to change the draft provision into a less restrictive one, so that the threat of a crisis needs not to be *immediate* but only *evident*, and that the (widespread) propaganda for aggressive war must be capable, without doing it *clearly*, of increasing the danger that Finland might be drawn into war. Such changes having been made, Finland might consider withdrawing its reservation to Article 20 (1).

As regards reservations to the Convention on Discrimination Against Women based on the idea of traditional patriarchal relationships between men and women, they are not consistent with the human rights standards of the CSCE. The CSCE could well pay attention to this matter. The reservations in question should be withdrawn.

It is a widely accepted principle in present day international law that reservations to human rights conventions have to be read narrowly. This is stated, for example, by the Inter-American Court of Human Rights and the Inter-American Commission on Human Rights.[15] The reason is that since individuals and groups are the beneficiaries of human rights conventions, these conventions shall not be interpreted detrimentally to them. In addition, since it is prohibited to make reservations incompatible with the object and purpose of conventions, most reservations to human rights conventions are of only limited significance. However, the existence of many reservations complicates the creation and identification of human rights standards within the CSCE. It is in the interest of the CSCE to stress that states should withdraw any reservations which clearly complicate the creation and identification of human rights standards within the CSCE.

6. Consent of CSCE states to international monitoring, supervision and dispute settlement

Nearly all human rights conventions listed in Tables 13.1 and 13.2 provide for procedures of international monitoring or supervision of the observance of the convention concerned or procedures for the international settlement of disputes. It is important that States Parties consent to international monitoring, supervision and dispute settlement, because their acceptance of such mechanisms makes it more difficult for them to act contrary to their obligations under human rights conventions than if they choose not to submit to those international procedures.

It has been noted above that all the 23 member states of the Council of Europe have ratified the European Convention on Human Rights. The European Convention provides for an individual complaints procedure to the European Commission of Human Rights. Complaints may be brought from the Commission to the European Court of Human Rights for compulsory judgment or to the Committee of Ministers for a compulsory decision. The other international procedure is the procedure of inter-state complaints, which may also lead from the Commission to the Court or to the Committee of Ministers for compulsory judgment/decision. These procedures of international supervision and dispute settlement have operated

---

[15] Regarding the Court, see *International Legal Materials*, 1981, p. 1424, and regarding the Commission, see doc. OC/83, Series B, No. 3, pp. 12-13. See also Buergenthal, 1985, pp. 19-20.

relatively well. The procedure of individual complaints has been resorted to actively by individual persons from different States Parties to the European Convention (*Stock-taking on the European Convention on Human Rights*, Supplement 1988, Council of Europe, 1989, pp. 99–118).

However, the ratification of the European Convention does not mean that the ratifying state is automatically bound by the individual complaints procedure and by the compulsory jurisdiction of the European Court of Human Rights. Separate expressions of acceptance are required by Articles 25 and 46 of the Convention. By the beginning of 1990, the parties to the European Convention and to its four Protocols have accepted the two optional procedures with few exceptions. All the 23 parties to the European Convention have now accepted both optional procedures *vis-à-vis* the Convention. The few exceptions are the following: Turkey has limited with a reservation the right of individuals from Turkey to make complaints to the European Commission,[16] and a few States Parties to Protocols 4 (Cyprus) and 7 (Greece, Luxembourg) have not accepted the optional procedures *vis-à-vis* those Protocols.

Thus, before we proceed to examine international monitoring, supervision and dispute settlement procedures under those human rights conventions which are open to ratification to all the states of the CSCE, we are already prepared to conclude that the states of the Council of Europe have displayed their determination to take seriously their obligations under the European Convention on Human Rights and its Protocols by submitting to the international supervision and dispute settlement procedures provided by the Convention.

The following kinds of international monitoring, supervisory and dispute settlement procedures can be found in the human rights conventions listed in Tables 13.1 and 13.2:

— Under many conventions, disputes between States Parties relating to the convention concerned are submitted either to arbitration or to compulsory settlement by the International Court of Justice, or just to compulsory settlement by the Court.

— The ILO has its own system of supervision of the observance of ILO conventions and of the settlement of disputes. Acceptance of this system is in most ways compulsory for the parties to the different ILO conventions.

— Certain important human rights conventions take as the primary or only form of international monitoring or supervision the obligation of the parties to report to an international organ on the measures they have adopted in order to give effect to the rights

---

[16] Since Turkey's reservation was subject to criticism in the light of the Belilos case (see Cameron, 1988, and Bourguignon, 1989), Turkey modified the reservation on 9 March, 1990.

recognized in the human rights convention concerned and on the progress made in the enjoyment of those rights. These conventions include the two Covenants of 1966, the Convention on Racial Discrimination, the Convention on the Discrimination Against Women, and the Torture Convention. The international organs concerned have only limited and recommendatory powers to respond to state reports. For example, as yet, they have not directly criticized individual reporting states for apparent violations of human rights. However, the development of these procedures is leading to the expression of concluding observations on individual state reports by persons who are members of the various international monitoring bodies.

Under the Covenant on Economic, Social and Cultural Rights (and the European Social Charter) state reports to the appropriate international organ and its issuing recommendations on the reports is the only form of international monitoring and supervision. In the Convention on Discrimination Against Women, there is also a second international procedure: settlement of disputes between the parties by arbitration or in a compulsory way by the International Court of Justice. The other three conventions mentioned here provide additional procedures, as can be seen below.

— The Covenant on Civil and Political Rights has two additional international procedures both of which are optional. Thus, the States Parties do not submit to them just by ratifying the Covenant. The first is provided for in Article 41: inter-state complaints to the Human Rights Committee. The second is provided for in the Optional Protocol to the Covenant: individual complaints to the Human Rights Committee. In its handling of complaints under these two procedures the Human Rights Committee has only recommendatory powers.

— In addition to the submission of state reports to the Committee on Racial Discrimination, the Convention on Racial Discrimination provides for three other international procedures:
  1. inter-state complaints: every State Party submits to this procedure automatically on ratification of the Convention;
  2. individual complaints: parties may accept this optional procedure through a separate notification (Article 14);
  3. settlement of disputes between parties by the International Court of Justice.

In the case of procedures 1 and 2, the Committee on Racial Discrimination has only recommendatory powers; in the case of procedure 3, the Court has compulsory jurisdiction.

— The Torture Convention has procedures concerning international supervision and settlement of disputes similar to those of the

Convention on Racial Discrimination, except that submission to the system of inter-state complaints to the Committee on Torture is optional, i.e. dependent on a separate notification.

— No international organ has been granted the authority to supervise the observance of the 1949 Geneva Conventions on the protection of war victims, even though the International Committee of the Red Cross (ICRC) in practice acts as the guardian of the observance of these conventions. However, because the supervisory work of the ICRC is unofficial, it is beyond the scope of this chapter. Instead, it is advisable to discuss the attitudes of CSCE states towards the International Fact-Finding Commission of Article 90 of Additional Protocol I of the Geneva Conventions. This Commission has competence with regard to those States Parties of Additional Protocol I which have given a separate notification accepting the competence of the Commission to inquire into any facts alleged to be grave breaches of the Geneva Conventions or of the Protocol and to facilitate, through its good offices, the restoration of an attitude of respect for these instruments. A party naturally gives its acceptance to the competence of the Fact-Finding Commission only reciprocally *vis-à-vis* those parties which have given a similar notification of acceptance. The Commission has only recommendatory powers.

To answer the question to what extent have the CSCE states consented to international monitoring, supervision and dispute settlement procedures provided by human rights conventions, it is particularly important to examine the extent to which the CSCE states have consented to *optional* procedures. A number of international procedures are not optional, but all *individual complaints* procedures dealt with here are optional. In practice, individual complaints procedures have been vital; individuals have actively claimed states have violated their rights.

On the other hand, *inter-state complaints* to international organs supervising the observance of human rights conventions have been rare. Thus, for example, the International Court of Justice has only relatively seldom dealt with human rights. However, it would be incorrect to say that the procedures set forth in human rights conventions for handling inter-state complaints and disputes are of minor significance and need not be dealt with here. CSCE states have adopted different approaches when deciding whether or not to consent to international procedures provided by human rights conventions for the settlement of inter-state disputes. For example, a number of states have lodged reservations denying the compulsory jurisdiction of the International Court of Justice. The Warsaw Pact states did consistently so prior to the glasnost period.

Thus, in Table 13.4 we have listed two types of international monitoring, supervisory and dispute settlement procedures provided by human rights conventions: optional procedures and compulsory settlement of disputes by the International Court of Justice (ICJ). On the other hand, Table 13.4 does not include procedures followed under ILO Conventions, as these conventions provide the States Parties with a very restricted range of options *vis-à-vis* ILO procedures of monitoring, supervision and dispute settlement.

Table 13.4 examines the CSCE states' submission to fourteen international procedures. The Chart lists the acceptances and refusals of each of the 35 CSCE states of the procedures of those conventions which they have ratified.[17] The CSCE states are grouped again into four groups as in Table 13.1.

7. Observations on the consent of CSCE states to international monitoring, supervisory and dispute settlement procedures

1. The first general observation to be made of Table 13.4 is that NATO states and neutral or non-aligned states have taken a positive attitude towards international monitoring, supervision and dispute settlement procedures provided by human rights conventions. The second general observation to be made is that among the Warsaw Pact states there have recently emerged a number of acceptances from the earlier policy of rejections. The third general observation is that although the mini-states have only a limited number of acceptances, there are nevertheless more acceptances than rejections.

2. A closer look at NATO states reveals that they have a positive attitude towards the compulsory jurisdiction of the International Court of Justice in human rights matters. One can find three reservations to the Court's jurisdiction. One of these reservations raises some worries, the reservation of the United States to the Genocide Convention. The United States, which had earlier taken a positive attitude towards the Court's compulsory jurisdiction, denounced some years ago its submission to the Court's compulsory jurisdiction (*American Journal of International Law*, 1986, pp. 163–5), when it became evident that the Court would condemn its activities against Nicaragua (as the Court, indeed, did; see *International Court of Justice: Reports of Judgments, Advisory Opinions and Orders*, 1986, p. 14ff.) When the United States ratified the Genocide Convention in 1988, it demonstrated

---

[17] In Table 13.4 the acceptance by CSCE states of the jurisdiction of the Committee on Torture to handle inter-state complaints (under Article 21) and individual complaints (under Article 22) are recorded in one single column. This solution was adopted, because only one state (the United Kingdom) has accepted only one of the two procedures. This one case is marked as follows: +/no and signifies that the United Kingdom accepted the inter-state complaint procedure but not the individual complaint procedure.

its cold attitude towards the Court by lodging a reservation. (The reservation itself is not without problems; see paragraph 6 below.)

Table 13.4 records quite many rejections of optional procedures by NATO states. Many NATO states have refused to accept the individual complaints procedure under the Convention on Racial Discrimination. As far as the limited number of rejections of the optional procedures of the Covenant on Civil and Political Rights are concerned, the rejecting NATO states have accepted effective international supervision of civil and political rights in the European Convention on Human Rights.

3. The record of the neutral or non-aligned states in Table 13.4 is quite similar as that of the NATO states. However, none of the neutral or non-aligned states have lodged any reservations to the compulsory jurisdiction of the International Court of Justice. Because Yugoslavia is not a party to the European Convention on Human Rights, Yugoslavia's acceptance of the optional supervision procedures of the Covenant on Civil and Political Rights would be welcome.

4. A general assessment of the acceptance by Western states of international monitoring, supervision and settlement of disputes procedures provided by human rights conventions is clearly positive — a weighty indication that Western states, or at least a great majority of them, take their obligations under human rights conventions seriously. The three Scandinavian states have accepted all the fourteen procedures of Table 13.4; many others reach at least ten acceptances. On the other hand, the United States, Turkey, Malta and Cyprus have accepted less than half of the procedures listed in Table 13.4. These states should move towards accepting a greater number of these procedures.

5. Although most Warsaw Pact states have not yet accepted many of the procedures listed in Table 13.4, Hungary has accepted eleven of them. Hungary has recently accepted various optional procedures and accepted the compulsory jurisdiction of the International Court of Justice under several human rights conventions, in some cases by withdrawing its earlier reservations to the Court's compulsory jurisdiction. The Soviet Union is also improving its record of acceptances. Of its five acceptances to date, four accept the compulsory jurisdiction of the International Court of Justice, the result of withdrawals of earlier reservations. The fifth acceptance is a most remarkable one: the Soviet Union is the first and only military power, i.e. a state with a strong army, to accept the competence of the International Fact-Finding Commission under Article 90 of Additional Protocol I of the 1949 Geneva Conventions.

It seems apparent that the record of acceptances of the Warsaw Pact states will look quite different five years from now, the number of acceptances outnumbering the number of rejections.

6. It is not common for CSCE states to object to the reservations by

Table 13.4 CSCE states: acceptance of international supervision and dispute settlement (by state)

	NATO states									
	Bel	Can	Den	Fra	FRG	Gre	Ice	Ita	Lux	Neth
1. Covenant on Civil and Political Rights, Art. 41; HRC: inter-State complaints	x	x	x	n	x		x	x	x	x
2. Optional Protocol of the Covenant; HRC: individual complaints	n	x	x	x	n		x	x	x	x
3. Convention on Racial Discrimination, Art. 14; CC: individual complaints	n	n	x	x	n	n	x	x	n	x
4. Convention on Racial Discrimination, Art. 22; ICJ	x	x	x	x	x	x	x	x	x	x
5. Convention on Discrimination Against Women, Art. 29; ICJ	x	x	x	n	x	x	x	x		
6. Genocide Convention, Art. 9; ICJ	x	x	x	x	x	x	x	x	x	x
7. Convention Against the Taking of Hostages, Art. 16; ICJ	x	x			x	x	x	x		
8. Torture Convention; CC: Art. 21 (inter-State complaints), Art. 22 (individual complaints)	x	x	x		x		x	x		x
9. Torture Convention, Art. 30; ICJ		x	x	x			x		x	x
10. Refugee Convention, Art. 38; ICJ	x	x	x	x	x	x	x	x	x	x
11. Refugee Protocol, Art. 38; ICJ	x	x	x	x	x	x	x	x	x	x
12. Convention on Stateless Persons, Art. 34; ICJ	x		x	x	x	x		x	x	x
13. Convention on the Reduction of Statelessness, Art. 14; ICJ		x	x		x					x
14. Additional Protocol 1 of the Geneva Conventions, Art. 90; International Fact-finding Commission: inter-state complaints	x		x			n	x	x	n	x
Total	8	11	14	9	9	9	10	13	9	12

x = acceptance
n = non-acceptance

CC = Convention Committee
HRC = Human Rights Committee
ICJ = International Court of Justice

						Warsaw Pact states							Neutral or non-aligned								Other states				
Norw	Por	Spa	Tur	UK	USA	Bul	Cze	GDR	Hun	Pol	Rom	USSR	Aus	Cyp	Fin	Ire	Mal	Swe	Swi	Yug	Holy S	Liech	Mona	San M	Total CSCE states
x	n	x		x		n	n	n	x	n	n	n	x	n	x	x		x		n				n	16
x	x	x		n		n	n	n	x	n	n	n	x	n	x	x		x		n				x	16
x	n	n		n		n	n	n	x	n	n	n	n	n	n		n	x		n	n				8
x	x	n		x		n	n	n	x	n	n	n	x	x	x	x		x	x		x	x			22
x	x	x	n	x		n	n	n	x	n	n	n	x	x	x	x		x	x						19
x		x	x	x	n	n	n	n	x	n	n	n	x	x	x	x	x	x		x			x		23
x	x	x		x	x	n	n	n	x				n	x	x			x	x	x					17
x	x	x	x	x/n		n	n	n	x	n			n	x	x			x	x	x					16½
x	x	x	x	x		n	n	n	x	x			x	x	x			x	x	x					18
x	x	x	x	x					x				x	x	x	x	x	x	x	x	x	x	x	x	27
x	x	x	x	x	x				x				x	x	x	x	x	x	x	x	x	x			27
x				x									x		x			x	x	x					15
x				x										x				x		x					9
x	x			n				n					x	x	n	x		x	x	x	n	n		x	14
14	8	10	5	10,5	2	0	0	0	11	1	0	5	12	5	12	8	4	14	7	7	3	3	2	1	

other CSCE states denying the compulsory jurisdiction of the International Court of Justice under human rights conventions. However, the Genocide Convention provides an interesting exception to this rule. Belgium, the Netherlands and the United Kingdom have objected to the reservations of a number of states, including Warsaw Pact states, denying the compulsory jurisdiction of the International Court of Justice under the Genocide Convention; the Netherlands do not consider the reserving states as parties to the Convention. The apparent reason for the objections has been the definition of genocide as an international crime, which in turn arguably makes the denial of the Court's compulsory jurisdiction ill-founded and incompatible with the object and purpose of the Convention. When in 1988, the United States entered a reservation to the Genocide Convention denying the compulsory jurisdiction of the Court, the Netherlands and the United Kingdom responded in December 1989 with objections to the reservation (UN doc. C.N.342, 1989). The Netherlands stated that it does not regard the United States as a party to the Convention.[18]

7. A state's submission to international supervision of its observance of its human rights obligations is a weighty indication that the state takes its obligations seriously.[19] Because Warsaw Pact states both opposed the establishment of any far-reaching supervisory procedures in the preparation of human rights conventions and avoided submitting themselves to any optional supervisory procedures, Western states considered this to justify insisting that the CSCE focus strongly on the human rights situation in participating states. The discussion on human rights conducted by Western states in the CSCE in the 1970s and in the early part of the 1980s was in many ways over-politicized, pointing to 'their' problems but forgetting 'our' problems. However, this discussion had a real basis, because Warsaw Pact states attempted to hide their human rights problems, which may be characterized as substantial, from international publicity. The CSCE was one of the few inter-state forums where the human

---

[18] Even if this reservation has received less objections than the other reservation of the United States to the Genocide Convention (see section 4 in this chapter above), it can be concluded that the CSCE community would welcome the withdrawal of both reservations of the United States. Also the Warsaw Pact states should follow the example of Hungary and the Soviet Union and withdraw their reservations to the Genocide Convention concerning the compulsory jurisdiction of the International Court.

[19] From the practice of the Human Rights Committee, one can find examples that not all states which have accepted the individual complaints procedure have taken their obligations under the Covenant on Civil and Political Rights seriously. This is especially true of Uruguay; see the annual reports of the Human Rights Committee for the years prior to 1985.

rights problems in Warsaw Pact states were given considerable attention.

The CSCE's record in human rights matters is clearly a positive one, notwithstanding these tendencies of over-politicization. However, the CSCE's capability to promote and implement human rights operates much more effectively if there exists mutual trust between the participating states than if the atmosphere is that of a political confrontation. At the beginning of the 1990s, there appears to exist quite a lot of mutual trust among CSCE states.[20] In the development of mutual trust, political rapprochement is naturally of primary importance, but in the field of human rights an important factor is whether CSCE states are ready to ratify human rights conventions, observe their obligations under these conventions and consent to international supervision. When there is mutual trust in this field, the chances of the CSCE process to promote and implement human rights and to create even higher human rights standards are promising. That time may be near, if there are no major political setbacks in Eastern Europe.

Bibliography

Bourguignon, Henry J., 1989. 'The Belilos Case: New Light on Reservations to Multilateral Treaties', *Virginia Journal of International Law*, vol. 29.

Brownlie, Ian, 1979. *Principles of Public International Law*. Oxford: Clarendon Press.

Buergenthal, Thomas, 1985. 'The Advisory Practice of the Inter-American Human Rights Court', *American Journal of International Law*, vol. 79.

Cameron, Iain, 1988. 'Turkey and Article 25 of the European Convention on Human Rights', *International and Comparative Law Quarterly*, vol. 37.

Frowein, Jochen Abr., 1988. 'Reservations to the European Convention on Human Rights', in Franz Matscher (ed.), *Protecting Human Rights: The European Dimension. Studies in Honour of Gérard J. Wiarda*. Köln: Carl Heymanns Verlag.

Hannikainen, Lauri, 1984. 'Prohibition of War Propaganda', in Kaarle Nordenstreng with Lauri Hannikainen, *The Mass Media Declaration of Unesco*. Norwood, NJ: Ablex Publishing Corporation.

Hannikainen, Lauri, 1988. *'Peremptory Norms (Jus Cogens) in International Law: Historical Development, Criteria, Present Status*. Helsinki: Finnish Lawyers' Publishing Company.

Horn, Frank, 1988. *Reservations and Interpretative Declarations to Multilateral Treaties*. The Hague: T.M.C. Asser Instituut.

Imbert, P-H., 1981. 'Reservations and Human Rights Conventions', *The Human Rights Review*, vol. 6.

Karapuu, Heikki and Allan Rosas, 1988. 'The Juridical Force of Economic,

---

[20] Even Albania which has been the only European state to stay outside the CSCE made it known in May 1990 that it would be interested to participate in the CSCE.

Social and Cultural Rights — Some Finnish Examples', *Mennesker og Rettigheter — Nordic Journal on Human Rights*, vol. 6.

MacDonald, R.St.J., 1988. 'Reservations under the European Convention on Human Rights', *Revue belge de droit international*, vol. 21.

Nieminen, Liisa, 1990. *Perusoikeuksien emansipatoriset mahdollisuudet* (with an English summary). Helsinki: Finnish Lawyers' Publishing Company.

Rikoslain kokonaisuudistus II. Rikoslakiprojektin ehdotus. *Oikeusministeriön lainvalmisteluosaston julkaisu* 1/1989. Helsinki, 1989: Government Printing Office.

Schindler, Dietrich and Jiri Toman (eds), 1988. *The Laws of Armed Conflicts: A Collection of Conventions, Resolutions and Other Documents*, 3rd edition. Geneva: Henry Dunant Institute.

Sinclair, Ian M., 1983. *The Vienna Convention on the Law of Treaties*, 2nd edition. Manchester: Manchester University Press.

Sulkunen, Olavi, 1988. 'Työelämän oikeudet ja Kansainvälinen työjärjestö', in Marjut Helminen & K.J. Lång, *Kansainväliset ihmisoikeudet*, 2nd edition. Helsinki: Finnish Lawyers' Publishing Company.

Tomuschat, Christian, 1985. 'Human Rights in a World-Wide Framework: Some Current Issues'. *Zeitschrift für ausländisches öffentliches Recht und Völkerrecht*, vol. 45.

Tupamäki, Matti, 1989. 'Extradition of Terrorists and the Conventions of the Council of Europe', in *Diplomacy, Conciliation and International Adjudication: Essays on International Law in Honour of Bengt Broms at his 60th Birthday 16.10.1989*. Helsinki: Ius Gentium r.y.

Valticos, Nicolas, 1979. *International Labour Law*. Deventer: Kluwer.

Zayas, Alfred de, Jacob T.H. Möller and Torkel, Opsahl, 1989. 'Ihmisoikeuskomitea kansalais- ja poliittisia oikeuksia koskevan yleissopimuksen soveltajana sopimuksen valinnaisen pöytäkirjan nojalla', *Oikeustiede — Jurisprudentia*, vol. XXII.

Table of Cases

This table includes both international and domestic cases. Page numbers refer to pages in this book.

Aguilar-Amory and Royal Bank of Canada Claims, see *Tinoco* Case
Antelope Case, 10 Wheat. 66 (U.S. 1825) 158
Austria v. Italy, European Commission of Human Rights, Yearbook IV (1961), application 788/60 348
Barberà, Messegué and Jabardo, Case of, Publ. E.C.H.R., Series A, vol. 146 (1989) 118
Barcelona Traction Case, ICJ Report 1970 137, 141, 296-7
Belilos v. Switzerland, Publ. E.C.H.R., Series A, vol. 132 (1988) 353, 357
Benthem Case, Publ. E.C.H.R., Series A, vol. 97 (1986) 115
Boeckmann v. Belgium, European Commission of Human Rights, Yearbook VI (1963), application 1727/62 115
Bönisch Case, Publ. E.C.H.R., Series A, vol. 92 (1985) 113, 124
Bricmont Case, Publ. E.C.H.R., Series A, vol. 158 (1989) 120
Brozicek Case, Publ. E.C.H.R., Series A, vol. 167 (1989) 120
Campbell and Fell Case, Publ. E.C.H.R., Series A, vol. 80 (1984) 114, 121
Colozza Case, Publ. E.C.H.R., Series A, vol. 89 (1985) 127
Creole Case, 4 Moore, International Arbitration 4349-4378 (1898) 142
Crociani et al. v. Italy, European Commission of Human Rights, Decisions and Reports 22 (1981), applications 8603/79, 8722/79, 8723/79 & 8729/79 93, 115
De Cubber Case, Publ. E.C.H.R., Series A, vol. 86 (1984) 117
Duncan v. Louisiana, (1968) 381 U.S. 479, 85 S. Ct. 1678, 14 L.Ed. 2d 510 93
Eckle Case, Publ. E.C.H.R., Series A, vol. 51 (1982) 117
Feldbrugge Case, Publ. E.C.H.R., Series A, vol. 99 (1986) 113
Filartiga v. Pena-Irala, 630 F.2d 876 (1980), U.S. Court of Appeals, Second Circuit 139
Free Zones Case, Reports of the Permanent Court of International Justice, Series A/B, no. 46 (1932) 351
G. v. United Kingdom, European Commission of Human Rights, Decisions and Reports 35 (1984), application 9370/81 122
Glasenapp Case, Publ. E.C.H.R., Series A, vol. 104 (1986) 190
Golder Case, Publ. E.C.H.R., Series A, vol. 18 (1975)) 115
Greco-Bulgarian Communities Case, Reports of the Permanent Court of International Justice, Series B, no. 17 (1930) 351
Great Britain v. Costa Rica, see *Tinoco* Case
Gregg v. Georgia, 448 U.S. 153, 96 S.Ct. 2909 (1976) 136, 149
Hauschildt Case, Publ. E.C.H.R., Series A, vol. 154 (1989) 130
Kamasinski v. Austria, Report of the European Commission of Human Rights of 5 May 1988, application 9783/82 124
Kitok Case, Human Rights Committee, Communication no. 194/1985 31

Klass and Others, Case of, Publ. E.C.H.R., Series A, vol. 28 (1979) 154
Kommunistische Partei Deutschland v. Federal Republic of Germany, European Commission of Human Rights, Documents and Decisions, vol. I (1955-57), application 250/57 43
König Case, Publ. E.C.H.R., Series A, vol. 27 (1978) 117
Kosiek Case, Publ. E.C.H.R., Series A, vol. 105 (1986) 190
Kostovski Case, Publ. E.C.H.R., Series A, vol. 166 (1989) 130
'Lawless' Case (Ireland v. United Kingdom), Publ. E.C.H.R., Series A, vol. 2 (1961) 348
Lingens Case, Publ. E.C.H.R., Series A, vol. 103 (1986) 77
Le Louis Case, 2 Dodson 210 (1817) 158
Lubicon Lake Band Case, Human Rights Committee, Communication no. 167/1984 31
Luedicke, Belkacem and Koc, Case of, Publ. E.C.H.R., Series A, vol. 29 (1979) 124-5
Mathieu-Mohin and Clerfayt, Case of, Publ. E.C.H.R., Series A, vol. 113 (1987) 26, 42, 47
Mbenge v. Zaire, Human Rights Committee, Communication 16/1977 127
Mikmaq Tribal Society Case, Human Rights Committee, Communication no. 78/1980 31
Military and Paramilitary Activities in and against Nicaragua, see *Nicaragua v. United States of America*.
Minelli Case, Publ. E.C.H.R., Series A, vol. 62 (1983) 118
Morris v. United Kingdom, European Commission of Human Rights, Decisions and Reports 35 (1984), application 9818/82 125
Neumeister Case, Publ. E.C.H.R., Series A, vol. 8 (1968) 113
Neves e Silva, Case of, Publ. E.C.H.R., Series A, vol. 153-A (1989) 130
Nicaragua v. United States of America, Merits, I.C.J. Reports, 1986 34, 360
Nielsen v. Denmark, Report of the European Commission of 15 March 1961, Yearbook IV (1961), application 343/57 112, 128
O.F. v. Norway, Human Rights Committee, Communication 158/1983 120
Ofner v. Austria, European Commission of Human Rights, Yearbook III (1960), application 524/59 120
Pakelli Case, Publ. E.C.H.R., Series A, vol. 64 (1983) 121
Penry v. Lynaugh, - U.S. - 109 S.Ct. 2934, 106 L.Ed. 2d 256(1989) 136, 149
Piersack Case, Publ. E.C.H.R., Series A, vol. 53 (1982) 115
Pinkney v. Canada, Case of, Human Rights Committee, Communication 27/1978 117
Reservations to the Genocide Convention (Advisory Opinion), I.C.J. Reports 1951 348
Ringeisen Case, Publ. E.C.H.R., Series A, vol. 13 (1971) 117
Roach and Pinkerton Case of, Resolution no. 3/87, Case 9647 United States, Annual Report of the Inter-American Commission on Human Rights 1986-1987 136-7, 144, 155, 157-8
Raúl Sendic v. Uruguay, Human Rights Committee, Communication 63/1979 123
Soering Case, Publ. E.C.H.R., Series A, vol. 161 (1989) 137, 146, 153-4
Stanford v. Kentucky, - U.S. - 109 S.Ct. 2969 (1989) 136, 149
Sunday Times Case, Publ. E.C.H.R., Series A, vol. 30 (1979) 110
Thomas v. Oklahoma, - U.S. - 108 S.Ct. 2687 (1988) 149
Tinoco Case (*Aguilar-Amory and Royal Bank of Canada Claims*) (1923), Reports of International Arbitral Awards, 1948, vol. I 22

Tyrer Case, Publ. E.C.H.R., Series A, vol. 26. (1978) 110
Unterpertinger Case, Publ. E.C.H.R., Series A, vol. 110 (1987) 119
W.X.Y.Z. v. Belgium, European Commission of Human Rights, Decisions and Reports 2 (1975), applications 6745 and 6746/74 26
Weems v. United States, 217 U.S. 349 (1910) 144
Western Sahara Case, ICJ Reports, 1971 32
Viana Acosta v. Uruguay, Human Rights Committee, Communication 110/1981 121
Wight v. Madagaskar, Human Rights Committee, Communication 115/1982 121
X v. Luxembourg, European Commission of Human Rights, Decisions and Reports 16 (1979), application 8366/78 116
X v. The Netherlands, European Commission of Human Rights, Decisions and Reports 27 (1982), application 9433/81 113
X v. United Kingdom, European Commission of Human Rights, Collection of Decisions 40 (1972), application 5076/71 119
Young, James and Webster, Case of, Publ. E.C.H.R., Series A, vol. 44 (1981) 42, 197, 277
Zwaan-de Vries, Case of, Human Rights Committee, Communication 182/1984 188

Table of Treaties

1926 Slavery Convention and 1953 Protocol. Concluded: 1926, entered into force: 1927. 60 LNTS 253.
1930 Forced Labour Convention (ILO 29). Concluded: 1930, entered into force: 1932. 39 UNTS 55.
1948 Convention on the Prevention and Punishment of the Crime of Genocide. Concluded: 1948, entered into force: 1951. 78 UNTS 277.
1948 Freedom of Association and Protection of the Right to Organise Convention (ILO 87). Concluded: 1948, entered into force: 1950. 68 UNTS 17.
1948 Inter-American Convention on the Granting of Political Rights to Women. Concluded: 1948, entered into force: 1949. OAS Treaty Series No. 23.
1949 Conventions for the Protection of War Victims Concerning:

1. Amelioration of the Condition of Wounded and Sick in Armed Forces in the Field,
2. Amelioration of the Condition of Wounded, Sick and Shipwrecked Members of Armed Forces at Sea,
3. Treatment of Prisoners of War,
4. Protection of Civilian Persons in Time of War.

Concluded: 1949, entered into force: 1950. 75 UNTS 31.
1949 Right to Organise and Collective Bargaining Convention (ILO 98). Concluded: 1949, entered into force: 1951. 96 UNTS 257.
1950 Convention for the Protection of Human Rights and Fundamental Freedoms. Concluded: 1950, entered into force: 1953. 213 UNTS 221.
1951 Convention Relating to the Status of Refugees. Concluded: 1951, entered into force: 1954. 189 UNTS 150.
1951 Equal Remuneration Convention (ILO 100). Concluded: 1951, entered into force: 1953. 165 UNTS 303.
1953 Convention on the Political Rights of Women. Concluded: 1953, entered into force: 1954. 193 UNTS 135.
1954 Convention Relating to the Status of Stateless Persons. Concluded: 1954, entered into force: 1960. 360 UNTS 117.
1956 Supplementary Convention on the Abolition of Slavery, the Slave Trade and Institutions and Practices Similar to Slavery. Concluded: 1956, entered into force: 1957. 226 UNTS 3.
1957 Abolition of Forced Labour Convention (ILO 105). Concluded: 1957, entered into force: 1959. 320 UNTS 291.
1958 Convention on the High Seas. Concluded 1958, entered into force: 1962. 450 UNTS 82.
1958 Discrimination (Employment and Occupation) Convention (ILO 111). Concluded: 1958, entered into force: 1960. 362 UNTS 31.

1960 Convention Against Discrimination in Education and 1962 Protocol. Concluded: 1960, entered into force: 1962. 429 UNTS 93.

1961 European Social Charter. Concluded: 1961, entered into force: 1965. ETS No. 48.

1961 Convention on the Reduction of Statelessness. Concluded: 1961, entered into force: 1975. 989 UNTS 175.

1964 Employment Policy Convention (ILO 122). Concluded: 1964, entered into force: 1966. 569 UNTS 65.

1966 International Convention on the Elimination of All Forms of Racial Discrimination. Concluded: 1965, entered into force: 1969. 60 UNTS 195.

1966 International Covenant on Civil and Political Rights, including Optional Protocol. Concluded: 1966, entered into force: 1976. 999 UNTS 171

1966 International Covenant on Economic, Social and Cultural Rights. Concluded: 1966, entered into force: 1976. 999 UNTS 3.

1967 Protocol Relating to the Status of Refugees. Concluded: 1967, entered into force: 1967. 606 UNTS 267.

1968 Convention of the Non-applicability of Statutory Limitations to War Crimes and Crimes Against Humanity. Concluded: 1968, entered into force: 1970. 754 UNTS 73.

1969 American Convention on Human Rights. Concluded: 1969, entered into force: 1978. 1144 UNTS 123.

1969 Vienna Convention on the Law of Treaties. Concluded: 1969, entered into force: 1980. 1155 UNTS 331.

1971 Workers' Representatives Convention (ILO 135). Concluded: 1971, entered into force: 1973. 883 UNTS 111.

1972 Convention for the Prevention of Marine Pollution by Dumping from Ships and Aircraft. Concluded: 1972, entered into force: 1974. UKTS 119 (1975).

1973 International Convention on the Suppression and Punishment of the Crime of Apartheid. Concluded: 1973, entered into force: 1976. 1015 UNTS 243.

1975 Human Resources Development Convention (ILO 142). Concluded: 1975, entered into force: 1977. 1050 UNTS 9.

1977 European Convention on the Legal Status of Migrant Workers. Concluded: 1977, entered into force: 1983. ETS No. 93.

1977 Protocol Additional to the 1949 Geneva Conventions and Relating to the Protection of Victims of Non-international Armed Conflicts. Concluded: 1977, entered into force: 1978. 1125 UNTS 609.

1979 Convention of the Elimination of All Forms of Discrimination Against Women. Concluded: 1979, entered into force: 1981. UN Doc. A/RES/34/180.

1979 International Convention Against the Taking of Hostages. Concluded: 1979, entered into force: 1983. UN Doc.A/RES/34/146.

1979 Second ACP-EEC Convention of Lomé (Lomé 2). Concluded: 1979, entered into force: 1981. UKTS 3(1983).

1982 UN Convention on the Law of the Sea. Concluded: 1982, entered into force: UN Doc.A/conf./62/122.

1984 Convention Against Torture and Other Cruel, Inhuman or Degrading Treatment or Punishment. Concluded: 1984, entered into force: 1987. UN Doc. A/RES/39/46.

ETS   = European Treaty Series
LNTS = League of Nations Treaty Series
UKTS = United Kingdom Treaty Series
UNTS = United Nations Treaty Series

Index

actio popularis 313, 316
administrative proceedings
    (jurisdiction, courts) 280-284
aliens, *see* foreigners
apartheid 34, 139, 292, 296, 298, 309
arrest and detention 353
asylum 191; *see also* foreigners

capital punishment, *see* death
    penalty
censorship 63, 69, 75, 83
children (rights of) 39, 294, 347
civil and political rights (freedoms)
    1-3, 17, 26, 37, 44, 51, 70, 247,
    293, 313, 335
collective rights 1, 4, 8, 24, 30, 66,
    206, 210
communications, *see* individual
    complaints
communism 6, 8, 13, 65, 75, 180
conscientious objection 224
CSCE process 1, 4, 36, 45, 46, 72,
    163, 189, 204, 211, 241-263, 264,
    268-269, 276, 287, 317, 334, 365
customary law 59, 92, 137-143, 147-
    148, 164, 171, 176, 233

death penalty 3, 136-171, 342, 347,
    351
democracy 4, 6, 8, 12, 17-53, 220,
    334, 346
denial of justice 99, 102
derogations, *see* non-derogable
    rights
détente 224
disarmament 220, 354-355
discrimination 40, 42, 66-68, 177,
    188-191, 206, 213, 293, 295, 298,
    322, 340, 350, 358
domestic remedies 264-288, 322-
    323; *see also* local remedies
    (exhaustion of)
due process 93-94, 144

economic, social and cultural rights
    1-3, 37, 49, 70, 176, 179, 185-
    186, 231, 252, 267, 293, 299, 313,
    335, 344, 350, 358
elections 23-24, 26, 27, 29, 32, 41,
    43, 46, 342, 346
equality 6-7, 19, 26, 37, 38, 52; *see
    also* discrimination
European Community 47-48, 49,
    154, 178, 194, 262
European legal space 263

fact-finding 299, 301-303, 305-307,
    311-312, 315-316
fair trial 4, 89-113, 269, 279-284
foreigners 39, 99, 188, 190-191, 342,
    346-347
freedom of
    assembly 17, 20, 28, 36, 37
    association 8, 17, 20, 28, 37, 69,
        341
    expression 4, 8, 17, 20, 28, 36, 37,
        43, 58-86, 247, 249, 259-260, 350,
        354
    movement 9, 37, 256-257, 259,
        342, 346
    opinion, *see* freedom of
        expression, freedom of religion
    religion 58, 246, 254, 256, 259-60
    speech, *see* freedom of opinion
French Revolution 6, 12, 19, 95

general comments 32, 44, 307-309
general principles of law 59, 90-93,
    96, 353
genocide (prohibition of) 35, 164,
    204, 214, 292, 296, 340, 344-345,
    350-351, 360-361
glasnost 71, 81, 162, 256, 334

handicapped 198
Helsinki Final Act (1975) 40, 72,
    203, 205, 243-251, 261

hostages 340, 344–345
humanitarian intervention 34; *see
  also* intervention
humanitarian law 103–106, 140,
  221, 341, 345–346, 351–352, 354,
  359, 361

implementation (of human rights)
  264–288, 290–330, 334, 356–365
incorporation (of treaties) 271; *see
  also* self-executing treaties
indigenous populations 209, 211;
  see also minorities
individual complaints 1, 31, 214,
  294–295, 317–329, 356–364
industrial democracy 49
inquiry procedure, *see* fact-finding
interference, *see* non-interference
international crimes 292, 296, 344–
  345
inter-state complaints 35, 295, 299,
  313–317, 329, 356–364
intervention 34, 225, 246; *see also*
  non-interference

judicial remedies 279–284, 322, 349;
  see also due process, fair trial,
  rule of law
jus cogens 35, 137–143, 148, 164,
  171, 345

law of war 103; *see also*
  humanitarian law
limitation clauses 17, 25, 26, 28, 37,
  42, 256, 260; *see also* non-
  derogable rights
local government 7, 20, 47
local remedies (exhaustion
  of) 314–315, 319, 321, 322, 325

Marxism (marxist theory) 4, 6–14,
  73, 78, 180, 270
minorities (protection of, rights of)
  4, 36, 37, 40–42, 202–214, 250,
  256, 259, 347
multi-party system 43, 45

natural law 7, 217, 270
New Deal 2, 231
non-derogable rights 33, 139, 221, 234
non-discrimination, *see*
  discrimination

non-interference 45, 202, 243, 245–
  246, 252, 256, 297–298
non-recognition, *see* recognition of
  governments
nullum crimen, nulla poena 111
Nuremberg Trial 101–102

Ombudsman 3, 267, 284–287
one-party system 43–45, 129
ordre public 61, 63–64, 65, 74, 78,
  107

pacta sunt servanda 91
peoples (rights of) 4, 216–218, 225,
  234–237; *see also* right to self-
  determination
peremptory norm, *see jus cogens*
pluralism 3, 24, 26, 28, 36, 40, 42–43,
  51–53
political participation 1, 17, 21, 23,
  37, 49
political rights 17–53
popular participation 49, 235–237
popular sovereignty 18–22, 23–34,
  28, 50–52
Prokuratura 67, 277–279, 284, 287
property 20–21, 41, 52–53, 70, 182,
  342, 346, 353
public emergency 33; *see also* non-
  derogable rights
public order, *see ordre public*

recognition of governments 22, 34,
  36
referendum 29, 46–47, 50
refugees 40, 210, 341, 345; *see also*
  foreigners
reporting systems 4, 294–295, 298–
  312, 328–329, 357–358
reservations (to human right
  treaties) 28, 31, 213, 334, 348–
  356
resistance, *see* right to resist
right to
  development 37, 49, 218, 225, 229–
    237
  education 37, 267, 342, 346
  environment 53, 218, 226–229
  life 4, 163–171, 176, 309, 355; *see
    also* death penalty
  resist oppression 23–24, 33, 36, 51,
    225

peace 218-226, 235-237
self-determination 1, 22, 29, 30-
    37, 50-52, 207, 210, 213, 224,
    247, 296, 318
work 4, 66, 174-199
rule of law 3, 17, 22-23, 26, 36-37,
    43-44, 51, 98; *see also* judicial
    remedies

self-defence 34-35, 221, 291
self-determination, *see* right to self-
    determination
self-executing treaties 89, 178, 267,
    272-273
slavery 139, 142-143, 158, 296
socialism (socialist theory) 1, 6, 12,
    14, 175, 270, 272, 290, 322, 334;
    see also communism, Marxism
solidarity 12-13, 216
sovereign equality 245, 290; *see also*
    non-interference
subjective rights of

individuals 269-271, 293-294,
    313, 320, 327

torture (prohibition of) 139, 143-144,
    176, 293, 295, 306, 340, 344-345,
    358-359
trade union rights 42, 197, 254, 267,
    277
Tokyo Trial 101-102

universal suffrage 6, 8-11, 20, 23,
    27, 41
universality 89-90, 95, 111, 293, 328

war crimes 101, 159, 161, 340, 345,
    351
war propaganda 61-62, 64, 213, 349,
    355
women (rights of) 27, 29, 46, 48, 50,
    52, 184, 293-295, 305-306, 340,
    344, 350, 354, 355-356, 358